MASTERING **WEDDING**

PHOTOGRAPHY

MARK CLEGHORN

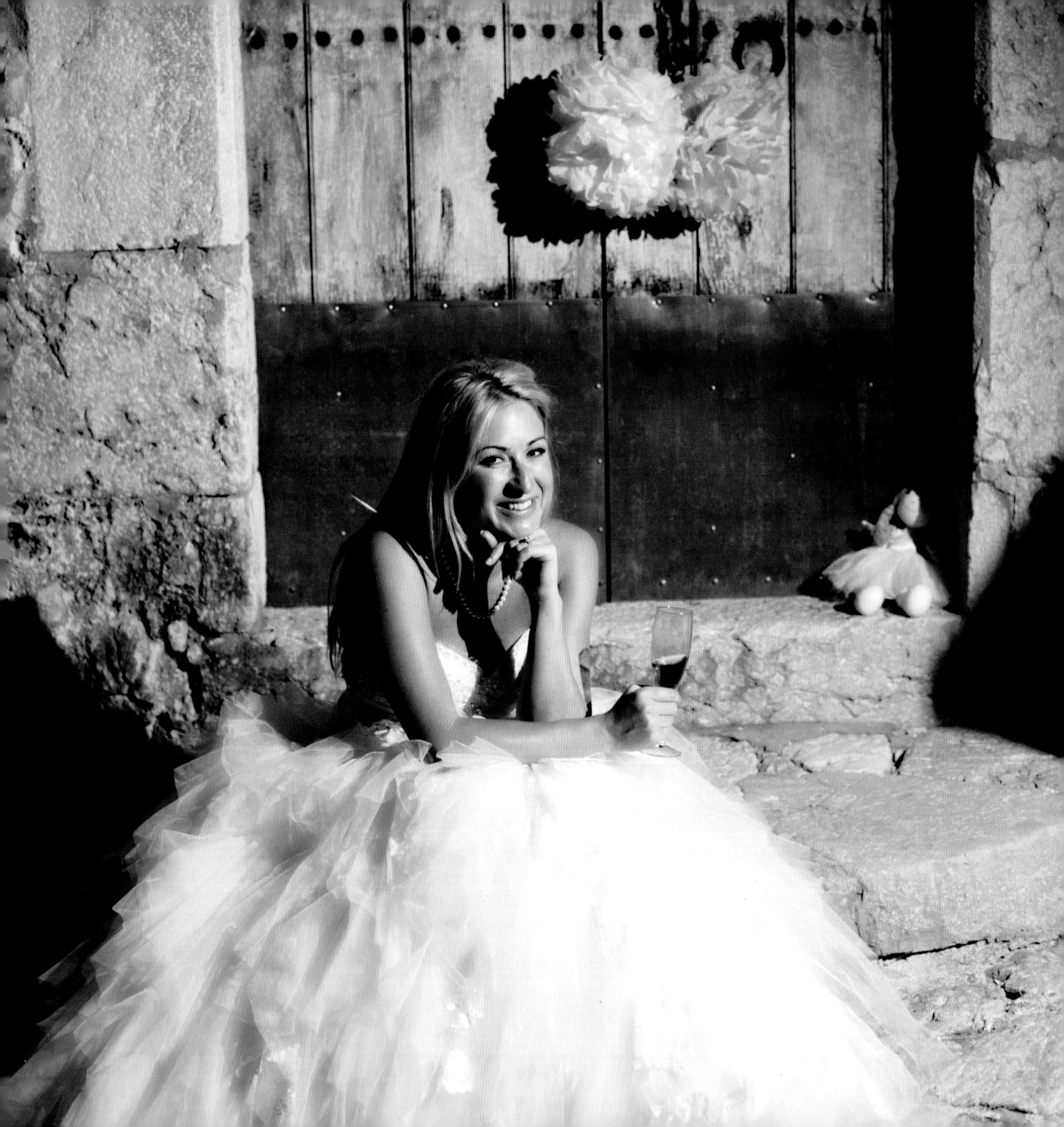

MASTERING **WEDDING**
PHOTOGRAPHY

MARK CLEGHORN

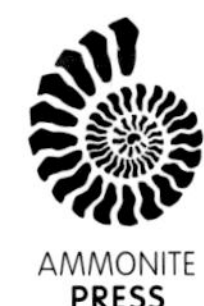

AMMONITE
PRESS

First published 2015 by
Ammonite Press
an imprint of AE Publications Ltd
166 High Street, Lewes, East Sussex, BN7 1XU, UK

Product photography: © Apple Inc (146 left); © Canon (16);
© Panasonic (17 top left); SanDisk (146 right); Sony (17 top right).

ISBN 978-1-90770-853-4

British Library Cataloging in Publication Data: A catalog record of this
book is available from the British Library.

Editors: Rob Yarham, Freya Dangerfield
Series Editor: Richard Wiles
Designer: Robin Shields

Typeface: Helvetica Neue
Color reproduction by GMC Reprographics
Printed in China

Page 2: Wedding style is invariably influenced by the bride—
whether it's classically formal or a whimsical fairytale romance.
This is her special day and she will want to look her very best
for her husband-to-be.

Contents

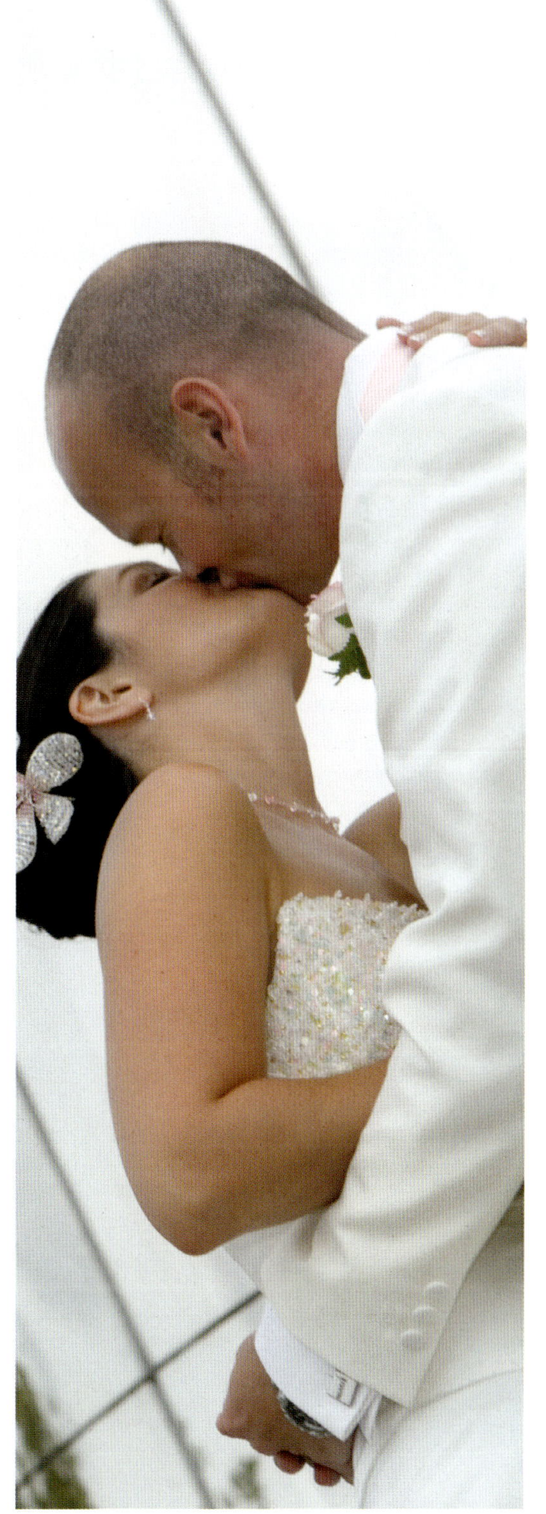

Introduction

Ask any bride what she wants from her wedding photographs and I guarantee she will use words such as "relaxed," "fun," "informal," and "details." Ask her what is most important to her and she will say friends and family, and not forgetting her husband-to-be, of course. Ask her about how much time is being allowed for the bride-and-groom portraits, and she will probably say anything from 15 minutes to an hour. Ask about the budget and it will never be enough, but ask her how she wants to look on the day and she will definitely use the word "slim."

And that is what this book is about: what the bride really wants!

After shooting weddings for over 30 years—I think it is more than 1000 to date—I have covered probably most types and styles of wedding, but every wedding still seems different. People skills and time management are the keys to mastering wedding photography, and you can only make the most of these skills if you are familiar with all the timings and procedures of the wedding itself, and have complete confidence in your camera equipment and your own shooting techniques.

In this book I shall cover all the key skills and information to help you shoot weddings successfully, while making sure the bride and groom are happy that they chose you to photograph the most special day of their lives. So whether it is your very first wedding or your 100th, *Mastering Wedding Photography* will help you to take your ideas and photography techniques to a new level.

Right: Keeping the bride and groom happy on their big day is the essence of successful wedding photography.

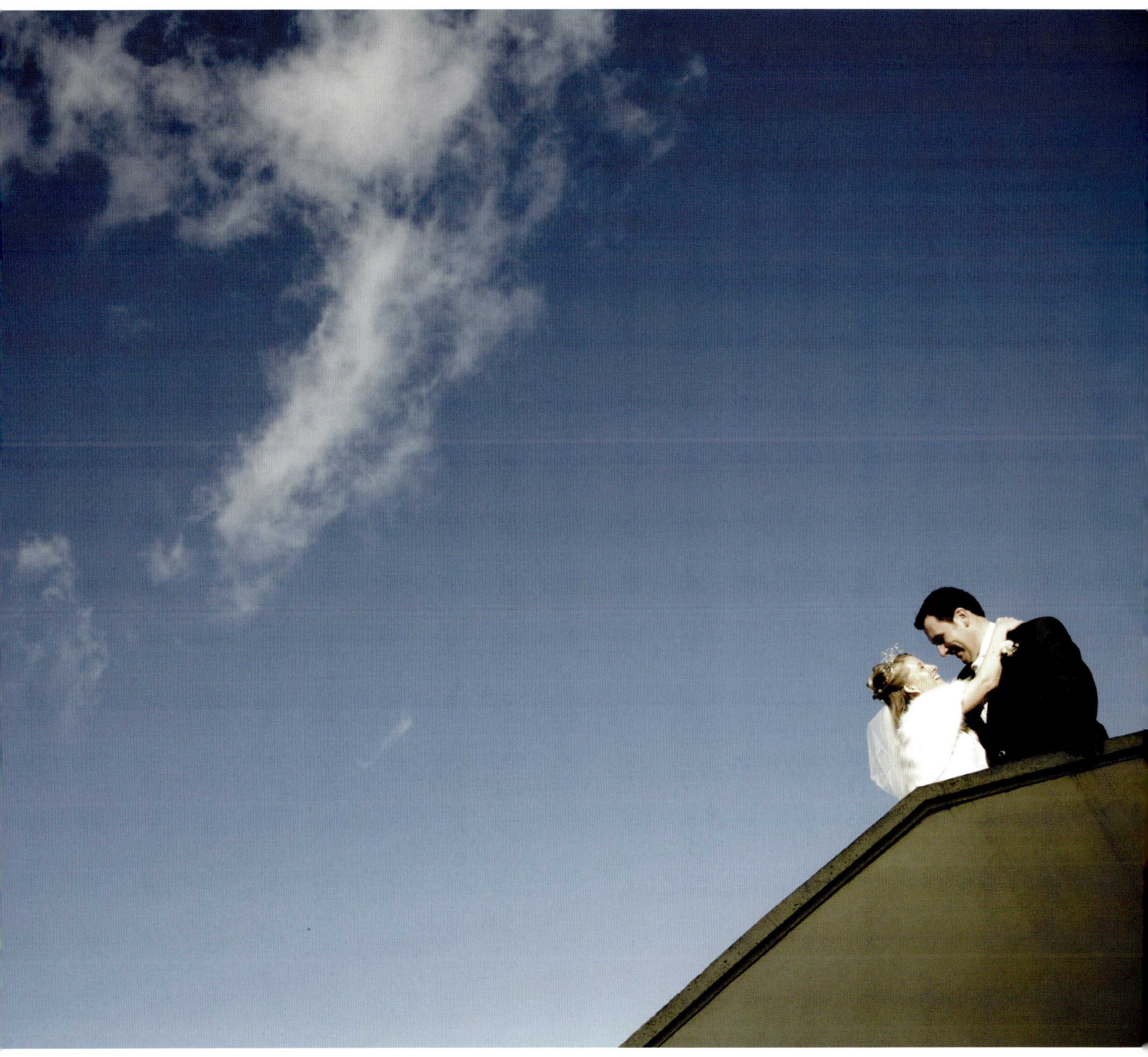

Changes in Approach

Once upon a time, there was no such thing as a full-time wedding photographer, only photographers who braved shooting weddings on a weekend. Weddings were an essential source of income for many photographers, but it was in addition to a busy working week, which may have included portraiture, commercial shoots, and the photojournalistic commissions.

Not all photographers took on wedding photography because of the pressures and time involved. In the past, a wedding photographer would have covered something like four or five weddings on a Saturday alone—giving rise to the true, complimentary meaning of the term "weekend warrior." However, all wedding photographers were really part-time because, even though weddings were held almost every day, there were still not enough to provide full-time work for a professional photographer.

In the first two decades of my career, it was not uncommon for me to shoot two weddings on a Saturday, praying that one wedding would not finish late, or that traffic would prevent me getting to the start of the next one in time. When I began to employ other photographers it brought the obvious benefit of enabling us to shoot multiple weddings on one day, ensuring that there would always be one of us to start and finish a wedding, no matter how many we had to shoot on the day. If we were lucky, we would also be able to shoot a few Friday and Monday weddings as well, but this was unusual, except for public holidays or special festivals.

Things changed in the UK in the late 1990s, with the introduction of the civil ceremony. This

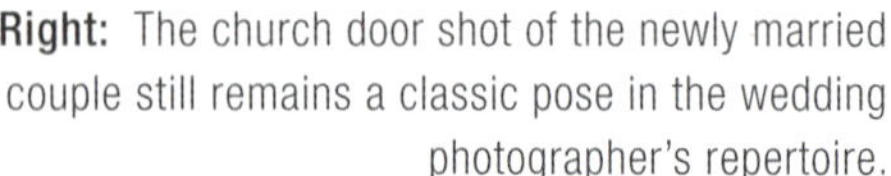

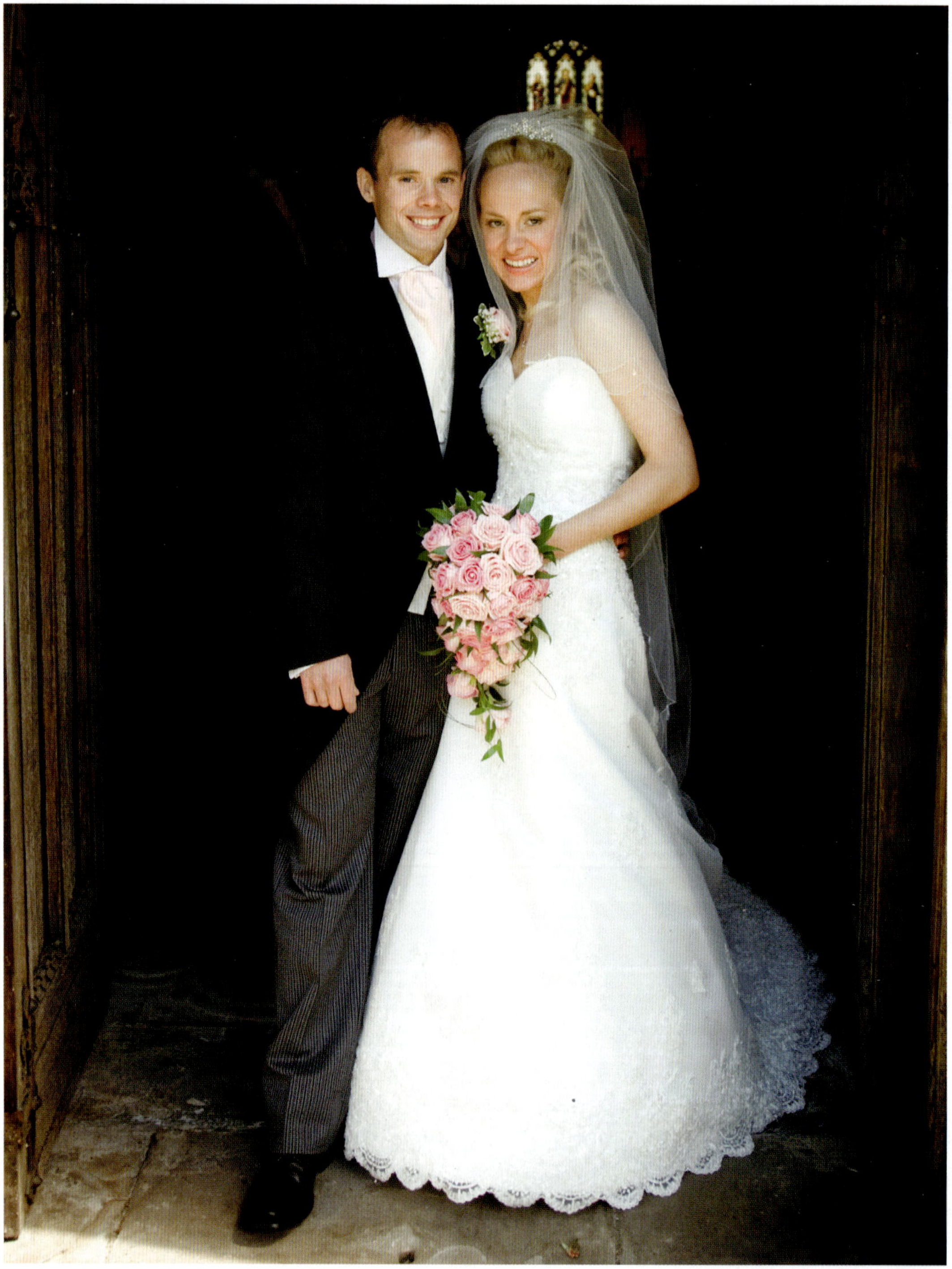

Right: The church door shot of the newly married couple still remains a classic pose in the wedding photographer's repertoire.

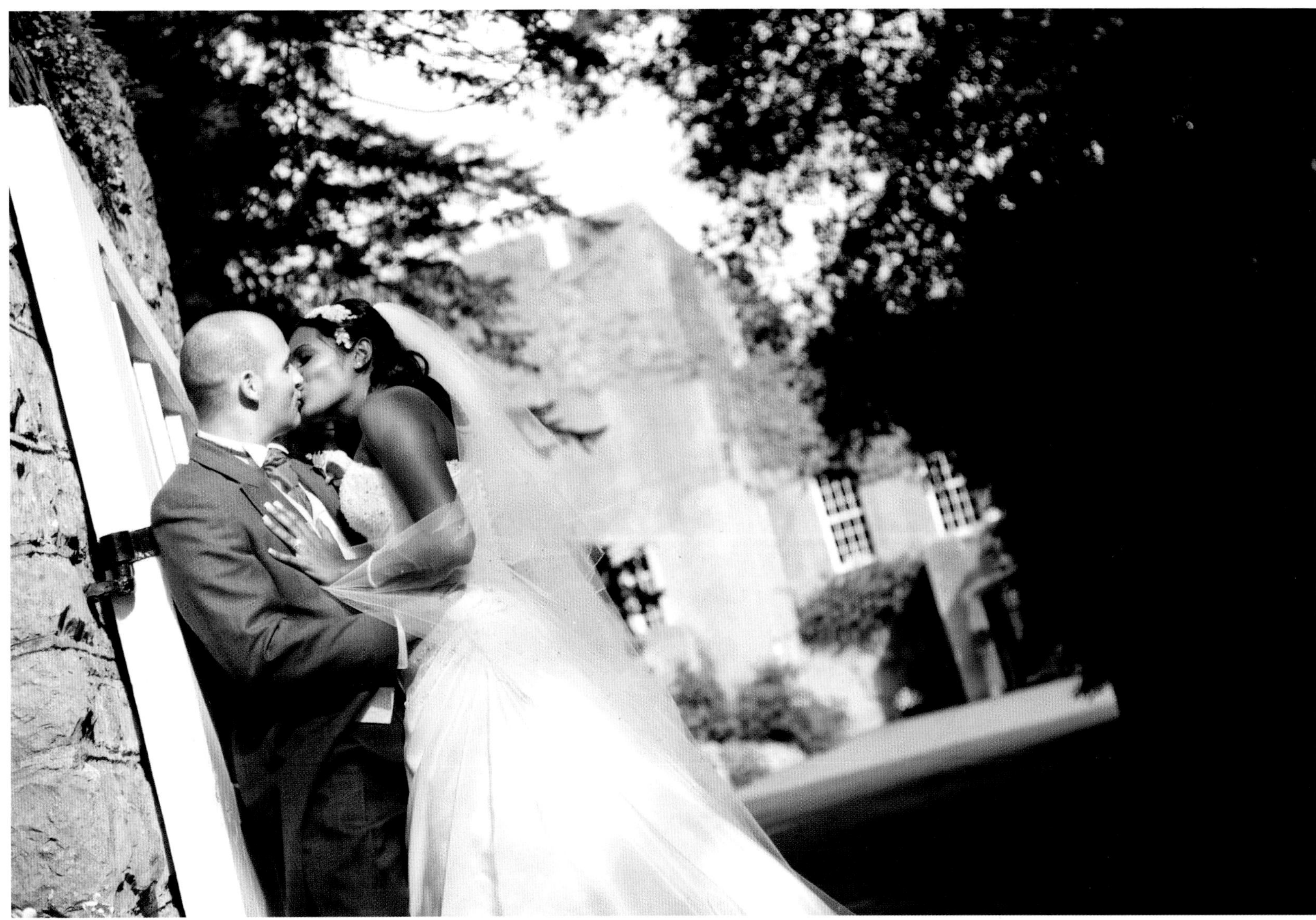

Above: Over the years, couples have become more demanding in what they expect from their photographers.

allowed couples to get married in registered locations other than churches or registry offices, and so the wedding floodgates were opened. For the first time I found myself shooting a wedding almost every day in the summer, and not just on a weekend. This change enabled photographers to specialize in weddings full-time for the first time.

Not only were there new locations for weddings, but also brides and grooms began to become more demanding for their wedding day, planning more complex events, and this also changed wedding photography—brides began to require their photographer to spend more time at their wedding. This, in turn, led to the one-wedding-per-day photographer, but for some this had a crippling effect. Many photographers had been able to offer a low price as a result of being able to photograph more than one wedding in one day. Even the higher-priced wedding operator was affected, as couples required more coverage for a similar price.

Changes in Skills

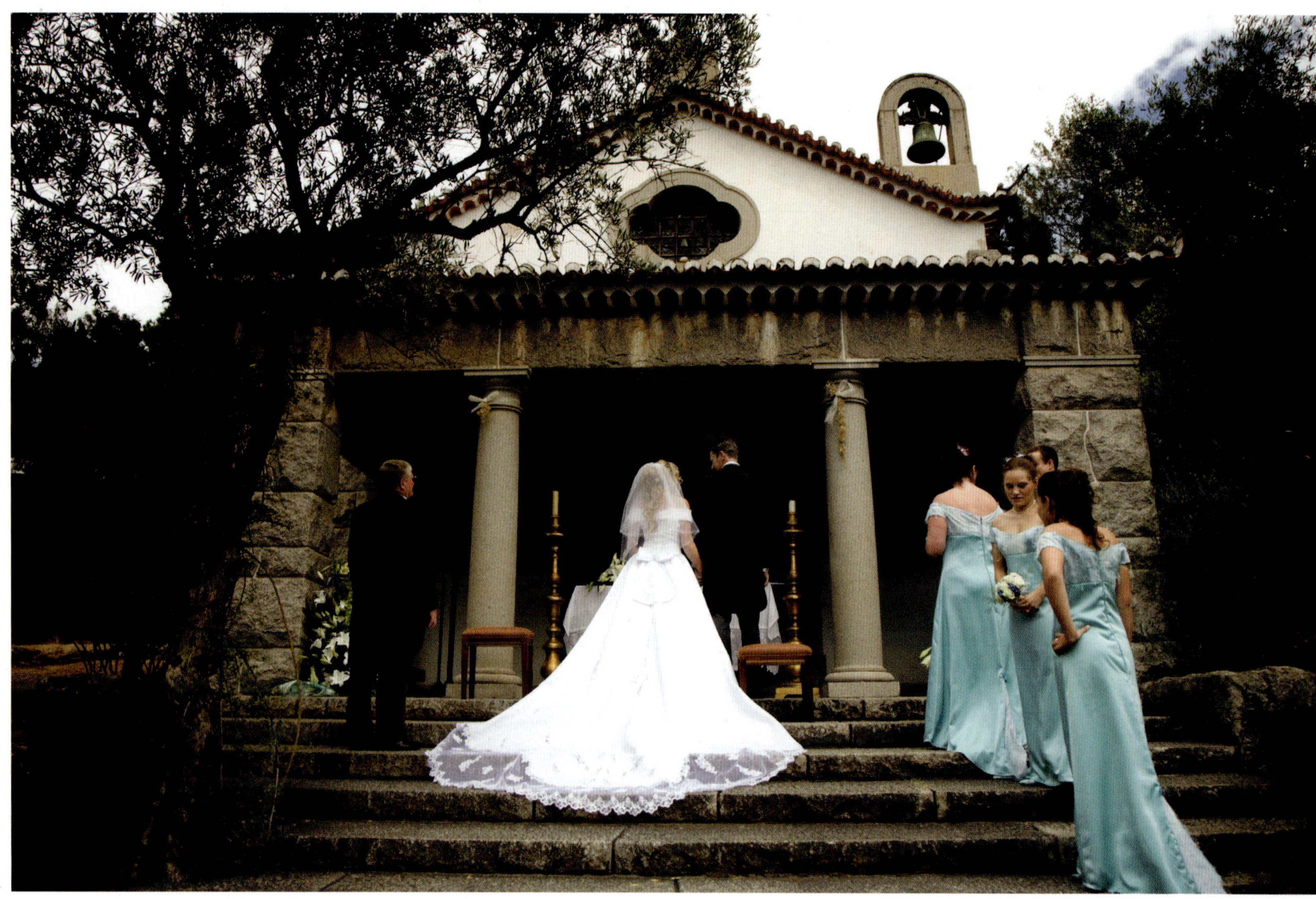

Digital capture was another big change in wedding photography, and it is a huge benefit for the photographer. Now, not only can you see what you shoot immediately, but also, more importantly, every photograph no longer costs you money in film and processing. The other obvious benefit for the wedding photographer is that it enables him or her to try new techniques, to experiment, and to be more creative on the wedding day itself.

Recently, the advent of same-sex marriages and civil partnerships has increased the number of weddings. Shooting same-sex weddings requires new people and posing skills—for instance, the happy couple will not want to look like two groomsmen or bridesmaids having a laugh and a giggle with each other.

Overseas weddings are also becoming more popular, perhaps because of the accessibility of

Above: Overseas weddings have become increasingly popular in recent years.

finding new, romantic, "paradise" locations, or simply because the couples are chasing good weather. Again, new skills are needed, especially for dealing with harsh sun and hot climates, along with flash control when the sun sets, to create subtle, flash-lit images that add to the scene's lighting and do not wash out detail.

Overseas weddings are very glamorous—we all love to do them—but pricing can be an issue. Remember that these commissions will need you to spend a lot of time traveling and away from your business. It is important that you do not become a "busy fool," working too hard for too little money, especially if this is to be your profession.

Today, I believe that being a full-time wedding photographer—and earning a decent standard of living—means that you need to shoot about 50 weddings per year, but this will obviously depend on your pricing and profit strategy. You can also supplement this income with other people photography, of course, including couples, children, and family portraiture.

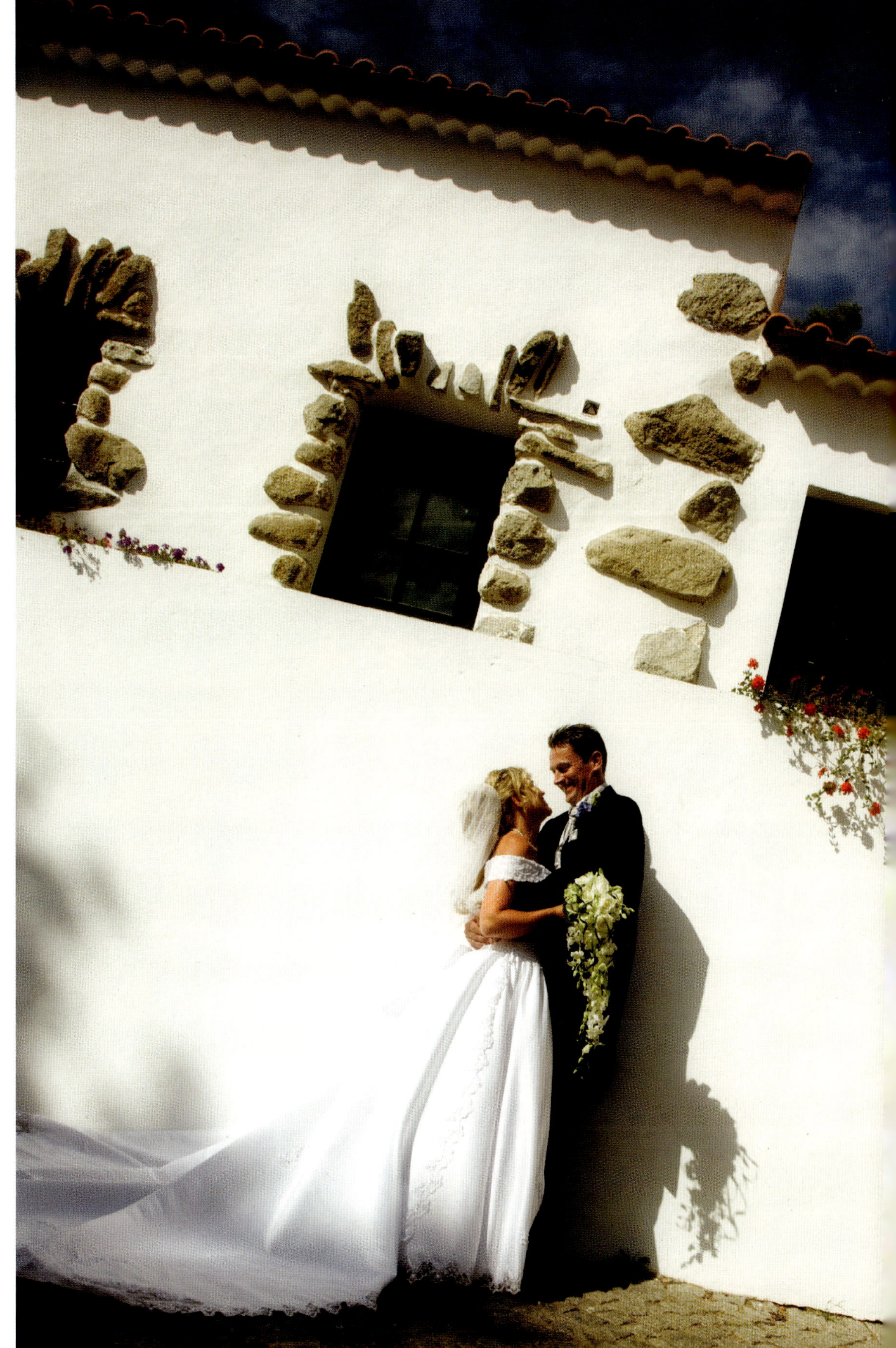

Right: Digital capture means that you can afford to become more creative with techniques.

Remember the Basics

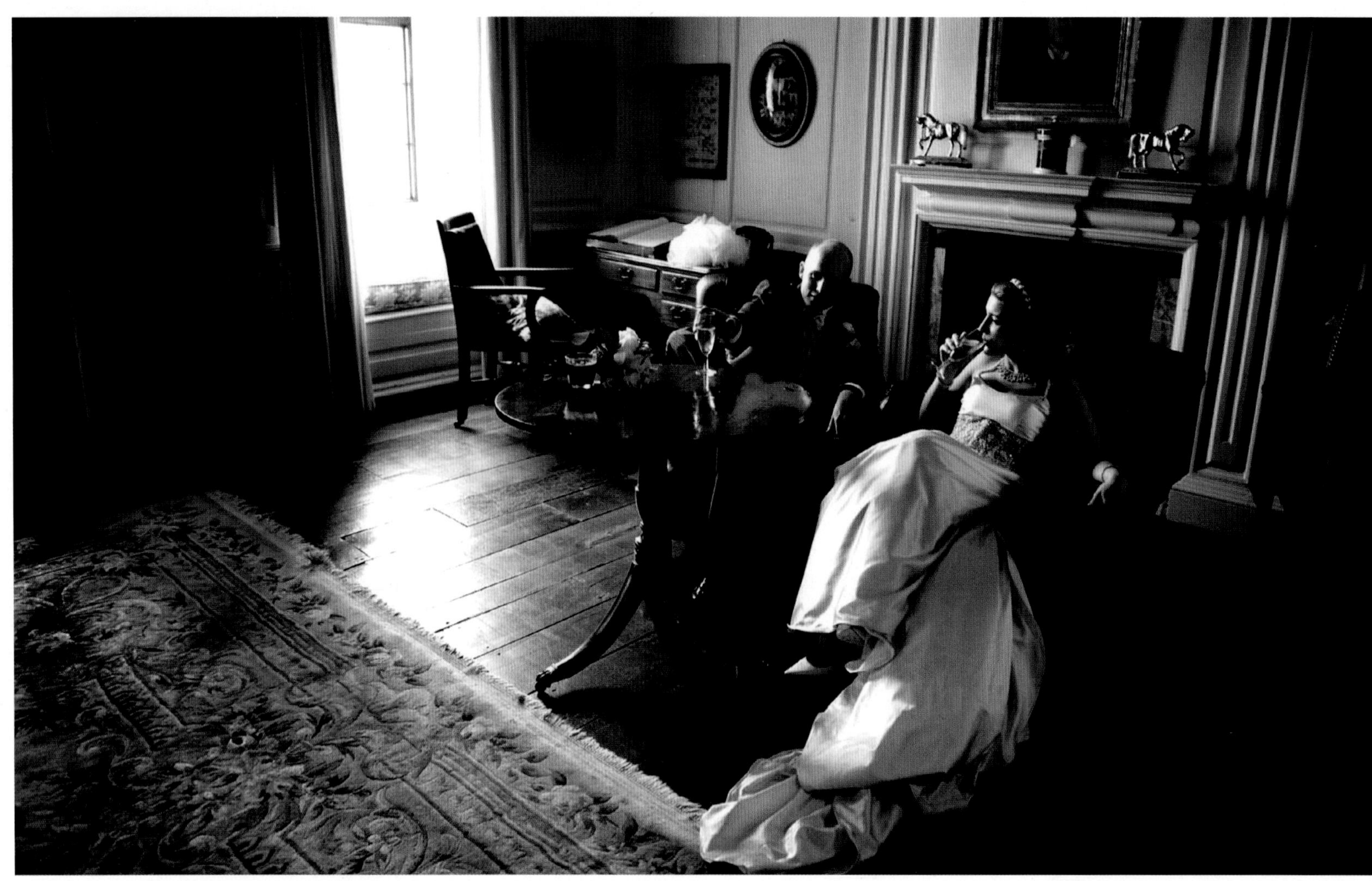

As weddings have changed, so it was inevitable that the wedding photography itself has had to evolve. Once it was the photographer who led discussions about what images were needed, but today the bride is definitely in the driving seat.

In addition, new blood has transformed the wedding photography business, with young photographers adopting a "no fear" approach to trying new trends and techniques. Just as in art, the once stiff and boring pictures, which simply record the people and the day, have been replaced by more realistic poses and storytelling, and by pictures with a touch of romance, fairytale, and imagination.

In spite of the many changes, there are still basic skills that the wedding photographer must master, and storytelling is one of the main techniques I try to teach in wedding photography tutorials. When combined with realistic-looking poses and great lighting, whether natural or artificial, wedding photography can look like stills from a magazine advertisement, or even a movie.

Above: The photojournalistic style has become popular, and is one to explore once you have mastered the basic skills.

Brides and grooms now have access to thousands of photographers on the Internet at the click of a mouse, so it is more important than ever to keep in touch with the trends in magazines. If you are at the beginning of your career in wedding photography, however, don't be afraid to mimic photographers whose styles you like or wish to emulate. Once you have started to build a basic repertoire, and as your confidence grows, you can start to develop your skills and style in new directions and create your own distinctive brand.

If you can discipline yourself to concentrate on the basics initially—such as posing and lighting— you will quickly be able to build and change your portfolio as your experience allows. The basics are sometimes ignored or even dismissed, but all the most successful wedding photographers automatically use these key skills, at times forgetting to even talk about them when teaching other photographers, assuming that they have already learnt them.

We all want to concentrate on the artistic side of photography, but it is essential to remember that we should all remember the basics, and keep pushing our working technique forward. With an understanding of the key skills it becomes easier to identify any problems quickly, and tweak your techniques to move your photography to a different level.

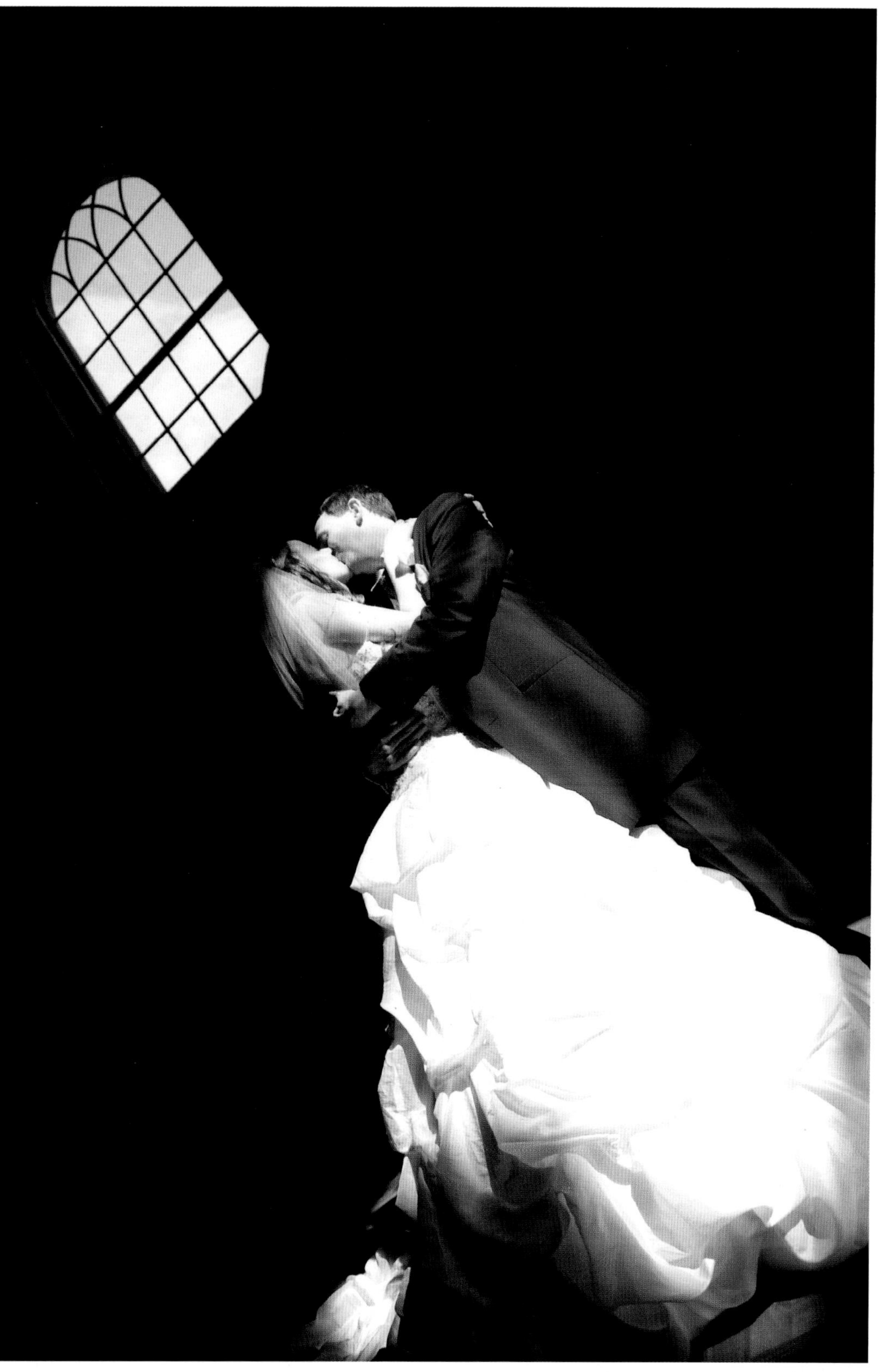

Right: An understanding of the basics, such as lighting, will ensure that you get the very best out of your subjects. Here the couple were asked to kiss—this avoided them looking straight at the camera in difficult lighting conditions.

Chapter 1
Equipment

Typically, we photographers tend to lust after new photographic toys. It's not that they will actually make us any more creative, but we come to believe we cannot live without a new camera, lens, or lots of different flash accessories. We fill our bags with new, glittering kit, which may get used for a while, but soon starts to collect dust in a bag or a cupboard. So in this chapter I outline the basic equipment you'll need to master wedding photography—the kit that will make a real difference—and what's in my bag at every wedding.

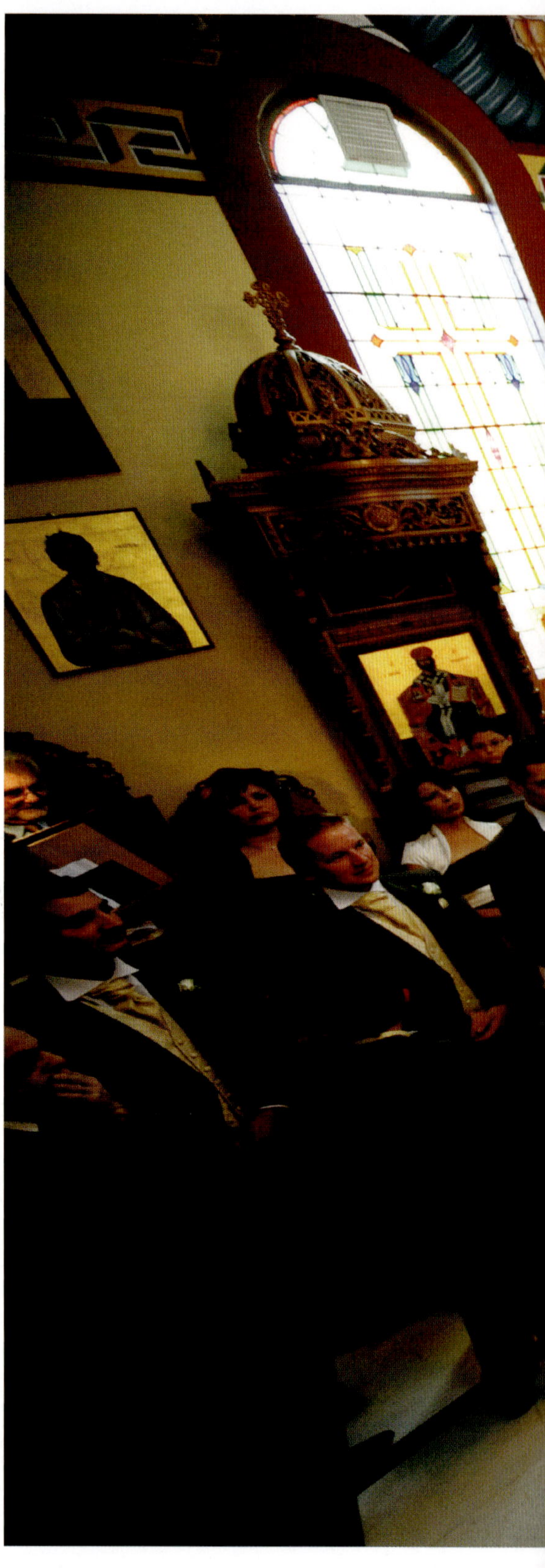

Right: A full-frame sensor allows you to make use of the full field of view of a wide-angle lens. A 24mm lens will give a true 24mm view instead of being magnified as a result of the cropped frame—up to a third in some cases—making the 24mm lens the equivalent of a 32mm lens.

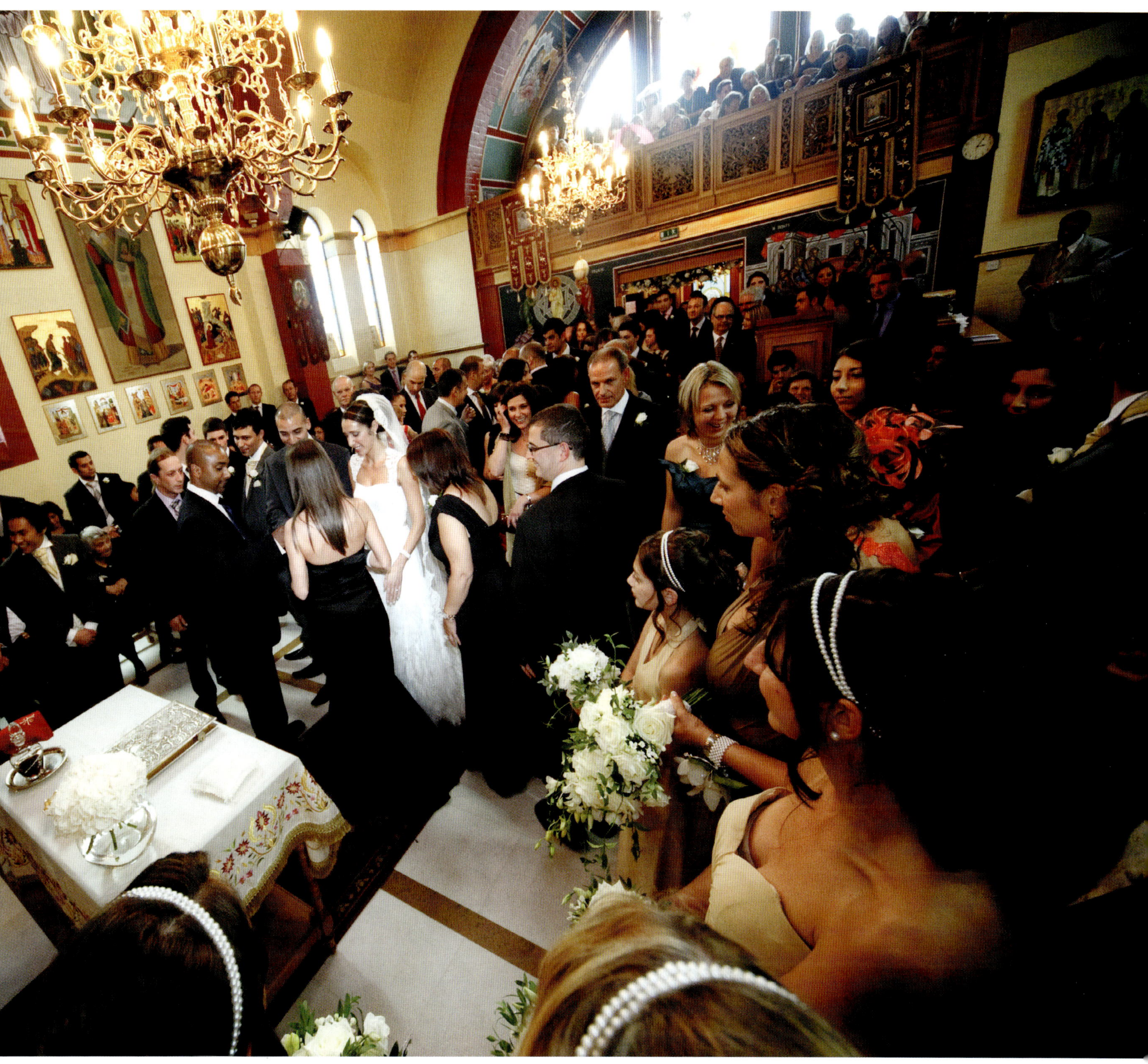

Cameras

The digital single lens reflex (DSLR) "system" camera is the professional wedding photographer's camera of choice. System cameras allow you to swap lenses and add additional equipment such as flashes, battery packs, and other accessories to expand their capabilities. Because of this, they are far more versatile than bridge, compact, and cell phone cameras. The sensor is often far larger as well, which means it will have a wider dynamic range and offer higher ISO settings than a compact model, without compromising image quality to the same extent. System cameras also tend to allow you to use a greater range of aperture and shutter speed settings, as well as supporting Raw files, which means you can tweak factors such as white balance in postproduction without a loss of image quality.

DSLR

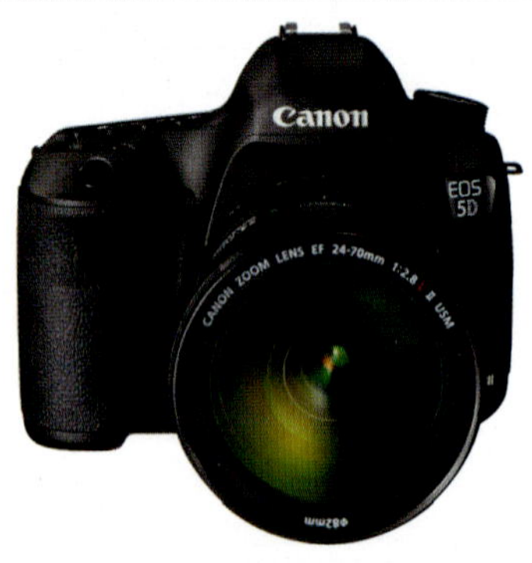

Above: The Canon EOS 5D Mk III is a full-frame DSLR that is popular with outdoor photographers because of its rugged, weather-sealed body.

DSLRs are the type of camera used by just about every professional photographer and the majority of enthusiasts. The main camera manufacturers have also been doing their utmost to tempt beginners to this type of camera, by manufacturing DSLRs with built-in help guides and a host of technological advances that significantly increase the likelihood of taking flawless photographs in almost any situation.

Although DSLRs are generally heavier and more expensive than compact and bridge cameras, they pack a whole host of incredible features into a robust, contoured body. Thanks to some clever engineering, photographers can manually control every aspect of the picture-taking process, from ISO sensitivity to metering, focusing, and drive modes. These functions can be accessed easily, while the less commonly used features are stored in electronic menus.

The main advantage of a DSLR is the ability to change lenses, offering the maximum level of flexibility and potential for the system to grow with you as your photography improves. From 14mm super wide-angle, to 105mm macro, and 600mm super telephoto, the choice of optics and accessories is extensive—not only from the camera maker itself, but also from third-party manufacturers. However, the accessories for one camera system will rarely be compatible with those from another. This makes it easy to get "locked in" to a particular camera system and expensive to change if you wish to switch to a different brand.

In general, DSLRs fall into three broad categories. Top-end, or "pro spec" DSLRs are often heavy and rugged, as they're designed for daily professional use (and abuse). They will typically feature weatherproofing seals on the camera body and around the lens mount to prevent the ingress of water and dust, and many use a high resolution full-frame sensor for optimum image quality.

At the opposite end of the DSLR spectrum are entry-level DSLRs. These tend to be smaller and lighter than their professional counterparts, and often feature a host of user-friendly automated shooting modes, such as Full Auto and Portrait, Landscape, and Sports Scene modes. However, this doesn't mean that an entry-level camera is limited—many match their more expensive stablemates in terms of the features they offer, whether that's sophisticated exposure metering or fast, multi-point autofocus (AF) systems.

Between these extremes are mid-range DSLRs, which tend to be more solid than the entry-level offerings, with slightly more advanced features—a higher frame rate or faster AF, for example—to satisfy advanced amateurs and some professional photographers as well.

Bridge camera

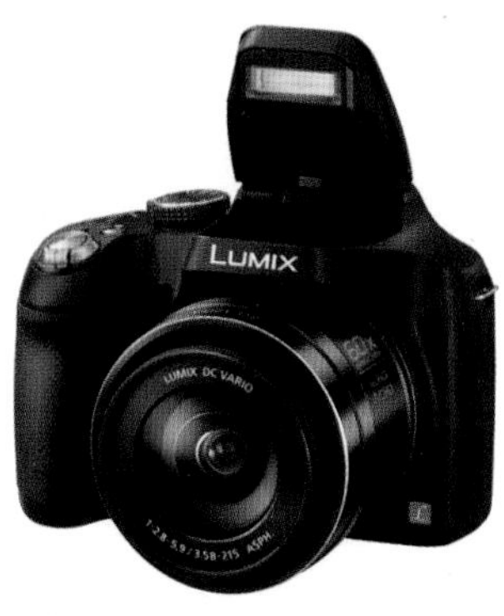

Above: A true superzoom bridge camera, Panasonic's FZ70 boasts a 60x optical zoom lens with a focal length of 20–1200mm.

Bridge cameras "bridge" the gap between compact and system cameras. Usually bigger and better specified than compacts, some use sensors that are the same size as those in system cameras. ISO, aperture, shutter speed, file size, white balance, and metering systems can be changed with ease. Many also shoot Raw, and most can take an external flash and have a filter thread on the lens.

The zoom lens is fixed, but this is compensated for with a huge optical zoom range, suitable for just about any shooting situation. To create such an impressive lens, compromises are made in design, and image quality suffers as a result.

Compact camera

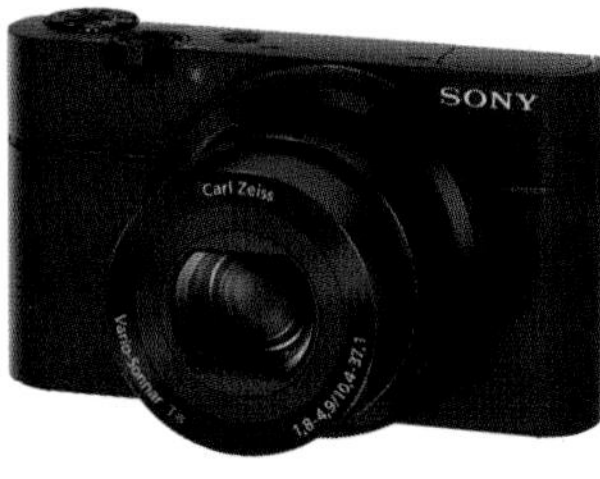

Above: Sony's Cyber-shot RX-100 is a highly regarded compact camera.

Smaller cameras are perfect for the photographer who wants to be more discreet. The advantages of the size of compact and compact system cameras include quiet mode options, which make them the perfect partners for shooting a wedding. The only problem is that they tend to have a slight shutter lag—a fraction of a delay between pressing the shutter-release button and when the camera actually takes the picture.

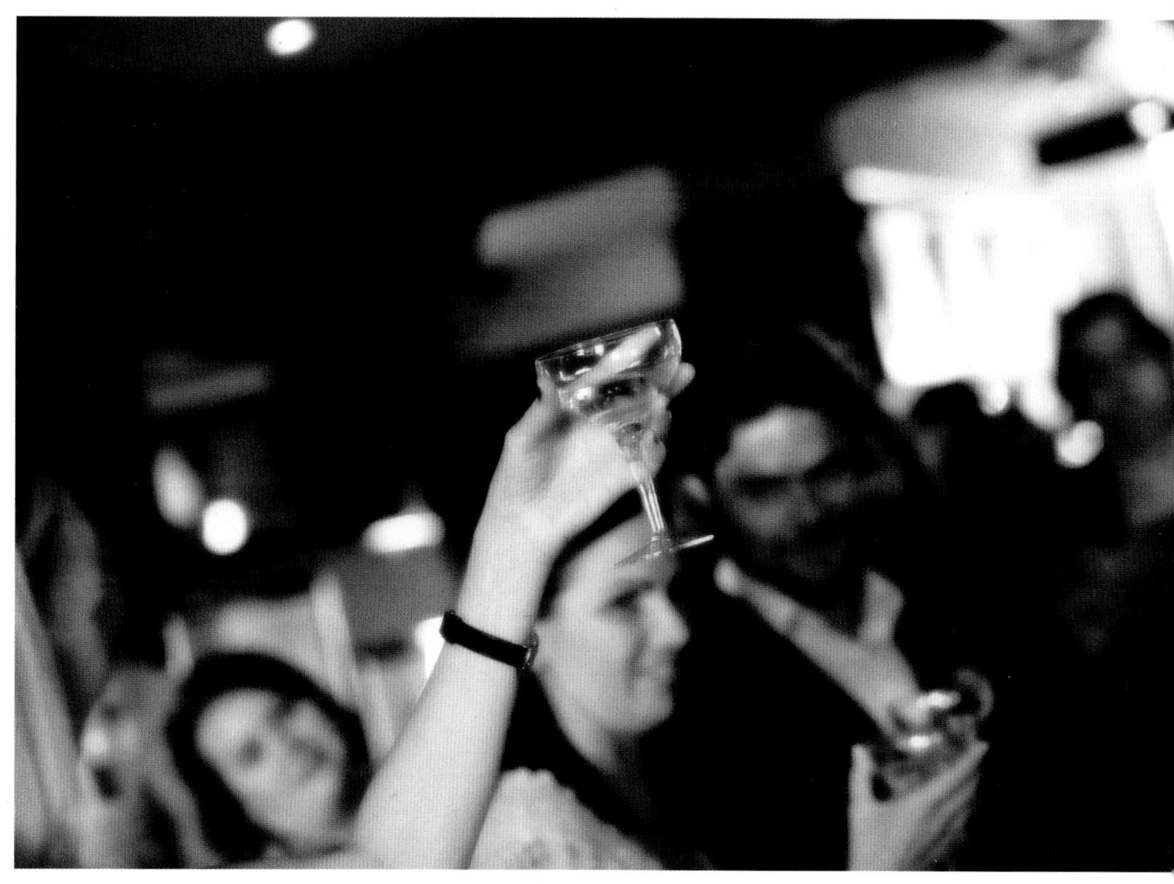

Right: A camera that offers a wide range of ISO settings will allow you to shoot in a range of lighting conditions— from the sunniest of days to the darkest of rooms. Be aware, though, that just because it is claimed that a camera has high ISO settings, it does not mean that the quality of images taken at those high settings is usable—they may contain "noise," which looks like grain.

Lenses

The choice of lens can make or break an image, so if you are in the habit of opting for a zoom all the time I hope this section will inspire you to think a little more about which lens you use and why.

When I bought my first SLR film camera at the age of 15 it came with a basic 50mm f/2.8 prime lens and, after reading all the photo magazines and drooling over the lens catalogs, I dreamed of owning a telephoto zoom. It was not long after a lot of hard work and saving that I bought my first 70–200mm zoom lens. This lens was my favorite, as it allowed me to get up close to a subject in a way that I dared not physically. Today, however, after buying many cameras and many lenses, I find myself more often than not reaching for an updated version of that original 50mm lens.

Why? The prime lens is a powerful tool, with apertures as wide as f/1.4 enabling you to create images that are impossible with a short or long zoom lens. The exaggerated drop in focus from working with a wide aperture—either at wide-angle or close up—creates milky skin tones on the subject, and, at the same time, separates them from the background in an almost three-dimensional way when the light is right.

However, every lens must have a specific job to do because they all take up valuable real estate in my bag, as well as add to the weight I carry around with me all day.

Zoom lenses

For many photographers, given the choice between a prime lens and a zoom lens, they will opt for a zoom every time. You can understand why, as one zoom lens is the equivalent of many primes in the bag, plus it is much quicker to use than having to change lenses all the time.

A medium zoom lens such as the Canon 24–105mm lens, is my favorite all-round zoom for a wedding because it provides the option of zooming from a wide-angle to a medium-telephoto shot with a twist or push of the barrel. The f/4 option is acceptable, but it is not as good as the f/2.8, which performs well in every shot, from small or large groups to the basic portraits of the bride and groom and the wedding party.

A telephoto zoom lens is also one of my preferred lenses for candid portraits and for most of the bride and groom images, as the extra compression gained from the 70–200mm f/2.8 lens captures good detail when shooting wide open, and also throws the background out of focus quickly enough to separate the subjects from the background through shallow depth of field.

The widest lens I use is Sigma's excellent 12–24mm wide-angle zoom lens, which helps me to get a very wide view in the church or at the reception, and creates different-looking images with a slight wide-angle distortion. This lens is perfect for shooting large groups in small side rooms or very tight spaces. I use it sparingly during a wedding to get specific shots, rather than to dominate the style across the whole day, as the images can be an acquired taste.

Prime lenses

A fixed focal length lens has a different image quality to a zoom lens. Even though you have to use your feet more, to move closer to or farther away from the subject, a prime lens provides high-quality and distinctive results at large apertures, adding a creative edge to even the most basic of images.

Note that the following lens properties and characteristics relate to their use with a full-frame-sensor camera. Using a crop-sensor camera will increase the lens telephoto amount according to the sensor size.

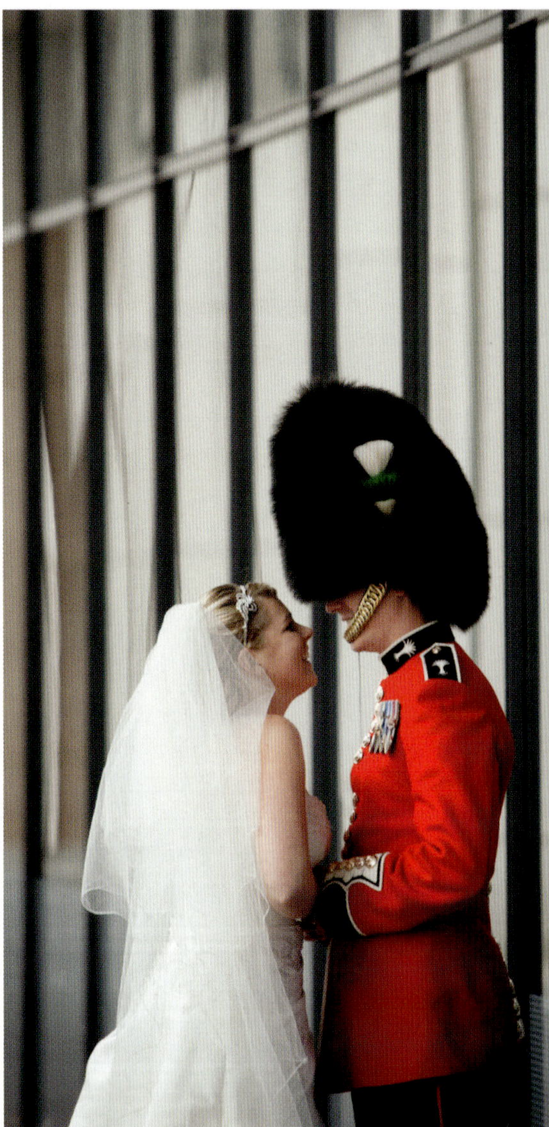

Above: My 70–200mm f/2.8 telephoto is the zoom lens I use for all my bride and groom portraits, as its ability to compress the backgrounds and control the focus depth is exceptional. The lens is also great for shooting candid portraits at a distance.

24mm

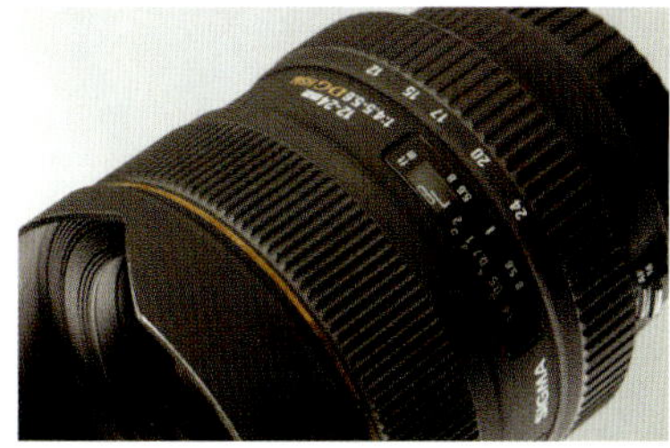

Above: This 24mm wide-angle lens offers no real distortion and is perfect for shooting groups and candid portraits, when I want to show the subjects in the scene but at the same time separate them from the background with a shallow depth of field.

50mm

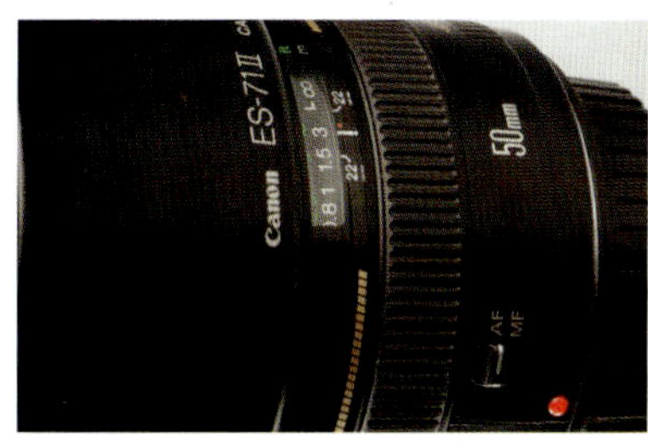

Above: Every bag should contain a 50mm lens, as it is way more useful than any other prime lens, and offers great scope for creativity at apertures between f/2.8 and f/1.4. This lens allows me to separate small groups and subjects from the background by controlling the depth of field.

85mm

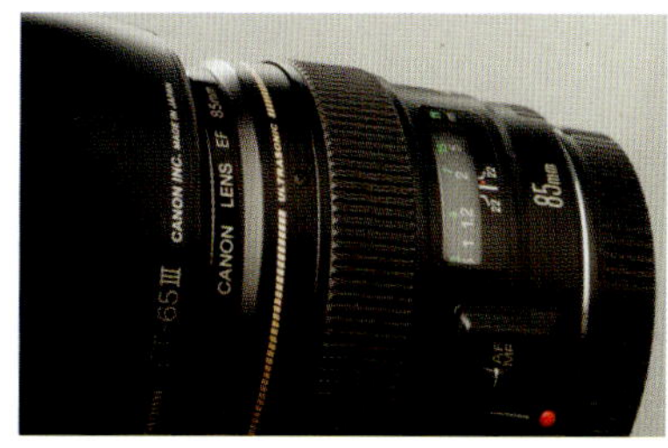

Above: This 85mm is an excellent lens for portraits—some would say the best. The focal length is perfect for head-and-shoulder and three-quarter-length portraits, but is too shallow for groups. The lens gives subjects' skin a "milky" quality when it is used wide open, and it is at its best with details, close-ups, and head shots.

100mm macro

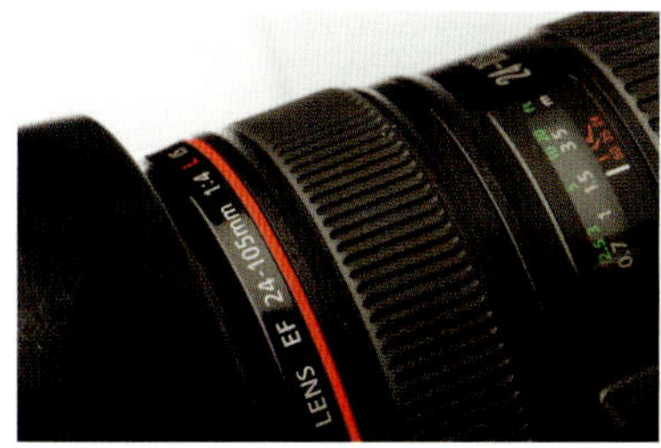

Above: A more specialist lens, this 100mm macro is useful for shooting a lot of detail shots, as well as three-quarter and head-and-shoulder portraits. If space for kit is limited, I would opt for this lens instead of the 85mm, which has difficulty focusing very close.

Super-wide zoom

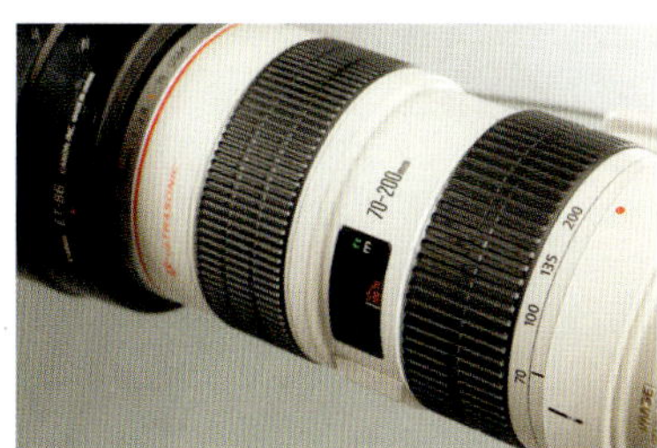

Above: Super-wide zooms are useful when space is tight or you have very large groups.

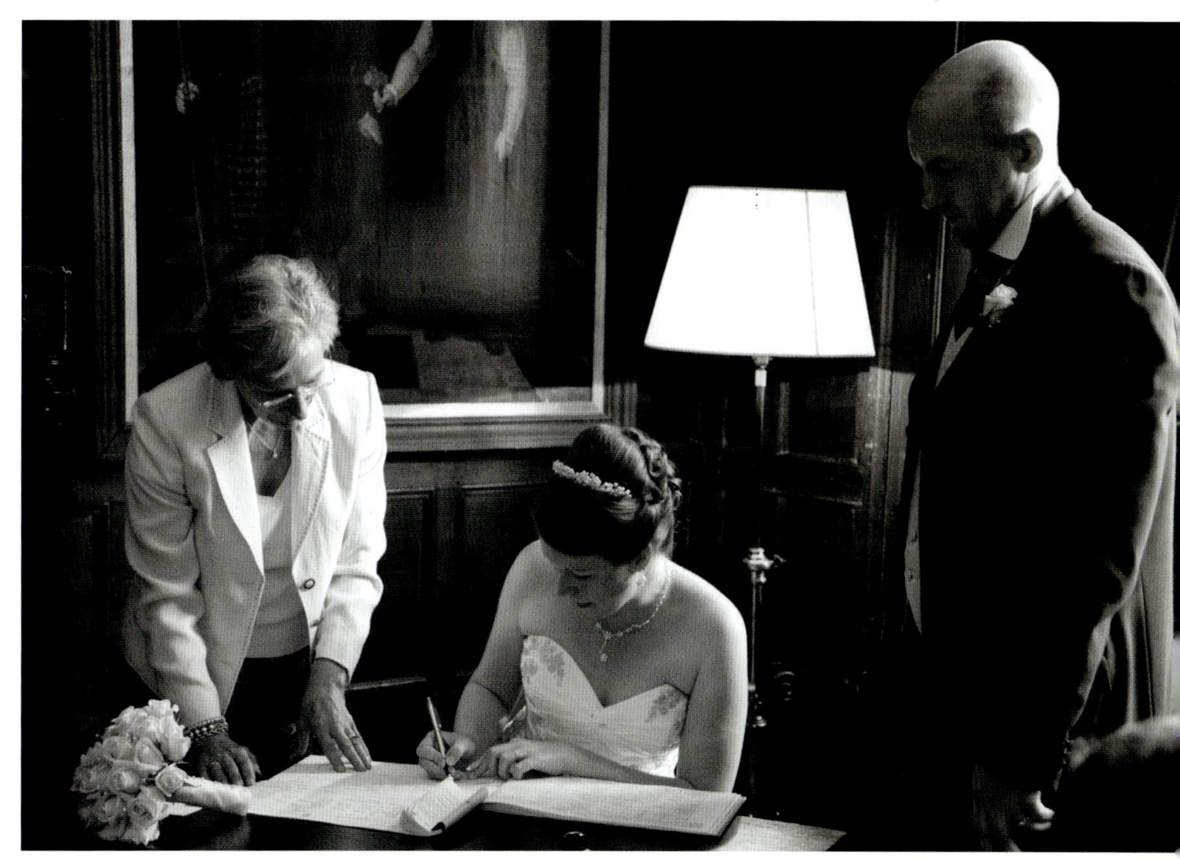

Above: A standard lens can be different for everyone as it is a matter of style, but a standard lens by definition for a full-frame DSLR camera is a 50mm lens.

Flash

The variety of locations you will encounter at each and every wedding means that using some form of flash is going to be essential at some point to illuminate your subjects. Flash, in any form, is an expensive accessory, but one you will always need. There are many things to take into account when purchasing a flash system, and these are the main ones you will need to understand.

Swivel-and-tilt head

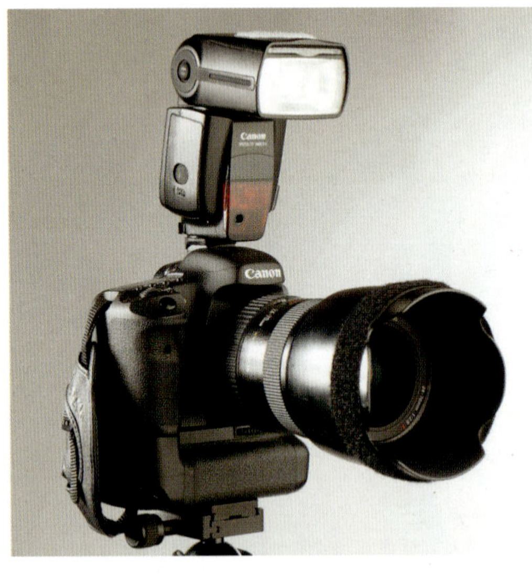

Above: Canon's Speedlite flash units tend not to be updated very often. In 2012 Canon provided a significant update with the Speedlite 600EX—a fully wireless flash instead of the infrared-based connection of previous units. This change allows more options for connecting flash units, including being able to hide a flash unit out of sight and still trigger it.

A movable flash head redirects the flash in an angled direction instead of straight at the subject. By swiveling the head from side to side or up and down, you can redirect the flash to bounce off a surface like a wall.

Bounce card

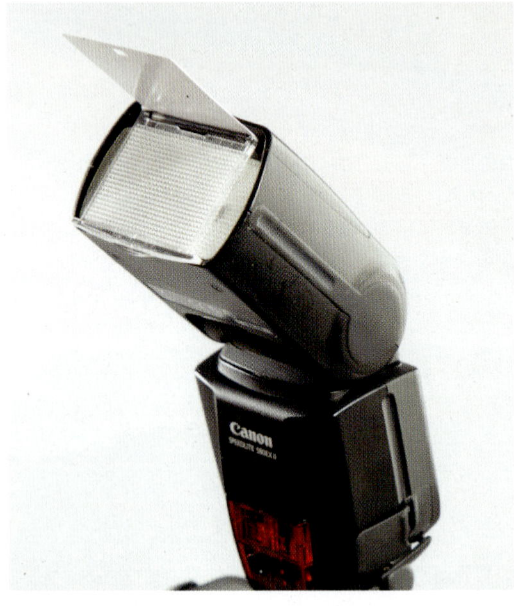

Above: Canon's Speedlite 580EX II functions as a wireless master or slave flash. It features a 24–105mm zoom head with 14mm pop-up bounce card diffuser to redirect some of the flash output toward the subject.

This is a small, pop-up card on the flash unit that can be used to redirect some of the flash toward the subject. This will result in a better position of the catchlight in the eye and more frontal illumination onto the subjects' faces, such as under a lady's hat.

Diffuser

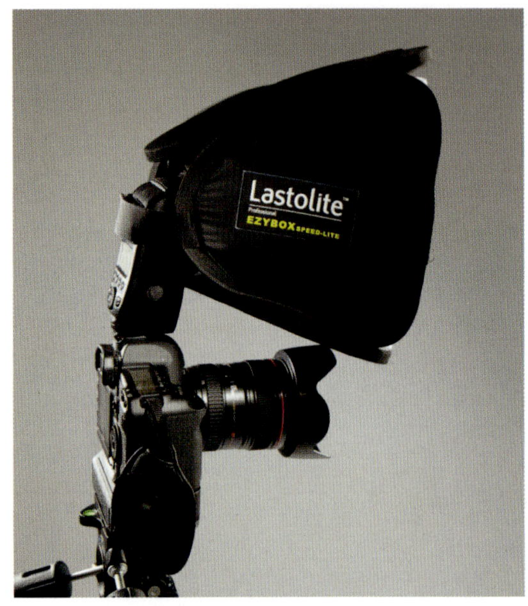

Above: The Ezybox Speed-Lite is a 22 x 22cm (8.5 x 8.5in) mini softbox that attaches directly onto a flashgun whether it's on or off camera, and that folds for portability. It comes with removable inner and outer diffusers, which when used together, produce a 2-stop light loss for excellent softness of light.

The diffuser softens the flash. A diffuser cap is a detachable plastic cap that fits onto the flash head itself to diffuse and enlarge the flash. It is great for wide-angle images, as it increases the spread of the light and softens any shadows behind the subjects.

Additional power

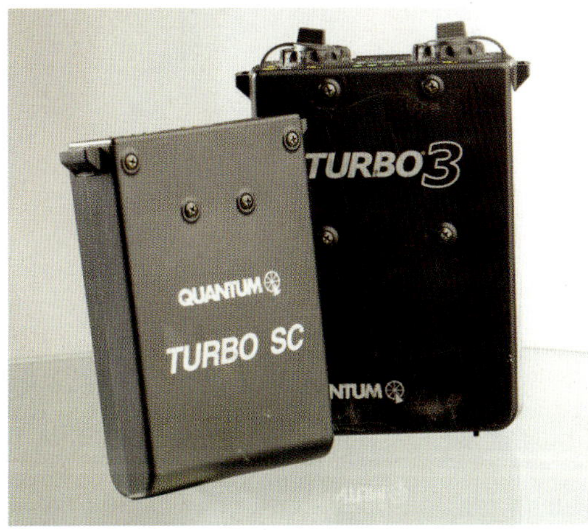

Above: The Quantum power packs for flash units have been an industry standard for more than 20 years. They can recharge a flash unit from full discharge to full recharge in around one second, while giving you over 1000 flashes at full power, making them the perfect accessories to any flash system.

An additional battery or power pack can be attached externally to the flash unit itself, or connected to it using a cable plugged into the power port. The extra power enables near-instant recharging of the flash unit, which is essential for shooting a quick succession of portrait or action shots.

Studio flash

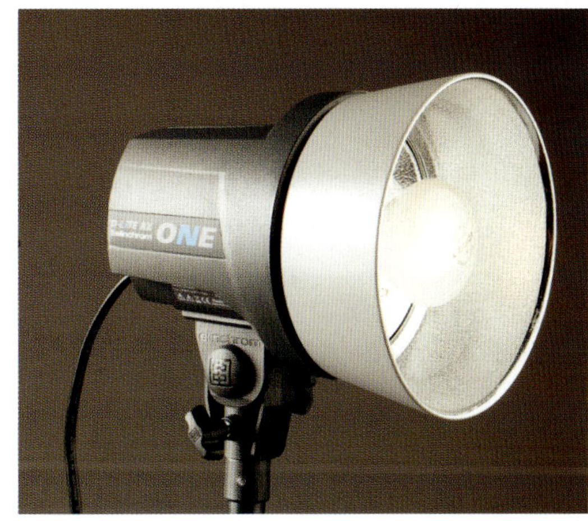

Above: The Elinchrom One is an ideal basic studio system.

It is worth considering taking a studio flash system to a wedding, but such a setup is not very portable because it relies on mains power. However, if you are planning a small, studio-style setup at the reception, I would definitely opt for the mains-powered flash because it will give you quicker recharging times and illuminate the scene much better, using flash modeling bulbs. The Elinchrom One flash, for example, is an ideal basic studio system, which allows you to grow your kit and accessories over time.

GUIDE NUMBER

The Guide Number (GN) denotes the power of a flash unit. This should allow a straightforward comparison of units, but different manufacturers base their Guide Number on slightly different situations, so check out the reviews on one of the specialist photography web sites.

Portable flash

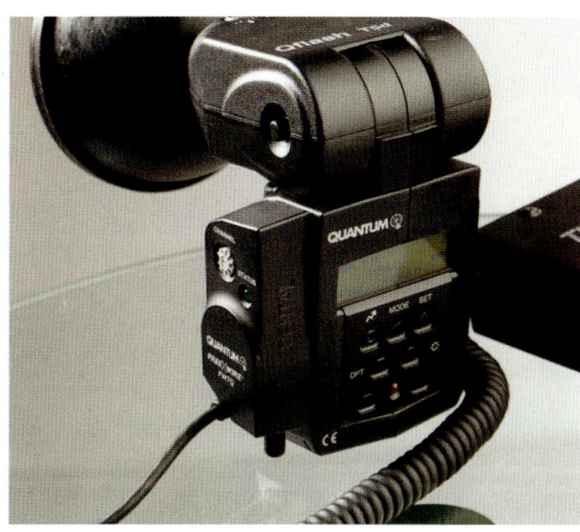

Above: The Quantum T5D Digital Flash Gun is a completely automated flash head with many advanced user-selectable operating modes. TTL flash exposures are possible with selected digital cameras. The Q Flash has a removable parabolic reflector for clean, even light spread.

There are more professional options for flash than a simple, standard flash unit, of course. The Quantum flash is a fully portable flash system that allows you to use a through-the-lens (TTL) function for automatic flash power selection to obtain the desired exposure.

The Q flash is more powerful than a simple flash unit, and its smaller sibling, the Quantum Trio, can be put on the camera hotshoe. Both units provide faster recharge times and a round light source, which is more pleasing to the eye. Each unit needs to be powered by a Quantum battery.

Elinchrom Quadra is a professional portable system used by many of the top professional photographers. However, because of its 400W power output and need for manual setup, it is more often used as a small, portable studio flash, for creative flash on location, or to light up big areas such as reception rooms.

Reflectors & Diffusers

Reflectors are available in different surface finishes to help adjust the level of reflectance and color. I tend to always carry a silver and white diffuser, as well as a deflector for very sunny days (a deflector is a combination of a diffuser and a reflector with narrow, silver stripes on one side). Harsh sunlight can be reflected into dark areas at great distances, and you can even use a second reflector to redirect light from your first reflector, but you will need to maximize the reflected light using a silver or gold surface.

Remember to meter again for the new exposure when you apply the reflector, or your exposure will be incorrect. You will also need to meter again if you change to a different type or size of reflector at any time during a shoot.

So when should you use which type of reflector? I use a silver and white reflector for much of the time, because of the predominantly overcast climate in the UK, to enhance and reflect as much light onto the subject as possible.

I use a gold and white reflector at winter weddings to warm up the natural blue light in the scene, especially on cold, snowy days. If this is too strong, I opt for a silver and gold-striped reflector—the Lastolite Sunfire—which still warms up the light but not quite as much.

On very sunny days, I use a white-surfaced reflector to soften the reflected light in combination with a diffuser. If I need to reflect the sun at greater distances from the subjects, or to provide a spotlight effect, I use a silver-surfaced reflector.

Right: A selection of foldable diffusers in a range of colors and sizes to suit all light levels.

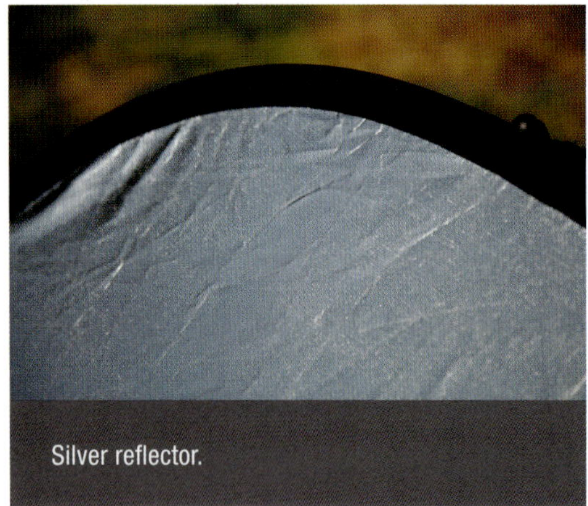

Silver reflector.

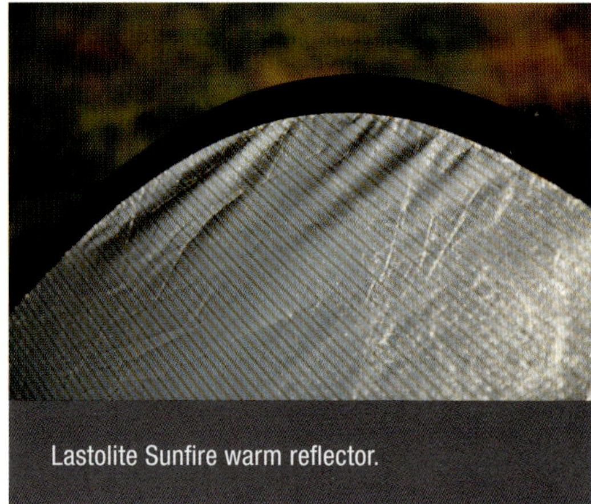

Lastolite Sunfire warm reflector.

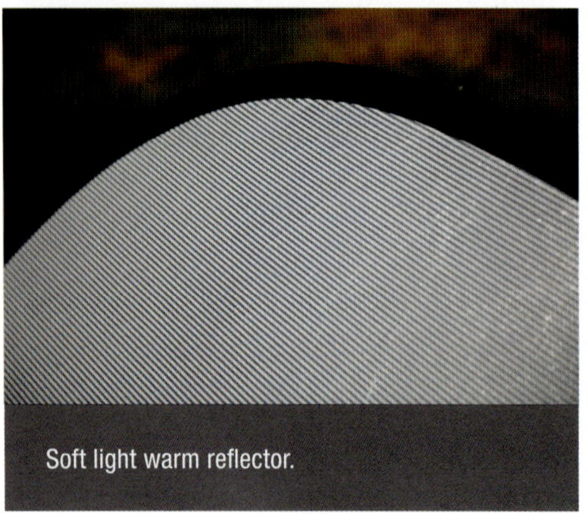

Soft light warm reflector.

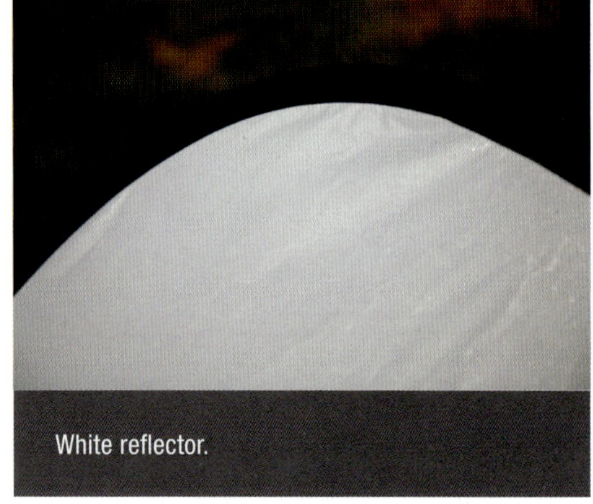

White reflector.

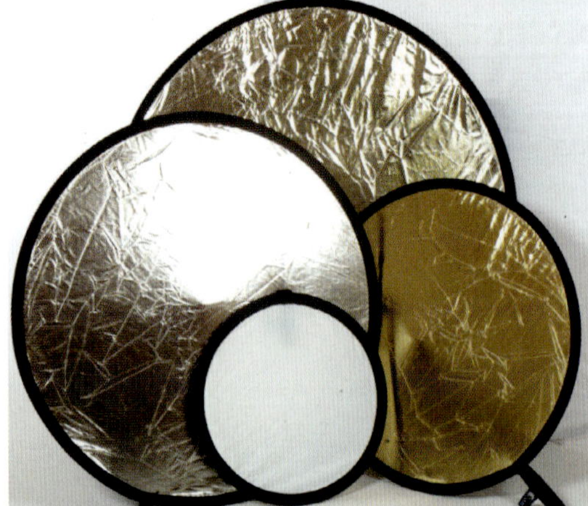

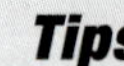

Tips

Avoid putting a reflector on the opposite side of the light source, as this will give an unnatural direction that will flatten the light and make the subjects appear fatter due to the lack of directional light.

In some circumstances a black "reflector" can be used to deaden the light on one side of the subject, a technique known as subtractive lighting. This technique also increases the modeling on the face.

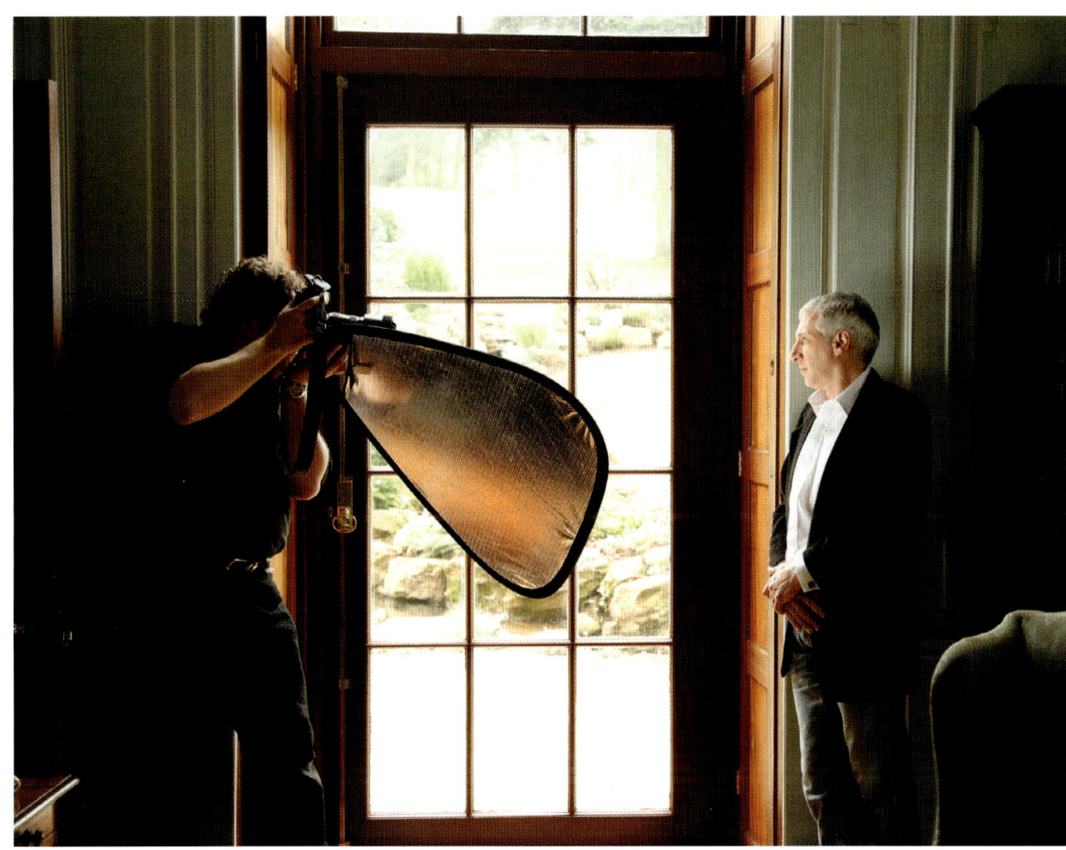

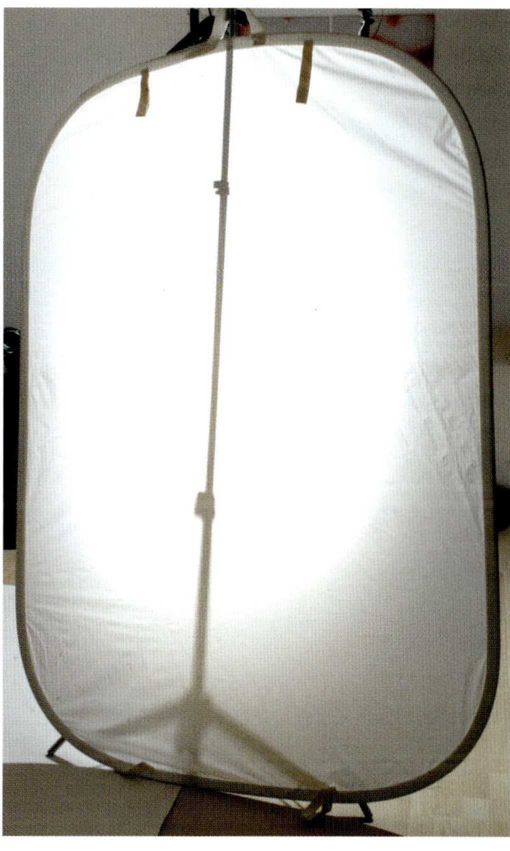

Above: If you are working alone, then a reflector that incorporates a handle allows you to direct the light where you want it without the need for assistance, stands, or supports.

Above: Used to diffuse harsh sunlight or off-camera flash, a large diffusion panel can make a real difference to the quality of light.

When I want to shoot outside in sunny conditions and I cannot easily reduce or diffuse the light, I use a diffuser. This is a type of reflector made from a material that allows the light through, but softens it. The diffuser is placed between the sun and the subjects being photographed. Once the diffuser is in place, take a new exposure meter reading to allow for the reduction of the light on the subject.

Diffusers come in different shapes and sizes. They also come in different materials that reduce the light passing through them in different amounts, usually by one or two f-stops. I tend to use the Lastolite TriGrip diffuser, which is triangular, and has a handle so you can hold it with one hand while still being able to shoot with the other. An assistant can hold the diffuser, but I am not afraid to ask a young bridesmaid, pageboy, or even a passing stranger in the street for help.

In addition, for my commercial photography, I have very large 2 x 2m (6 x 6ft) frames to which I can fit different reflective or diffusive materials—perfect for shooting family groups—although I don't use them at weddings myself because of the work involved in setting them up. However, I do know many photographers who shoot in very sunny conditions and rely on the Lastolite Skylite panels to get the job done.

Meters

Correct exposure is essential not only to image quality and detail, but also for a faster workflow and postproduction. Every slightly incorrect exposure needs to be corrected in some way, and this adds time, so it is important to get the exposure right in the first place, and this is why correct metering is essential.

There are two main types of light metering: in-camera and with a handheld meter. Both mean that you need to use the Manual mode on your camera to set exposure. The in-camera option may seem quicker and easier, but it often relies on you checking the preview image on the back of the camera—and the histogram or exposure warning—and making a slight adjustment. A handheld meter gives you a readout of the light falling on your subject and you then need to transfer the settings to the camera to obtain the correct exposure. A handheld meter usually has the facility to meter for your flash as well, which, of course, in-camera metering cannot do.

There are many types of handheld meter, so when investing in one think forward a little, as there will not be much difference from a basic meter to a professional meter in price, although the difference in functionality will be evident. The main facility the meter should have is an option for an ambient reading and another for flash power. If you plan to shoot with creative flash, a professional handheld light meter will become invaluable, as it takes all the guesswork out setting exposure.

The professional meters will often give you the option of choosing a reading based on either aperture or shutter speed. This is essential for me, as I always set my working aperture and ISO, and so the only aspect that changes is the shutter speed. I use the Sekonic L-358, which is an older model now, but gives me these options as well as being able set very specific metering in tenths of a stop for working with flash.

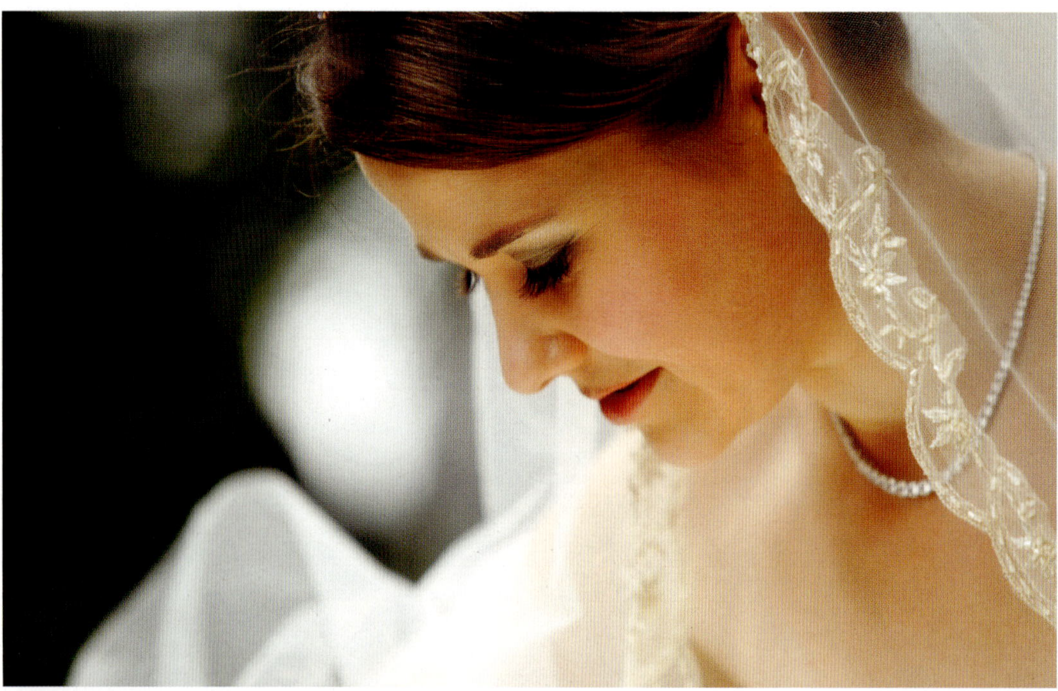

Above: Metering allows you to obtain an accurate reading even when the subject and background are totally different in tonality.

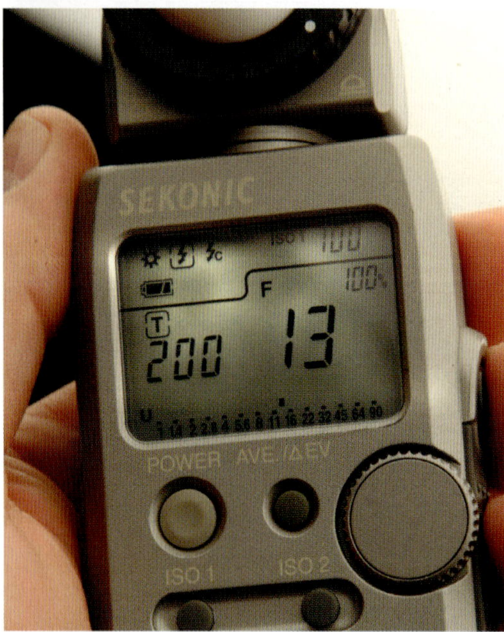

Above: A handheld meter has the ability to meter for flash.

METER SET IN AMBIENT MODE
When setting the meter to work in ambient light—whether you are shooting outside in daylight, or inside with a tungsten light or window light—the meter is set to the sun icon to record the exposure.

METER SET IN FLASH MODE
When you are shooting with flash you need to meter the flash output to give a perfect working aperture—a flash reading depends on which ISO and aperture settings you wish to work with. To measure flash, set the icon to the lightning bolt icon.

Tripods & Monopods

I only use a tripod now when I have to—in other words when the exposure is going to be longer than 1/15 sec. and there is no natural support around—but for over 20 years I always shot my main formal portraits with the camera on a tripod.

There are many types of tripod and monopod. For most, the deciding factor now is weight, so it is a good idea to opt for a carbonfiber model for that reason alone. Another function to look for is the ability to change the tripod or monopod height from a standing position, as this is makes life easier and the shoot faster.

Also use a tripod for any long exposures at night or interiors. This helps when you're having to add "pops" of white or colored flash around the scene to bring areas alive. Always use a monopod when shooting for long periods of time with a heavy and long 70–200mm lens, especially at the end of the wedding day for the speeches and candid portraits. By this time, you will be tired and also using slower shutter speeds to be able to use ambient light in the scene.

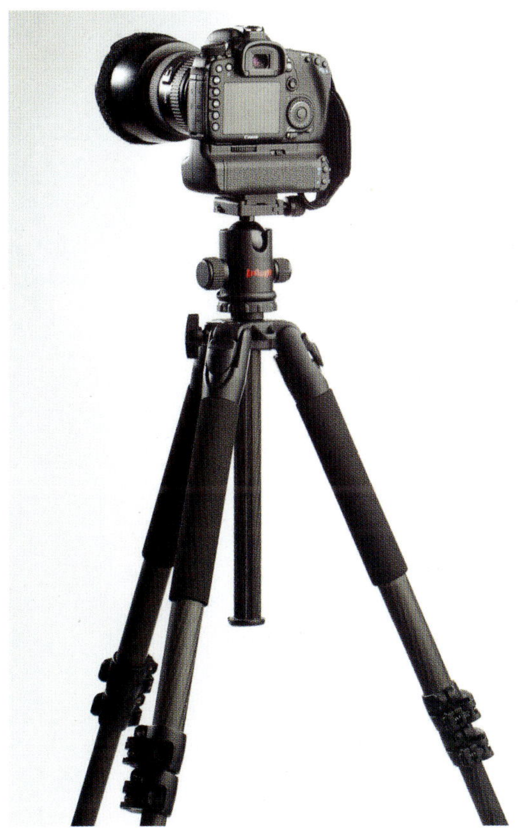

Above: Tripods are ideal for very long exposures—as well as for marking your "space" when shooting groups—but they can be a slow option at any other time.

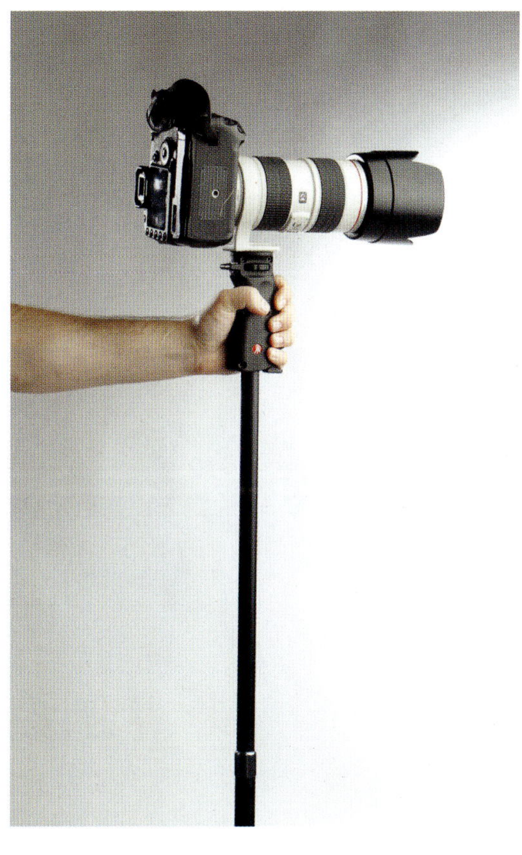

Above: A monopod is a good way to support a long zoom lens as it helps you take the weight, especially when shooting for long periods of time such as during the speeches.

Storage

If you are shooting Raw files, which I hope you are, you will need a large number of memory cards, depending on their capacity. I use around 24GB of storage each wedding, but I carry around cards amounting to 64GB, just in case.

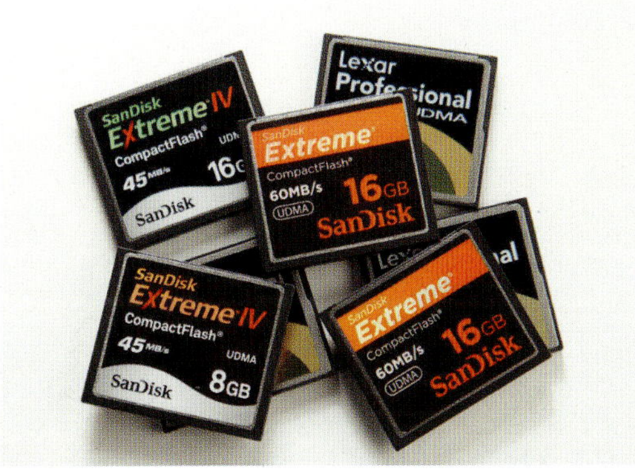

Left: Don't just buy the cheapest storage cards as you need reliability and quality. I buy either Lexar or SanDisk cards, as I have trusted their products for many years without any problems.

Bags

The biggest mistake you can make when shooting weddings, especially if you are working alone, is having too much or not enough equipment with you to complete the tasks at hand. This is why you must think through your choice of bag carefully, and not just grab the one you picked up for free years ago.

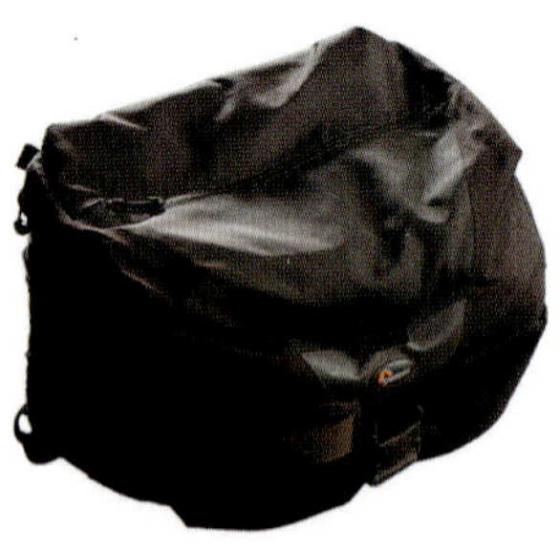

Above: The conventional bag is a great carry-all option, but the weight can be too much at the end of a long day, or where you have to walk a long way.

Large bag

If you are working with an assistant, you will probably use a large bag and keep more kit at hand, especially as you will probably end up shooting more creative images at some stage using specific reflectors and multiple flashes. Still make sure that you are not overloading the bag just for the sake of having everything with you, so for every wedding decide what equipment you need, based on the type of wedding and the locations. The great thing about a large bag is that you can put it down, and there is no way you will forget about it or miss it. It also acts as a useful "perimeter," or a way to mark your space when guests are milling around you or when you are shooting groups.

Sling bag

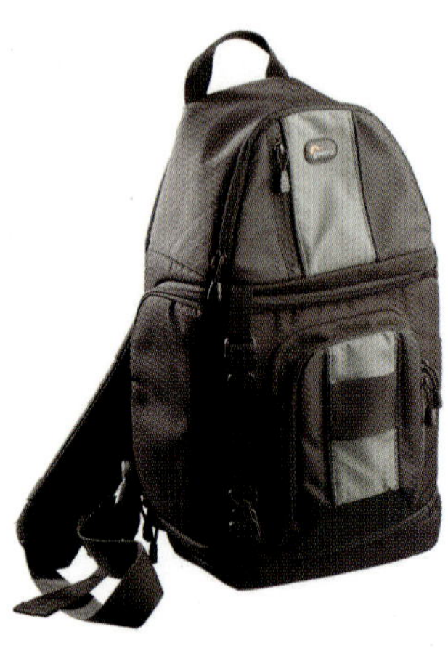

Above: When traveling light, a sling bag is perfect for carrying several lenses as well as flashgun, memory cards, and batteries—especially if you are leaving your spare equipment in a vehicle.

If you are working alone, you will often be working light, with minimal equipment at hand and with the backup equipment left in the car. This means that your bag needs to be just big enough to carry the essentials, including backups. So to travel light, a small sling bag or backpack may be enough for a few lenses, cards, and a spare flash—just make sure it is easy to get the equipment out in a real-case scenario, as sometimes when you open one of these bags everything just falls out.

Trolley bag

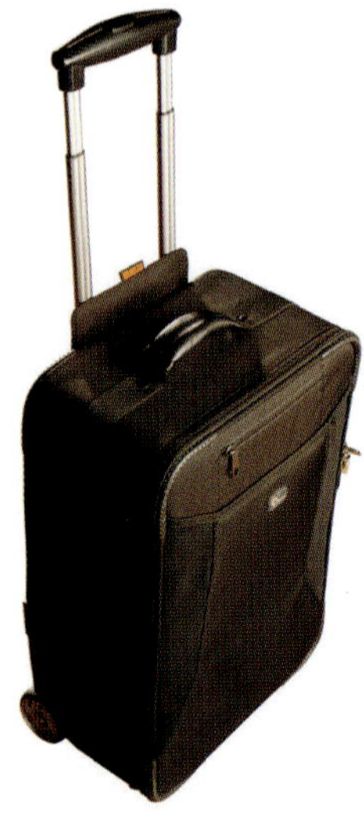

Above: Trolley bags are good, although they can be difficult if there are lots of steps or soft ground to travel over; however, they do make a safe and lighter option to carrying equipment.

If you are traveling abroad, a trolley bag designed for airplane cabins is ideal. You don't want your kit going through the hold in case it gets lost or damaged—which would be a disaster—and you may be traveling to a foreign country with no idea of how or where to buy new equipment in time for the wedding. Trolley bags are also useful when you have to walk long distances, but only across flat ground such as in a city center—they are useless for crossing fields and parkland.

Tip

When selecting a bag, always go into a camera store and get the feel of what it will take as well as how easy it is to carry. Trade shows are a good place to start planning your next bag purchase.

What's In My Bag?

Here I've listed the equipment I take with me to every wedding, which can serve as a guide to what you'll need. I use two different sets of equipment: in spring and summer I keep a minimum amount of kit to hand, leaving the backups and extras in the car; and in the fall and winter—during the dark months—I need to carry more kit, especially studio flash and extra flash units.

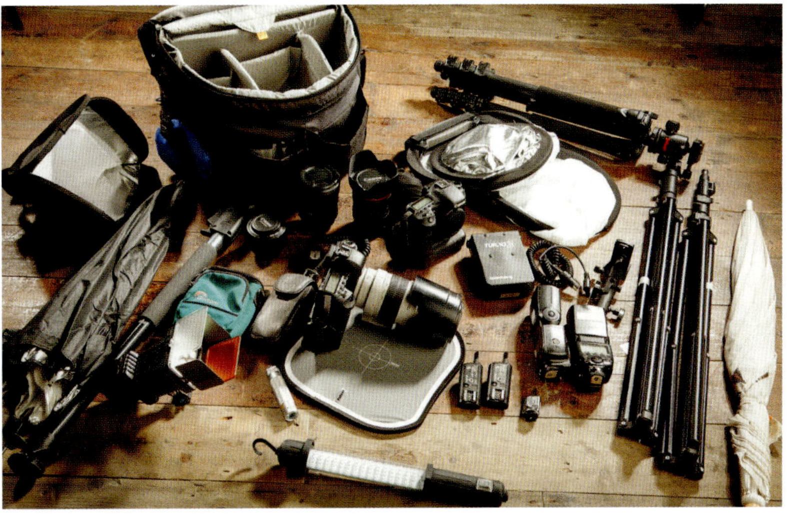

Right: Lay out all your equipment on the floor and check each item off against your list to ensure you never leave anything behind.

SPRING AND SUMMER	
Main kit	*In-car backup bag*
2 x camera bodies	Large bag
24–105mm lens	1 x camera body
70–200mm lens	2 x Canon Speedlite flash units
50mm lens	Stands
12–24mm lens	Flash coldshoe mounts
Sekonic meter	Gray card
2 x Canon Speedlite flash units	Lastolite Ezybox II softbox
1 x camera strap	Lastolite Universal umbrella
1 x Quantum battery	2 x triggers/receivers for flash
Lastolite TriGrip diffuser	LED lights
Lastolite TriGrip deflector	Tripod
Lastolite TriGrip silver/white reflector	Compact flash cards
Manfrotto monopod	Rain umbrella
Sling bag	Rain cover
Trigger/receiver units for flash	Raincoat
TTL cable	
Compact flash cards	

FALL AND WINTER	
Main kit	*In-car backup bag*
2 x camera bodies	Large bag
24–105mm lens	1 x camera body
70–200mm lens	2 x Canon Speedlite flash units
85mm lens, 50mm lens	Stands
12–24mm lens	Flash coldshoe mounts
Sekonic meter	Gray card
3 x Canon Speedlite flash units	Lastolite Ezybox II softbox
1 x camera strap	Lastolite Universal umbrella
2 x Quantum batteries	2 x triggers/receivers for flash
Lastolite TriGrip silver/white reflector	LED lights
Manfrotto monopod	Lastolite TriGrip diffuser
Large waterproof bag	Elinchrom One studio flash kit (two heads)
2 x trigger/receiver units for flash	Elinchrom Sky ports
TTL cable	Background support system
Compact flash cards	Gray mottled background cloth
Rain cover	Tripod
	Compact flash cards
	Rain umbrella
	Raincoat
	Change of clothes

Appropriate Clothing

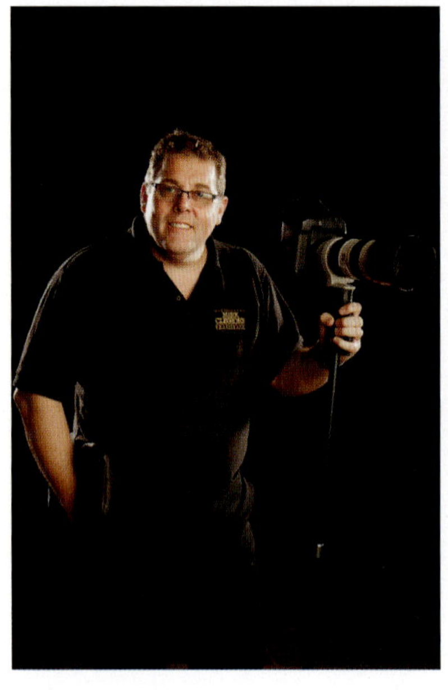 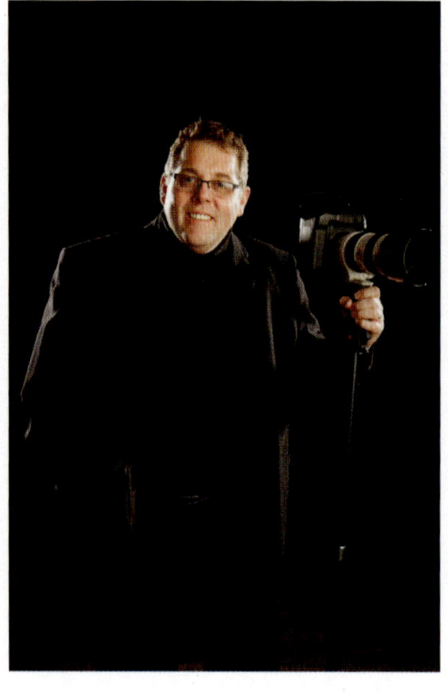 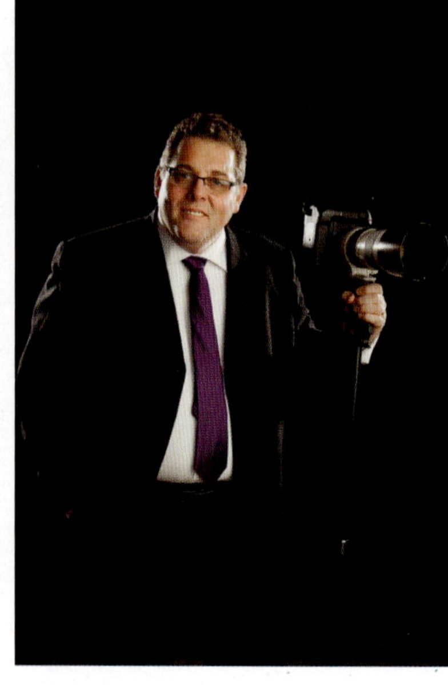 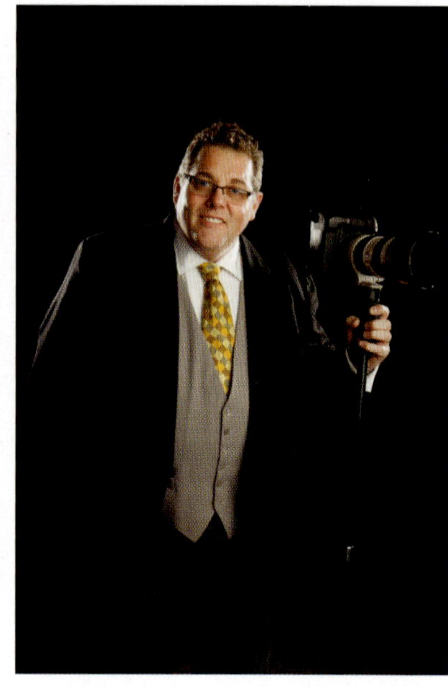

Above left & right:
Informal Dressing informally can make you feel a little underdressed at times, but it is essential to dress for the job and not to look nice.

Above left & right:
Formal I like to dress in a suit or in formals at weddings, but they become impractical in summer months.

Knowing what to wear to a wedding is one of those questions that I get asked a lot, and my answer, of course, is that it all depends on what type of wedding you are shooting.

The most important thing to consider is practicality during the wedding day, as kneeling or lying down on dirty or damp surfaces is not going to be practical, no matter what you wear and what the weather conditions are, plus your dry cleaning bill could become costly over 12 months.

I prefer to dress for the occasion, so if a wedding is more formal I wear either a morning suit or a normal suit. Never invest in tails, as these are far too formal for photography at a wedding, plus the tails would be in the dirt at some stage when you knelt down. I usually wear a shirt and tie with a suit, or with a simple rollneck sweater, especially in winter.

For summer and less formal weddings, you can wear a polo-style t-shirt, as you'll find it more practical, and you can swap shirts a few times on very hot days. The only thing I do miss when I am dressed informally is jacket pockets—they are useful for keeping things to hand. I always wear a pair of smart, black slacks, but I usually opt for a machine-washable pair rather than dry-clean only, because they will need a lot of cleaning. When working abroad in hot climates, opt for a less formal, summer look, and if the wedding is on a beach, and informal, you may feel it fitting to wear a pair of dress shorts.

I tend to wear predominantly black—a black suit, shirt, t-shirts, and so on—partly to stay in the background, but if you are more flamboyant then that is not a problem, as long as you don't outshine the couple or family on the day.

Lady photographers tend to work in a trouser suit or slacks, and wear a blouse rather than a dress—again for reasons of practicality—but if you feel you want to have a more feminine look, wear what you feel good in and just be aware of where and how you stand, sit, or lay—to avoid any embarrassment to you or others.

When you shoot a themed, costumed wedding, you should, of course, try to fit in, but you would have to pass on the cost of any costume hire to the bride and groom.

Tip

Remember that looking smart is said to start with your shoes!

Using an Assistant

There are advantages and disadvantages to having an assistant at a wedding, but the benefits will always outweigh the drawbacks. The only real negative in having an assistant is the cost element—you will need to pay the assistant and this extra cost might not be one you will recoup. But don't despair—a friend or a family member can always step in, even if it is to just carry your bag. The first step is to define the role: are they an extra photographer or a helper?

A second shooter will not have the time to assist you, so you will have to expect that you will lose the second pair of hands. The role of second shooter is an important one, and is not to be taken lightly, as I would expect them to concentrate on the shots I cannot get and not just duplicate what I am shooting. For instance, a second photographer should shoot at very different angles from the main camera, to completely change the look of the images. Usually, the images are shot closer in, filling the frame more, with more emphasis on the expressions and candid interactions of the family and guests, even picking out certain people from the crowd. A good second shooter can increase your reprint order by more than 100%, especially if you give them training before the wedding in what to look for and shoot.

Having an additional person in a pure assistant role will enable you both to concentrate on the task at hand, as they can start anticipating your needs for kit and accessories. A good assistant will make you look amazing, but a bad assistant can make you look a bit of a fool, especially if they are not paying attention to you. An assistant will also be under some stress at the wedding, particularly if they have had little or no training in the role, so make sure you run through some of the basic tasks beforehand. I always train my assistants in the art of using a reflector, as well as the basic setup of a flash and its menu system, as the extra pair of hands can really make a

difference to your images. The assistant will help you quickly create dramatically different images by moving the direction of the light in the scene, which can completely change the intensity and mood of the picture.

ASSISTANT

An assistant's role can be many things, but I ask them to take care of the kit as well as to anticipate my requirements, and be ready with reflectors and flash when needed.

HIRED HAND

As most of the time I work alone, it's not uncommon for me to ask a passer-by or a guest to help out. You can usually persuade a young person to help, and bribery works too!

Tip

Is the assistant going to be exactly that—an assistant—or are they going to be a second shooter? Whichever you decide, make sure you define their role and what you expect from them on the day.

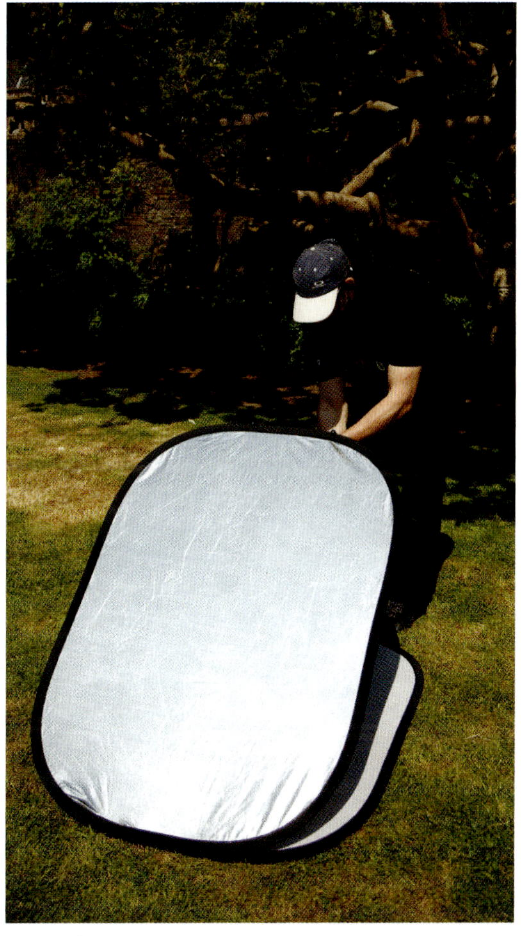

Above: It is important to train an assistant in the art of assembling and using a reflector.

Chapter 2
Basic Principles

As well as the bad habits that have been encouraged by digital photography, there are so many aspects that have changed for the better, and even those lazy habits can be fixed if we learn our craft and the way to use our equipment properly. However, it's vital that all photographers must first learn the basic principles and techniques concerned with exposure, ISO, and natural and artificial light—and how to manipulate them to create stunning and compelling images.

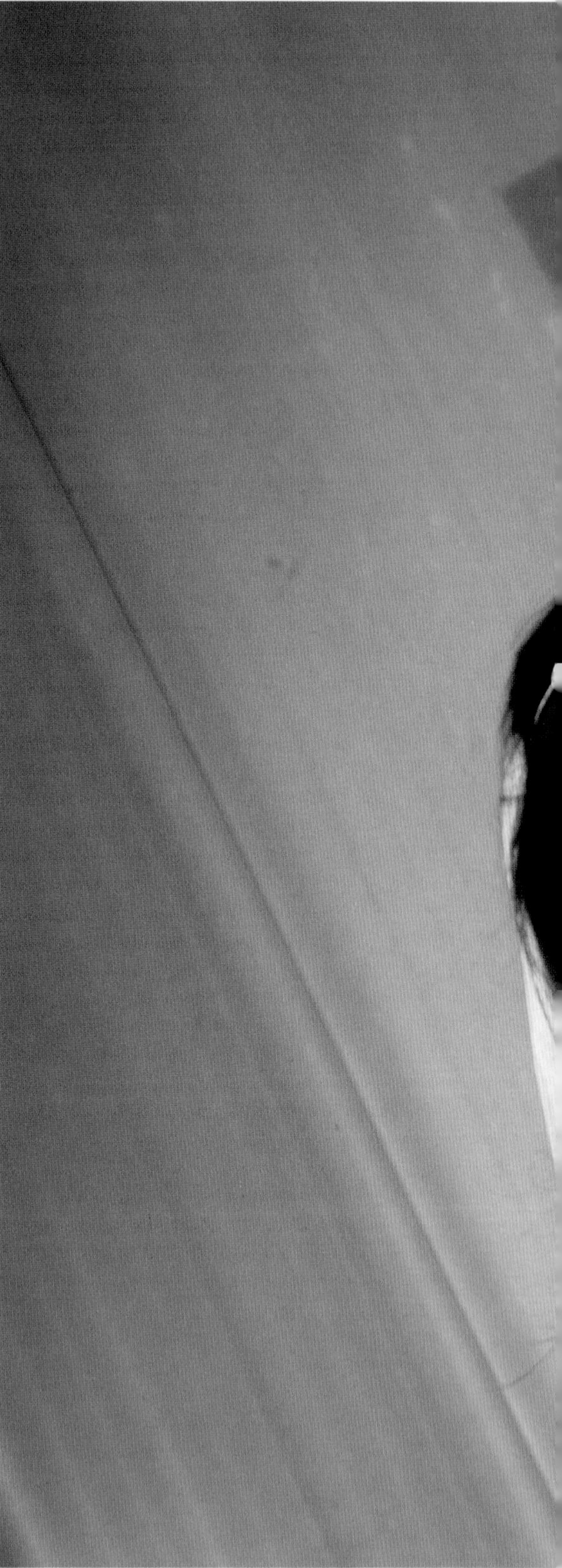

Right: Getting as much right in camera is vital, even creative crops such as the one shown here.

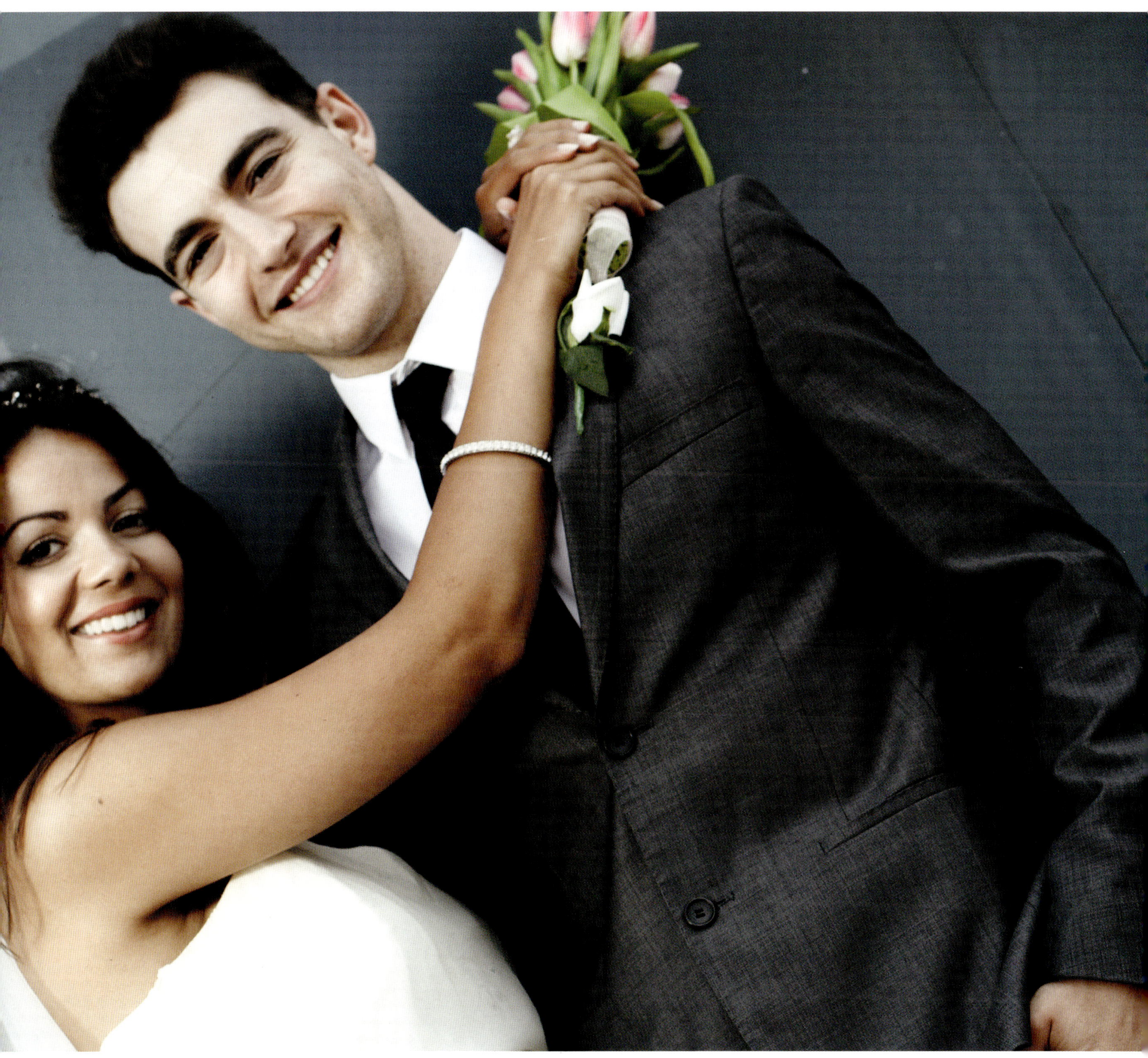

Exposure

Most cameras offer the option to set exposures automatically, but as your photographic skills improve you will want more control over an image. To do this you will have to apply your own exposure alterations, both for creative purposes and to obtain the ultimate in accuracy.

Exposure is a complex subject, and there are many books that cover in depth the relationship between aperture and depth of field, shutter speed and the representation of motion, and the interrelation between all the different variables. For that reason I will leave the fundamentals of exposure to other books and concentrate instead on how they are applied to wedding photography.

For the wedding photographer, a "correct" exposure is a combination of a technically accurate exposure and the creative application of exposure variables. Creatively, you should pay attention to the depth of field in order to position the envelope of sharp focus correctly, while the choice of shutter speed can be used to freeze movement or create motion blur as desired. The ISO rating can also be manipulated, not just as a subsidiary of the other variables or in order to obtain a correct exposure, but also to create noise. How the creative variables can be used is covered, where relevant, throughout this book.

Technically, wedding photographers should aim to retain as much detail as possible within most images. This can be challenging when faced with white dresses and black suits. Overexposed images lose detail in the highlights and generally suffer from too much contrast, giving little transition to tones and resulting in white blotches instead of graduated highlights. Underexposed images will appear muddy with little contrast and will need to be printed lighter, which can add to the flat look due to the lack of a true black in the photograph. Although some digital correction is possible, and even though Raw files allow more leeway, it is best to get it right in camera.

HISTOGRAMS

To make an accurate assessment of an exposure, you need to refer to its histogram (see right). Most cameras allow you to view a histogram of your photographs, either in "live view" before capture, or in playback after the exposure has been made.

A histogram is a graph showing the distribution of tones in your image. The horizontal axis represents the brightness levels, from black on the extreme left through to white at the right. Halfway across the histogram are tones that correspond to mid-gray. Subjects such as grass or stone roughly equate to mid-gray, so the histogram of a correctly exposed image of a rock face would peak in the middle. The vertical axis represents the number of pixels of each tone.

There is no ideal shape for a histogram, but if it is "clipped" (when the histogram leans against one end of the graph) the tonal range has exceeded the point at which detail could be recorded. When the histogram is clipped on the left, no detail will be recorded in the darkest parts of your photo; those areas will be pure black. When the histogram is clipped on the right, no detail will be recorded in the brightest parts of your image; those areas will be pure white.

When assessing a histogram, remember that a high number of pixels on the right-hand side is normal for scenes containing a lot of light elements, whereas a high number of pixels on the left-hand side is normal for scenes containing a lot of dark elements. When shooting average scenes, try to capture a full range of tones, with the majority of pixels to the left of center—underexposure is easier to correct in postproduction than overexposure, where detail is irretrievably lost.

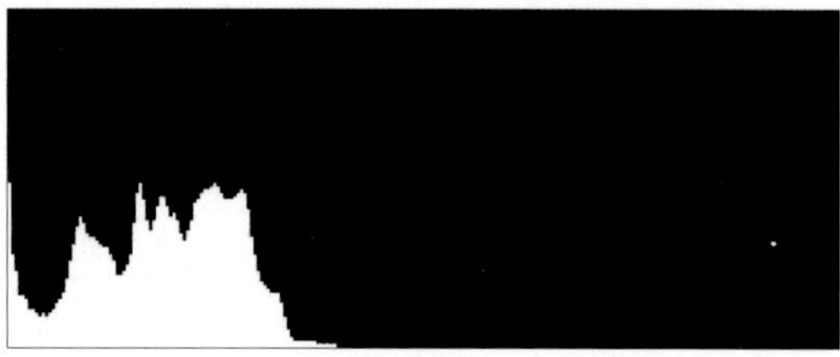

Above: This histogram is skewed to the left, with no tones lighter than mid-gray. This indicates that the photograph might be underexposed.

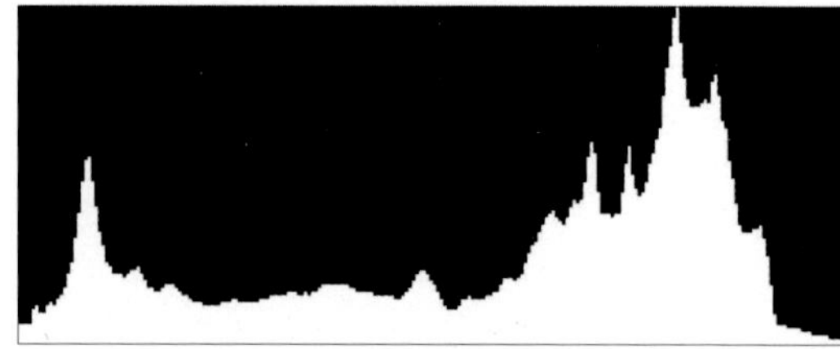

Above: The tonal range is better distributed in this histogram, with no clipping at either end. This is a good exposure.

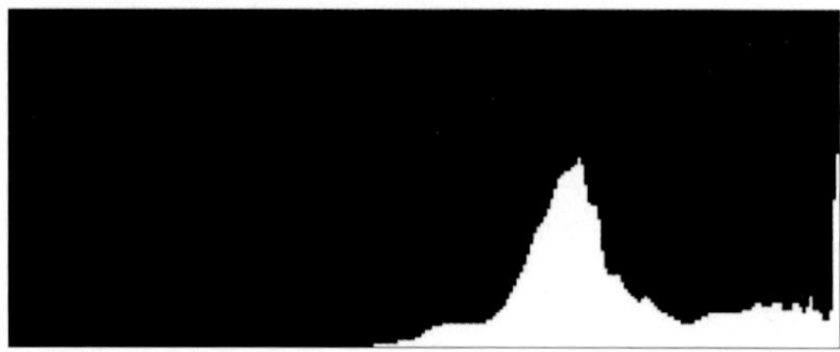

Above: There are few tones in this histogram that are darker than mid-gray and the highlights have been clipped. This could indicate overexposure.

Right: As you can see from this high-key image, the correct exposure is giving detail throughout all the whites and cream colors, as well as in the shadow areas of the hair. A perfect exposure, and consequently a perfect print.

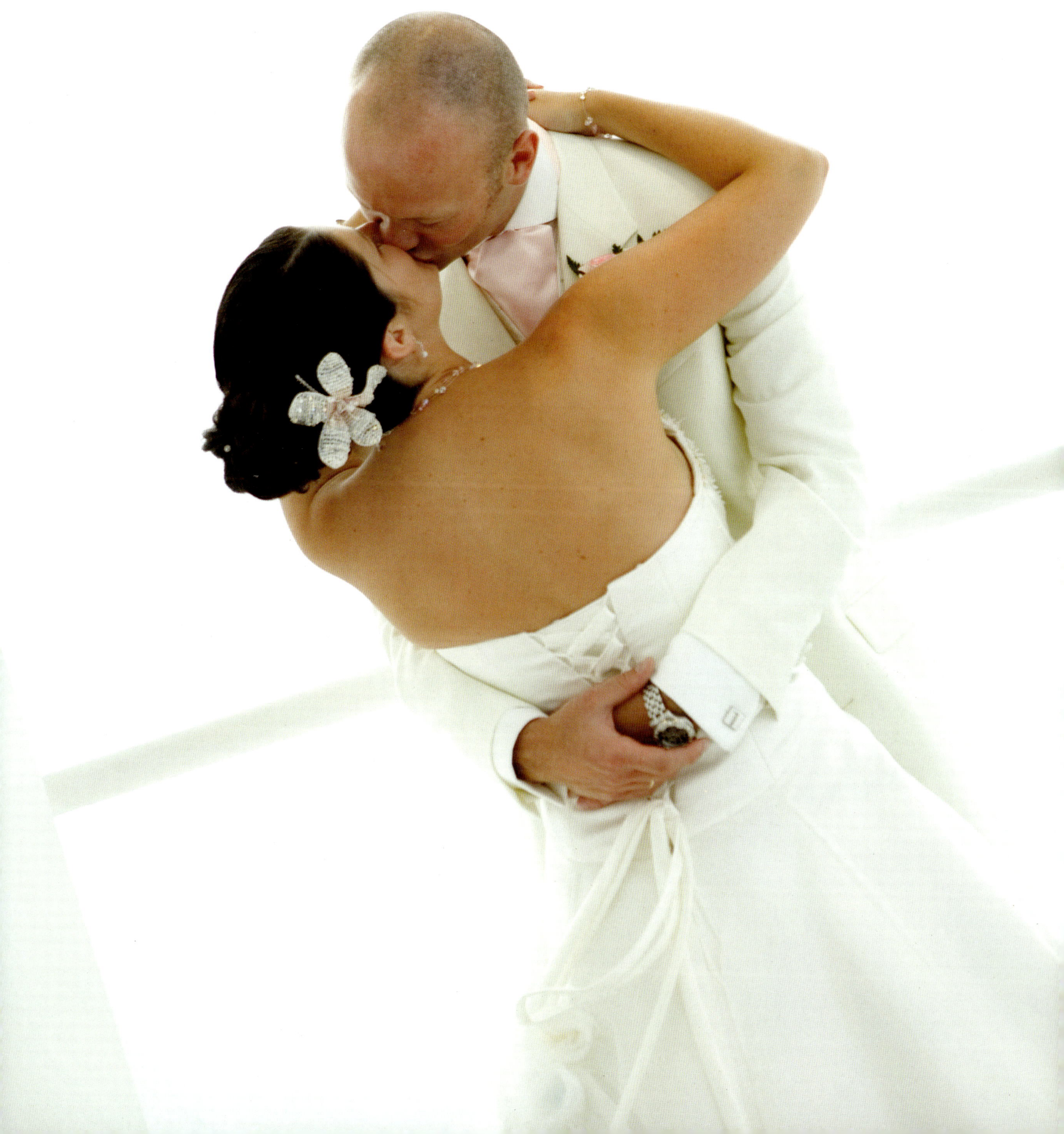

Right: I shoot in Manual mode most of the time when working with on-camera flash. Once I have a meter reading, using Manual ensures that I get the same exposure every time. This image needed two Canon Speedlites to give me the f/20 exposure, overpowering the ambient light and providing great depth of field.

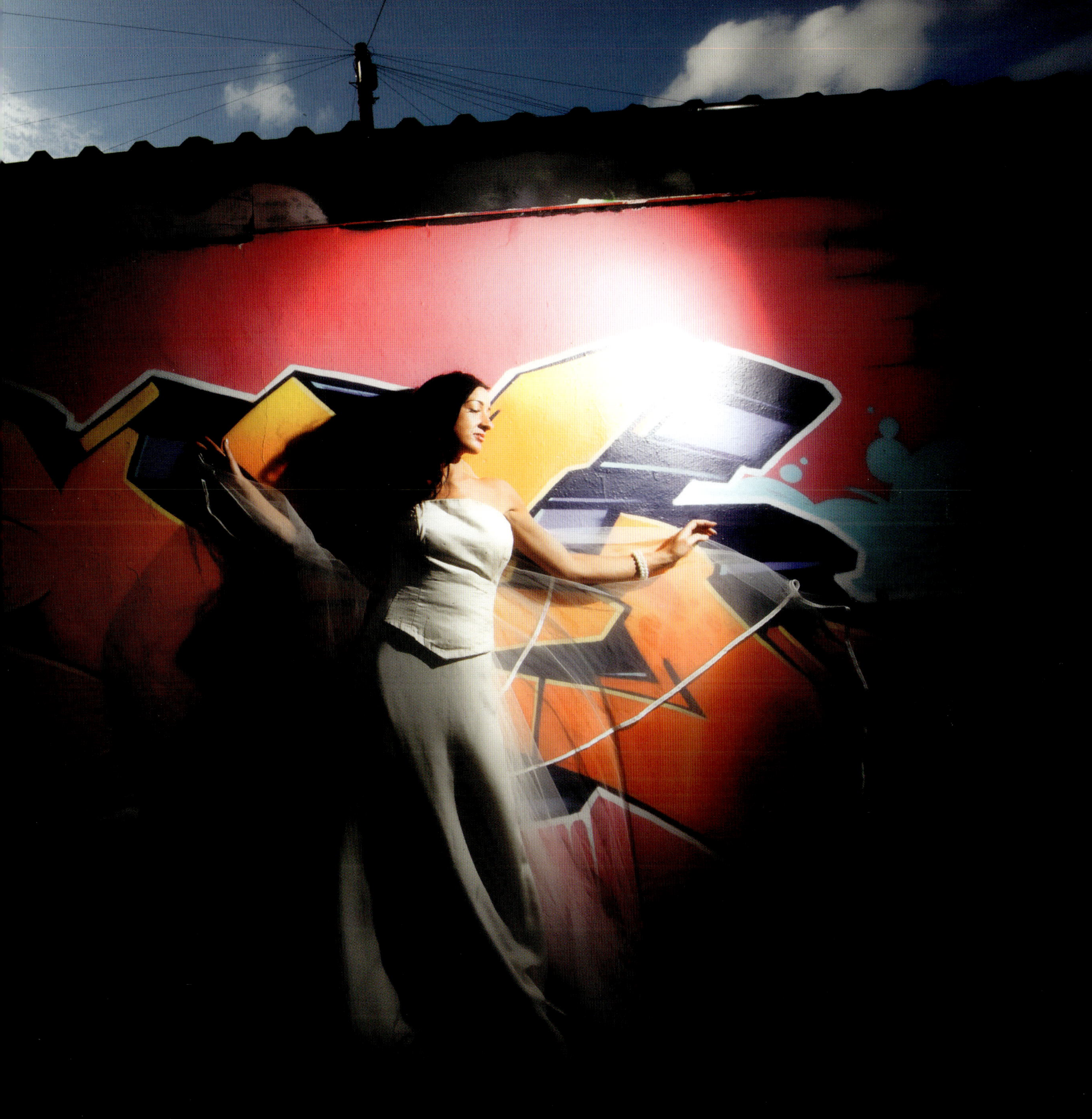

Choosing the ISO Rating

The ISO speed indicates how sensitive the sensor is to light, which determines how much exposure it requires to record a subject or scene accurately. The sheer ease with which you can flit from one ISO rating to another and back again means that it is just as much a useful exposure tool as aperture and shutter speed in influencing the creative mood of your images. Recent advances in noise reduction technology at high ISO ratings also mean that the low-light shooting capabilities of modern digital cameras are staggering. It is now feasible to shoot day and night, and come back with very usable images.

The lowest ISO speed on a camera is usually 100, which produces crisp images with rich detail and vibrant color. However, as the sensor/film is less sensitive, it needs to be exposed to light for longer, leading to slower shutter speeds and/or wider apertures. While long shutter speeds are not a problem for static subjects, they are of little use for capturing movement and handholding your equipment. In addition, the use of wide apertures reduces depth of field, which can be an issue for close-up subjects.

If you require a fast shutter speed (and the largest aperture available is not enough to allow one), boost the ISO to suit your needs. The highest ISO a camera is capable of also varies, and some cameras have the ability to almost see in the dark with ISO values in the hundreds of thousands. Many new DSLR cameras produce near-flawless images up to around ISO 800, and some high-end pro cameras boast upper ISO ratings of 102,400, which basically allows you to take photographs of subjects at night or in low light when you can't even see them with your naked eye! Increasing the ISO also facilitates faster shutter speeds (which is ideal for reducing camera shake or freezing a moving subject) and/or allow smaller apertures (increasing depth of field).

There is a cost to using a high ISO setting: sensors are designed to provide optimum quality at their base ISO, so as the ISO is increased, image quality decreases due to the intrusion of "noise." This means there is often a compromise that needs to be made between the usability of the camera and image quality: a slightly noisy (but sharp) image is often better than a cleaner image with camera shake because the shutter speed was too low.

As with aperture and shutter speed, ISO is measured in stops, so ISO 400 is 2 stops faster than ISO 100. In practical terms this means you could use a shutter speed of 1/500 sec. rather than 1/60 sec. in the same light conditions, or shoot using f/11 instead of f/5.6. As with aperture and shutter speed, ISO can frequently be set in ½- or ⅓-stop increments.

Your DSLR will almost certainly offer the facility of an Auto ISO setting, regardless of the exposure mode, but the ability to override this may only be available in Aperture Priority, Shutter Priority, Program, and Manual modes. In the increasingly common scene modes (which tend to be largely automated) you may not be able to set a specific ISO. The automation of the ISO setting can be extremely useful, provided you can determine a "ceiling" for the highest setting. When an ISO ceiling is selected, you can determine an exact aperture and an exact shutter speed in Manual exposure mode, leaving the camera to vary just the ISO setting in line with variations in meter readings. It will do this without the risk of the camera setting an ISO that results in unacceptable noise levels.

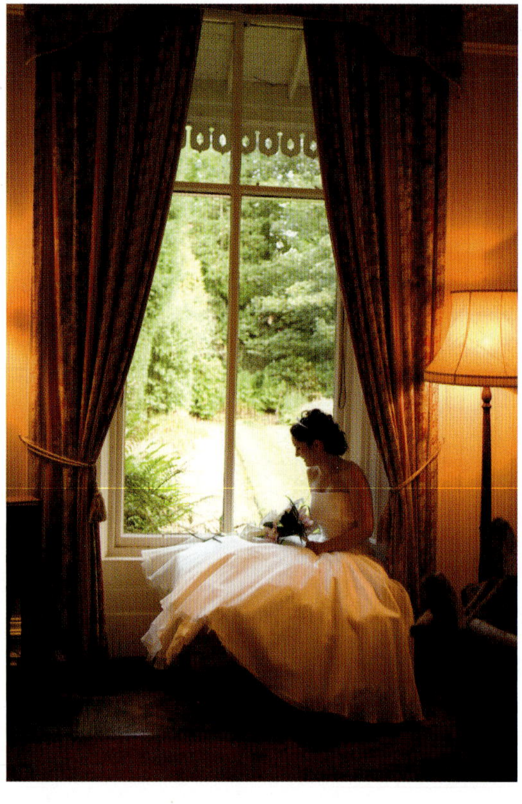

Above: Higher ISOs such as ISO 800 will start to make noise a bigger issue—you don't have to look too hard at the print to see the granular texture in the smoother toned areas.

Right: Shooting in very low levels of light is possible with today's digital cameras and the very high ISO values they offer, which increase the sensor's sensitivity.

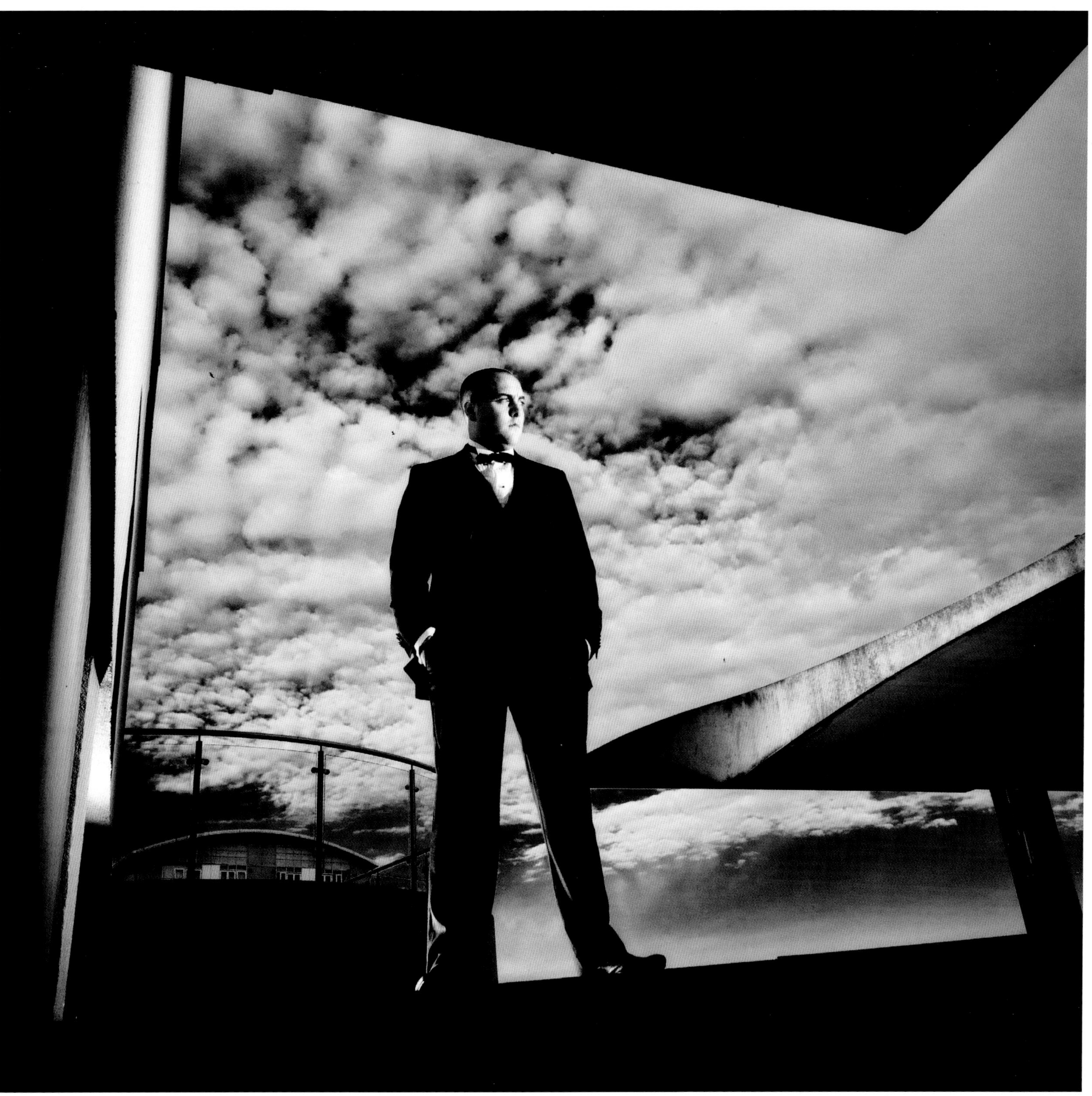

Shooting Modes

If you are to make full use of your camera's technology, it's essential that you understand its metering and exposure options, and some of the automatic or semi-automatic modes can be employed successfully in wedding photography. Aperture Priority (Av) and Shutter Priority (S or Tv) modes are both useful functions, offering a balance of flexibility and automation. However, I prefer to use full Manual (M) mode so that I can control the aperture directly, keeping an eye on the shutter speed, particularly in low light levels, in case a tripod is needed.

Automatic modes

New photographers have a tendency to set everything to "automatic." This means that you will no longer be learning many of the essential photography skills, such as exposure control, or understanding the control of tone in the scene— essential if you want to produce images with detail in both highlights and shadows without relying on postproduction to fix things.

Modern cameras also often offer specific automatic "scene" modes that are designed to make photography hassle-free, in addition to the more sophisticated shooting modes that will give you more control over the aperture, shutter speed, and ISO. See opposite for a brief description of the main automatic modes, but bear in mind that these should be treated merely as a learning tool by the aspiring wedding photographer, and should be avoided as an easy option.

AUTOMATED SHOOTING MODES

- **Full Auto** This is the mode commonly used by beginners. The camera makes all decisions with regard to aperture, shutter speed, and ISO. It is also likely to set file quality (to JPEG) and a range of other options—everything except focus. The user can't override many (if any) of these settings.

- **Scene modes** These modes are geared toward specific shooting situations such as Portrait, Party, Sports, and Close-up. An adequate aperture is selected automatically when the camera is switched to the relevant mode. Scene modes record images as JPEGs, removing many postproduction options.

- **Program mode** This offers more control than Full Auto and is often the next point on the learning curve for beginners. In this mode, the camera's meter determines the exposure and suggests a combination of aperture and shutter speed.

- **Aperture Priority mode** For complete control over aperture, this is the mode to use. For example, you may want to use a wide aperture for a restricted depth of field, blurring the background behind the main subject. Alternatively, you may want to use a small aperture to provide a greater depth of field, so the foreground, middle distance, and far distance are in focus. Having selected the aperture, the camera determines an appropriate shutter speed according to the meter reading. The difference between this and the more automated modes is that the user retains control over a wider range of settings.

- **Shutter Priority mode** This works like Aperture Priority, except that you set the desired shutter speed. This may be because you want a fast shutter speed to freeze movement in a fast-moving subject, or you want to deliberately blur the motion in an image by using a slow shutter speed. In both cases, the camera chooses the aperture.

Manual control

Only with the camera set to Manual mode will you really learn. With this setting, you'll be responsible for setting both the aperture and the shutter speed independently of one another. If the selected combination does not match the exposure reading suggested by the camera's meter, there will be a mechanism for indicating that overexposure or underexposure is likely. However, it is highly likely that you will already have determined the meter reading is inappropriate, which is why the camera has been set to Manual mode in the first place: the camera isn't always right!

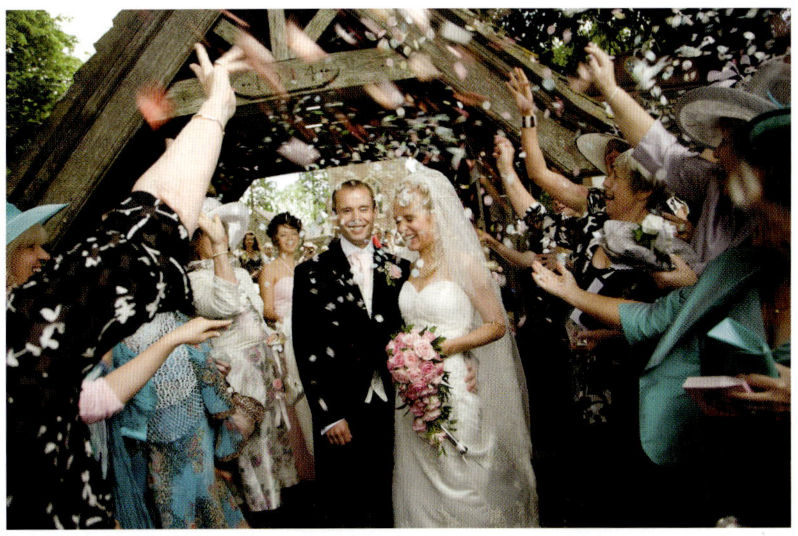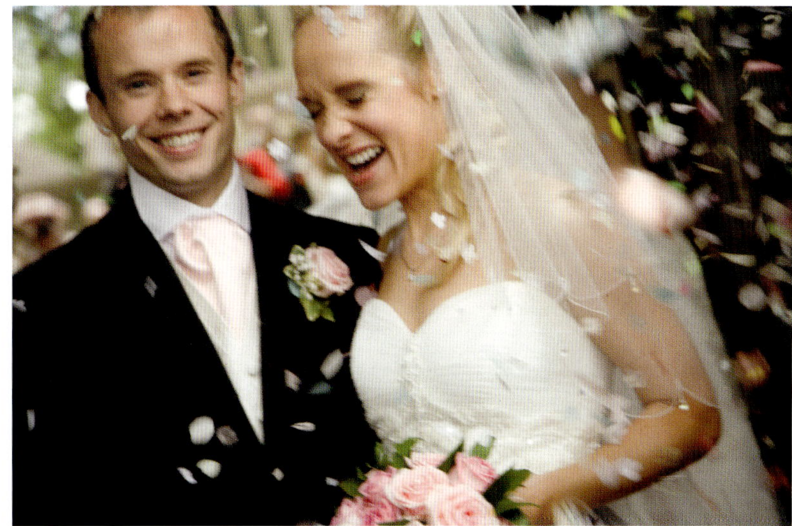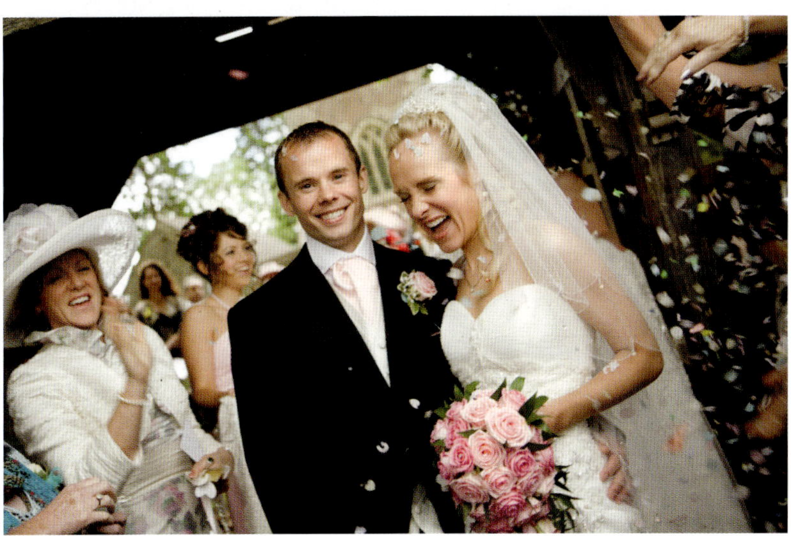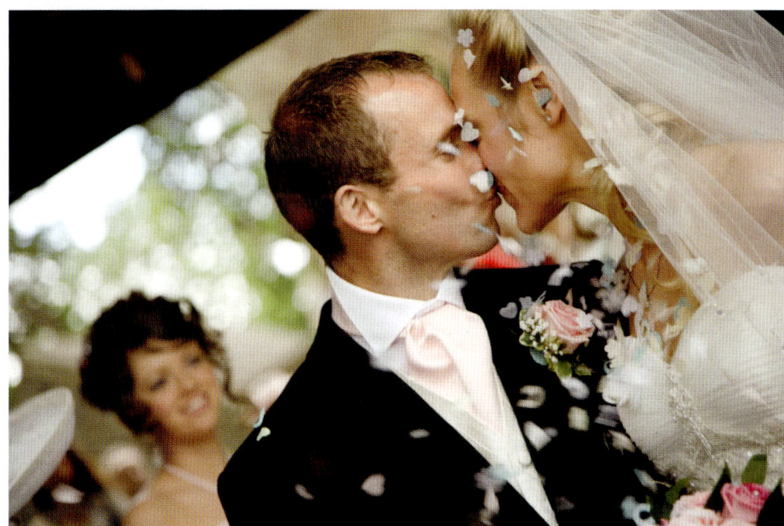

Burst shooting

Many photographers have begun to shoot in a machine-gun style, spraying the scene with the camera, hoping to get the image, instead of using a more traditional, sniper-style of shooting—waiting and then taking the images you wish to shoot.

Burst-shooting is slightly different, and this can pay off as a technique in situations such as the throwing of the confetti or the bouquet. Shooting in bursts helps to ensure the photographer gets the shot, as well as offering multiple, additional images that can be used in the final design and layout of the wedding album.

Burst shooting must not be confused with bracketing exposures. This has also become a habit for many, especially for photographers who shoot using automatic exposure modes. Even though bracketing helps to solve the problem of lost detail in a scene, by exposing at different steps of exposure compensation, the photographer still has to spend more time editing in postproduction, finding and selecting the right exposure. The other disadvantage of this technique is that you may miss exposing correctly at the right moment, and not get the shot of the perfect expression or position of your subject.

Above: The confetti-throwing is a perfect example of when to shoot in burst mode—this allows you to use a variety of images when designing the album layout.

Natural Light

I have a simple saying: "Natural light before reflector, reflector before flash, and flash as a last resort." If you follow this rule of thumb, you will learn to work faster and more efficiently, and be able to develop a style that is right for you and your clients.

So what is natural light? Natural light is anything already available in the scene—it could be from the sun at an outdoor location, from the light coming in through a window, or even from the artificial room lights. I class all of these constant light sources as natural light, as you cannot control the different quantities, qualities, or color temperatures.

The natural light can be hard, creating extremes of contrast, or soft if the light is diffused, creating little contrast. In addition, light usually has a direction to it, even when it is very diffused. Understanding the direction of the light is fundamental to people photography, as the direction of the light will either complement your subject or not.

As wedding photographers, we often work in open light, in the middle of the day, which can cause problems. At this time of day, the light is from directly above, which causes ugly, high-contrast shadows on our subjects, such as in the eye sockets, and under the chin, bust, or stomach. You can use a reflector to redirect the light into these shadow areas, reducing the contrast and lifting the detail, or you can use flash. So with this in mind, we need to know when and how to control natural light to make it work for us instead of against us.

Overcast light

The perfect type of day for many photographers is an overcast or cloudy day, as this reduces the problem of the high-contrast sunlight casting deep shadows—the clouds diffuse the light. Diffused sunlight does not completely cure the problem, however, as the direction of the light will still be from above, unless you are shooting early or late in the day when the sun is lower in the sky.

Diffused sunlight is perfect for large groups, and easier to work with than direct sunlight. Adjusting for the correct exposure is easier in diffused lighting. Although you will still need to take two separate exposure readings—metering for the light falling directly on the subjects' faces and for when shooting against the light—the resulting exposures will be within just 1 f-stop of each other.

On the other hand, if you want to give the light more direction, and your images more contrast, you can reduce the amount of diffused light coming from above. Shooting beneath the branches of a tree, for instance, or using a black reflector will absorb some of the light from above, and strengthen the sidelighting in your images.

The color temperature of diffused daylight is slightly cooler than direct sunlight, and you can use the "cloudy" color setting on your camera, which will adjust the color temperature, warming the overall image slightly. However, I tend to shoot everything in Raw, with the camera's color temperature set to the daylight or flash setting. This means that when I use flash—which emits a light similar in color temperature to direct sunlight—I will achieve an overall consistency of color in all the images. If any images need adjusting, I can batch-process the color temperature changes when I edit the images later on.

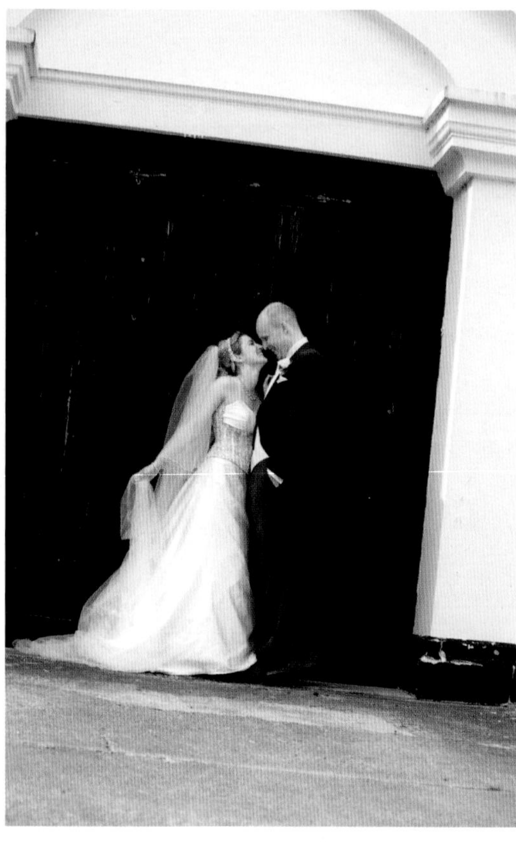

Above: In overcast conditions, depending on the amount of cloud cover, the light can be fairly uniform, creating soft shadows and diffused highlights.

Right: Where possible, I prefer to use natural light before anything else, as this allows me to put the subject in the scene and then shoot with the minimal of technical fussing around.

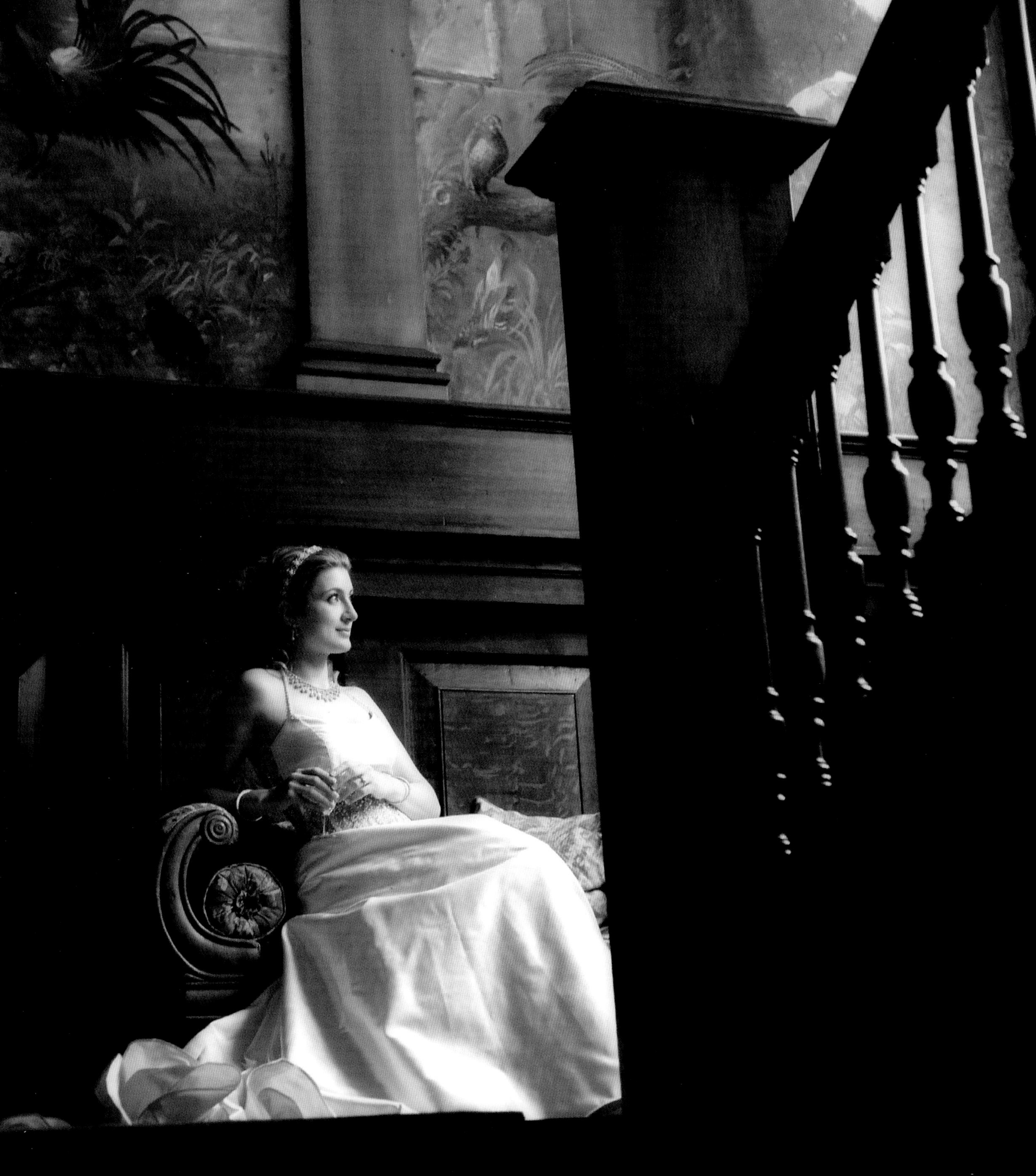

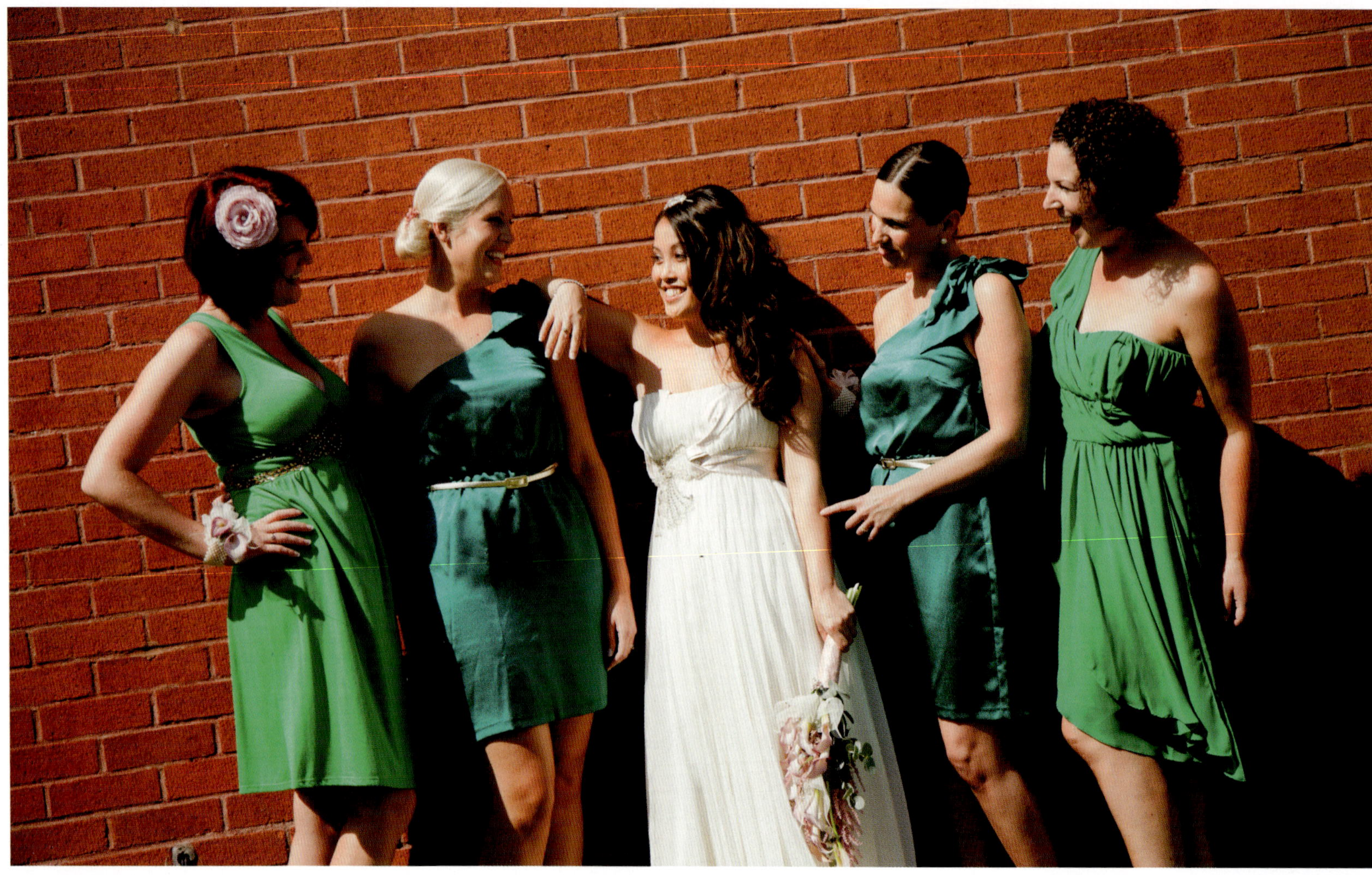

Sunlight

Strong sunlight is my favorite lighting for creativity, but my least favorite lighting for groups, especially when they are facing the sun. However, even with this drawback, I always prefer to shoot in full sunlight.

Bright sunlight will create heavy shadows, which help to make the image look three-dimensional. Even though it causes extreme contrast between the shadows and the highlights, this type of lighting also helps to create a feel-good factor in the images, especially as it also brightens the colors, creating deep blue skies and lush green grass.

The only problem with direct sunlight is when subjects are looking directly into it, causing them to squint and make strained expressions. The simple solution to this is to ask your subjects to look at each other or away from the camera just before you take the picture. So never be afraid to shoot in direct sunlight, just be aware of the problem and how to get over it.

To shoot a series of formal portraits of your subjects looking at the camera, turn their backs to the sun. I call this working with a forward shadow, because your subjects will cast the shadow in front of them. This throws a softer light onto the subjects' faces, and helps to separate them from the background. The meter reading taken from their faces will result in an exposure probably

Above: Ask your subjects to look away from the camera to avoid strained expressions from the direct sunlight.

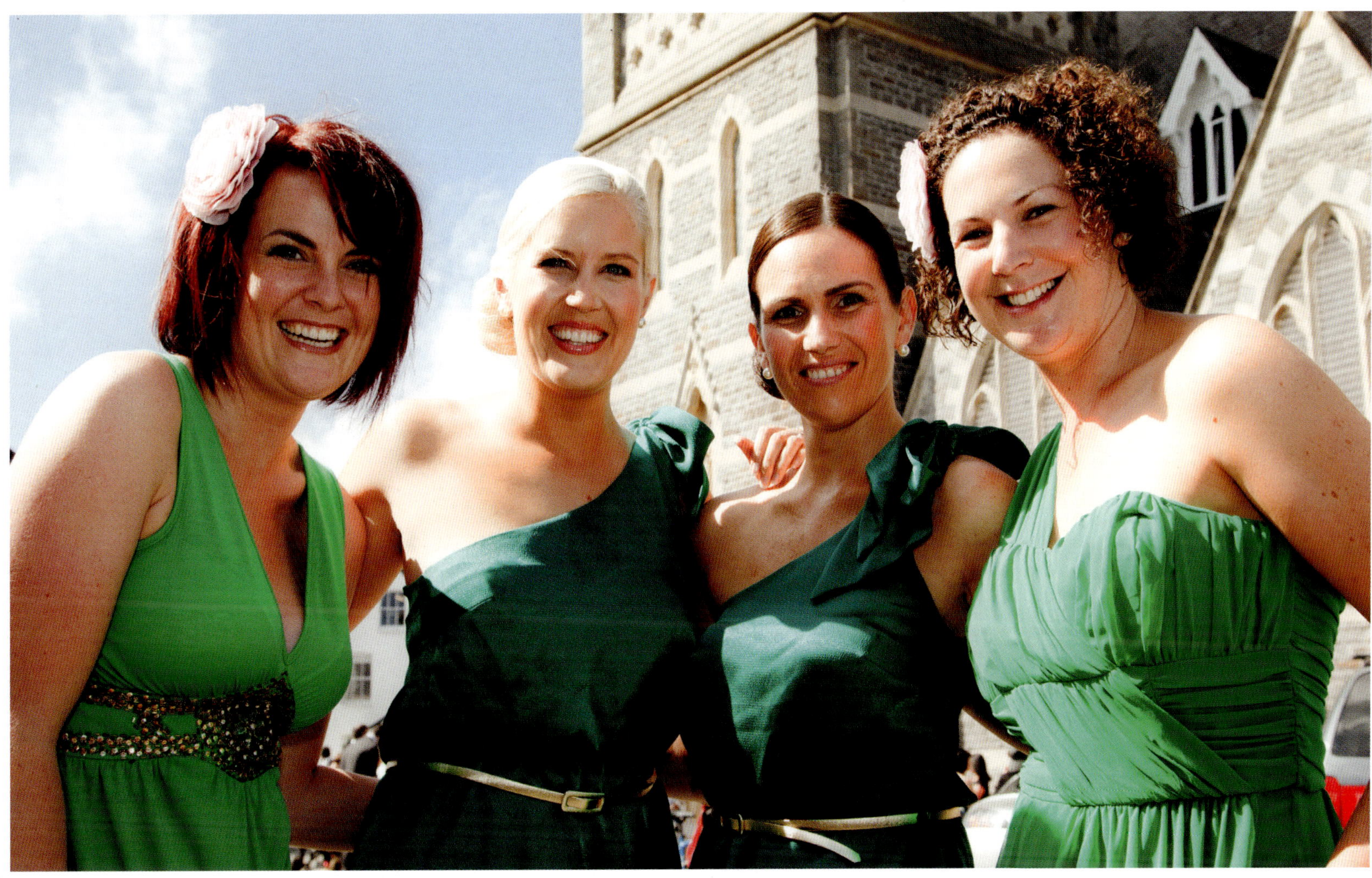

closer to two or three stops different from the direct sun reading. In these conditions, make sure that the subjects' faces do not have any bright highlights where they catch the sun—any detail in these areas will be burnt out and lost, even if shooting in Raw.

Exposure readings on a sunny day are easy to determine, especially if there are no clouds to change the exposure intermittently. You should need only two basic exposure settings in any one scene—one for sunlit subjects and one for backlit subjects.

My color balance for a sunny day is set to "flash," but the "sunny" icon setting will give you a similar color. Be aware that image colors will differ between the camera's LCD and a calibrated computer screen, so always test the colors on new cameras to make sure you get the color balance right in-camera, saving you time later on. Getting the color right is especially important if you prefer to shoot in JPEG, as these compressed files contain much less information than Raw files and therefore offer limited options for color-correcting later on.

Above: For subjects looking directly at the camera, turn their backs to the sun.

Tip

The golden hour is a term given to the time of day when the sun is either rising or setting. The angle of light, even though it is lower, creates a beautiful, soft, and colorful light with a slight sharpness.

Reflected light

Reflecting light onto your subjects will not only brighten the ambient light and increase illumination of your subjects, but it will also give the light direction and increase contrast. At a wedding a portable reflector enables you to redirect the sunlight onto the subject, bringing a sharpness to the light. This is especially useful when the light source is far away and the light is "muddy" or diffuse, lacking in contrast.

An example of when to use a reflector is when photographing backlit subjects with a forward shadow. Positioning the reflector in the 4 to 5 o'clock or 7 to 8 o'clock position is perfect for redirecting and adding contrast to the light, brightening your subject and creating a three-dimensional shadowing on the face. It will also create a 2 or 10 o'clock catchlight in the subjects' eyes. Another example of when to use a reflector would be when shooting a couple in a wooded location or inside a reception room away from the main light source. Here, you can use a reflector to redirect the dappled light through branches, or from a window onto the subjects' faces.

For perfect lighting, the couple should be posed with their backs to the sun, creating a forward shadow. You can then use a reflector on the bride's side at 5 o'clock, adjusting its height and angle to create a 2 o'clock or 10 o'clock catchlight in her eyes. This will enhance the light falling on the five main surfaces of her face—the forehead, chin, both cheeks, and nose. The shadow from her nose should meet the opposite side of the top lip.

It is easy to get into the habit of reflecting light only from below, instead of from above. Often, if you reflect the light from below you will create a catchlight at around 4 or 8 o'clock in the eyes and push the shadows on the face upward, causing the nose shadow to fall towards an eye, which appears to deform the face.

Below: If you are working alone, a Lastolite Uplighter on an adjustable frame will allow you to tilt your reflectors at different angles and maximize their effects.

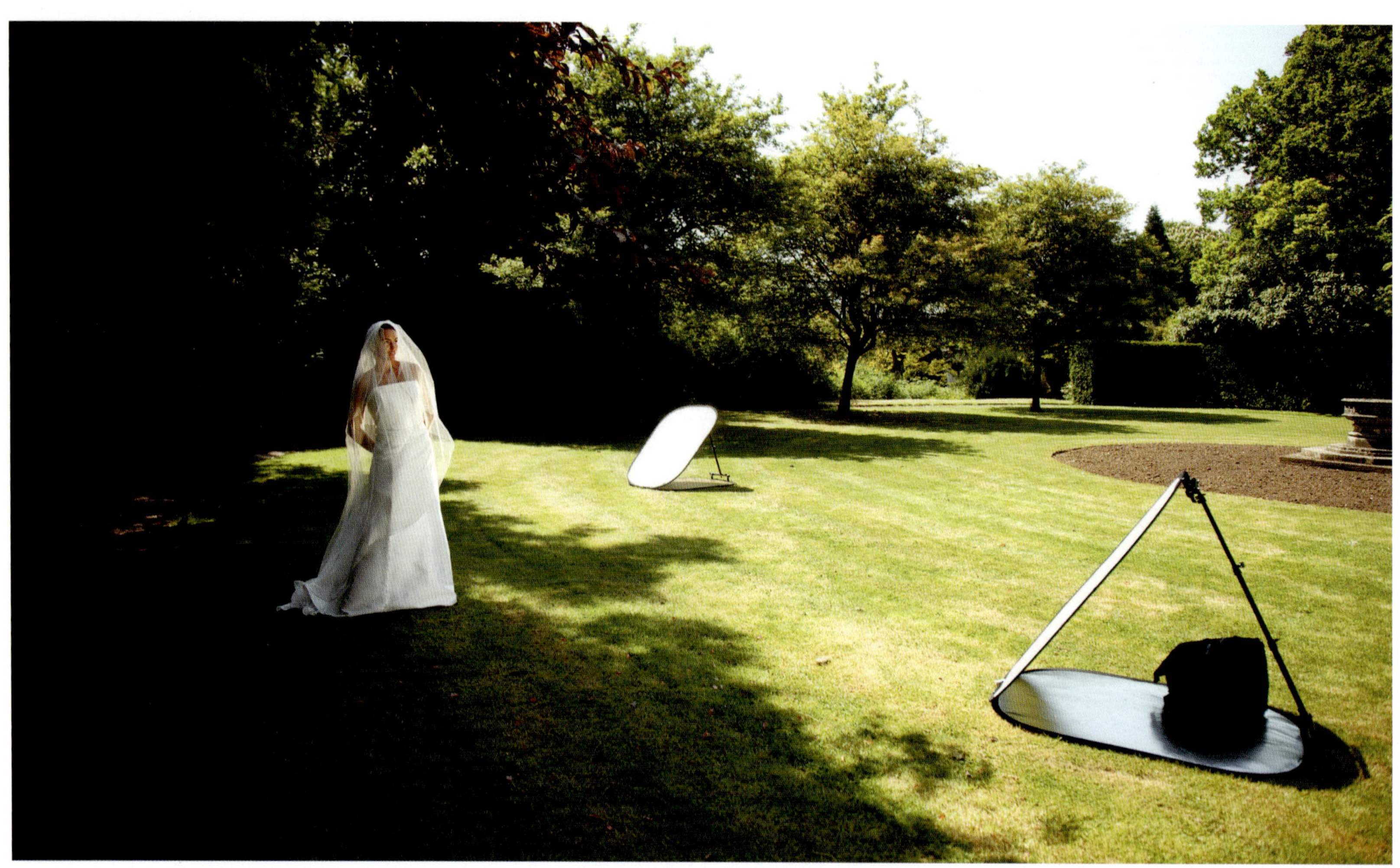

Window light

When working in a room at the bride's home or at the reception, I try to work as close as possible to a window. This is so I can maximize the amount and quality of the light, and have some control over its direction. Master the basics of this technique and you will be able to consistently produce images with impact, no matter what the weather conditions are outside. You can even use a window as a setting at nighttime if you wish, just by using flash instead of daylight.

A window is an opening that restricts how much light enters the scene, and from which direction. I always opt for shooting by the largest window—unless it is in full sunlight—as this will create a bigger flood of light for shooting the three-quarters portraits as well as the head-and-shoulders images. A large window will also provide more soft light to help you shoot small groups more easily.

There are disadvantages to window lighting, which you have to learn to work with. The quality—the intensity and color—of the light through a standard-sized window is better around the waist than on the face, but with a small window the better quality light will probably be nearer the floor. So be aware when shooting portraits that the light will be better when the subject is sitting down than it will be if they are standing—this is no different to working in a studio with a low ceiling. Also, if your subject is looking at the camera, the further you move the camera into the room, the darker your subject's face will appear. Therefore, to make the best use of the light through a window, using the classic "C" lighting pattern to light your subject (with the light to one side, in front, and behind the subject), you must place the camera along the same line as the window—shooting along the line of the window wall.

You can achieve several different lighting effects by simply positioning and then repositioning the subject near the window. The five basic window lighting positions are set out above. All of these images can be shot with a

similar exposure as the same quantity of light is being used each time, but you are controlling the amount that falls on to the subject by changing their position. After you have covered these basic shots, don't forget to move further into the room to shoot a silhouette profile, using the window to frame the subject.

POSITION	DESCRIPTION
The feather	The feather is the best position as it produces the softest light on the subject, and is achieved by standing or sitting the subject just in the shade of the drapes.
Directional	With the subject standing next to the drapes, there is more contrast in the image, but the light is still usable.
Split	With the subject standing in the middle of the window, the lighting will be split on the face when they look at the camera, with one side being very dark.
Profile	If the subject stands on the side of the window closest to the camera, make sure you turn their back to you and then shoot the profile and three-quarters portraits.
Dramatic	When the subject is in the feather position nearest to the camera, the profile will become more dramatic and much lower key because there is no reflected light spilling onto the face. This shot looks great in black and white.

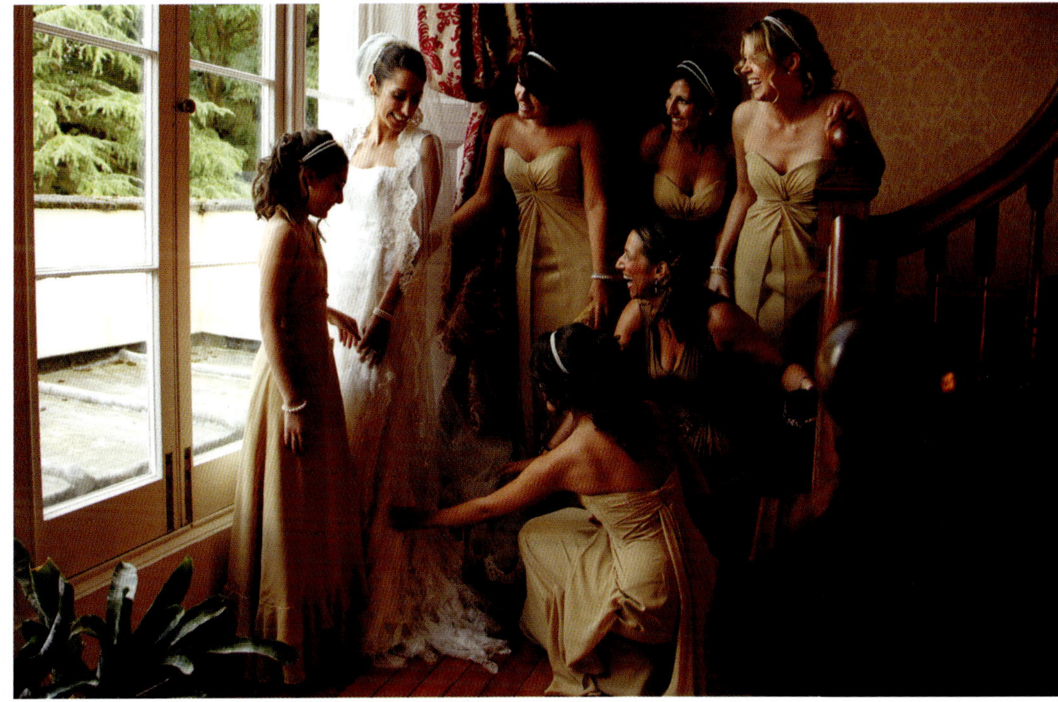

Above: A large window is perfect for shooting groups, even if it is in direct sunlight. Window light gives a timeless, almost old-master-painting quality when used well, casting deep shadows on the subjects and in the scene.

Tip

When using the feather lighting technique, be careful not to shade the subject too much, because the light will become "muddy," with little or no contrast.

Mixed Light

You can achieve some weird and wonderful results with mixed lighting, and working with mixed lighting in a scene tends not to be a problem, as you can correct any color cast in postproduction. However, problems do occur when you have two light sources with two different color temperatures lighting your subjects separately. The easiest way to solve this is to always have one light source that dominates your subject.

LED & ambient

I use a combination of different lighting devices to enhance my pictures and, even though flash is quick to use and set up, there are times when I prefer not to use it. For other forms of lighting, I use everything from a simple LED torch, or LED inspection light, to an LED video light. LED is now so affordable and is powerful enough to give a quick boost of light in a scene. This brightness means you can use LED lighting at realistic shutter speeds and ISO settings when shooting inside, but it is simply not bright enough for shooting outdoors or in a brightly lit room—this is where you should turn to a flash or a reflector.

For adding an accent light to a subject's skin, to separate them slightly from the background, I opt for a small, dimmable LED light. With LED light you can also preview the effect and change it before you shoot because, unlike flash, it is always on.

Set white balance on the camera to Daylight if the LED light is dominant, but to Tungsten if the room lighting is dominant with the LED only adding accent lighting. In the latter situation, also place a tungsten gel over the LED light so everything has the same color balance.

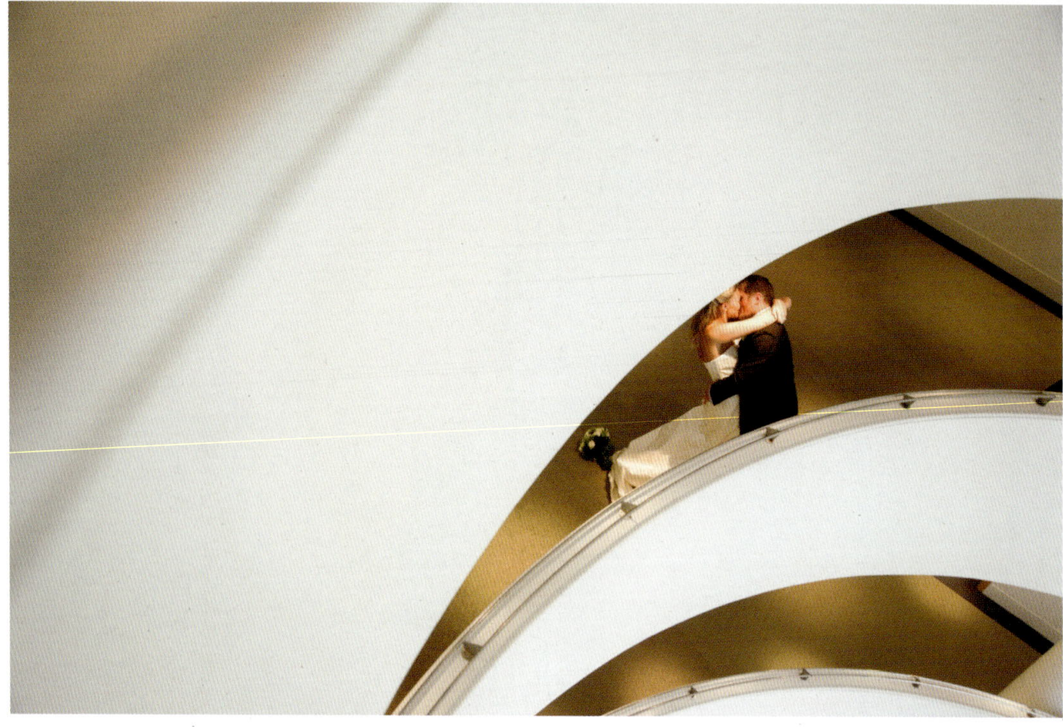

Daylight & ambient

If you're using the window light to light the subjects, set the camera white balance to Daylight, but the farther you take the subject into the room, the more they will be lit by tungsten-colored light. If the tungsten light becomes too strong, use an LED light on the faces or opt for a bit of flash to balance it out. By using Daylight white balance in a tungsten-lit reception room, the image will appear to have a rich, warm color.

Flash & ambient

For shooting in a bright, daylight-lit reception room, such as a conservatory, set the camera to Daylight or Flash color balance the whole time, as there will be little color cast. However, if there is any doubt

Above: The combination of daylight and tungsten lighting is the same as flash and tungsten lighting, the only difference being that you can control the color temperature of your flash, but you can't control the color of the daylight.

about the color, use a gray card to help set a custom color balance on the camera.

If you want the flash to dominate the ambient lighting in the scene, then use your shutter speed to control the ambient light—the aperture setting controls the flash power until it equals the same level as the ambient lighting.

Tungsten flash & ambient

In the winter months, or when shooting near dusk, add a color temperature orange (CTO) tungsten gel to the flash. This sets the flash

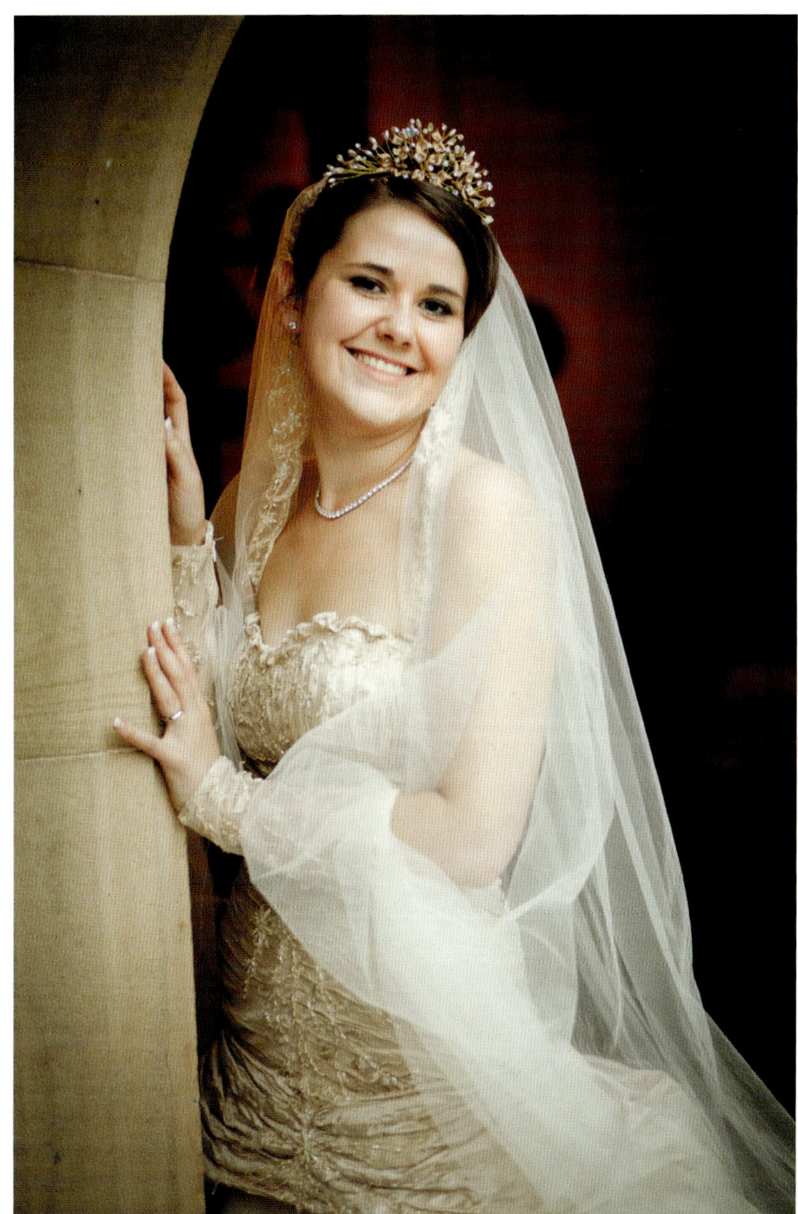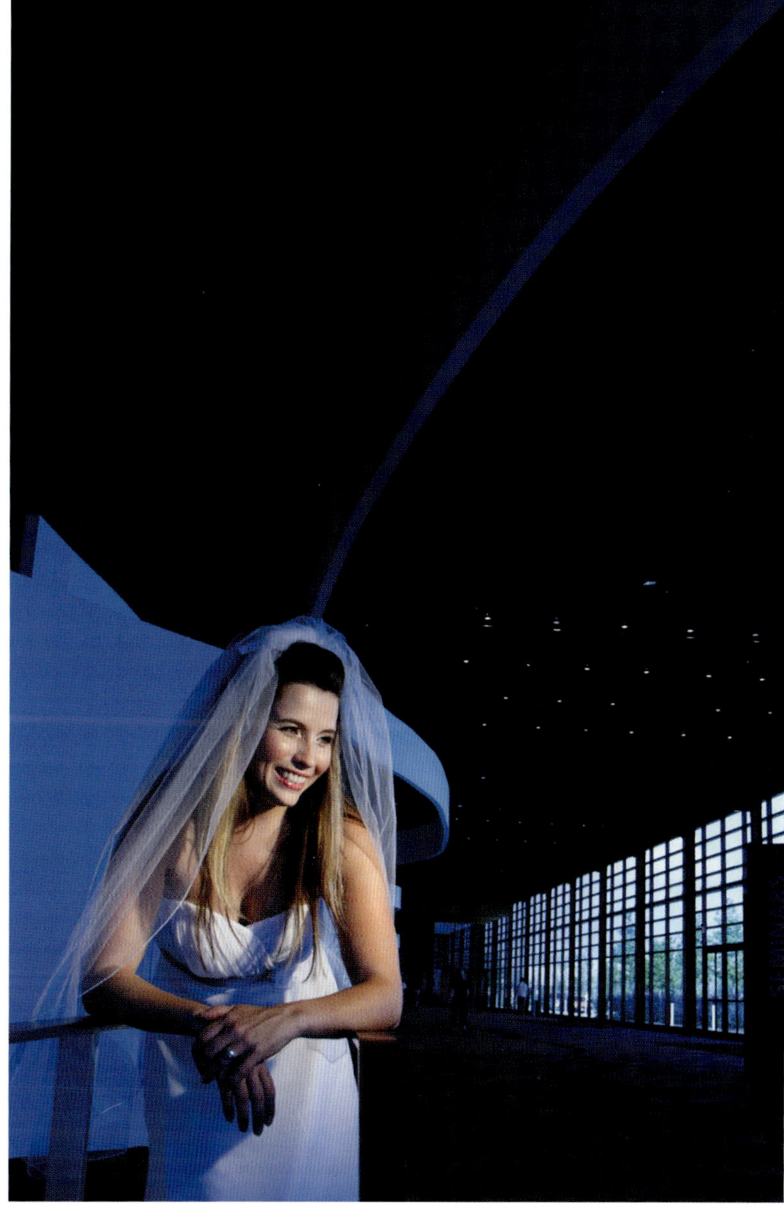

to the tungsten color balance, so also set the camera's white balance to the little Bulb. Once you are using this color balance, any daylight that is visible in the scene—including light coming through any windows or accent flash—will appear blue. The more that you set the flash to dominate the ambient light by using a higher shutter speed, the deeper and richer the blue daylight will become.

Above left: When mixing two color balances, you must make one dominant or you will have a color cast in the image that cannot be fixed. I use flash for the shots of the bride coming down the aisle for two reasons: the first is to help freeze the movement, and the second is to illuminate her dress with white light to ensure color accuracy.

Above right: Try using gels on your flash, such as a tungsten CTO, then set your camera to tungsten and watch the daylight in the scene turn blue.

Tip

A simple way to use an accent light in a reception is to invest in a small LED light, torch, or video light. These are small, easy-to-control daylight-balanced lights for adding accent lighting.

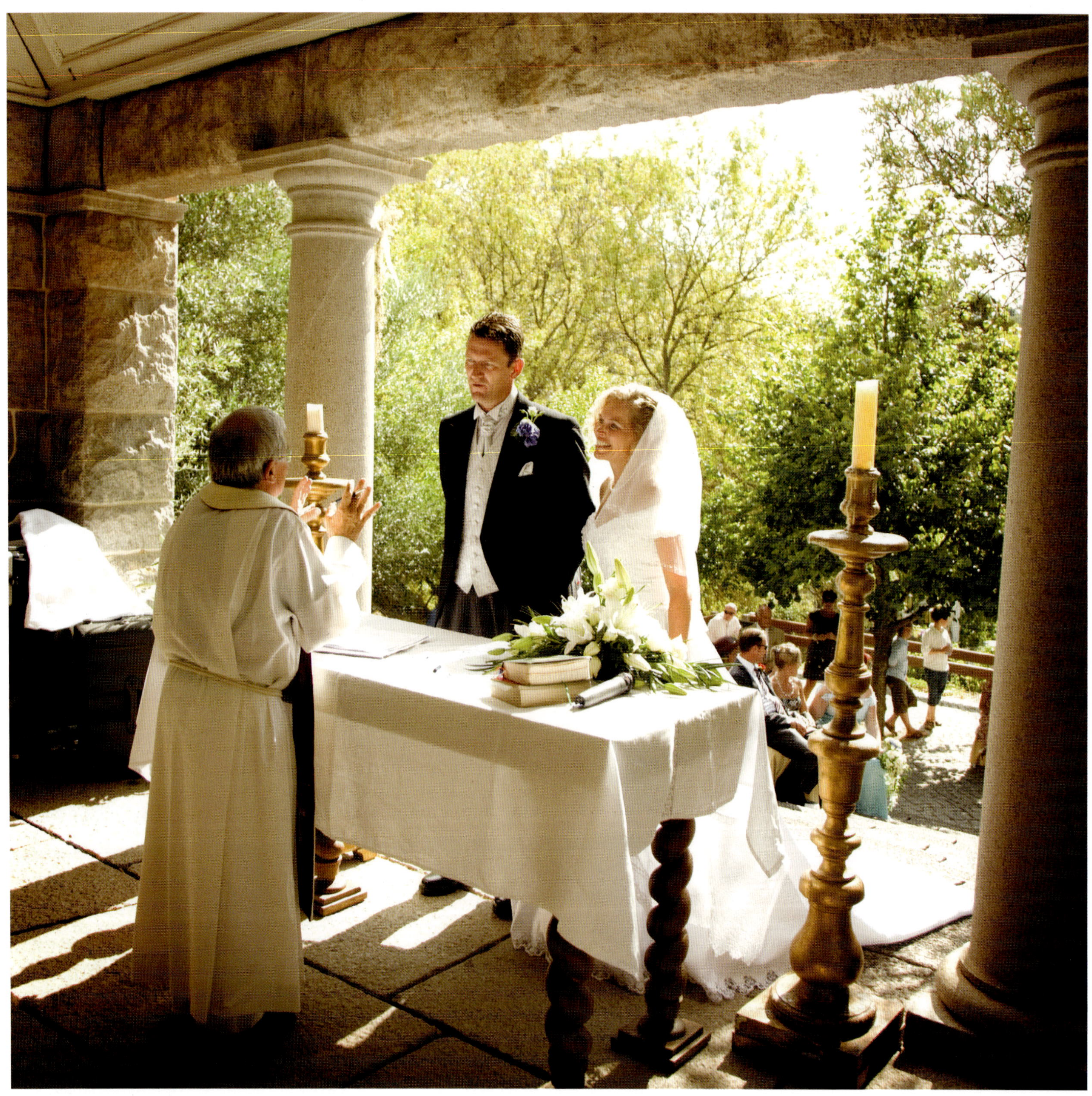

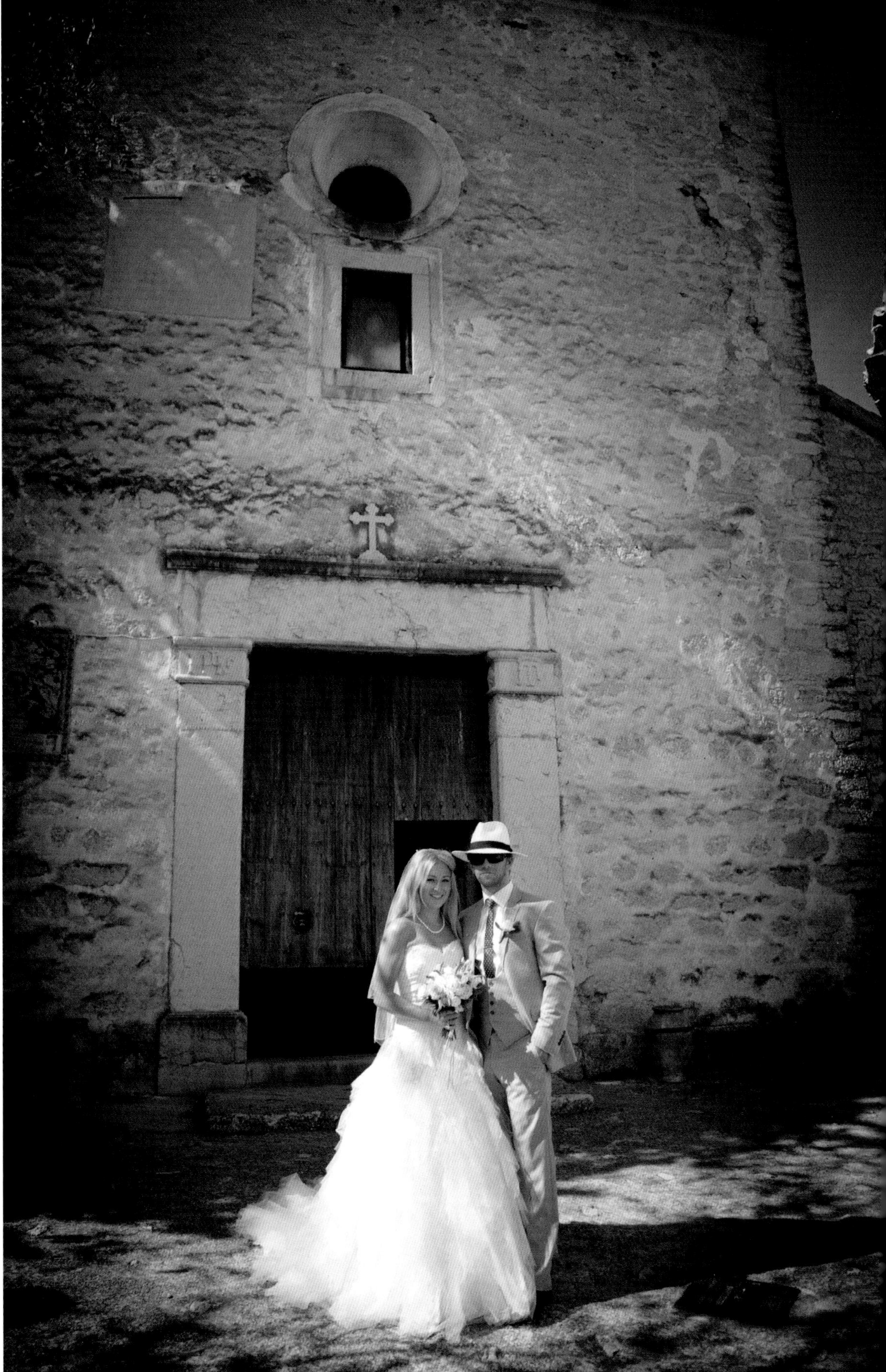

Left: Photographing weddings in hot, sunny climates presents a new set of problems for the photographer. In this shot it was necessary to balance the bright sunlight beyond the pillared chapel and the pure white of the bride's dress, while not losing detail of the building's interior.

Right: An ancient Spanish stone church provides a romantic backdrop for this image of the bride and groom. The dappled light filtering through nearby trees illuminates the white dress and the groom's light colored suit, while bathing the entire scene in a soft, dappled light.

Flash Light

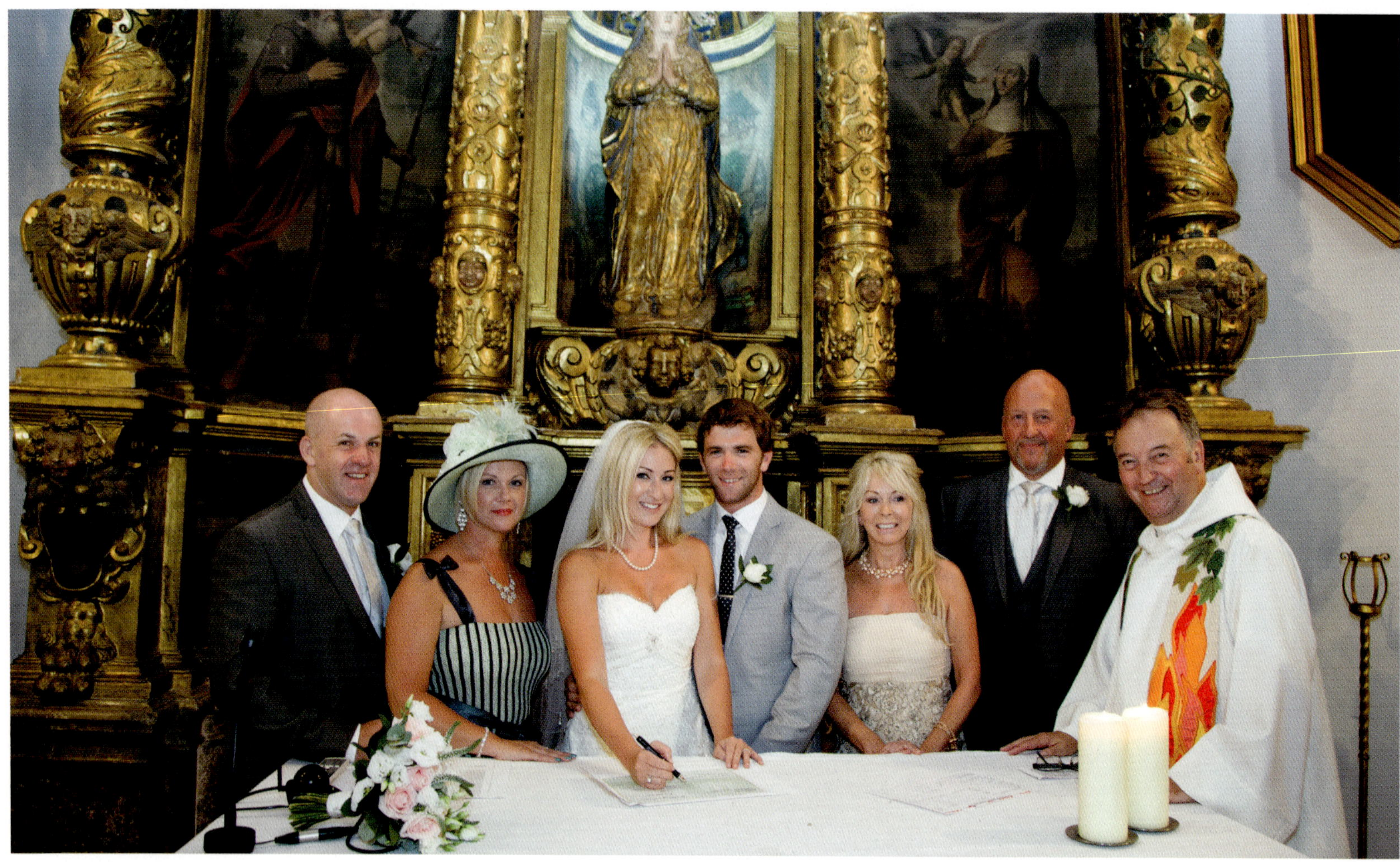

The question I am asked the most on workshops and seminars is: when do you use flash? Well, the easy answer is: only when you need to. As previously explained, I always prefer to use the natural light in some way before using flash. This is because I want to make use of the mood and atmosphere of the scene created by the ambient lighting.

That is in an ideal world, of course. In the real world, I need to freeze motion, create more light where there is not enough, and enhance the subject with a better quality of light in contrast and color, and that is where the flash unit comes into play.

Since the flash unit became "intelligent" in the early 2000s, along with the advent of digital photography, the combination of being able to view the image on the back of the camera and fire a small flash unit off-camera really has brought more creativity to the world of photography in general, and to wedding photography in particular.

The latest, small flash units allow even the inexperienced flash user to get better results, more consistently, thanks to in-camera metering and TTL (through-the-lens settings). The TTL function makes sure that the flash does what you tell it to—

Above: On-camera flash—whether it is the small pop-up flash built into the camera or a separate flash unit fixed to the accessory hotshoe—is a perfect way to illuminate small groups or scenes, helping to achieve the correct exposure, as well as providing clean light and some contrast.

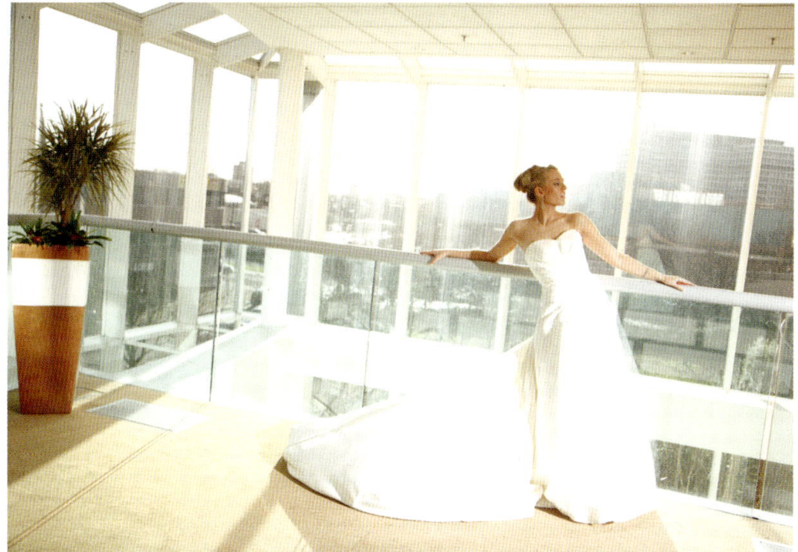

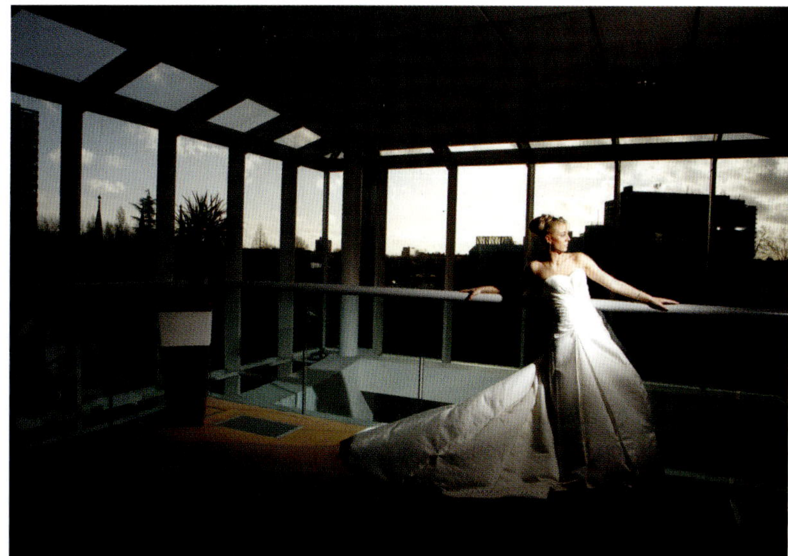

Above & left: When using flash, the shutter speed is only really used to lighten or darken the scene, as the exposure is based on the aperture and ISO combined with the burst of flash. The working exposure will depend on the amount of flash power used, as well as how close the flash is to the subjects.

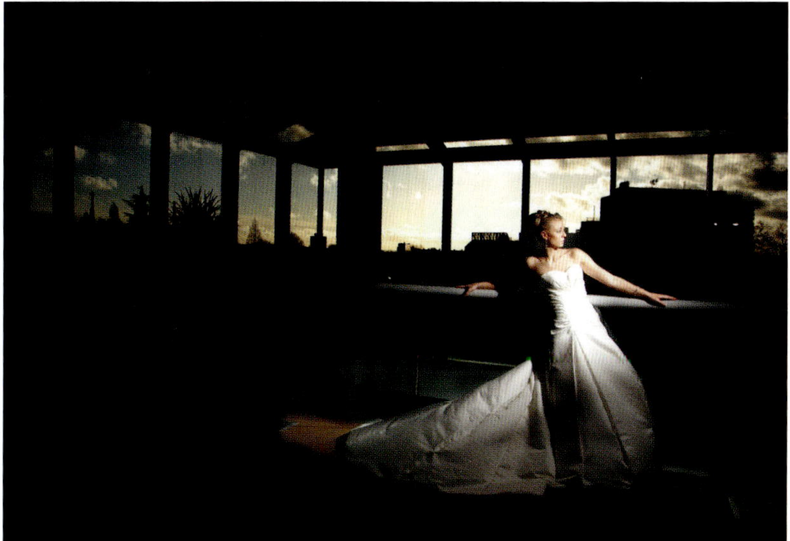

Tip

Get used to the flash unit settings, as weddings wait for no photographer. If you are having a problem with exposure, you will need to know how to adjust the flash settings instantly.

to blend its output with the ambient light, to fill in the shadows, or to dominate the whole exposure. The flash unit fires a small pre-flash from which the camera and flash both determine the amount of light to emit, based on your settings, making flash simple to use as well as more predictable in achieving accurate exposures.

When I use flash, it is mostly to correct the ambient light falling on the subjects. For instance, if the subjects are being lit by direct sunlight, this will cause heavy shadows under the brim of a hat. This dark shadow would mean that the image is unlikely to sell to the family or guests, because people naturally prefer seeing all of their faces in a picture and not just parts of it.

The flash also works as a fill-light, at about one stop less than the ambient light exposure, again lifting shadow detail to produce a more pleasing picture. Without fill-flash, the images would need to be printed lighter or adjusted in editing software, such as Adobe Photoshop, to show more detail.

Flash can also be used to dominate a subject in a dark scene, and although you can use this creatively, it may be the only lighting option for some shots. This technique is perfect, for instance, for the shot of the bride and groom walking up the aisle, where there is little or no light to capture their expressions, without resorting to very high ISO levels or very slow shutter speeds. It is also used in this way to freeze the subjects in motion. To dominate the scene with the flash as the main exposure, as a rule the setting should be 1 stop higher than the ambient lighting level.

Using on-camera flash settings

Flash units will differ slightly between manufacturers, but they all have similar settings in some way, so let's cover the basics of how they work and some simple techniques to create better flash images.

The TTL function is a form of exposure metering and is called a variety of names by different manufacturers—for instance Canon call it E-TTL. TTL used in conjunction with the plus or minus exposure adjustment is the most popular flash technique used on a wedding day. This is because using TTL metering enables you to change from one shot to another, with different exposures, while allowing the camera and flash to automatically control the flash output. TTL also allows you to shoot with wide apertures such as f/2.8.

One of the biggest problems you will encounter with TTL is generating too much or too little flash for your exposure. Too much flash makes the background go dark, which is caused by choosing a fast shutter speed, a large aperture (between f/8 and f/11), or a combination of both. Too little flash will result in an underlit subject and an underexposed shot, which will ultimately produce a washed-out image that lacks in contrast after you try to correct it in postproduction.

Most of the cameras with built-in, pop-up flashes have a TTL function. However, these units lack the power of a separate flash unit and they often underexpose groups that are too far away from the camera flash. So it is important to learn how to control exposure with TTL settings using the plus (+) and minus (–) adjustments. The + and – steps represent ⅓-stop exposure adjustment. TTL+ is used to add more flash, which is perfect for shooting groups and when the flash is being reflected off a surface. TTL– is used when you want to reduce the amount of flash, such as for fill-light when shooting against the sun, or when you want the flash to just lift detail on the subject and scene next to a window. To improve the accuracy of TTL flash, increase the distance between the flash and your subject.

Manual is another setting that you need to understand how to use—even though this is a little more complicated to use, it will pay off in the long term. To use the Manual setting properly you should use a flash meter, but if you don't have one of those, you can gauge the exposure by looking at the camera's LCD preview screen. The benefit of the Manual setting is that it fires the exact amount of flash you request every time it triggers, instead of trying to calculate the exposure automatically itself. Manual is ideal for shooting large groups when you need all the power of the flash, for shooting with reflective surfaces behind the subjects, such as glass or mirrors, and for manual control when shooting with off-camera flash.

High-speed sync (HSS) is usually represented by a lightning bolt symbol, and this allows the flash to be used at a shutter speed higher than the usual camera sync speed of about 1/200 sec. You will lose some of the flash power as you

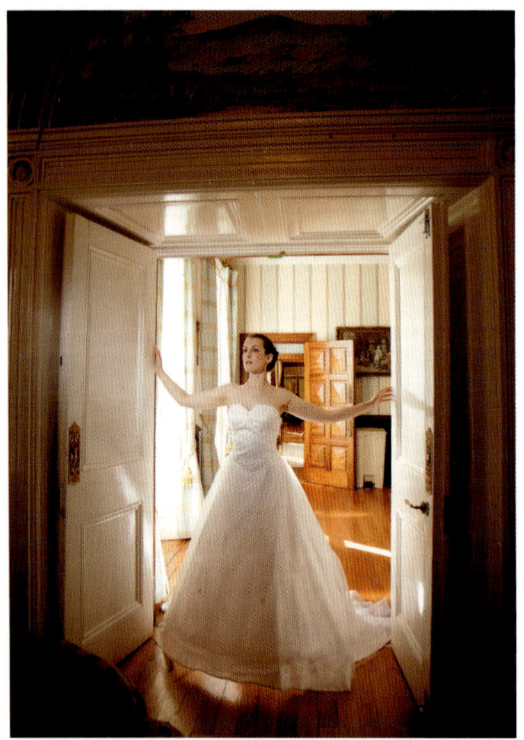
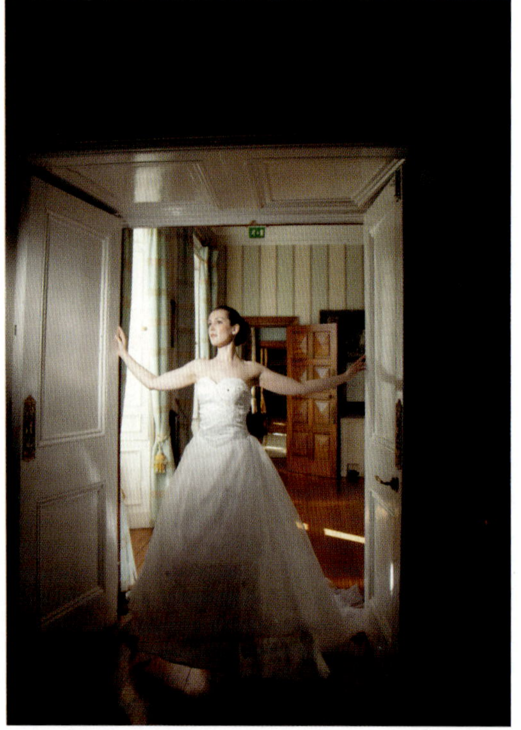

Left: When you've mastered the basics of TTL flash, using small + or – adjustments, you can then start to develop your technique with simple but effective adjustments of your shutter speed. These two images were shot within seconds of each other with the only change being the shutter speed. The first image, which is light and bright, made more use of the ambient light in the scene with a shutter speed of 1/60 sec. at f/4. The second image was shot using a shutter speed of 1/400 sec., using the flash to dominate most of the ambient light in the foreground.

increase the shutter speed above 1/200 sec. because the camera shutter is not giving the flash enough time to expose for the full flash that's required. HSS is useful when working outside, as it stops the camera from automatically changing your shutter speed back to 1/200 sec., which will often cause overexposed images on sunny days or when working with wide apertures. Use HSS for darkening the skies on sunny days—if you can dominate the ambient light by one stop or more—or shooting in harsh sunlight and using flash for fill-in light.

Second-curtain sync (SCS) is the opposite of HSS, and is represented by a double lightning bolt icon. This setting tells the flash to fire at the end of the exposure, which helps with a moving subject in low light. I always switch from the HSS setting to SCS as soon as I walk into an area where the shutter speed is below 1/60 sec.—for instance, a reception room or the church. SCS is perfect for shooting indoors, and working in low light.

Tip

Learn how to use the plus and minus settings on your flash to control its output more accurately.

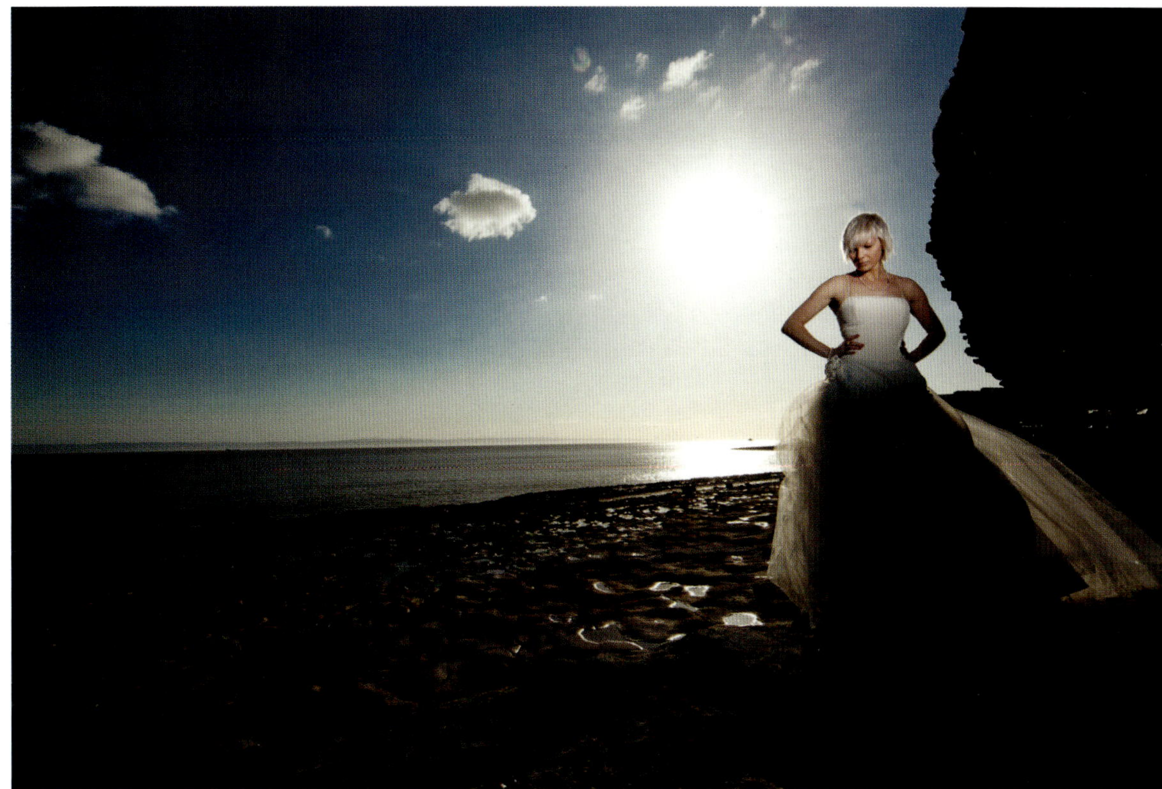

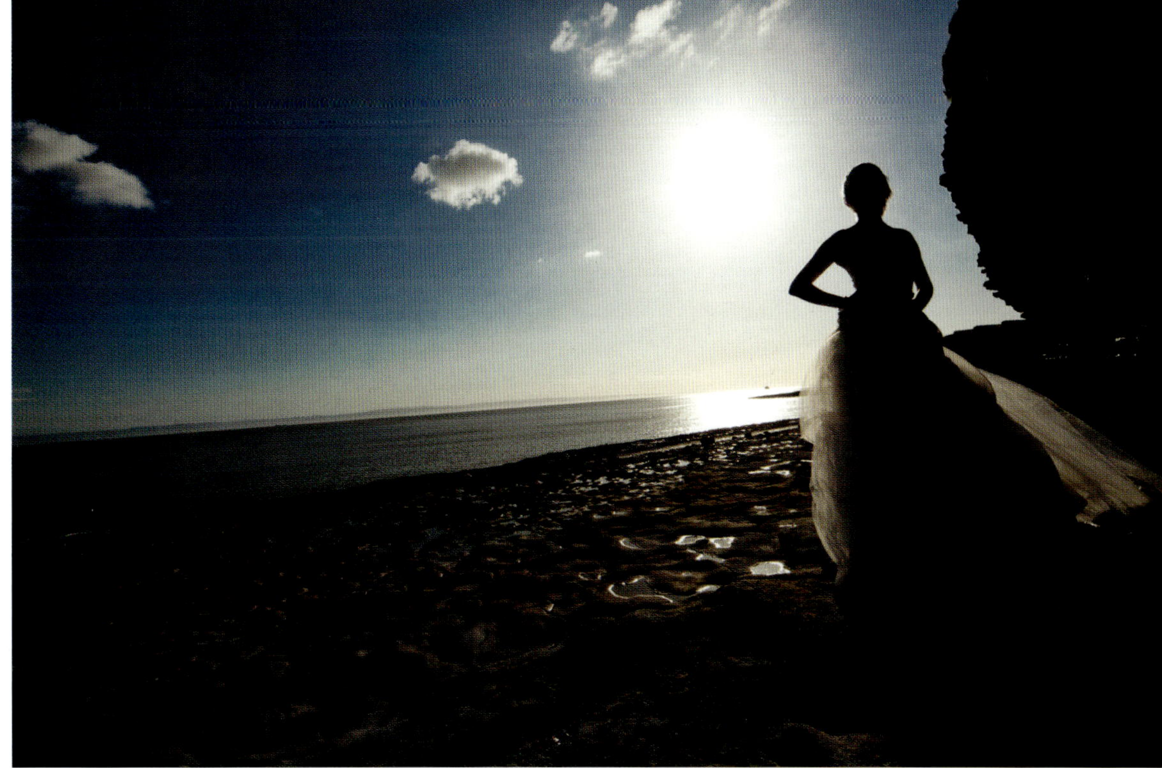

Right: Flash can be used to equal and even overpower the ambient light if used properly. The technique relies on high-speed sync with the flash unit, enabling you to use high shutter speeds to achieve the right exposure. It can also help you shoot at the end of the day, when the sun is setting, so you can shoot with less flash power. These two images show the difference between shooting with and without flash.

Bouncing & zooming flash

Another way to improve your flash photography is to avoid using direct flash on the subject, as this can result in ugly shadows behind it.

The bounce flash technique is probably the most used flash technique because it does several things that benefit the image. Firstly, it increases the size of the light source by reflecting the light from the flash off a larger surface—and this has the secondary effect of softening the light. Secondly, it solves the problem of shadows behind your subjects because the direction of the light and the diffused, softer light make the shadows more faint and less visible.

Swivel the flash head to either the left or the right to bounce the flash off a wall, or tilt the flash head upwards to bounce it off the ceiling. Accessories such as bounce cards act as bounce surfaces to create a similar effect as a wall or ceiling surface. Of course, bounce cards are small so they will only increase the size of the flash a little. However, larger reflectors, which also act as bounce surfaces, are available and these do spread the flash. Reflector panels also come in different surfaces, which bounce the flash in different ways—for instance, a silver reflector will reflect the flash like a mirror, creating sharper, more specular light, whereas a white reflector will soften the light.

Using bounce flash does have some disadvantages. The light from the flash has farther to go to reach the subject and so the amount of light will be reduced, giving you fewer exposure

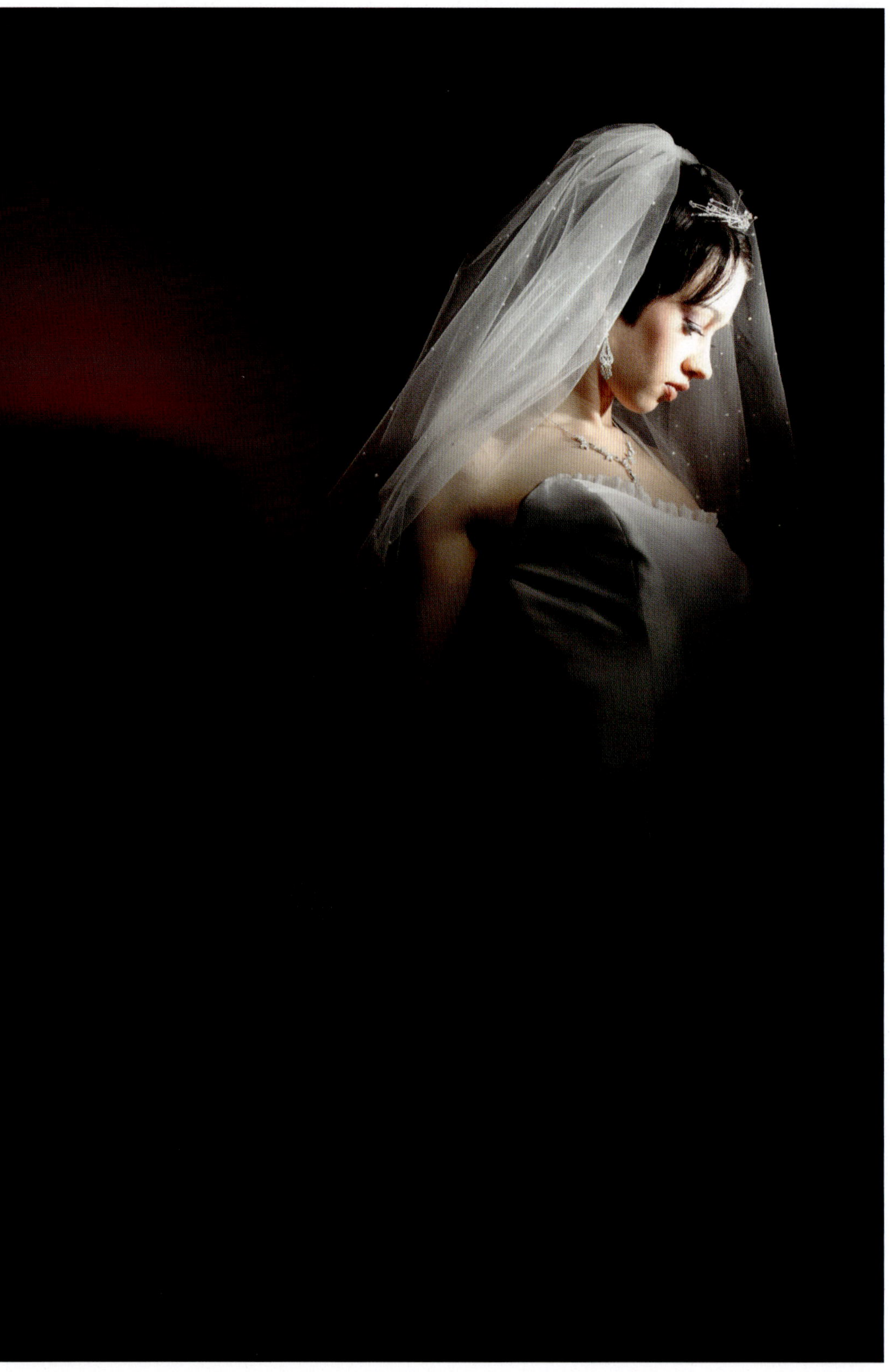

Right: To create a more dynamic image with on-camera flash, I often bounce the flash off mirrors in a room. There are times when the mirror magnifies the beam even more, helping to create a much better lighting effect.

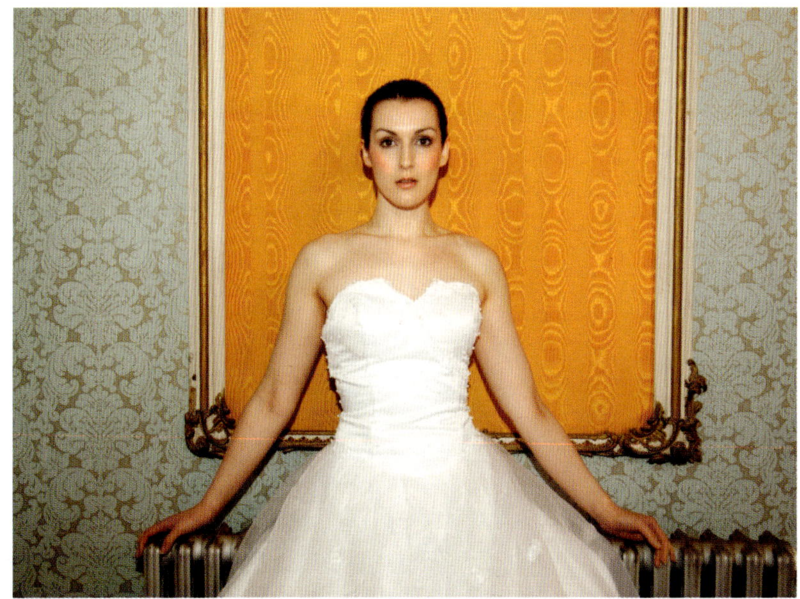

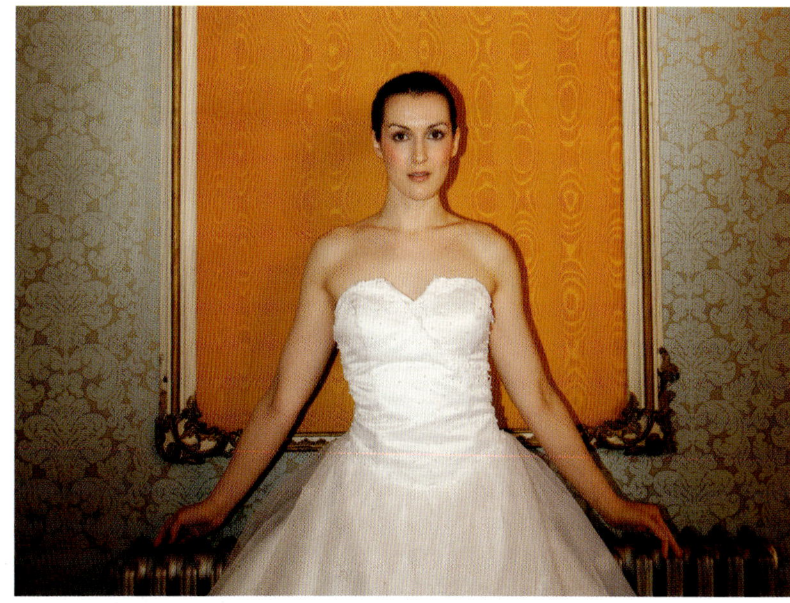

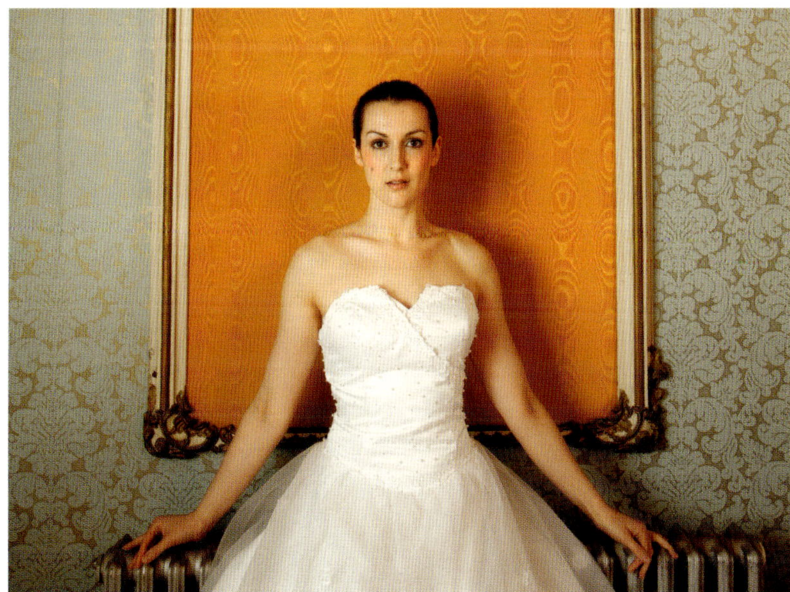

Top left: When the camera is in the horizontal position, and the subject is slightly lower than you are, the shadow created behind them will be subtle, even if they are very close to the background.

Top right: When the camera is turned vertically, the shadow will appear exaggerated on the opposite side. The only way to counter this is to take your flash off the camera hotshoe and place it on a special camera flash bracket.

Left: Bouncing the flash off a white wall or door can create a more pleasing flashed image. Bouncing the flash creates a larger source of light and a softer lighting effect.

options. Also, the increased angle of the light bouncing down from the ceiling sometimes causes dark shadows to appear under the subject's eyes.

The Zoom setting option on your flash unit will allow you to manually fool it into thinking you are using a telephoto instead of a wide-angle lens. This creates a spotlight effect, but make sure your subjects are in the middle of the frame for the flash to light them. Use the zoom controller to increase the telephoto range of the lens, so if you shoot with a wide-angle lens and a zoom of 105mm the subjects in the middle of the frame will "pop" out of the scene, especially if the flash is the dominant light source.

Remember to slightly move the flash head to the left or right if the bride and groom are offset to one side in the frame. If the effect is too strong, try reducing the telephoto range a little to increase the spread of the flash and illuminate more of the subjects and surrounding scene.

Tips

Bounce flash is perfect for lighting small groups, providing fill-in flash, shooting the cake, and shooting in a room with no natural light and white walls.

Flash zoom is perfect for shots of the bride and groom walking down the aisle, the first dance, and off-camera flash.

Off-camera flash options

Once you have mastered the basics of on-camera flash, the next step is to take the flash unit off the camera hotshoe and to position it elsewhere to angle the light. This is the first stage of learning to be creative with flash.

The more square a source of light is to the subject, the "flatter" the light, and the flatter and fatter the subject will appear. This is because the direction of the light is not suitable for creating three-dimensional shadows in the scene or on the subject. Small flash units help you to solve this because they are portable and easy to move around and angle—especially useful when you are learning your flash skills, unlike studio flash systems.

Remember that time is never on your side at a wedding, and the more complicated you make the flash setup, the more that can go wrong, and the more time you lose trying to get it to work. So keep your flash setup as simple as possible.

There are several ways in which you can fire your flash off-camera:
- use a TTL cable to fire the flash from the camera's hotshoe
- set up two flash units—one to act as a "master" or "commander" flash, and the other as a "slave"
- use a trigger and receiver set
- use a TTL trigger and receiver.

Cost always plays a part when you are first experimenting with flash, and you have to be really serious about professional off-camera flash systems before investing in them. Let's look at the options in rising order of cost.

A TTL cable will always be the cheapest option, and long cables are available that allow full TTL control from 3–5m (10–16ft) away. A cable will give you full control of all functions including high-speed sync and TTL power control. Although using cables can be restrictive and get in the way at times, if you are only shooting a few images of the bride and groom with off-camera flash during the day, then why spend more?

You can purchase a basic trigger and receiver

kit for not much more than a cable, but they will not have TTL control. You will have to shoot with the flash on Manual mode setting, using the flash meter to get an accurate exposure setting. Because most trigger and receiver kits use wireless forms of communication, you can place the flash units further away from the camera than with a TTL cable, as well as hide them around corners or behind walls.

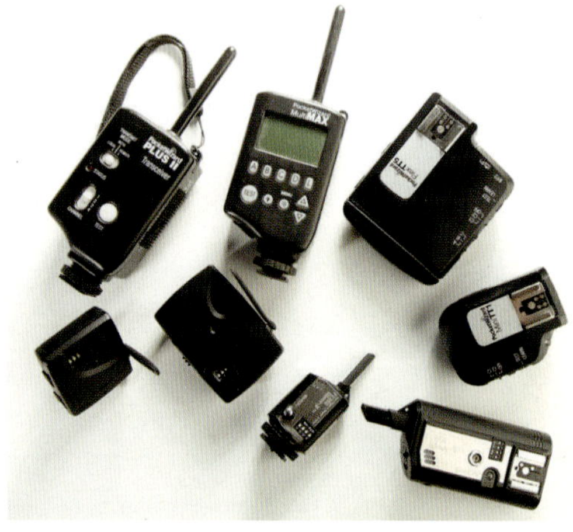

Above: Even when working with off-camera flash in full Manual mode you can capture great candid shots, as long as your assistant is paying attention to the distance between the subject and the flash.

Purchasing a second flash unit is a more expensive option, but it will give you a backup flash, which can be very useful. A second flash can be used as a slave to the master or commander unit on the camera. When buying a second flash, make sure that both units are compatible, as some can only act as slave units. Bear in mind that infrared systems require the flashes to "see" each other—so there is no obstruction between them—in order to communicate. Flash units that use other wireless technologies are now available but are more expensive.

First set the new unit to commander/master mode using a switch or menu on the flash. While setting the master flash, choose a group setting—

usually 1, 2, 3, or 4—so that your flashes will only communicate with each other and not someone else's. Next, choose your other settings, such as TTL or high-speed sync, as described earlier. Then set the second unit to slave mode, and select the same group setting as the commander flash.

You are now ready to shoot. If you are in TTL mode, use the + or − settings on the commander flash to change the slave flash's power output. If you are in Manual mode, you will need to use a flash meter to record the power output and the aperture achieved before adjusting the power to achieve your desired exposure.

The commander and slave flashes can be set to fire with different power outputs, by setting a ratio on the commander flash. For instance, you can set the slave flash to be more dominant, creating strong directional shadows, whilst the commander flash provides fill-light. You can also set the commander flash not to fire at all, to create more drama with enhanced shadows. Even when it doesn't fire, the commander flash still appears to, but this is just a preflash to instruct the slave units to fire.

A smaller commander unit is a slightly cheaper option than a full flash unit because it is only a controller device, with no built-in flash.

Tip

Remember that with an infrared-based triggering system, the commander and slave units need a clear line of sight between each other to work.

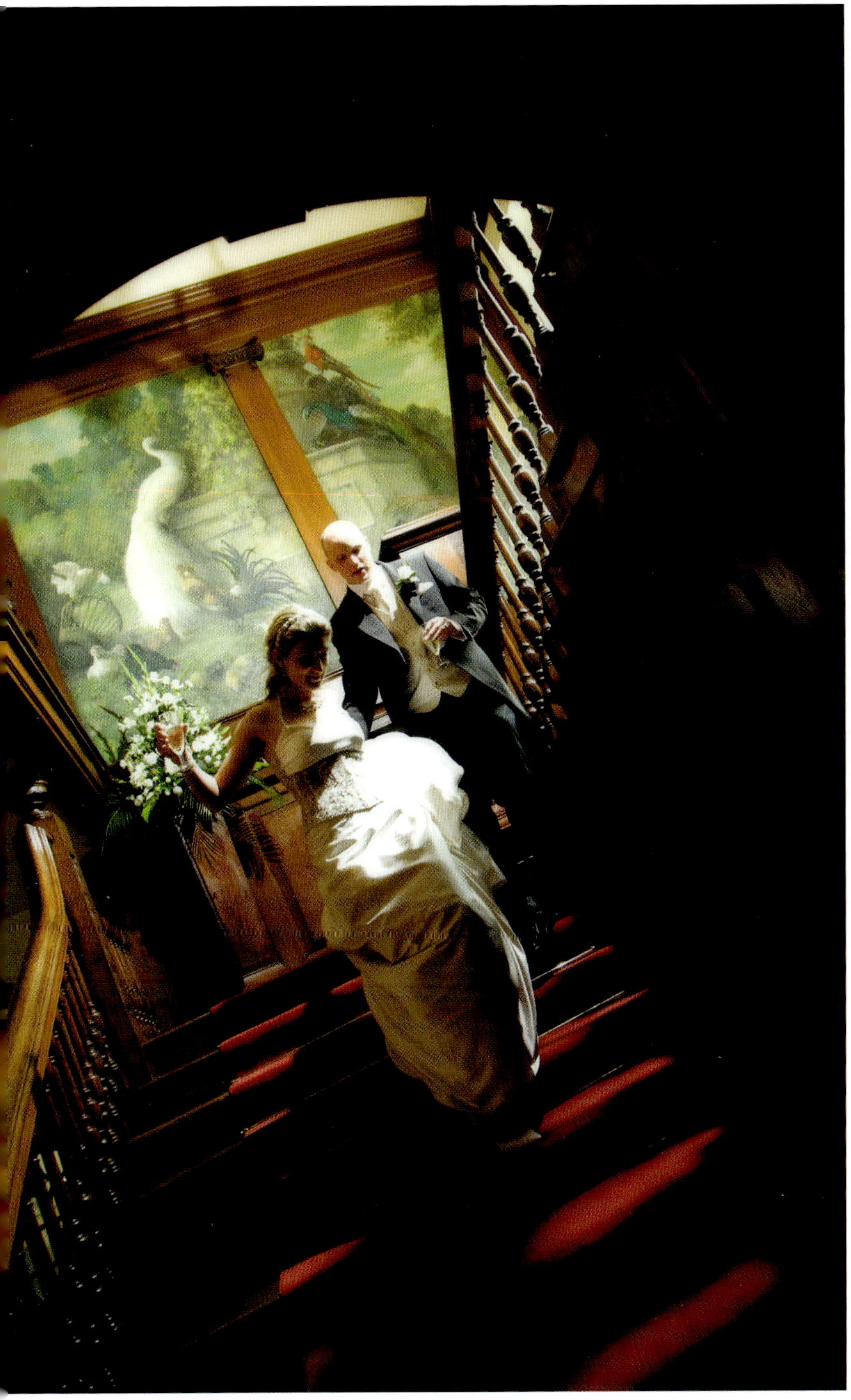

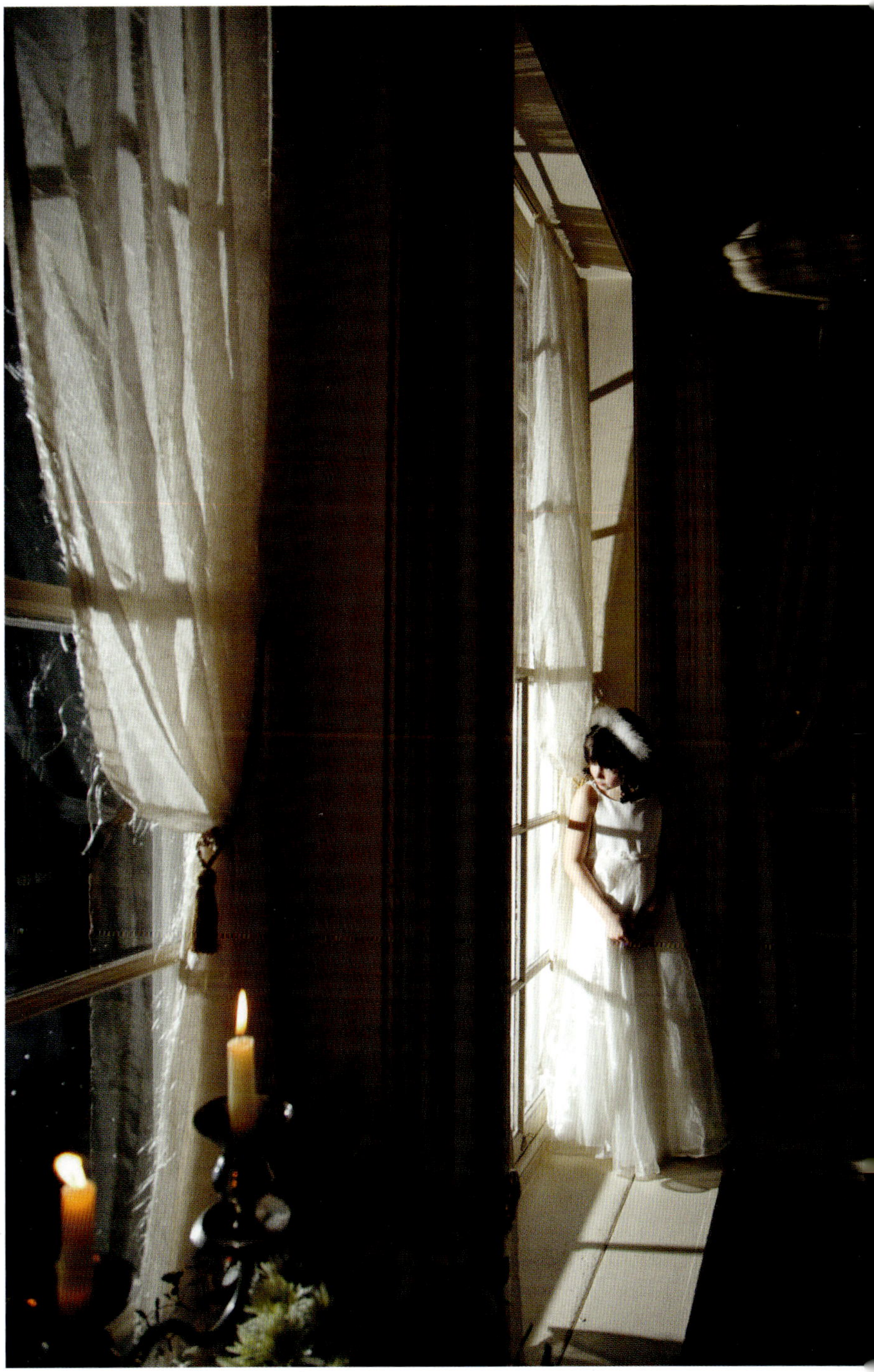

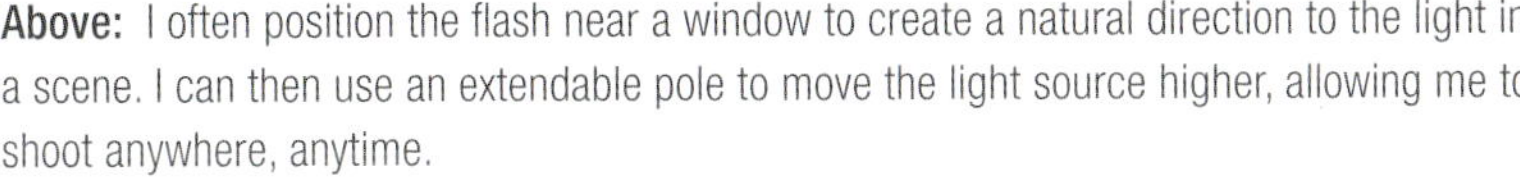

Above: I often position the flash near a window to create a natural direction to the light in a scene. I can then use an extendable pole to move the light source higher, allowing me to shoot anywhere, anytime.

Above: During the winter months, when natural light is not around for long, I ask my assistant to go outside with the flash, which provides an artificial external—and movable— light source.

Positioning off-camera flash

The key reason to use off-camera flash is to bring more dynamic lighting to the scene.

When I was learning about lighting and where to position flash, I was taught that 45 degrees was the most pleasing flash position for lighting a subject, whereas a position of 90 degrees added more drama to the lighting. This is not that easy to understand, however, particularly if you're only just learning to use flash, so I now use the clock face to explain flash positioning to my assistants and attendees on photography courses.

Imagine a clock face, with the subject being photographed at its center and the camera at 6 o'clock. Then split the clock face in half, along a line from 9 to 3 o'clock, to create two segments, which I call the Impact Zone and the Safe Zone.

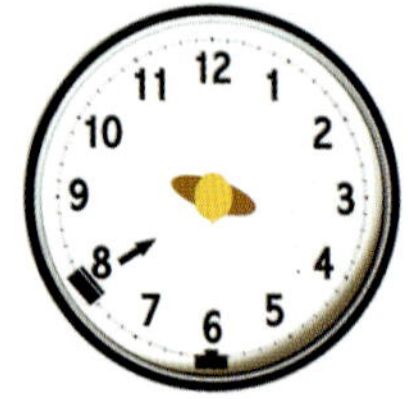

Above: The clock concept helps you to understand and remember where to position your light to produce a particular effect.

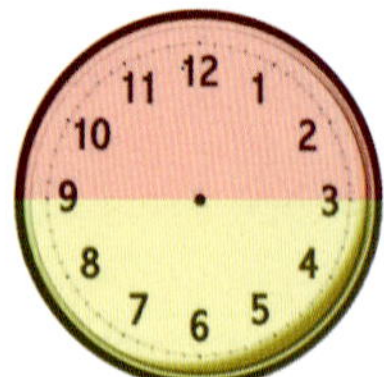

Above: The clock can be divided into two sections: the Impact Zone (pink) for lighting to separate your subject from the background and to create impact, and the Safe Zone (yellow) for safer, more flattering lighting of your subject.

Right: Positioning the flash at 10 o'clock will generate more shadow, making the subject of the picture appear more three-dimensional.

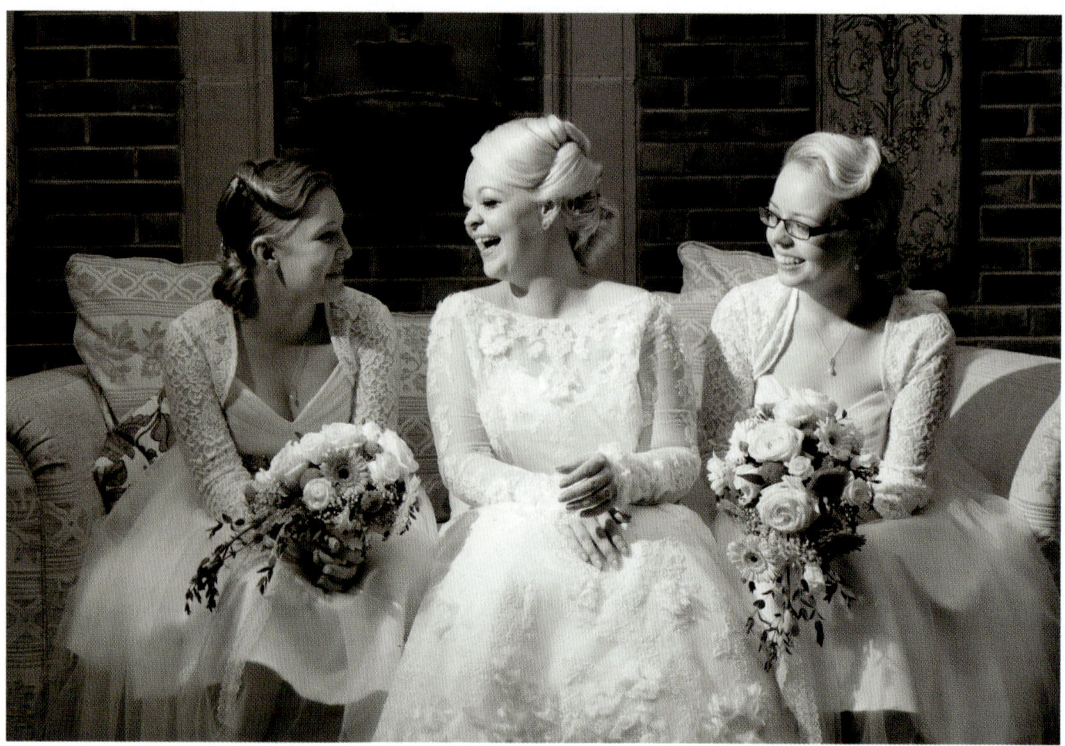

Above: Position the flash at 8 o'clock to soften strong lighting and generate a little more overall illumination, reducing the weight of the shadows.

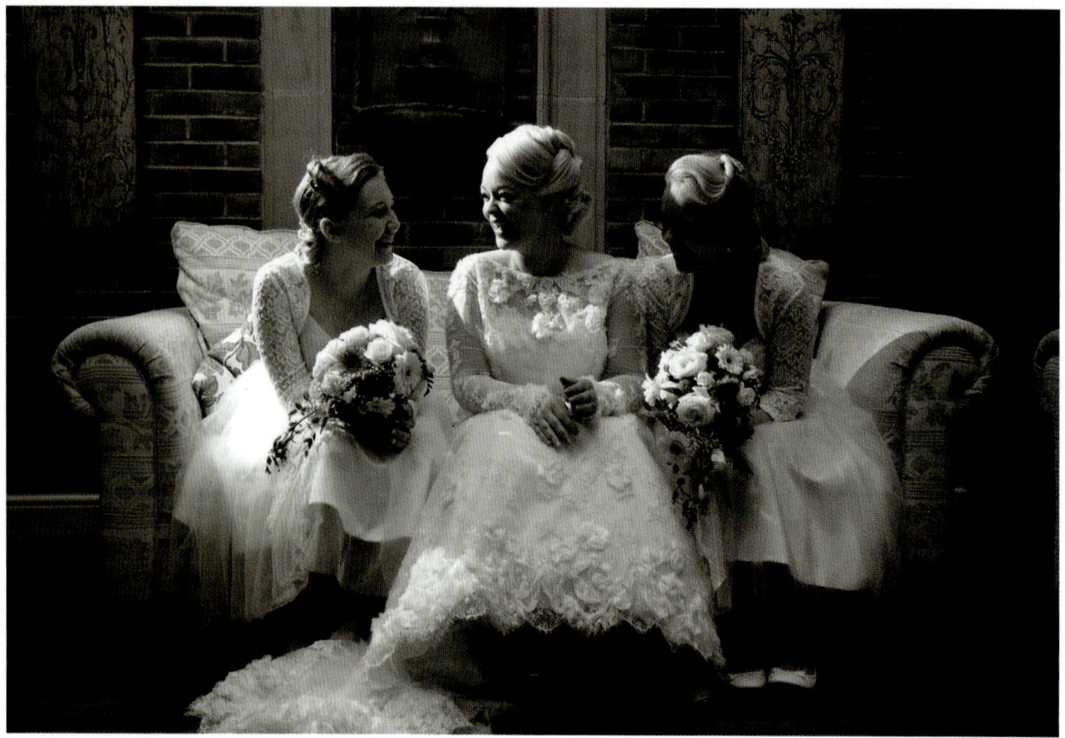

Impact Zone

Any flash light placed in the segment from the 9 o'clock to the 3 o'clock position will create more dynamic lighting, with little or no light on the subject's face, unless they turn towards the light. When the subject is looking at the camera, the light becomes an accent or a separation light.

Safe Zone

Any flash light positioned in the section between the 3 o'clock and 9 o'clock positions clockwise will create a usable light on the subject—which should create sellable images. The key positions are 4 o'clock and 8 o'clock, as positioning flash units at either of these points will create a dynamic shadow on the subject, slimming them and providing three-dimensional modeling. For shooting a couple or a small group, move the light to the 5 o'clock or 7 o'clock position, as this will lessen the shadow but still slim and shape the subjects. For large groups, use the 6 o'clock position to create a flatter light.

If you use on-camera flash, it is technically at the 6 o'clock position, in the Safe Zone, but the light from the flash will be so flat that it will not add any drama to the scene—except when zoomed. A quick way to change the look of the image is to bounce the flash off a side wall or a reflector, which effectively creates a new light source at the 7 to 8 or 4 to 5 o'clock positions.

Tip

When using multiple flashes for a photograph, place them opposite each other, so if your key light is at 4 o'clock place your accent light at 10 o'clock.

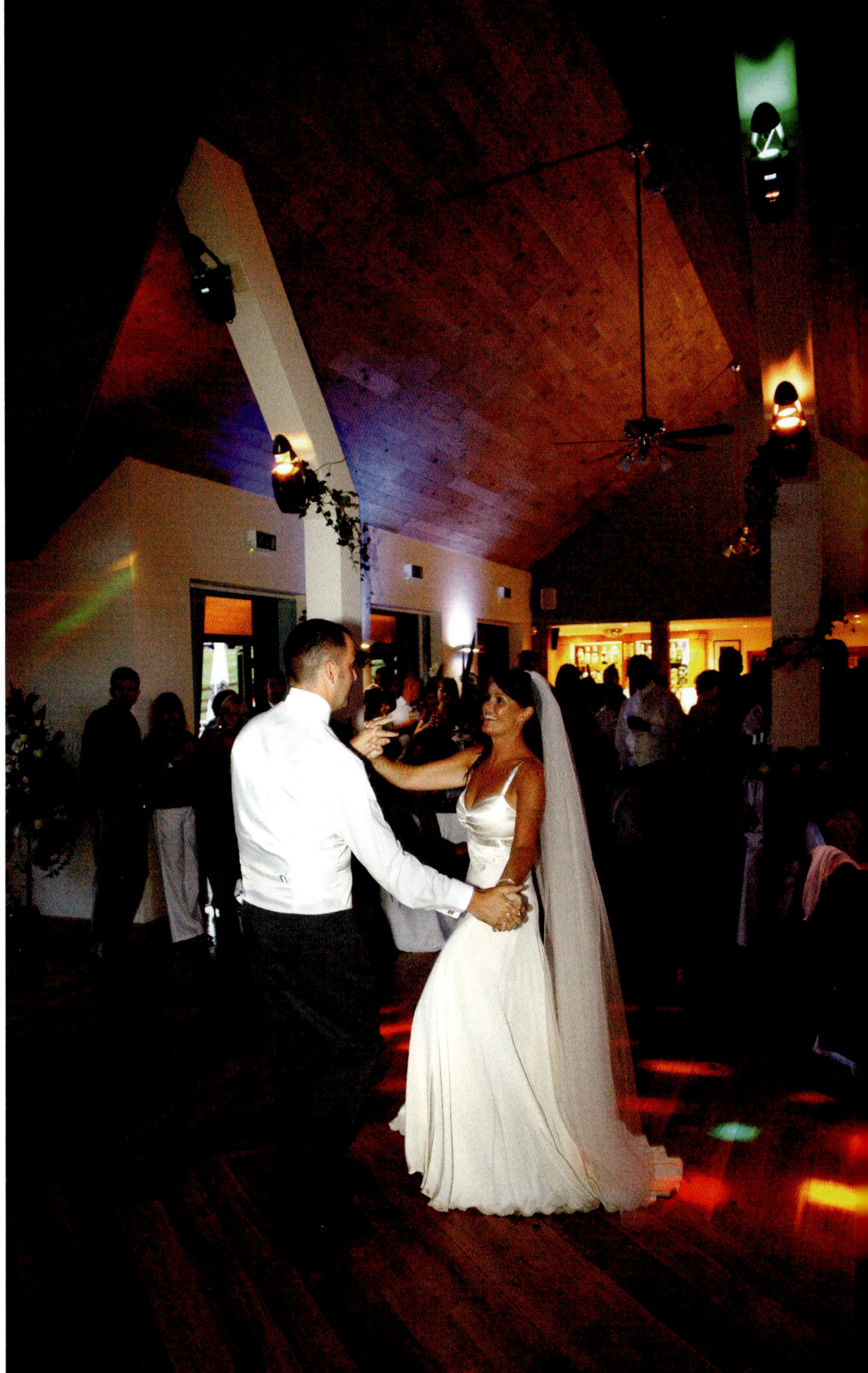

Right: On-camera flash should technically be positioned at 6 o'clock, but the lighting effect produced in this way is far from dramatic.

Chapter 3
Animation

I prefer to use the word "animation" rather than "posing," as it implies bringing your subjects to life instead of fixing them in stiff and rigid positions. But no matter what you prefer to call it, understanding how to position and move your subjects is crucial to improving your wedding photography. In this chapter I look at the most successful ways to animate your subjects, both as groups and as individuals.

Right: Use a flow of animations to achieve beautiful, natural-looking shots of the wedding couple.

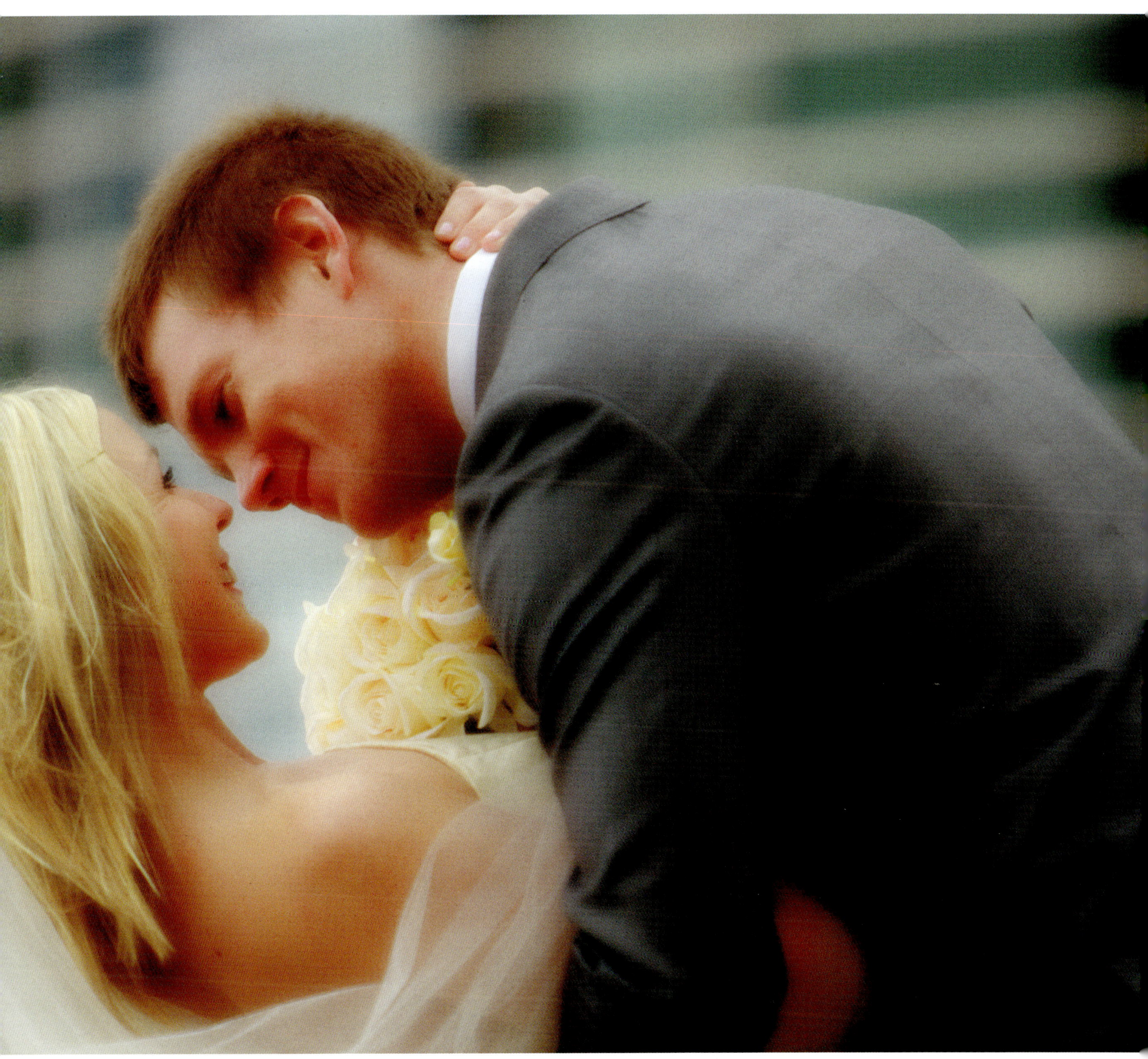

Basic Positions

Using a simple "flow" of animations will help you move your subjects from one position to another with a single move of a limb, enabling you to shoot a variety of different photographs in a short time. You can practice these positions, and the flow from one to the next, by using your friends, family, or even yourself in a mirror. Like anything in life, practice makes perfect. When I was first learning the basics of animation, I would practice my hand positions in the car mirror whilst stopped at the traffic lights, or try out body poses in the studio with my assistants when we had a quiet five minutes.

Even though you might not like the idea of structured animation and posing, the fact is the only way to get the client looking their best on the day is to control their shape using some simple postures. So let's start by looking at the basic animations that allow you to move from one position to the next with complete control.

Feet positions

Every pose begins with the feet because they provide us with our basic balance. When most people relax, they stand on one foot, putting most of their weight on that one leg and using the other for balance. This is exactly what we mimic when we pose our subjects. If they were to place equal weight on both feet, they would have a strong, upright posture that looks very stiff. Equally, if you were to ask your subject to just stand, they would do something similar and instantly look rigid and awkward.

So start by asking your subject to put all their weight on their back foot and then use the other as the "show" foot. For a woman this means placing the front foot slightly to one side, with the toes pointed, to exaggerate the line of the leg. Although you probably won't be able to see the bride's feet under the dress, you will notice when she isn't following this instruction, because she'll be standing awkwardly.

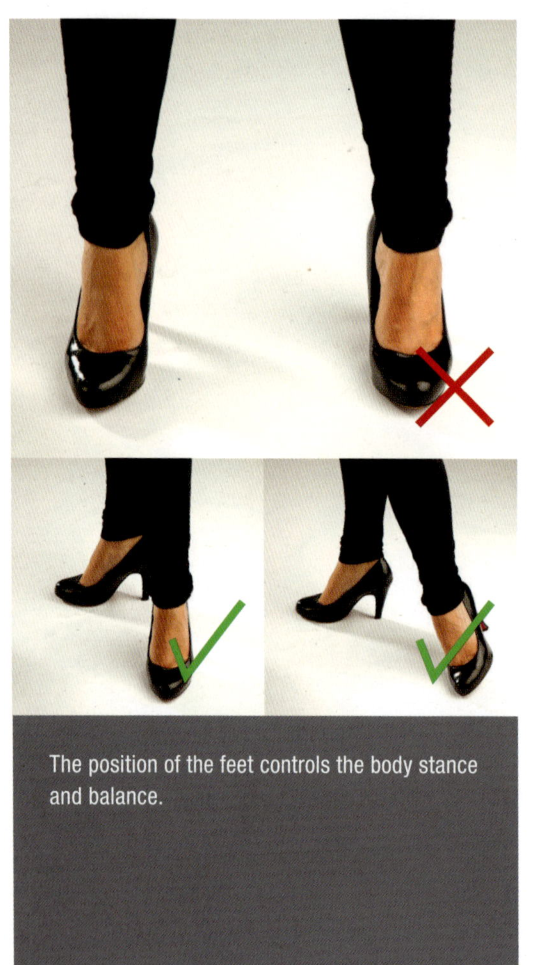

The position of the feet controls the body stance and balance.

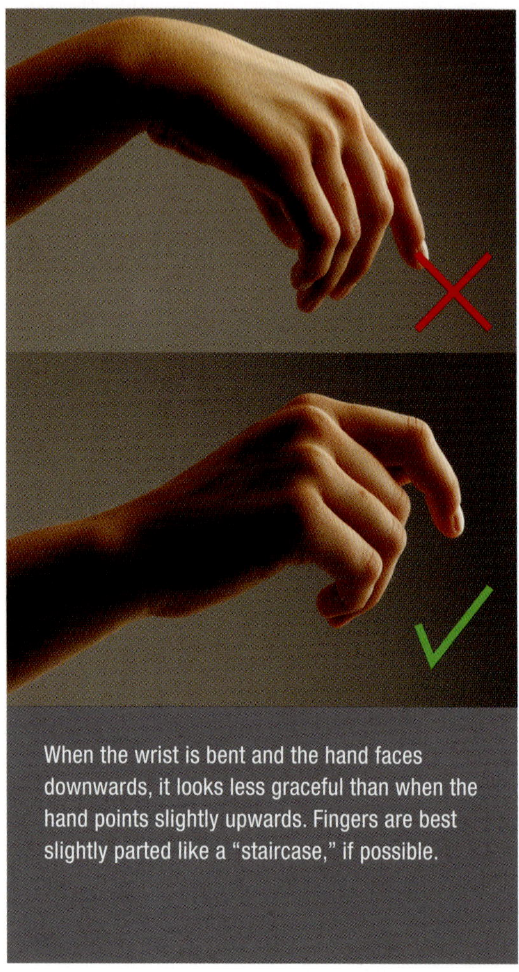

When the wrist is bent and the hand faces downwards, it looks less graceful than when the hand points slightly upwards. Fingers are best slightly parted like a "staircase," if possible.

Body position

Next, we look at the body position. Ensure the subject's back foot is turned to one side slightly, which will naturally turn the hips away and will appear to slim the body by around 25 to 30%. The rest of the body can then lean slightly towards the back foot for a relaxed pose, or even more for an exaggerated line, as you would see in a dancer.

For a more three-dimensional body—which also serves to flatter the female form—turn the torso and hips away from the light source. This helps to emphasize the bust shape using shadow. For a male subject, you can make them appear more bulky—and hence strong-looking—by doing the opposite, turning them into the light source.

If you have a heavier client, the body position will need to be slightly different. A bride can position a bouquet in front of her body, or you can ask her to turn back to face the camera square-on.

Hand positions

The hands should, if possible, always be seen from the side, as this reduces the amount of light they reflect to make them less of a distraction. If the front or the back of a hand is fully visible, the bright skin-tone will have the same visual weight in the picture as the subject's face, making it a major distraction in the picture.

All the limbs—including the wrist and fingers—should be slightly bent to create a graceful arc instead of a stiff, straight line. The wrist should be bent so that the hand is higher than the arm, pointing upwards. If the hand is below the waist it can be bent in the opposite way.

Head positions

The face will look slimmer if it is not square-on to the body. The classic two-thirds face position works well for a woman, whereas a man can turn his head to face the camera, again for that look of extra strength.

As well as positioning the face, ask your subject to tilt their head slightly for more animation and a softer line. Typically, you can ask a woman to tilt her head back to the lower forward shoulder, and a man to tilt his head into the forward position.

Eyes

Make sure that the eyes are in the middle of the eye socket. If you ask your subject to look off-camera too far without moving their head, this will create too much white in the eye closest to camera, which distorts it. The best solution is to ask your subject to look along the line of their nose.

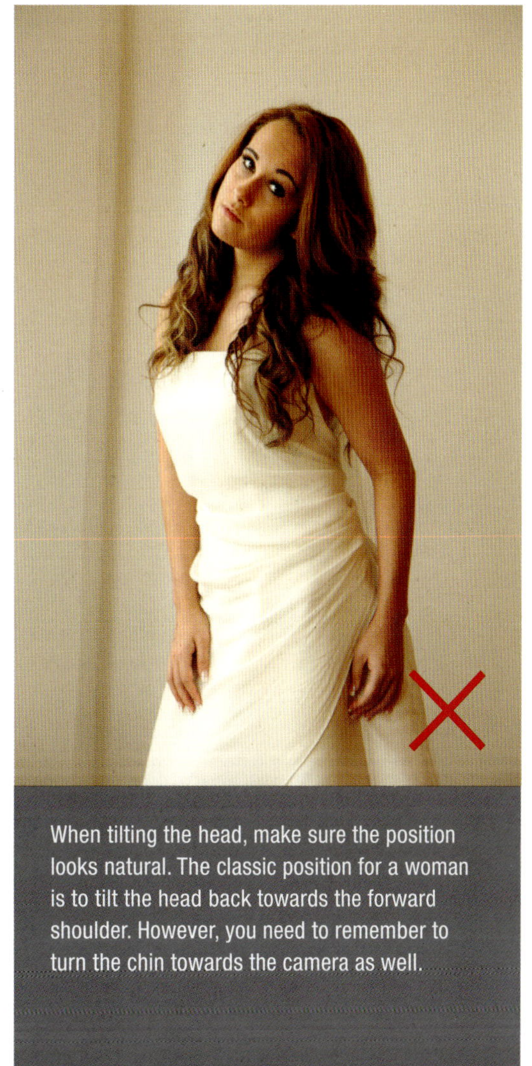

When tilting the head, make sure the position looks natural. The classic position for a woman is to tilt the head back towards the forward shoulder. However, you need to remember to turn the chin towards the camera as well.

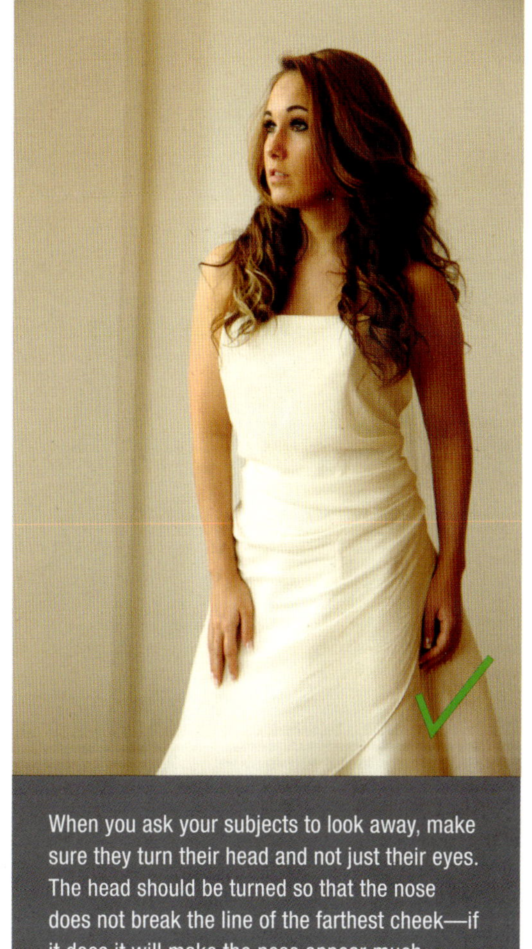

When you ask your subjects to look away, make sure they turn their head and not just their eyes. The head should be turned so that the nose does not break the line of the farthest cheek—if it does it will make the nose appear much bigger than real life.

Camera height

Be aware of the height of your camera in relation to your subject, as well as the effects of perspective from your lens. As a rule, the camera position for a full-length portrait should be slightly lower than the bride's bust, especially if you want to increase her leg length by shooting slightly upwards. However, you do not want to exaggerate this too much or you distort the proportions of the body, making it appear long, and the head appear small.

For the three-quarter portraits, shoot from the same height as the bride's bust or slightly higher, but make sure you don't appear to create "double chins" because the client is looking down instead of up.

For head-and-shoulders portraits, the camera needs to be at nose level or slightly higher, if possible. This will stretch the neck and create a more flattering eye line. When your subject looks up to a viewpoint with their eyes as well as their head, a little white of the eye will become visible just above the bottom eyelid—this is called a "canoe" and is thought to be a sign of flirtation and innocence, so is often used in female portraits.

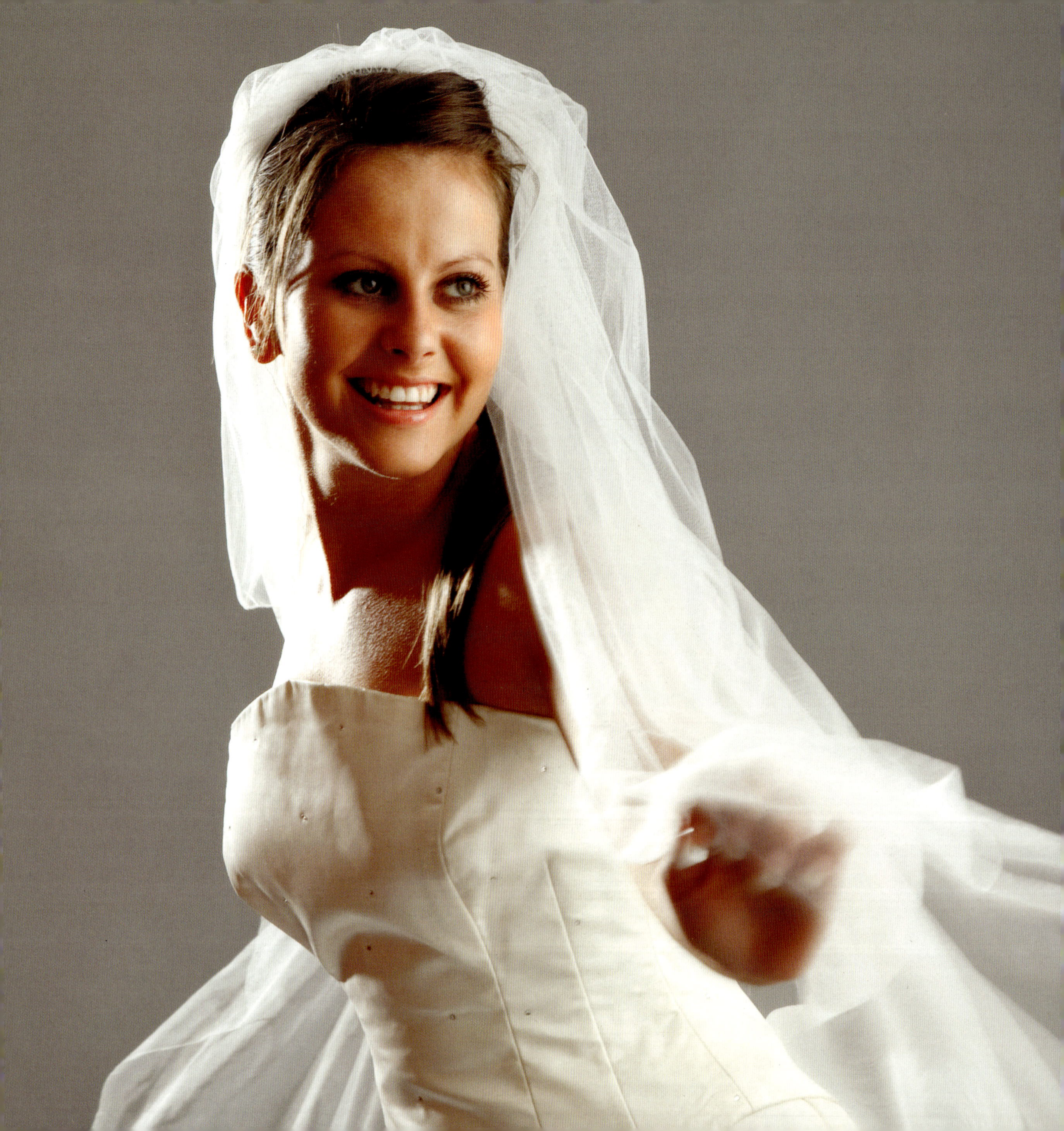

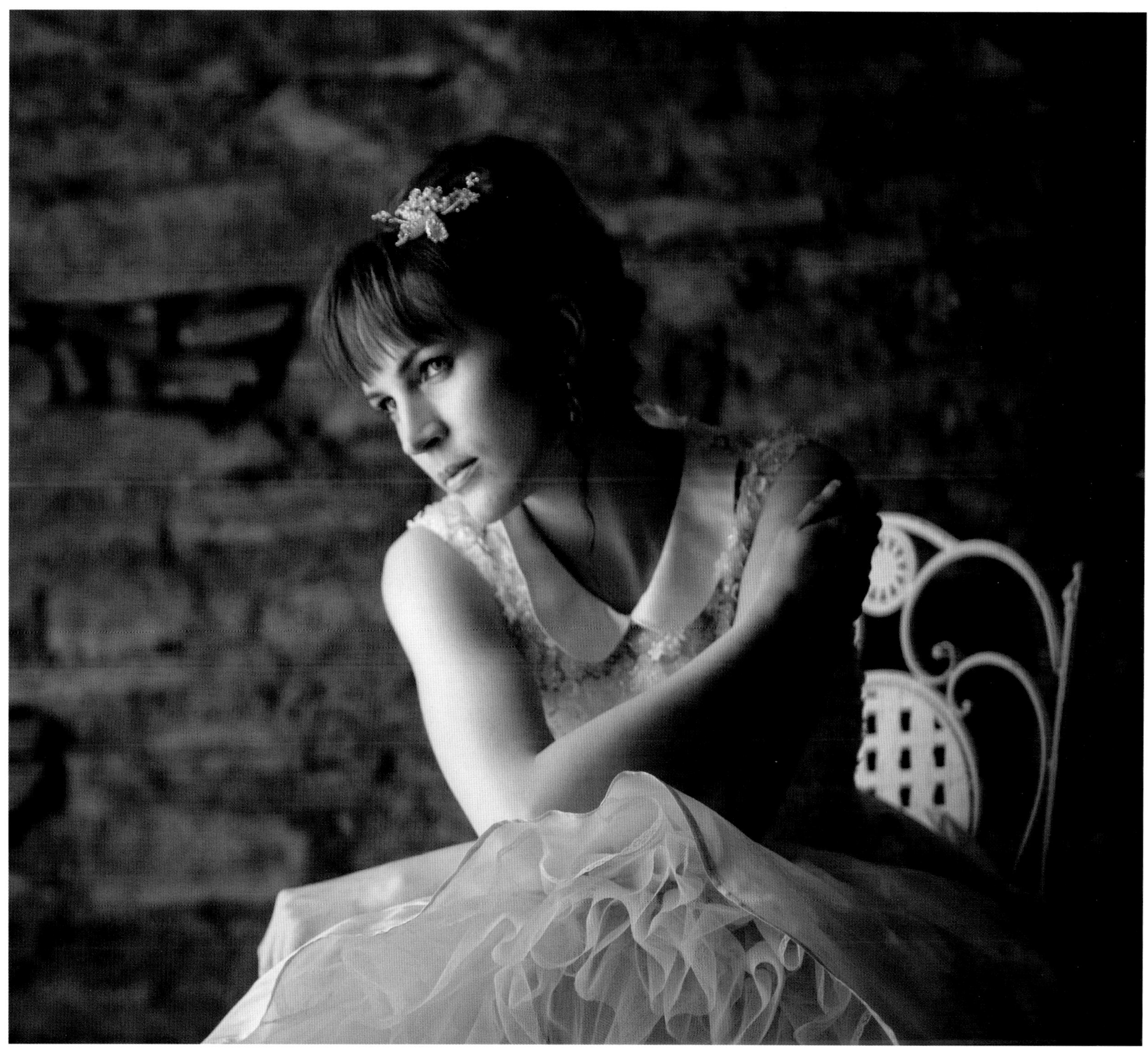

Left: When animating your subject, try to keep the eyes pointing along the same line as the nose to avoid too much white of the eye, which will appear too dominant.

Above: A dreamy, romantic look is created with subtle lighting and by asking your subject to tilt their head slightly to one side.

Basic Bride & Groom Portraits

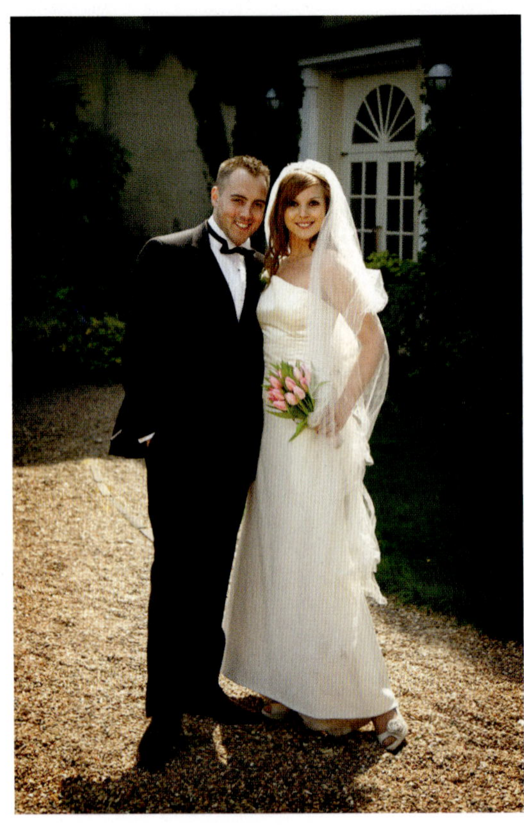

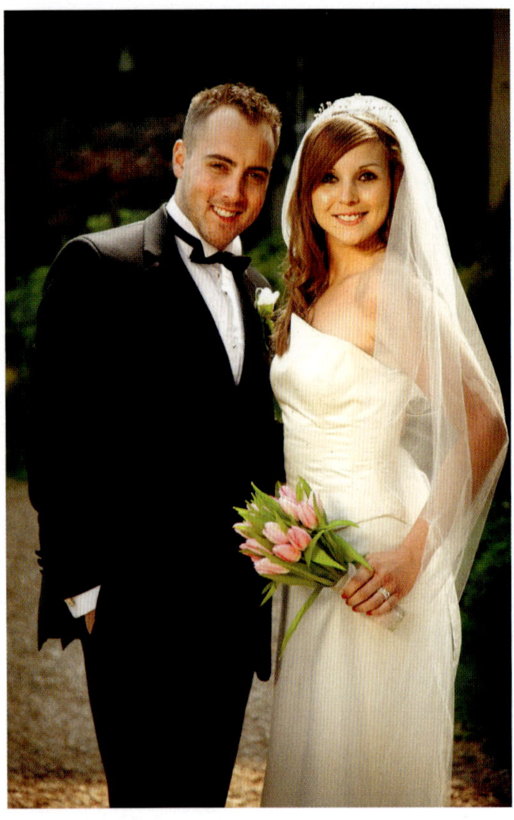

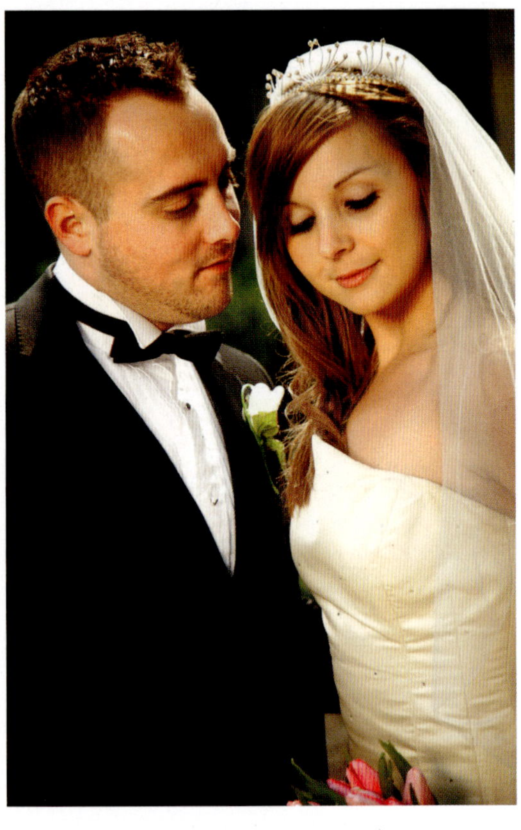

Above: For the full-length portrait of the bride and groom, posing, or "animating," always starts from the feet upward to ensure a good basic balance.

Above: The closer we get to our subjects the more that little mistakes in posing start to show, so it is still important to pay attention to the whole pose.

Above: If you are struggling to keep the subjects within the camera frame, try backing off a little and then ask the subjects to lean their heads in towards each other.

Here we look at simple, progressive shooting and posing of the portraits of the bride and groom. I use a series of images to demonstrate the flow of animations, but all these pictures could be achieved within a 20–30-minute period on a wedding day.

As with all animation, the subject is posed from the feet upwards—this basic balance is the most important element in any pose as it helps to create either soft or dramatic lines. The limbs are used to provide secondary balance and to add accents or a more dynamic shape. The head is the final element to the pose, with different degrees of tilt providing either submissive or aggressive emphasis.

Full-length portrait

To ensure a stable foundation to the pose (above left), most of the weight is placed over the back foot. This creates a slightly submissive and relaxed basic pose. In this case, the groom has most of his weight on his left foot and the bride's weight is mostly on her right foot. The front foot is then used as the "show" or "balance" foot. The show foot should be positioned slightly out to one side, often with a slight break of the ankle.

The groom's back foot is positioned at 90 degrees to the camera to hold his body in a position turned away from the camera slightly, and to help slim the body. The bride should also turn her body away from camera, but not too far or she will be turned to the profile position, making it awkward for fine-tuning the pose and making her look top-heavy if she has a fuller bust. The two-thirds body position is the most-used pose—because it helps to slim the subject's figure—but fine-tuning the pose for each subject is essential.

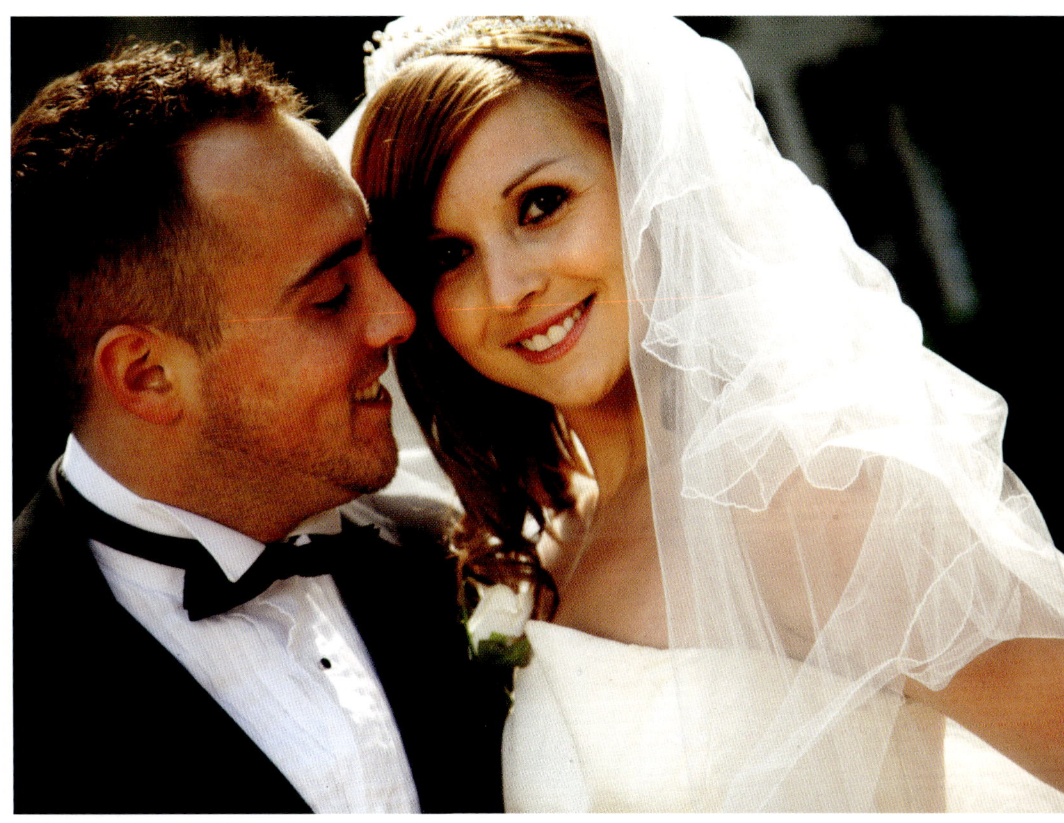

Above: Watch out for unintentional cropping of heads in-camera, as shown here, since this will be impossible to correct during postproduction.

Three-quarters portrait

The closer and tighter the pose (opposite, center), the more you need to concentrate, especially with in-camera cropping, as the last thing you want to do is crop limbs out of the picture by mistake. If you have achieved the full-length pose successfully, the three-quarters portrait should be simple to shoot, just by moving closer to your subject.

Arms and hands dominate the frame in close-ups, so it is important to pay more intention to what they are doing. There has been no deliberate adjustment to the pose here, but the bride has begun to slightly rotate to the profile body position—this can only be because she has moved her feet. The arms and hands should be bent to eliminate any sense of tension or stiffness in the body. A good rule to remember is "if it bends, bend it"—check this before you progress through a series of pictures to ensure a good position in all of them.

Again, always try to photograph the sides of the hands to make them look slimmer and smaller. However, there are times—as with this image—when there is no alternative to showing the back of the hand. The bouquet was quite heavy and the bride needed a firm grip to support it.

Providing a gap between the arm and body will also add a slimming effect, unless the subject is very large. This slimming effect can be increased further if you create some contrast between the bride and the background.

The basic hand pose for a man is quite simple in the three-quarters pose, although it can be easy to forget when we are so focused on getting the bride right. The easiest position for the hands is in the pockets, but here I have made sure that the hand does not disappear into the pocket completely—I've allowed it to protrude slightly and have lifted the jacket sleeve to show the shirt cuff and cufflink at the same time.

Head-and-shoulders portrait

The head-and-shoulders image (opposite, right) is once more a simple progression of the above poses—I usually start with the basic, full-length image and then move closer and closer to the couple, creating a rapid series of images, each with a small variety of simple head and glance positions.

How to crop is the biggest decision with the head-and-shoulders portrait. Both a vertical or horizontal crop seem to leave too much space around the subjects, whilst close-cropping leaves parts of the head out of the frame (left). The crop in this image seems to be a good balance between all the elements, especially as a "Dutch tilt" has been applied to the angle and composition. Dutch painters used to add more drama to their pictures by tilting the image from the vertical, hence the name. This technique adds tension and unsettles the viewer, and is used in photography for the same reasons.

Modern Bride & Groom Portraits

These days, clients often ask for more relaxed or candid images, but what they really mean is that they don't want to look posed, pompous, or rigid with false expressions. Every client is different, as is every wedding, but in the end the couple just wants to look their best—which is, after all, what all the preparation has been about. However, even when working with clients who want something different— whether more stylized, relaxed, or candid—we must still begin with careful posing of the couple.

Full-length portrait

For this full-length image (right) I chose an old barn door to use as the setting. The location was only a two-minute walk round the side of the hotel that featured in the last section—proof that there is another picture around every corner. I decided to give these images a fashionable, "arrogant" look, a style that has been used over many decades in photography. At the end of the day, it is always the expression that sells and everything else just adds polish to the portrait.

To find a different pose for the bride and groom here, I deliberately chose to contradict the classic use of balance and body postures. Instead, I asked both subjects to adopt the flat-footed pose, with even weight on each foot and their bodies facing the camera. This is the vertical "I" pose, which looks strong and rigid, and is perfect for this style. For this shot I refined the pose a little, by allowing the bride to soften her right foot with a bend, but a strong overall line is still achieved.

To complete the animation, the couple were asked to hold hands as if they were walking along a street, and positioned the groom's free hand in

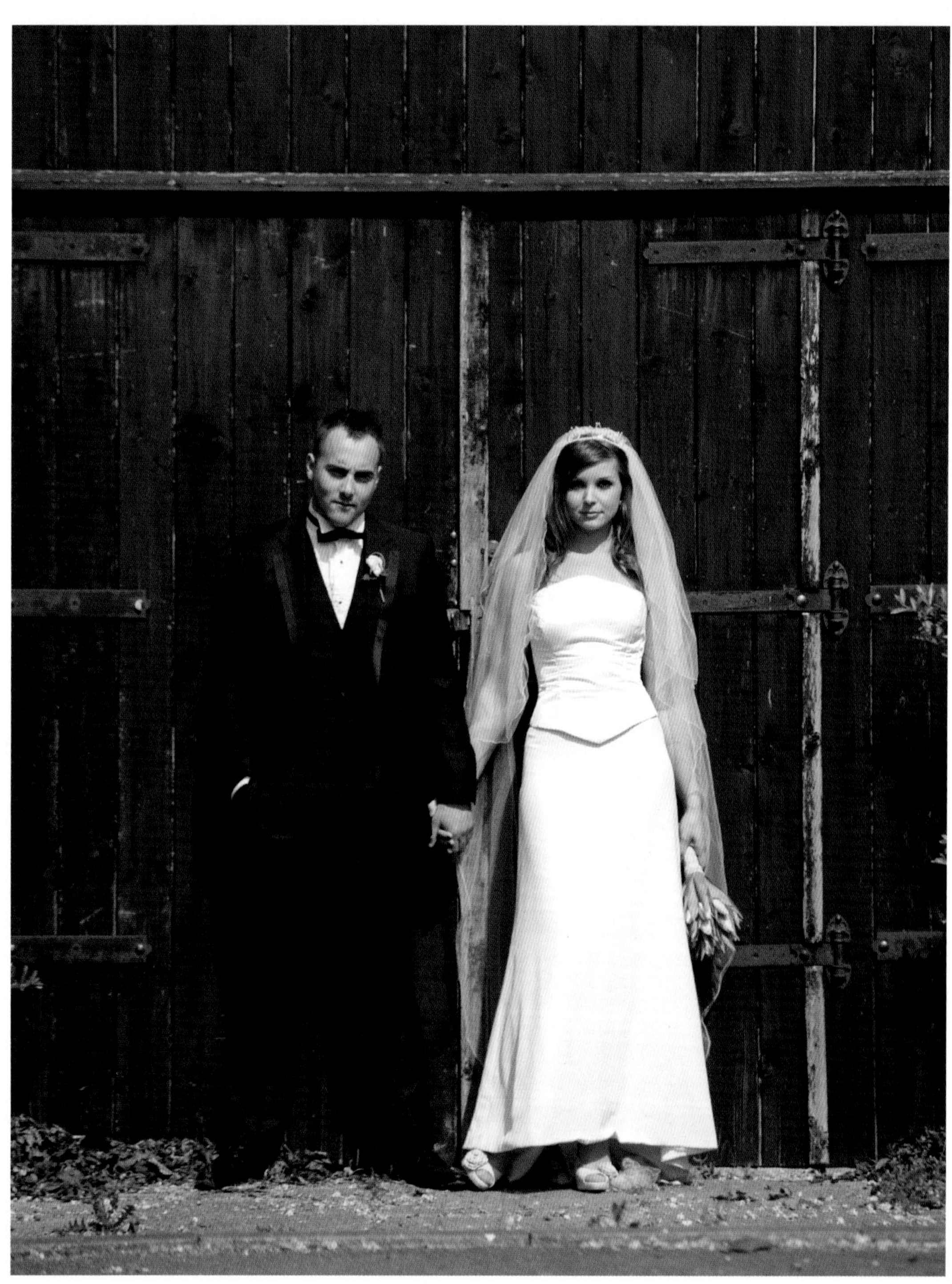

Right: Posing the couple to provide strong lines adds to the composition and complements the vertical design of the old barn door.

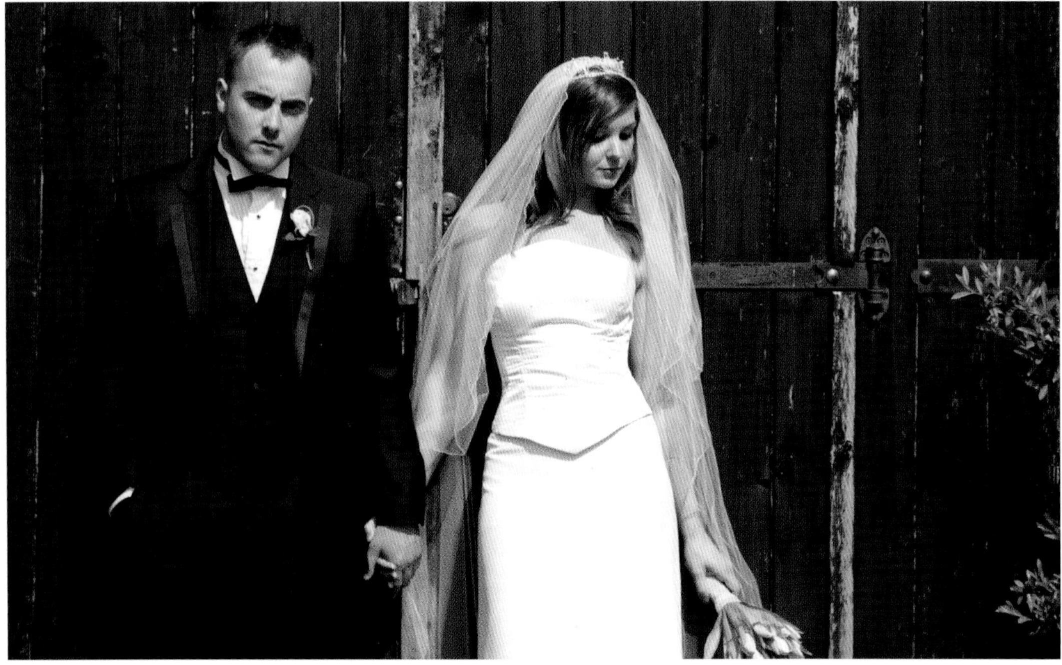

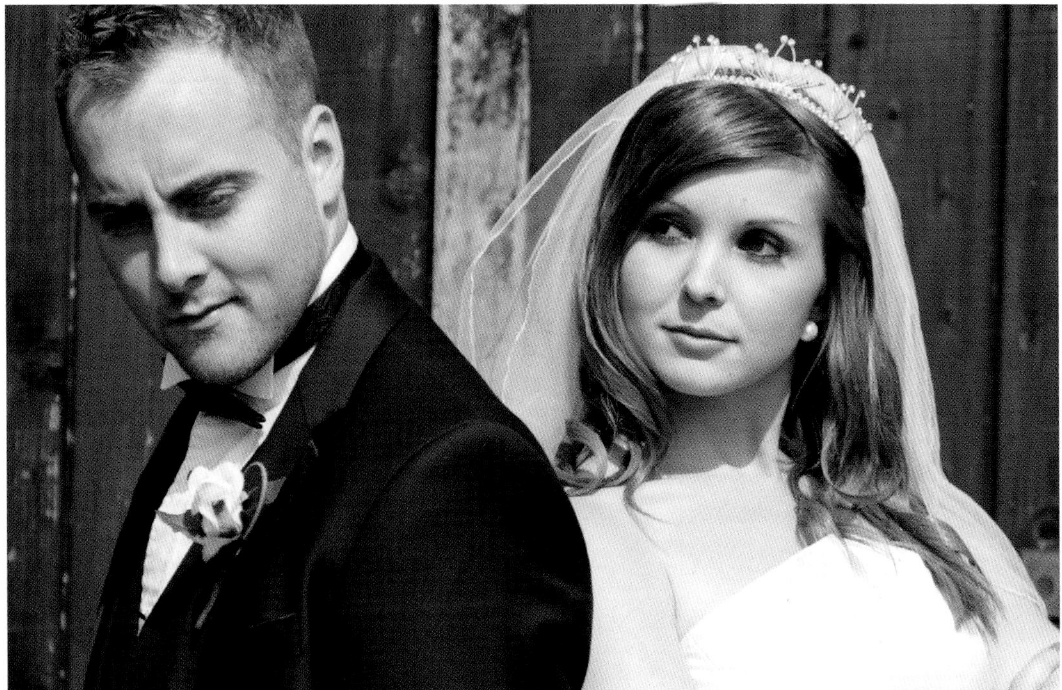

a pocket for a casual look. The bride's free hand, which was holding the bouquet, was just allowed to drop, again in a carefree manner. Even though the overhead sun cast heavy shadows in the subjects' eye sockets, the distance and style allowed me to get away with the strong lighting on the faces.

Three-quarters portrait

For the three-quarters shot (top left), I did not change any balance or limb poses. I asked the bride to look to the side and towards the floor, mainly to hide the bad lighting on her face. As you can see from the groom's eye sockets, the harsh sunlight from overhead casts the couple into shadow, creating an unsightly "panda-eye" effect with a lack of detail. The square-on pose again gives a strong line, but by allowing the bride to bend her foot slightly, her weight is pushed out her opposite hip, which adds to the fashion look of the shot.

Head-and-shoulders portrait

For the head-and-shoulders shot (left), I decided to turn the bodies completely away from each other, which is normally seen as negative body language. What this does is to give the couple a sense of carefree arrogance, especially as I had the bride cross her arms, another strong position with negative body language. However, a very tight crop was used to focus on the couple's expressions, which are a mixture of cheeky and defiant, but also humorous. Slight changes in body position and expressions will dramatically change every close-up image.

Tip

When shooting with strong lines in the background, such as these barn doors, applying a Dutch tilt to the composition may simply make the image look like a mistake, so use unusual tilts and crops carefully.

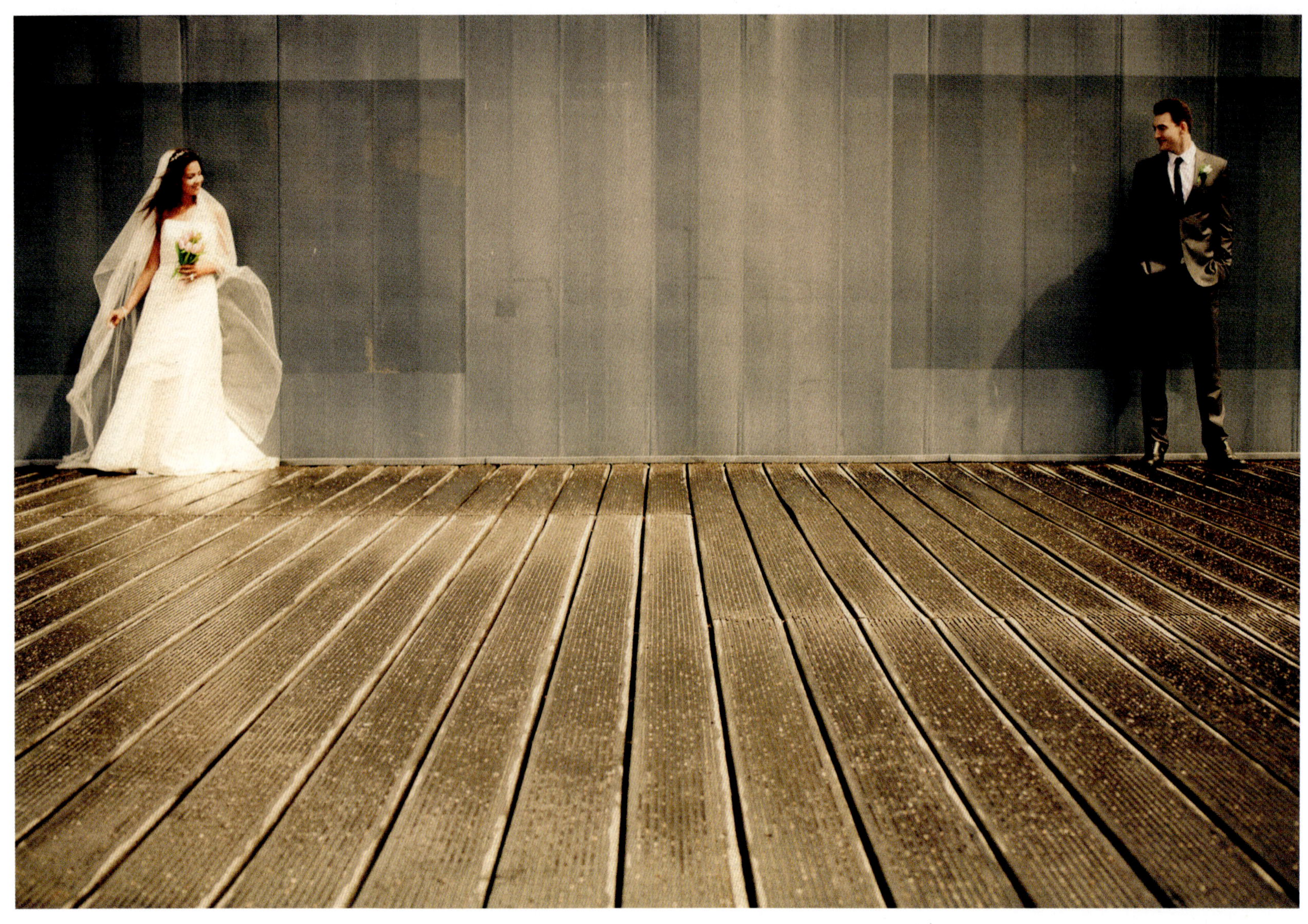

Above: Look for strong, even quirky, shots that will help to tell a story and convey a "fashion shoot" theme that is both stylish and humorous. It's important to discuss this style of photography with the clients initially, so they appreciate what you're endeavoring to do.

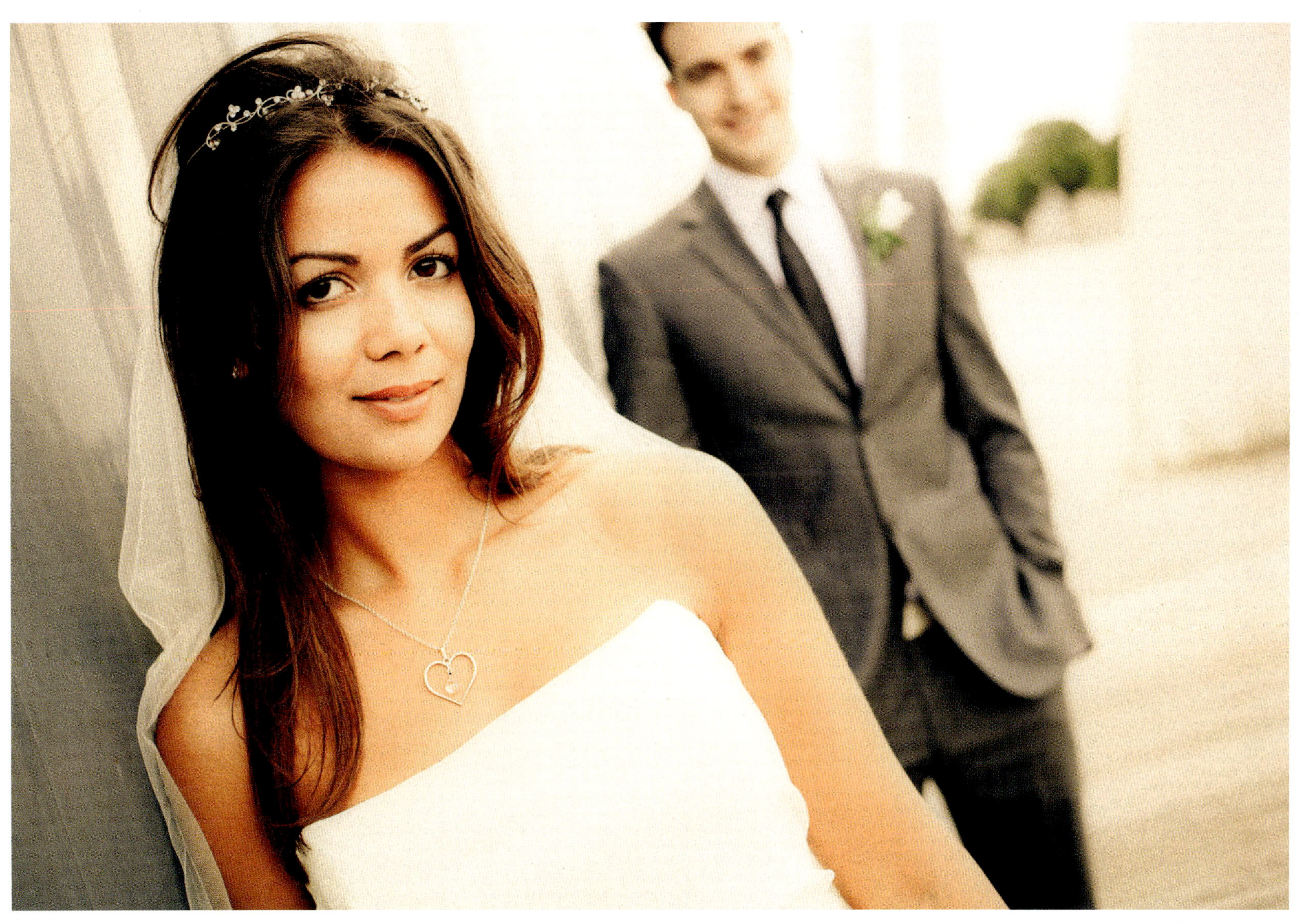

Above: Soft focus shots—perhaps adjusted in postproduction—can suggest a romantic feel that lifts a simple pose from being just a snapshot.

Controlling the Flow

Controlling the flow between images is important to maximize your time with the couple. This is a skill you will quickly develop through training, and in your own style. Some photographers like to make each and every image totally different, repeating the same shots in a flow for each and every wedding they shoot, but personally I find this a little robotic. Instead, I like to shoot a variety that brings the couple closer and closer together, while developing a range of expressions, from looking moody to laughing, but all the time trying to capture the couple's individual characters and emotions—and it's from this that you create a truly individual set of images.

Think of the flow in three simple sections: animating the couple for full-length images, animating them for a three-quarters series, and then taking a variety of close-ups. Also think ahead about how the limbs will be used—for balance or for show—as well as how you will crop the limbs when moving closer in.

All images: This flow of images was shot using a 70–200mm zoom and exposed using Manual camera settings. Because the couple were facing into the sun all the time, there was only one exposure at 1/2000 sec. at f/5.6.

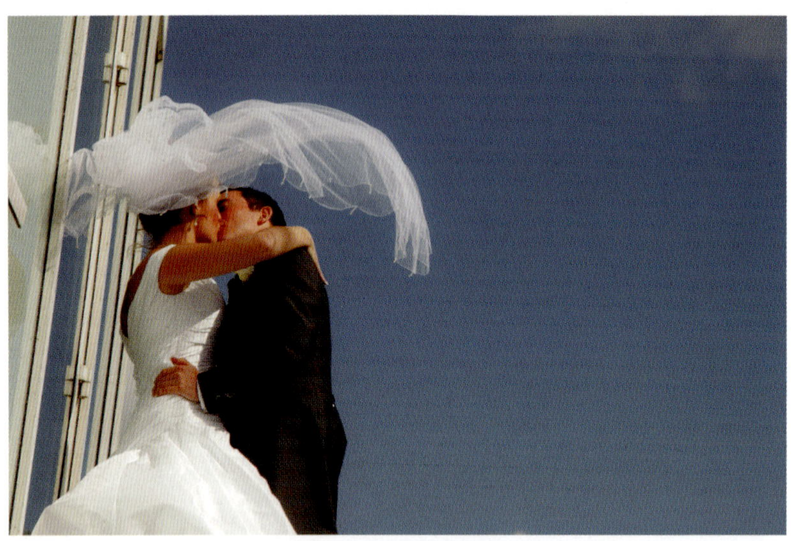

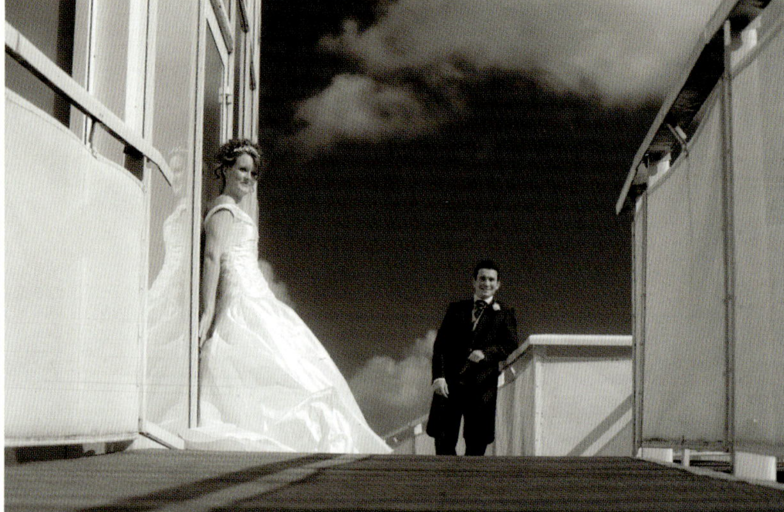

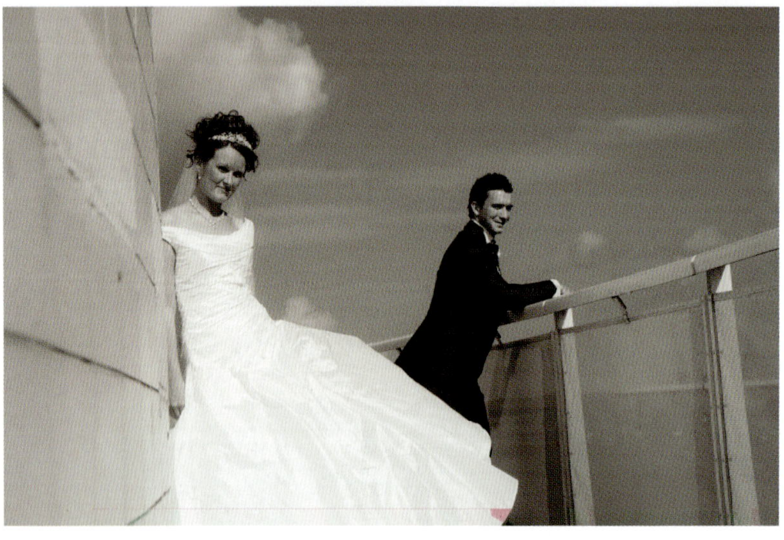

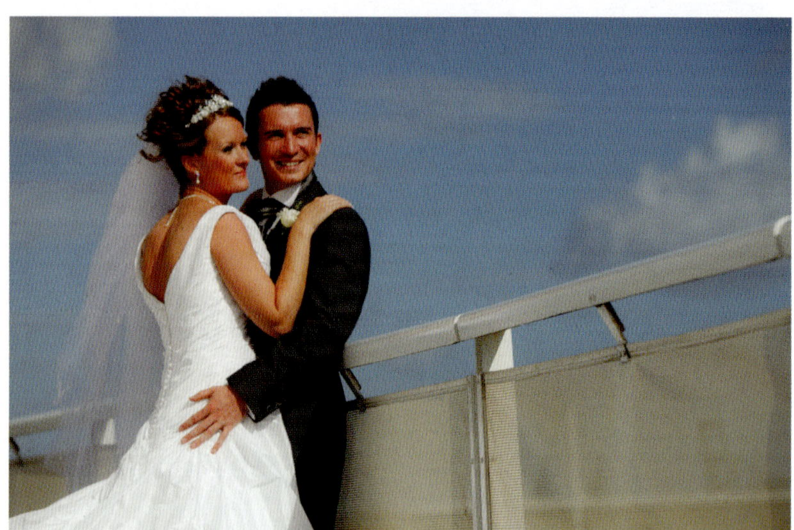

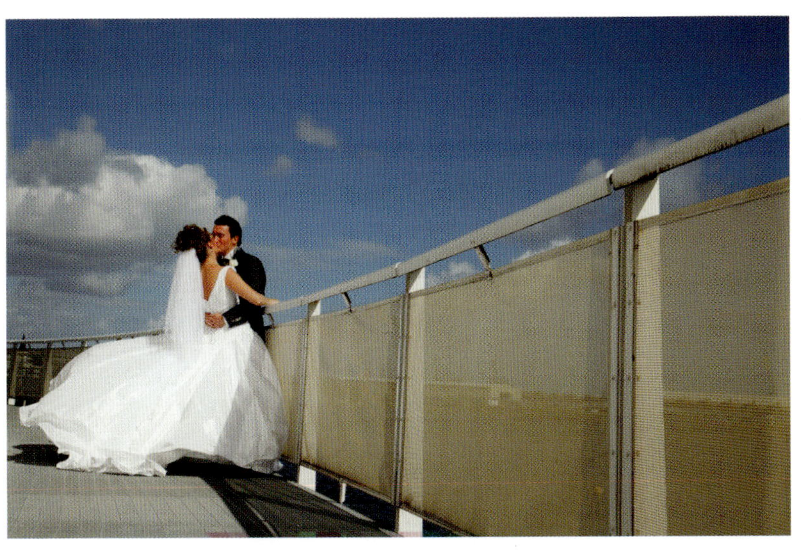
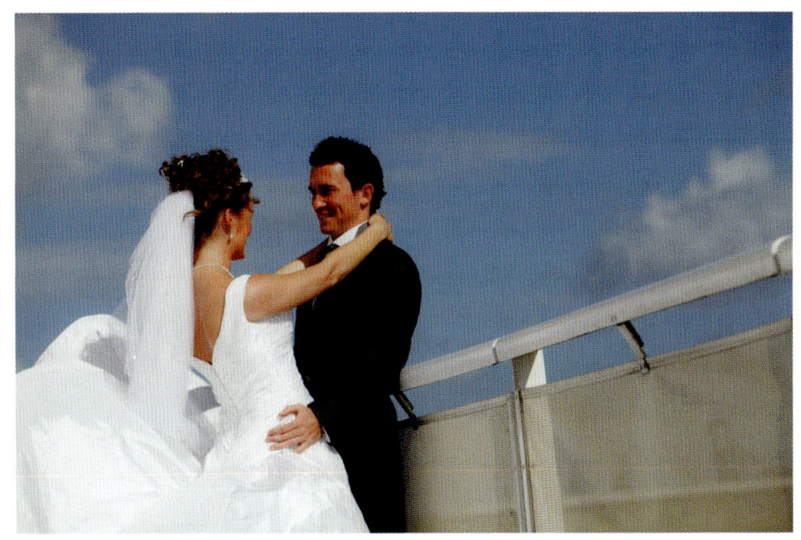
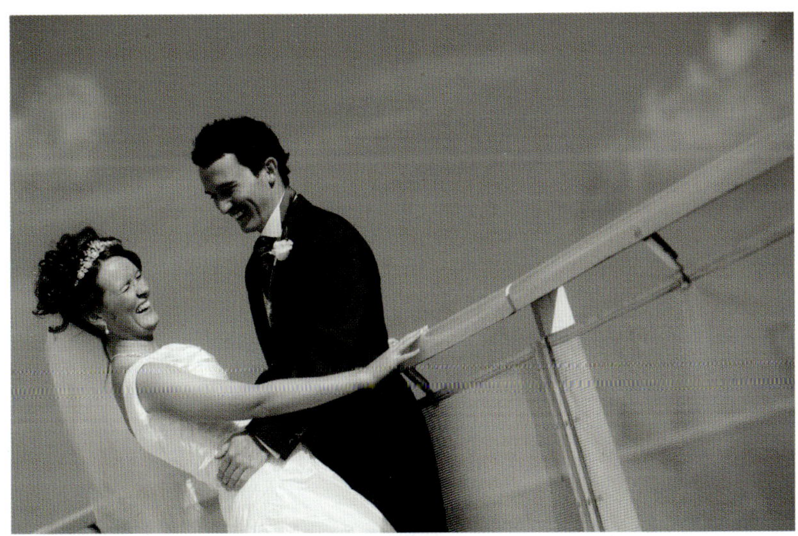
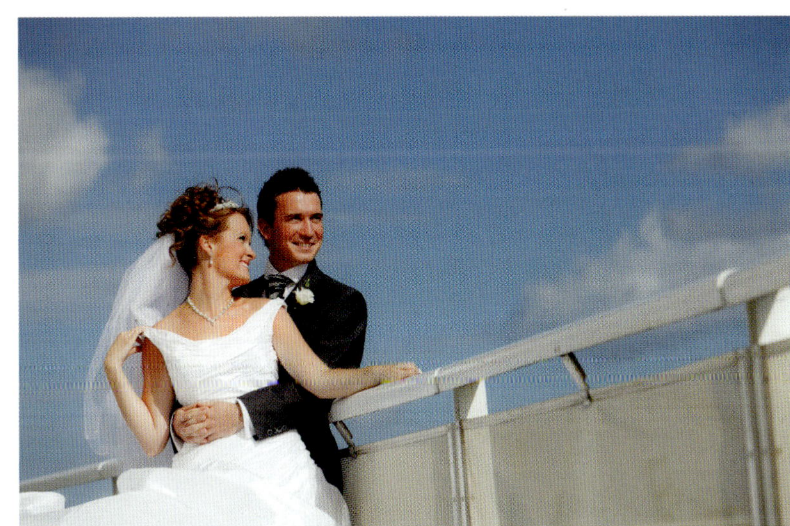
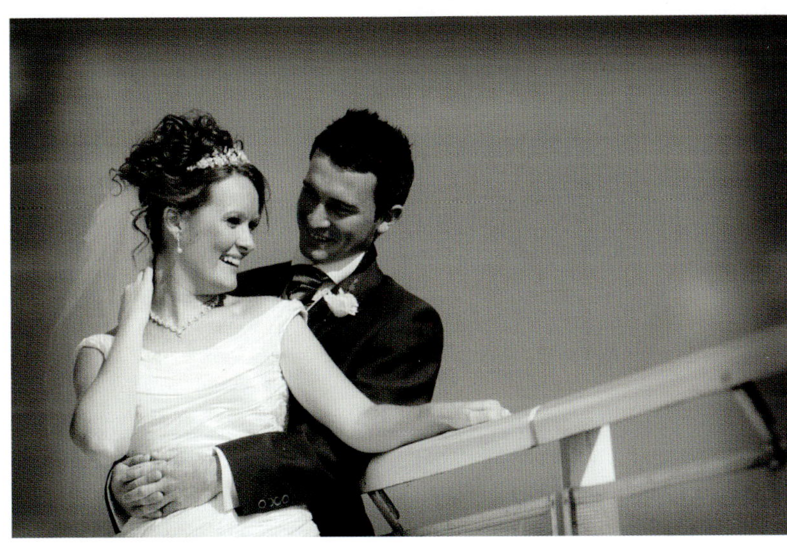
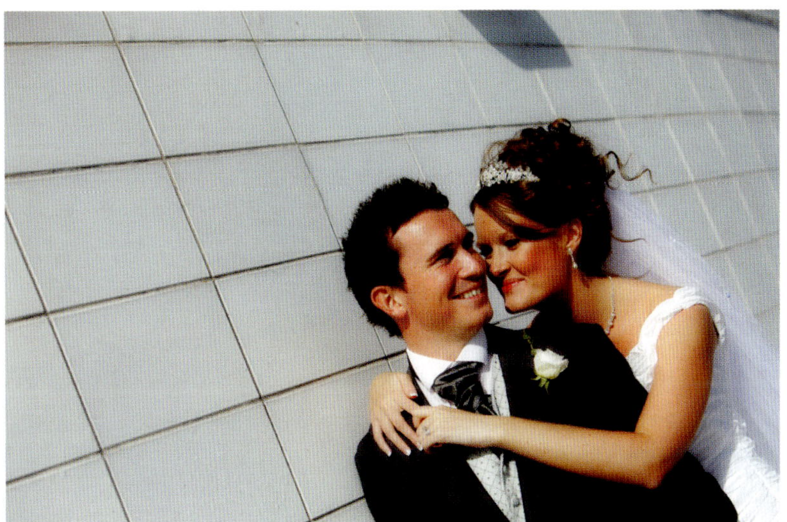

Bride Portraits

For the pictures of the bride, I try to keep the body looking slim, bring a softness to the limbs and her expression, and to make the whole animation look natural.

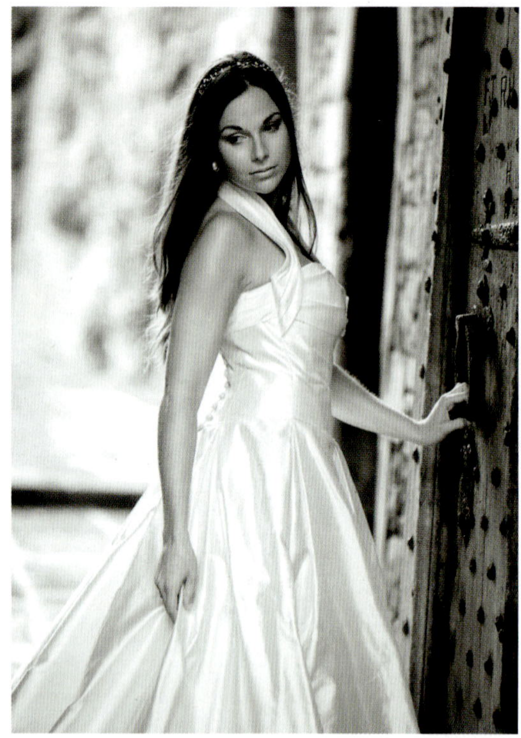

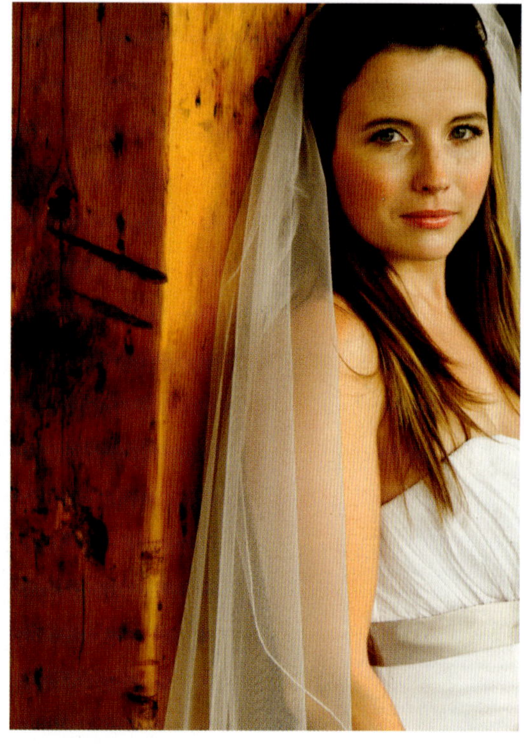

Standing

When the bride is standing, follow the principle of positioning her weight on the back foot, using the other foot to add balance and stability. Position the bride's limbs so they look graceful, paying particular attention to the hand and arm positions. Here, the body is in the two-thirds position, turned away from the camera and light, with the head tilting back towards the camera slightly. To complete the pose, make sure that there is a slight gap between the arms and the waist, as this will also help to slim the figure.

Sitting

With the bride seated on a chair, I have turned her body slightly away from the camera and the light source, with most of her weight on one side to create a natural lean. If the chair has arms, place the hand or forearm furthest from the camera on one chair arm, and the other arm slightly apart from the waist to slim it. The legs are slightly stretched towards the camera, with the knees together. Cross the ankles for a graceful line or place the feet apart for a more edgy pose.

Leaning

There are several ways to pose a bride leaning against, for example, a door or wall, but they all rely on a contact point. Lean the bride against the surface using her bottom, a shoulder, or a hand—but never more than two—and ensure that your subject has good balance and that you have enough space to move around. If your subject is flat against the surface, she will look uncomfortable and unnatural. If you are looking for a more feminine pose, the weight should always remain on the feet, so that even when she's leaning on a hand or shoulder, the subject's limbs are not bearing any real weight.

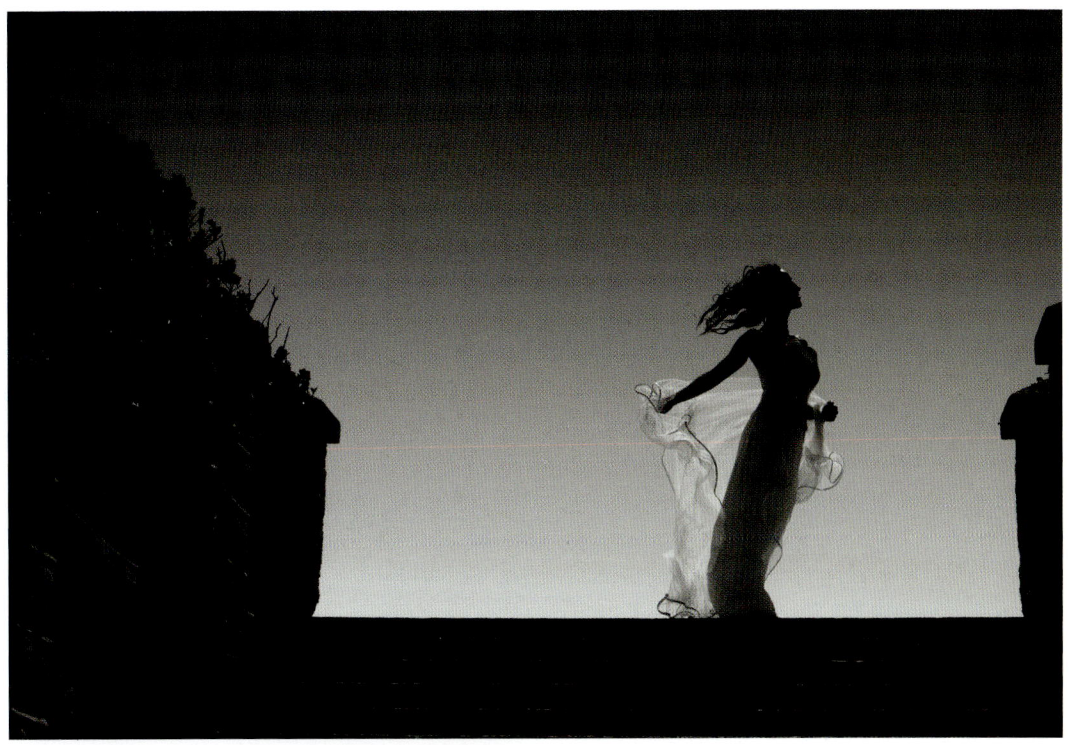

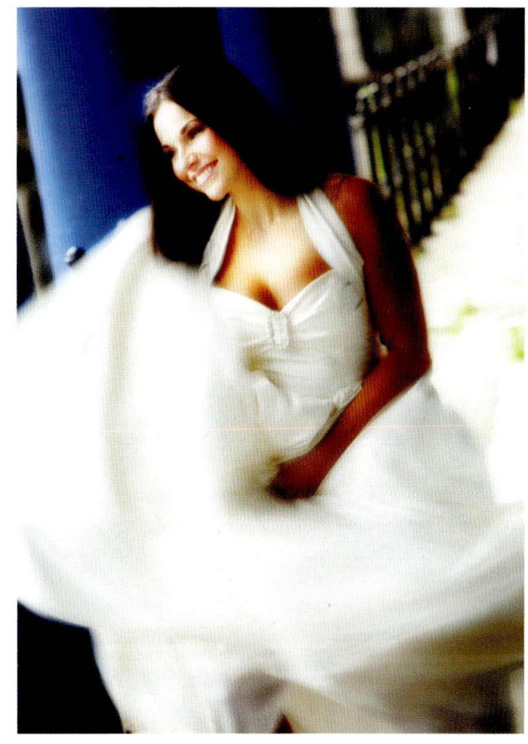

Dramatic

To add drama to any bride portrait, just position her weight away from the basic posture. This will make her naturally unstable and force her to create a new pose so she can keep her balance. This could be as simple as a very wide foot stance, or an exaggerated lean. The aim is create sharper, more dramatic or rigid angles and lines.

Fashion

For a fashion-shoot look, use a very low camera position, and pose the bride with a simple body line or an exaggerated angle—this makes the images look like a magazine shoot. A pre-wedding shooting session with the couple is essential to learn more about their characters—just because they appear to be modern and "funky" doesn't mean that they want to look different on their wedding day.

Fun

Adding movement and new expressions will instantly change the characters of your subjects, almost creating exaggerated caricatures of them. A wedding day is, after all, a posh fancy dress party, so it does not take much to get someone away from their normal selves. Running, jumping, and even falling over are all ways to inject some energy and new expressions into a shoot—just be careful not to break the bride or the dress!

 A dramatically posed and framed image with a distinctly theatrical air reveals a through understanding of composition—vital for the aspiring wedding photographer to ensure highly individual images that your clients will be thrilled with.

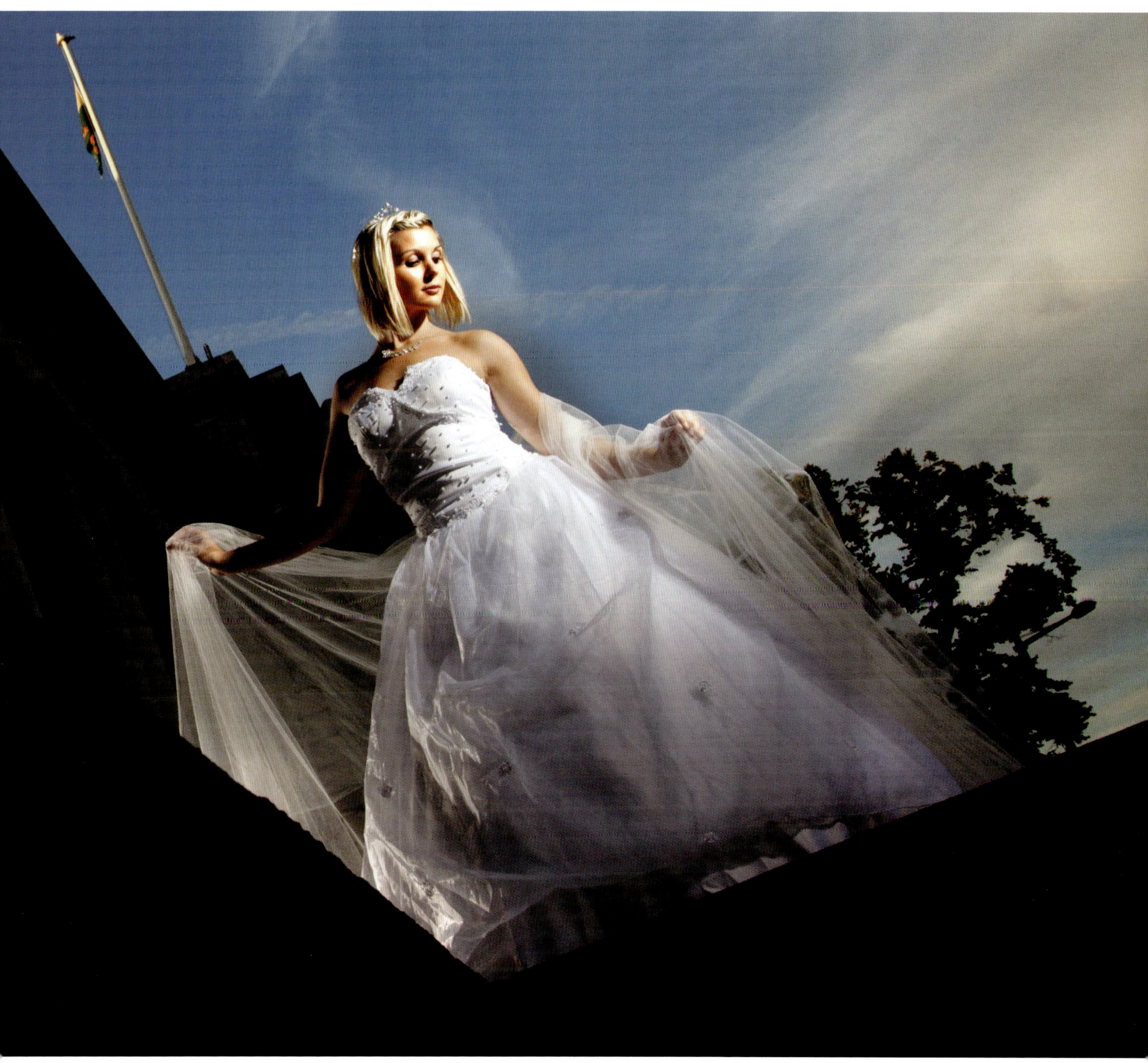

Groom Portraits

When shooting the groom, try to create a more exaggerated, masculine image by asking the subject to stand more square-on, facing the camera. Also, the expressions tend to be more serious and less over-the-top happy, as we try to create a "cooler" character.

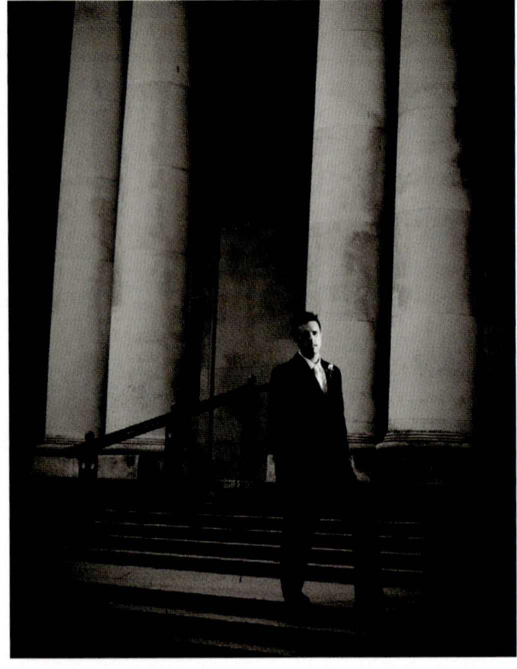

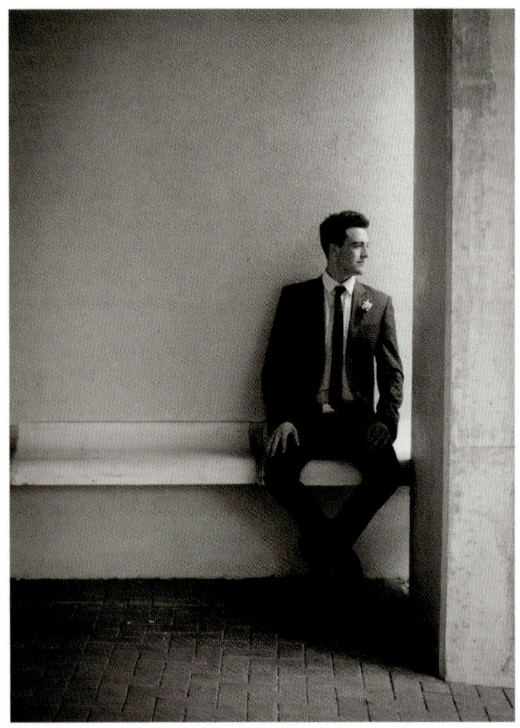

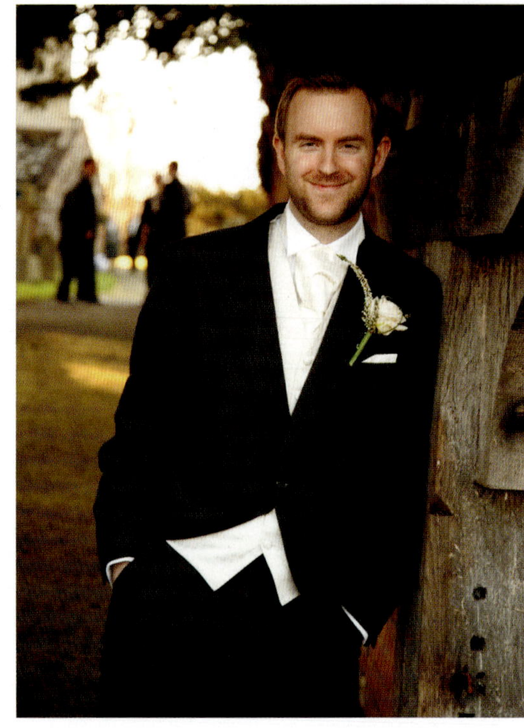

Standing

The male standing pose should look more powerful, so ask the groom to stand with both feet facing the camera, and with square shoulders to add "bulk" to his body figure. A wide-open stance creates a strong-looking pose. However, if the subject needs to be slimmed down a little, ask him to turn his feet and shoulders slightly away from the camera. The head position is usually square-on, again to give an impression of strength. However, make sure that the expression complements the pose, and the subject does not end up simply looking miserable!

Sitting

When shooting the groom in a seated position, you should aim for either a relaxed or an interested-looking pose. In the relaxed pose, the groom should lean back in the chair—the more he sits on the edge of the chair, and the further he leans back, the more relaxed or even arrogant he will look. The hands can be posed together in the lap, rest in the trouser pockets, or be placed on the top of the chair arms. Position him so his feet are wide apart or his legs crossed. Put all these together for an instant flow of animations from a simple starting point.

For an interested-looking pose, position your subject leaning forwards, with either the elbows or the forearms leaning on the thighs. If his feet are wide apart, he will look strong and dominant. The hands are usually clasped together with fingers intertwined to complete the simple and strong posture

Leaning

Probably the most natural pose for a man is a leaning pose, whether he is leaning on a bar or a gate. This natural stance implies a reassuring confidence. The most comfortable and natural-looking leaning position is to use the shoulder to lean against the surface or object, with the body directly facing the camera. The only way to get this pose wrong is if the subject's feet are too close to the surface or object he's leaning against.

Tip

Make sure you take these shots quickly as many men are very self-conscious, and often rebel at the thought of being photographed.

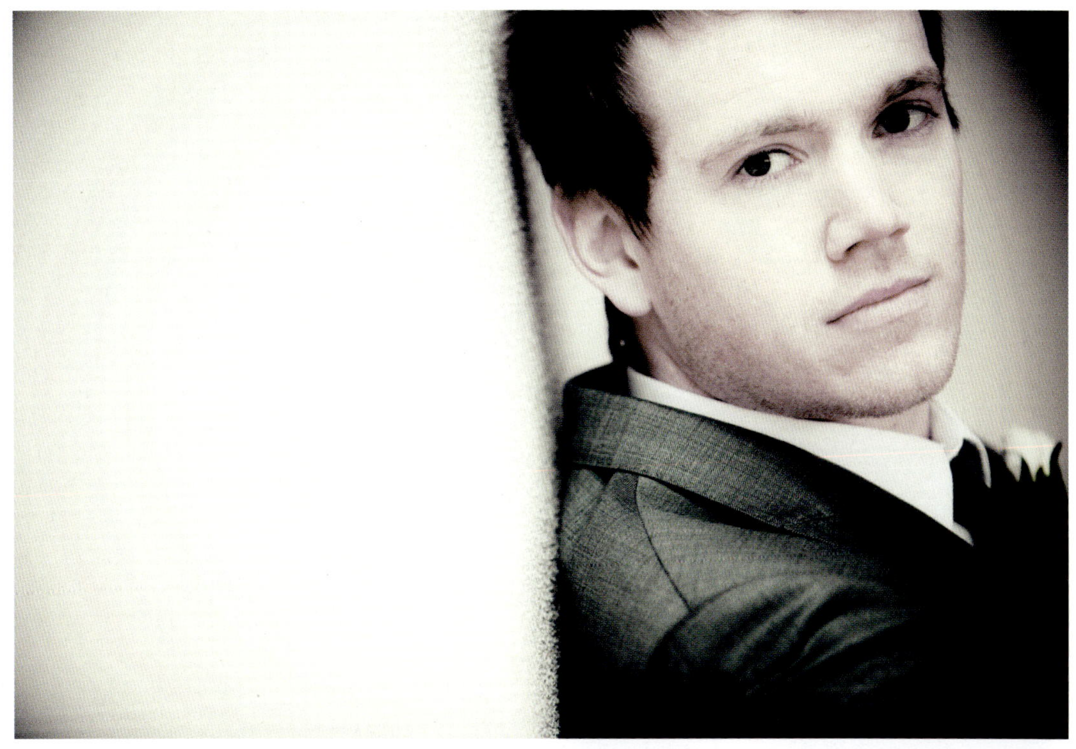

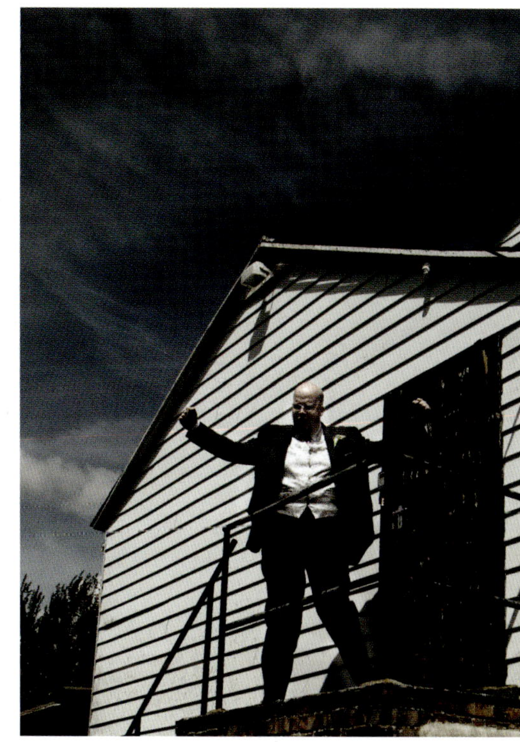

Fashion

Probably the quickest way to look for ideas to suit your groom is to look through magazine fashion portraiture or to search the internet. By using a few keywords you can find classic images—for instance, for an English gent look, you can use a hand to straighten a cuff or the tie. Don't forget to take care with the poses, though, as they can look tacky very easily.

I prefer to keep things simple, and often opt for placing the subject's hands in his trouser pockets, with either the thumbs or fingers on the outside to create some tension in the arms and shoulders. If you have a funky or fashionable groom, add a fashion look to your images by copying some of the poses you come across in men's style magazines—these can range from simple and classy to a bit more dramatic. Another quick way to make the groom look a little more like a fashion model is to use sunglasses.

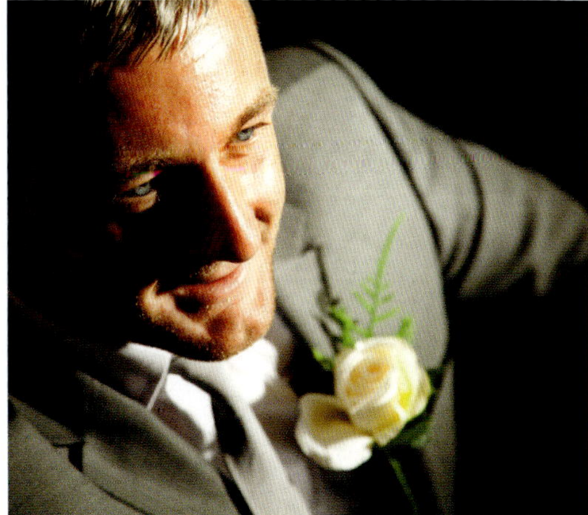

Dramatic

A very low or very high camera angle is a perfect way to add drama to an image, but the secret is in the angles of the limbs. It is best to animate the arms and legs in straight positions, or with dramatic bends, for an edgy look. You can also exaggerate the head position by asking the subject to look up very high or down very low—just be wary of creating double chins.

Fun

Running, jumping, leaning, and squatting can all help to create a fun series of images, but the "fun" element is more often found in the expressions of your subject. I often do a series of quirky close-ups to focus on the expression, and the series looks great in an album.

Don't be afraid to try unusual angles and viewpoints—even using a wide-angle lens can instantly make a difference. You can also use accent lighting with a reflector or a flash to change the style of a simple portrait.

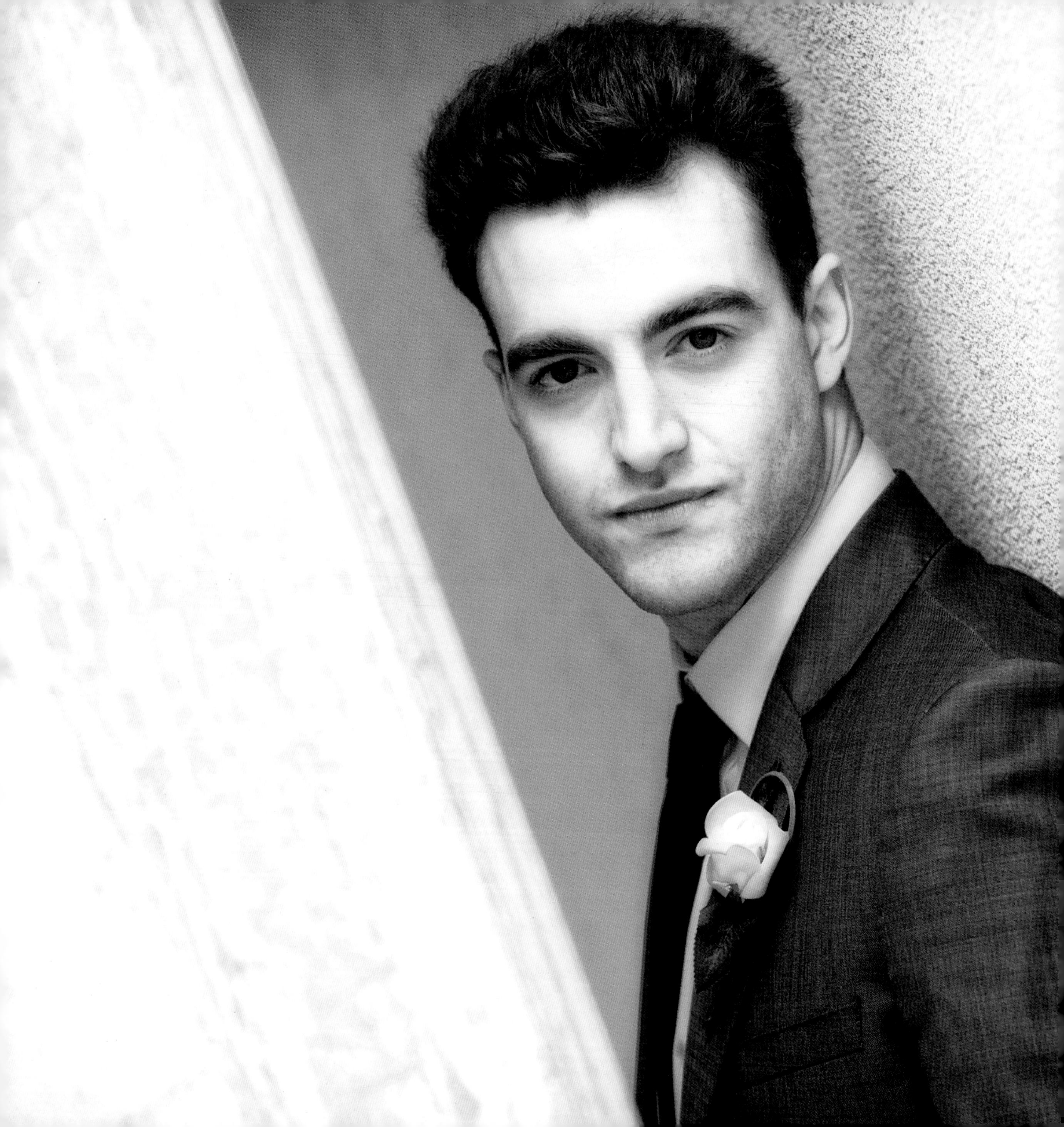

Left: Use fashion magazines as your inspiration to create some more contemporary shots of the groom.

Couple Portraits

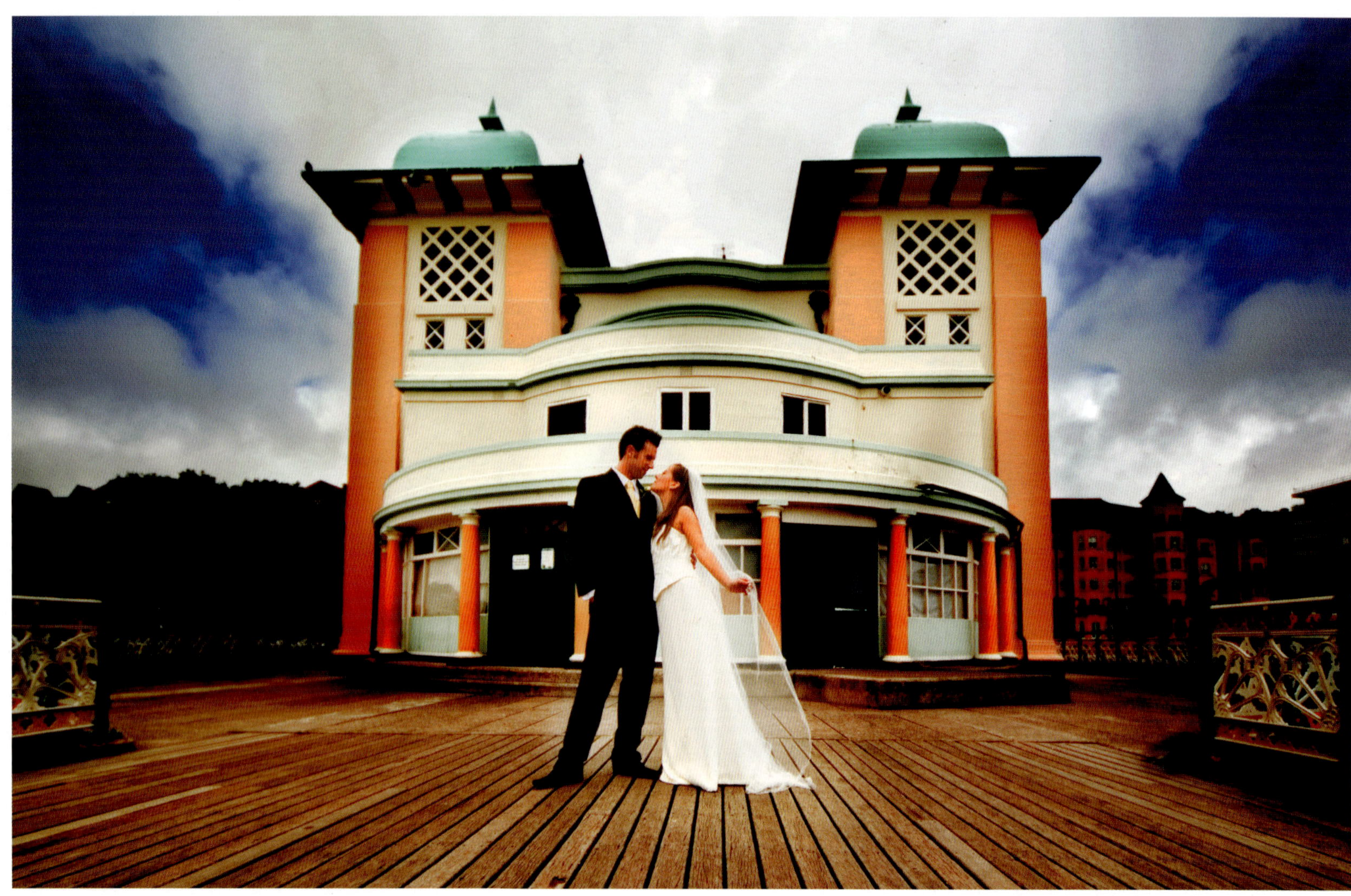

Once you have grasped the basics of animating a couple, you will want to develop this further.

Sitting

Sitting poses can be a little difficult to begin with, but once you have got the individual posing right, you can find ways to mix them so the couple fit together. The same principles apply as before—the aim is to make the bride look slimmer and the groom more masculine. Try starting with the groom and then position the bride next to him. This will allow the groom to take most of the weight of the joint pose, and the bride can relax without the fear of falling over or off the seat.

Leaning

A good leaning posture can be quickly adopted by simply exaggerating the basic couple pose. The key thing to remember here is to keep the gaps between the subjects' bodies to a minimum so they still look like a loving couple. As with the seated pose, make sure the groom takes most of the weight of the couple, and then focus on the bride's arm and hand positions to add some elegance.

Dramatic

Using low or high camera angles will add drama and, when combined with stiffer or more static poses, you can change the look of the portraits dramatically without a lot of work. I always find that the surroundings help me take the images to the next level of drama, so choosing a location that is more than a pretty backdrop is crucial to the success of this look.

Fashion

Probably the most difficult thing to shoot is a fashion-style portrait, especially if one or both subjects are not naturally at ease with being photographed. This is not uncommon, but don't necessarily dismiss a fashion-style series if one of them is a little more awkward—you can play on the strengths of the one, using the other as a secondary subject, which can work well.

Fun

A guaranteed series of shots at most weddings will be the fun pictures, and whether they are quirky or more fashion-like, they allow the characters of your couple to come through. Running shots work well, whether it is through an arch of confetti, running over a bridge, or the groom dragging his bride, as they are natural actions for anyone. And don't forget the close-up shots that concentrate on the couple's facial expressions, as these can be fun too, especially when you are working in confined spaces.

You don't just have to look for weird and wacky poses. You can also change a basic pose with a different perspective—for instance, by shooting into a reflective surface such as a mirror, glass, or even the polished chrome of an old car.

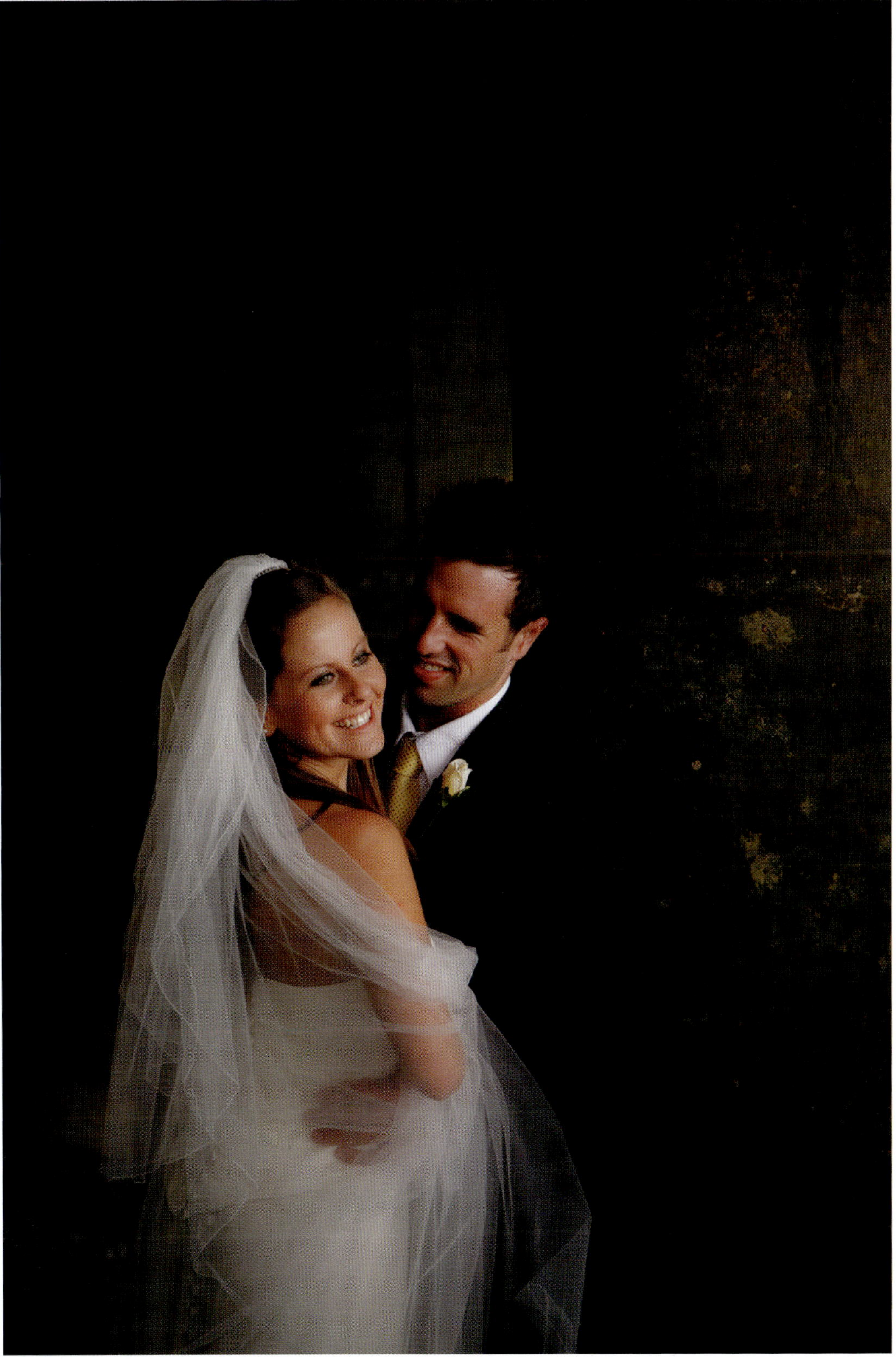

Group Portraits

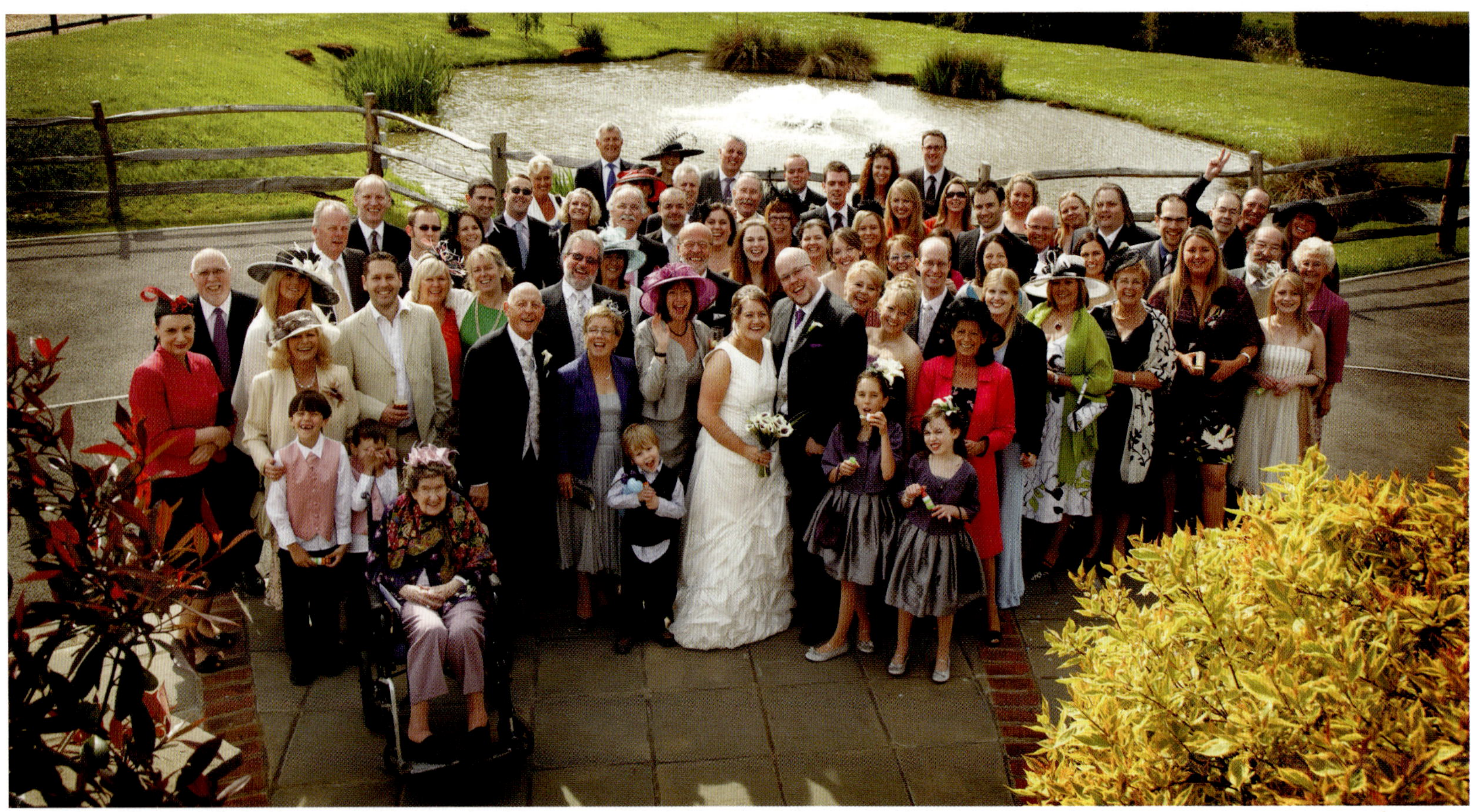

When shooting small or large groups it is important to take time to construct them carefully, otherwise the shots can look messy with little or no uniformity, and even hide people. Consider the background first, especially with large groups, as you will see a lot of foreground and background in the image.

The lighting also has to be taken into account so that the whole group is lit in the same way—if half of a group is in harsh sunlight and the other half is in shadow, you will have a terrible image that you cannot correct, even in postproduction. It is a good idea to shoot with the sun on the backs of the subjects so that everyone will have a basic overall illumination. If you have to use harsh sunlight on the subjects then you will need to work as close to them as possible to ensure the flash is better able to open up the shadow areas.

Apply the same basics of animation to the bride and groom or the central subjects. The couple should be turned in towards each other slightly, with the groom just behind the bride. Again, position them from the feet upwards, to allow for full-length images as well as close-ups if needed.

Once you have established the central subjects, you can now add and subtract people quickly and easily. This add-and-subtract method should allow you to shoot around 20 group portraits in 20 minutes—as long as you have planned the order in advance using a predetermined list.

Above: When shooting large groups consider the background and lighting first.

Two plus two

For adding the parents to the couple, use the boy-girl method so the mother stands next to the groom and the father is added on the other side. This works in the same way for close family, grandparents, and godparents. The secret to posing all of these groups is to ensure you can only see a part of the farthest shoulder, as it gets hidden slightly behind the person they are standing next to. Turning each member of the group slightly inwards compresses the group, and hides about 20% of their body mass.

Two plus four

For shooting both sets of parents, you should swap the fathers around—this is traditionally how the families would leave the church, with the groom's father escorting the bride's mother and the bride's father escorting the groom's mother. The mothers are positioned next to their respective child with the alternative father on the outside. This also happens to help with any awkward situations if any of the parents are divorced.

Remember that everyone's feet should be turned slightly inwards and their shoulders farthest from the camera should be mostly hidden. There are sometimes more than two sets of parents, and in these cases, I position the bride's parents and partners on her side and the groom's on his side.

Two plus bridal party

You can then add the bridesmaids and best man to the parent group. Position the best man on the groom's side of the line-up, and the chief bridesmaid on the bride's side. If possible, arrange the guests in order of height, from the tallest in the middle to the shortest at the sides. Very often you can place the bridesmaids and pageboys in front of the group, but never place them in front of the bride and groom. Add the groomsmen onto each side, trying to keep the group symmetrical with the same number either side. The groomsmen can be staggered behind very young bridesmaids if they are also on the end.

You can then develop this further in several steps. Firstly, remove the parents and close the gap by shuffling people in from the sides. Once you have captured this, you can then ask the groomsmen to step out quickly for a shot of the smaller bridal party, and then ask the bridesmaids to step out, adding the groomsmen back to the group for another quick shot.

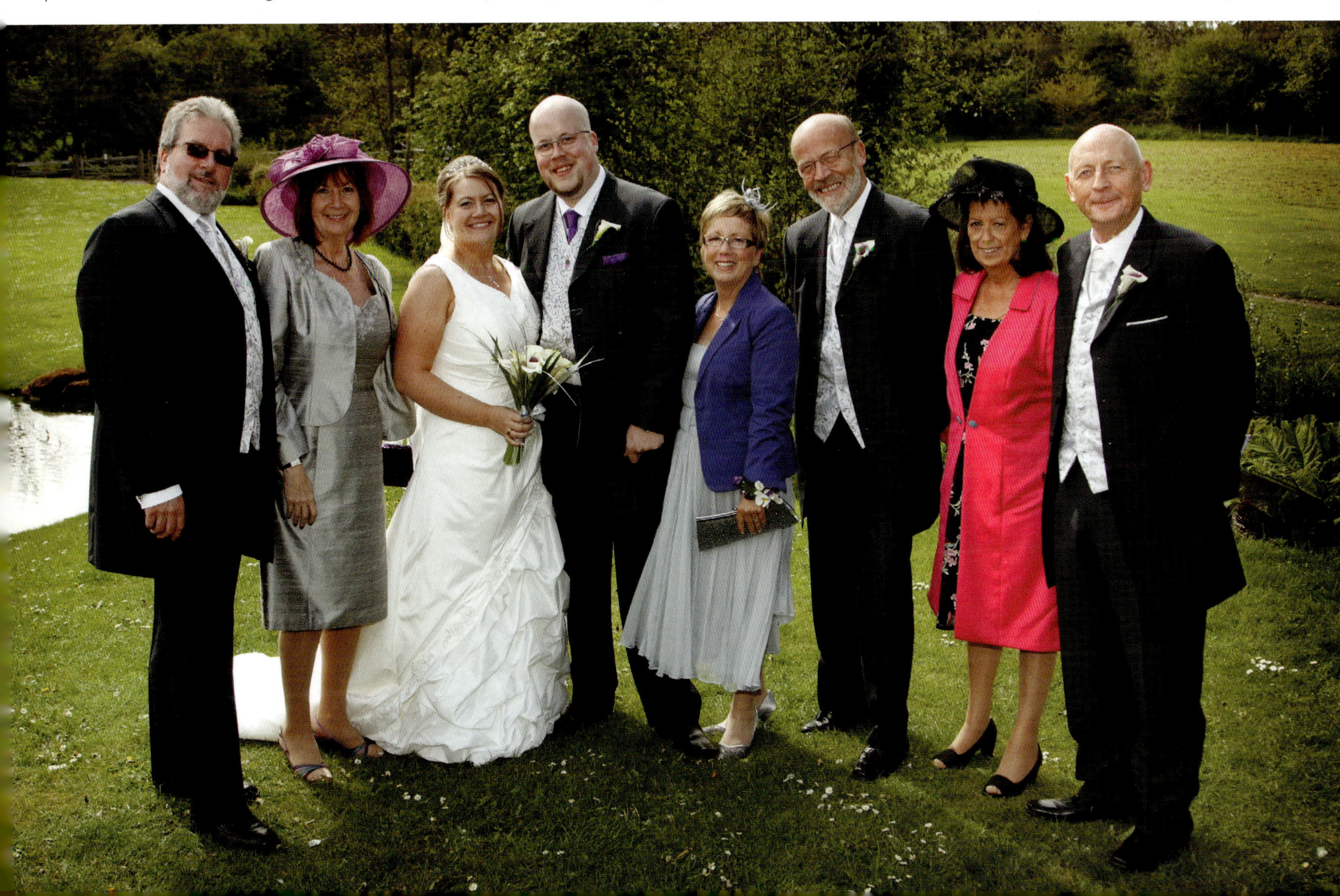

Below: Ensure everyone's feet are turning inwards and that their shoulders farthest from the camera are mostly hidden.

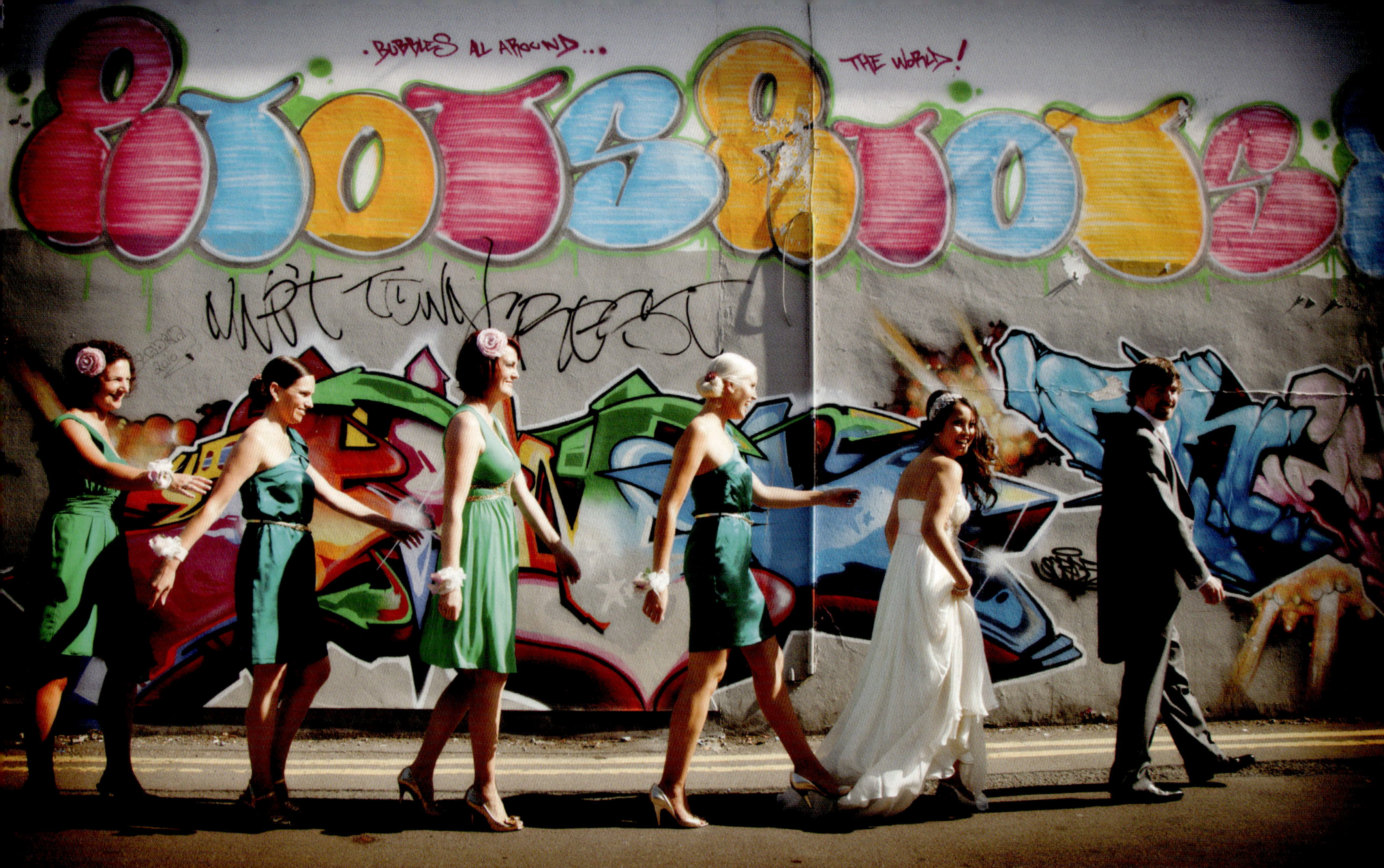

Two plus immediate family

Once the bridal party formal portraits have been completed, you can begin with one side of the family, which is usually the bride's, unless there are elderly or infirm guests who need to leave as soon as possible. With the basic "two plus parents" photograph setup and shot, you can add brothers and sisters evenly to each side, and then the grandparents to complete the immediate family.

Two plus large family

To complete the pictures for one side of the family, all you need to do after adding the grandparents is to include the aunts, uncles, cousins, and any other special people on your list of requests. If the group is large, add the ladies to each side of the group, all posed for the basic setup, and then position the men in front of them, asking them to kneel just before you take the picture.

If the family group is larger than that, then you can split them in half by first shooting the bride's mother's family, and then setting up and shooting the bride's father's family. Repeat these groups for the groom's family.

Two plus very large groups

For exceptionally large groups or the whole wedding party, I always try to find a high viewpoint from which I can shoot down on everyone. Starting once more with the bride and groom in the front and center, I gather the bridal party around them and then just allow everyone else to get as close as possible, making sure young children are towards the front of the group. After a few quick shots of the group looking up at me, I ask the ladies to kiss anyone they want, and this usually injects some new life into the group and produces a different series of pictures.

Seated groups

Using seating to pose groups is not uncommon at winter weddings, when you have to resort to shooting inside. Use a combination of seats or sofas in a slight, soft "U" shape, posing the groups in a similar way to above, but with ladies seated and men standing behind or sitting on the floor. Remember to pose the seated subjects as before, by turning them in slightly to close them up and lose body mass.

Fun groups

For the shots with friends, I tend to ease my control of the poses to allow things to be more relaxed and less organized, especially when trying to bring a fun element to the shot. After the main image is taken, get everyone to bunch up even closer, leaning on the person next to them to help get a tighter crop and focus on their expressions.

Bridesmaids

For the shots of the bridesmaids, you should aim to shoot a variety throughout the day, including full-length standing, three-quarter and seated pictures. In addition, of course, you should shoot a series of candid images, as well as shots of the bridesmaids running, walking, and chatting to each other, which are more animated and fun than the formal portraits.

Groomsmen

For the groomsmen portraits, I often resort to well-known movies for a particular fun look, including classics such as *The Godfather* for gangster cool, *The Blues Brothers* for quirky cool, or *Reservoir Dogs* for just cool. This helps to liven up the group, which may be feeling awkward about being photographed. Use a wide-angle lens and a touch of zoomed flash to capture these memorable, fun images.

Below: A touch of gangster cool eases any awkwardness in this shot of the groomsmen.

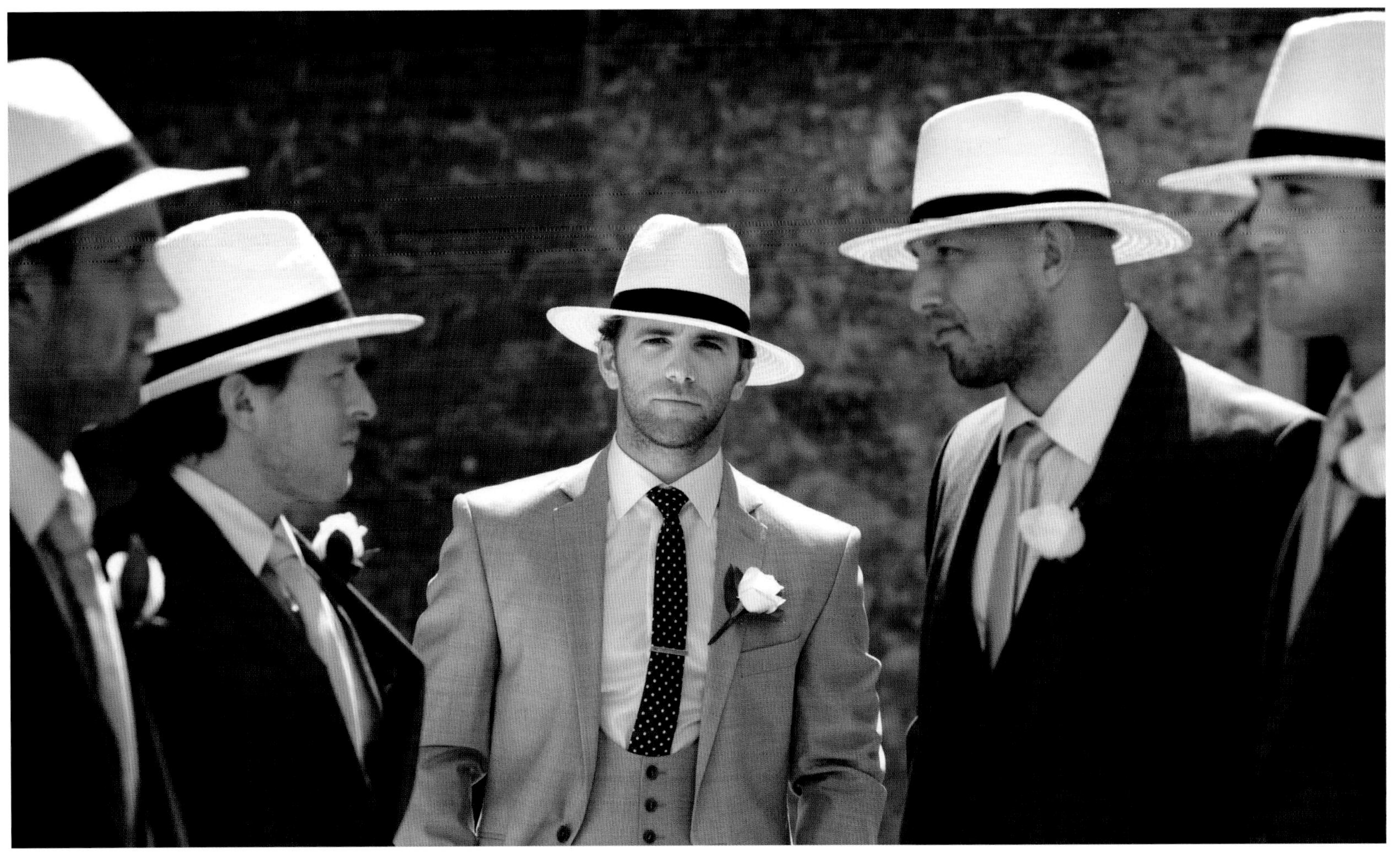

Chapter 4
Planning

When shooting a wedding, the two most important things for you to concentrate on are time management and planning. Without either of these you will not be prepared for the day, and will end up missing some important and unrepeatable shots. Here we'll explore both aspects, to understand these important stages and how to go about them.

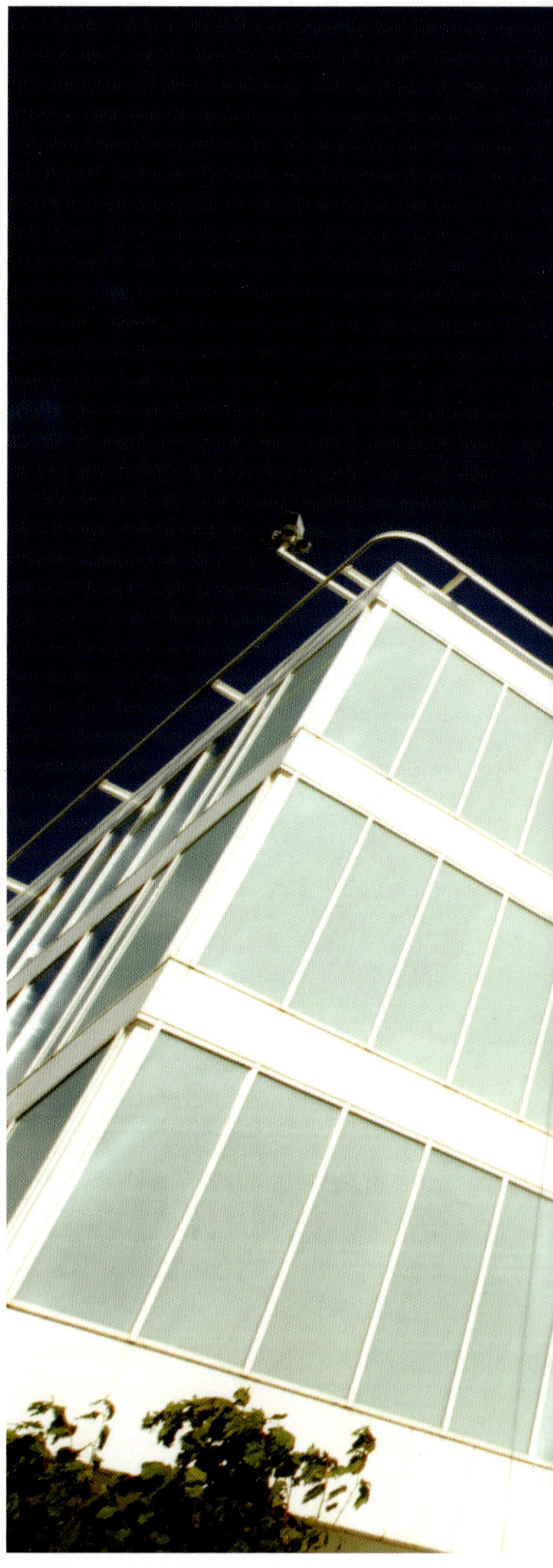

Right: The photographer has no control over the location and styling of the wedding, but he or she is responsible for reflecting the atmosphere of the occasion in a distinctive manner. Plan carefully by visiting the venue in advance of the day and be bold with your images.

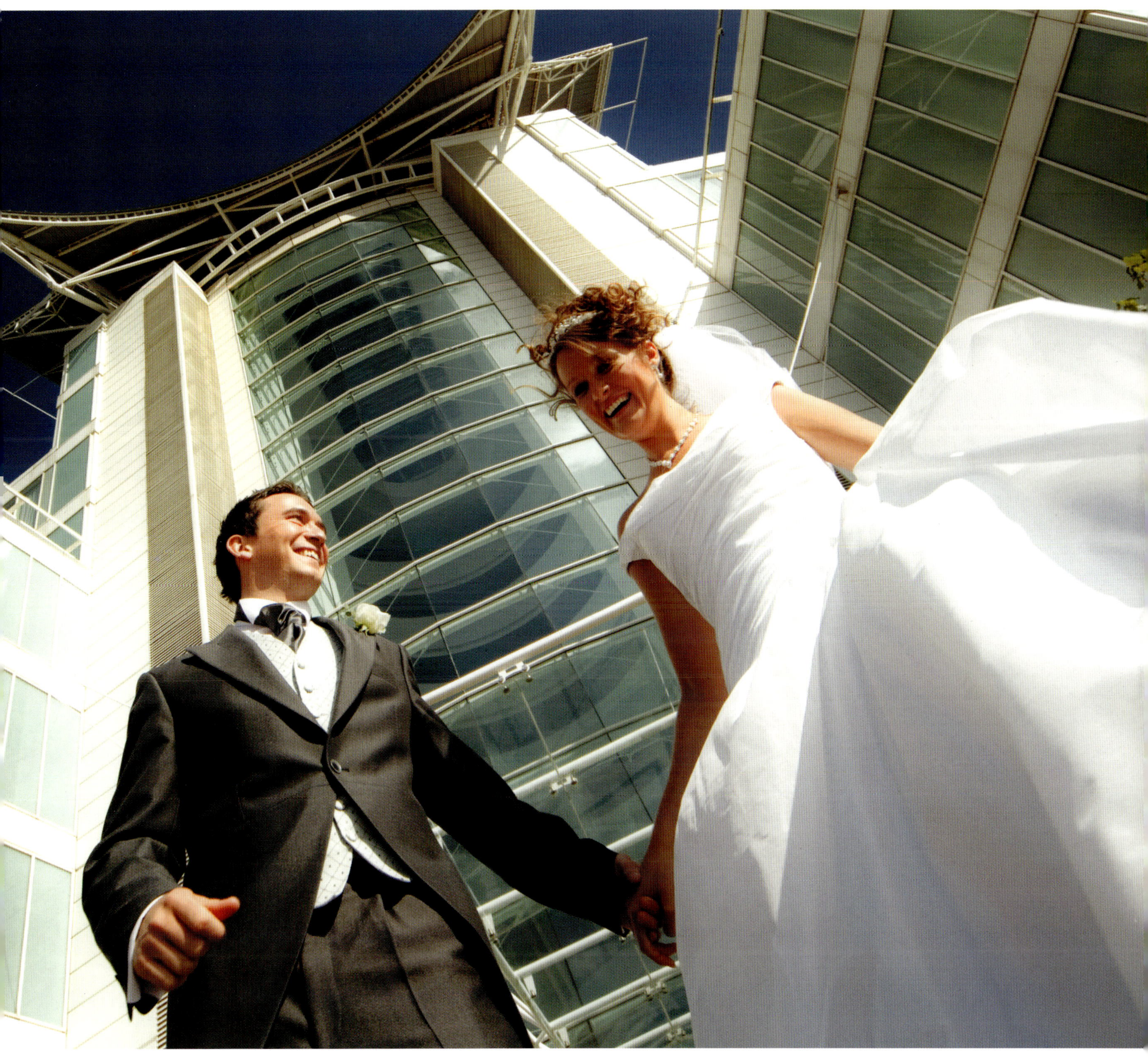

Meeting the Couple

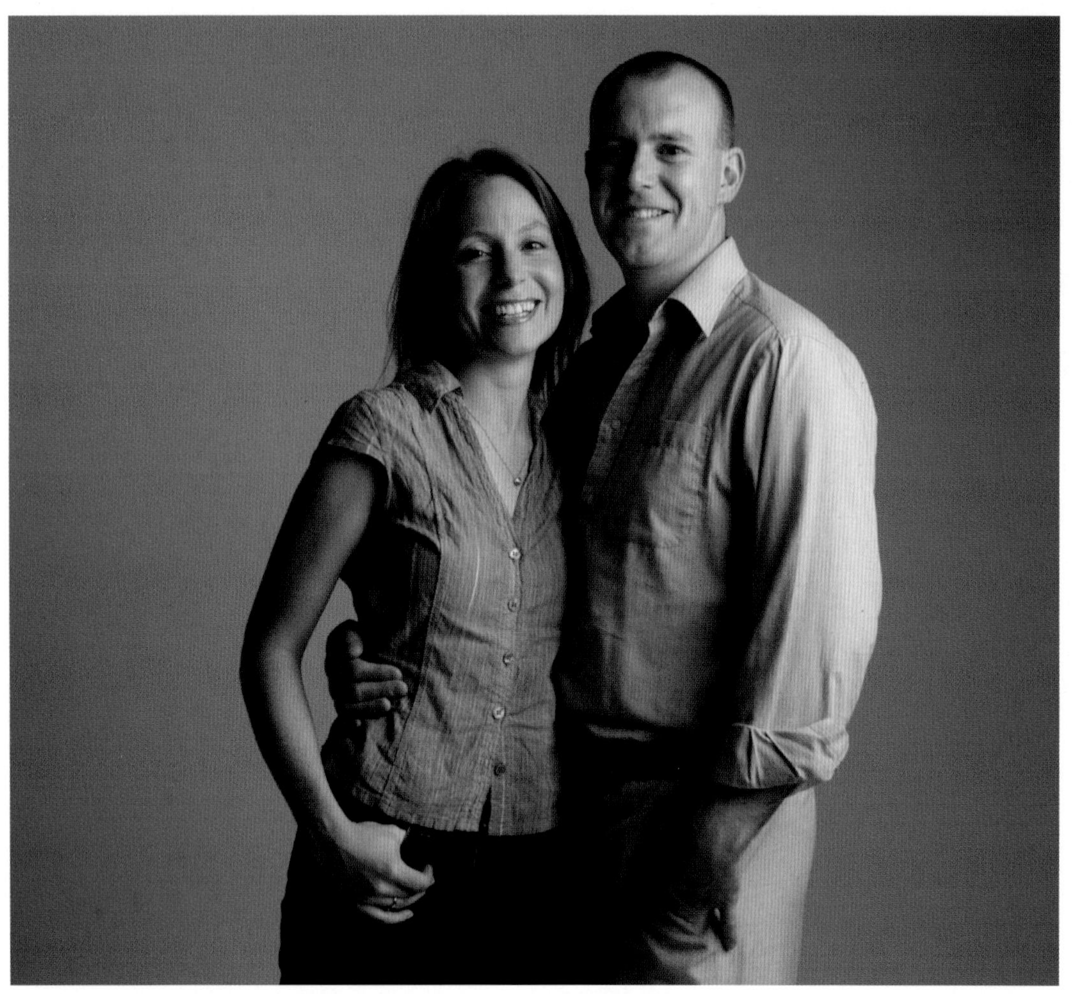

Meeting up with the bride and groom about six to eight weeks before the wedding will really help you with your to-do list of things to shoot, and will also help the couple with their final planning for the day, as the photographer is usually the only one person who is around for the whole wedding event. If you are intending to make the most out of every wedding you shoot—both financially and creatively—you will need to choreograph every step of the day. The couple will become very busy in the final weeks of preparation, so the closer you schedule the planning meeting to the event date the more difficult it will be to get together with them. I usually arrange these meetings in the evening, as this tends to suit couples better, and the meeting will benefit us all.

Start the meeting by running through the booking form (see above right) and checking that nothing has changed. Clarify the date, the time, the venues, and, of course, the people to be photographed. This might sound like common sense, but several times every year something drastic has changed and the couple have forgotten to inform me, so never take anything for granted. On the reverse of the booking form is the wedding contract, which the couple must

sign and date. Once the contract has been checked and confirmed, ask the couple to make the final decision on which package they want. This has to be done at this stage, as it will affect how long you spend at the reception and whether you need to visit the bride's morning location or not. You will usually have to run through most of your packages again, as it is probably 12 months or more since the couple enquired.

Then write down on a blank sheet of paper the basic shot requests in order. I know several photographers who have a shot list printed out and

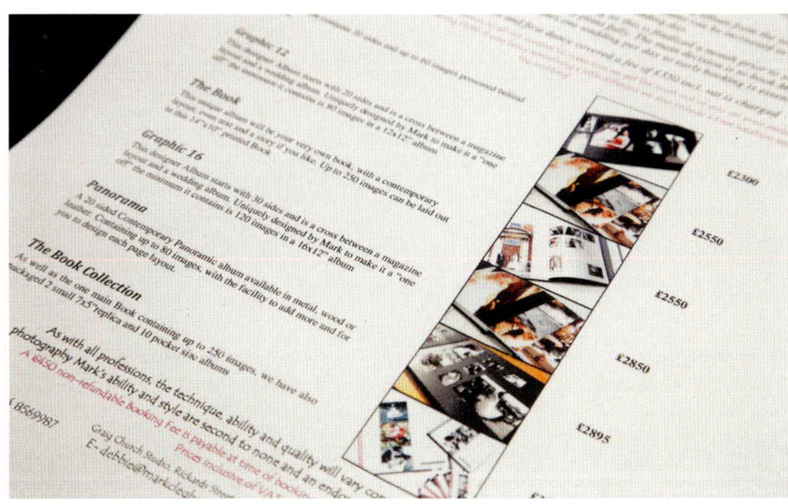

£2300

£2550

£2550

£2850

£2895

Above: In my business, we have price lists available for two years ahead, as many couples start searching for their photographer 12–24 months before their wedding date.

Far left: Meeting the couple again prior to the wedding is a vital stage in finalizing details—and you could also fire off some informal photos!

Right: Thank-you cards are a nice touch for the couple to send out to their guests, and are also a good promotional device for the photographer.

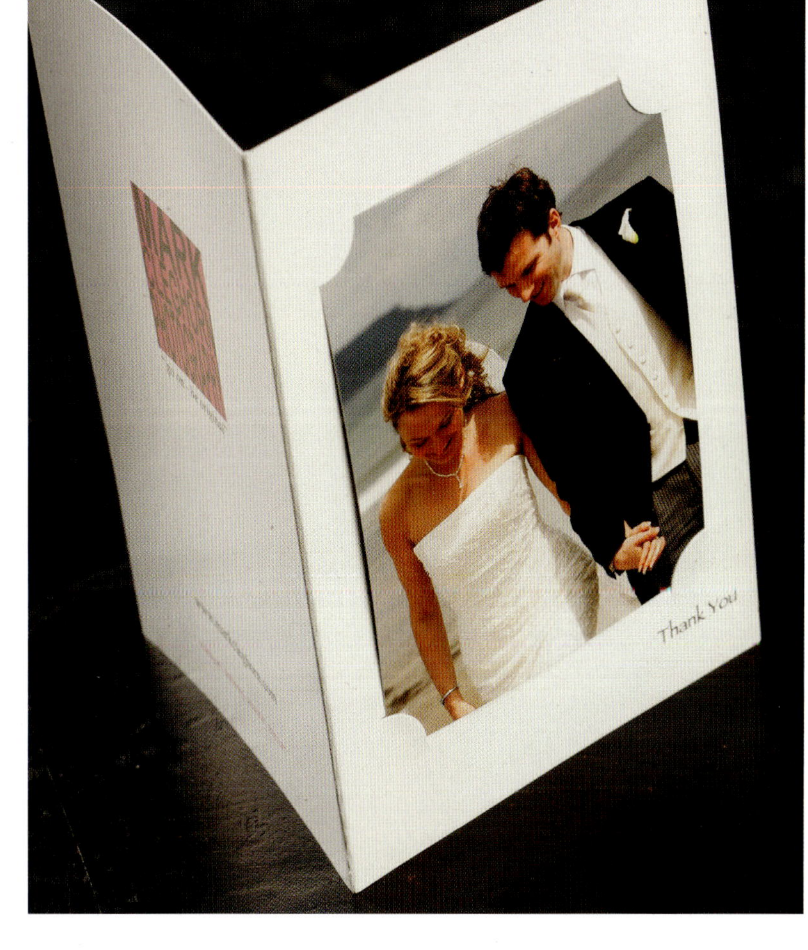

the couple tick the ones they want, but to me this seems a little impersonal and does not provide the "à la carte" experience I want my clients to enjoy. The list will start with the first location, so if you're shooting images of the bride getting ready, you need to know the address of the location, as well as a contact number at the house, in case cell phones are switched off. You'll need to arrive at the house approximately two hours before the start of the ceremony to complete shooting all the elements, so confirm with the bride when you need her to be ready—she will need to tell any hair or makeup people this "ready time," which differs from the leaving time.

The rest is pretty simple. The "who, when, and where" is a good way to remember the questions you need to resolve when planning your shoot list. You should also discuss the ceremony venue and times for the groom, as well as the group list—one of the most important things to get right—and when and where you recommend shooting all of these.

I always prefer to shoot groups at a church location as everyone is still together, and they have not yet scattered into different rooms or bars, so it is easy to shoot many different groups in a limited time. Also, remember that the reception venue grounds and rooms may be unsuitable for the groups, especially in winter or at wet weddings, because of inadequate space or poor backdrops inside or out.

Finally, ask the couple if they want you for the speeches and the first dance. Depending on the package they have chosen, this extra time will either be included or charged by the hour. However, if you are starting out as a wedding photographer, it is a good idea to shoot as large a variety as you can early on to grow your portfolio and experience.

Contracts

Contracts, agreements and insurance are all essential things to consider when you start charging for your services—they give the couple and you security.

Agreeing on what you are going to provide and in what format is only the start of an agreement. Remember that all the time you spend before and after the wedding, including any meetings, also have to be considered. It is always best to list everything, so all parties can see and agree which events are going to be shot and shown in the final album.

Personally, I do not list all the wedding images in any form in any of my packages, and I make this clear in the contract. In addition, I insist that the copyright to all the images remains my property, along with the rights to reproduce and copy them.

From the couple's point of view, they need a document that shows you are agreeing to shoot their wedding on a specific date and time, and that shows they are agreeing to pay you the specific fee. This is important for the photographer too, as the couple are also promising you that they will get married on that date and time, as well as agreeing to pay you the fee for your services and agreed products. This means that, if things go wrong and the wedding does not happen for any reason, you have a legal document to help you recoup whatever costs you may have incurred.

I recommend that all wedding photographers use a company that specializes in insurance for photographers. For instance, I use a company that offers a basic wedding contract, specifically written to protect the photographer as well as the rights of the couple themselves. At the very least, get your contract produced by qualified legal consultants to ensure that your rights, and your business, are protected.

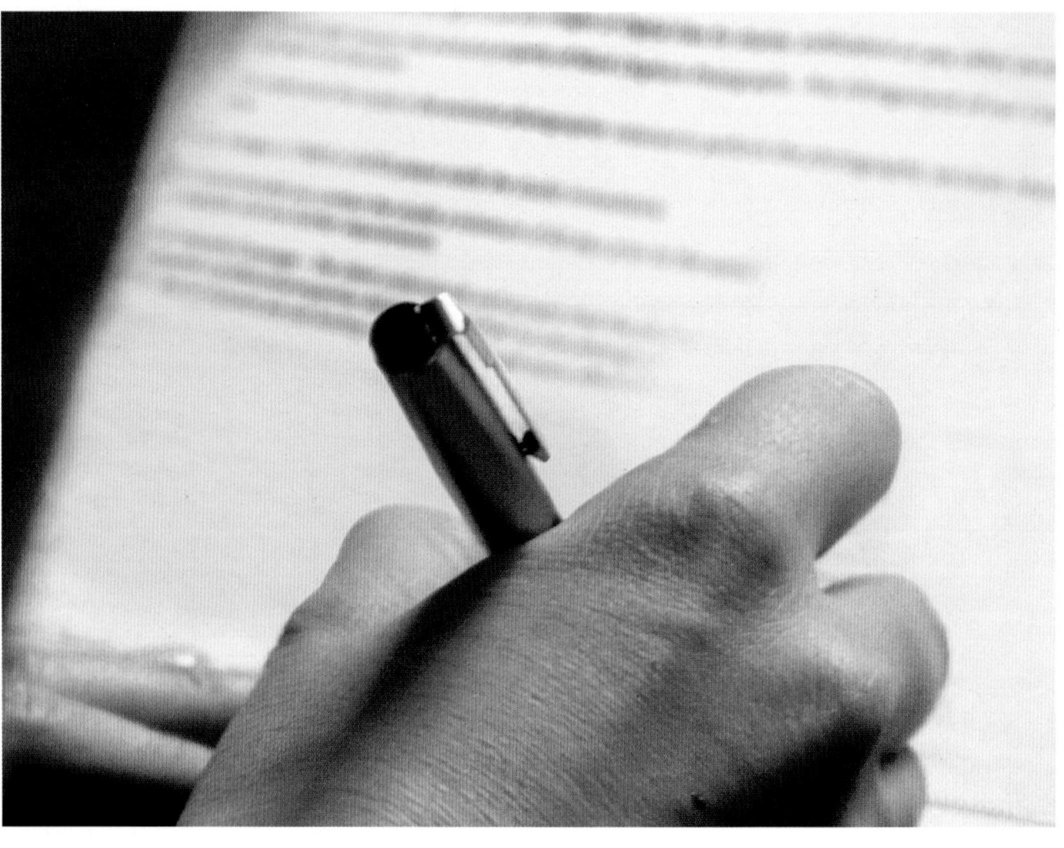

Above: Make sure you have even the most basic of contracts, including your price list, charges, and cancelation policy.

What if things go wrong?

When something has gone wrong in any way, the first things to address are how bad it is and what the outcome could be. If you're in any doubt, call your insurers first; there is big money in claiming against small companies today and, of course, it is important to protect yourself and your company. In over 30 years, I have only had to involve my insurers twice—on both occasions it was down to equipment failure—and they handled the situations on my behalf, taking over all correspondence until completion and relieving me of any worry or stress, and also looking after my clients with dignity and professionalism.

Tip

If you are charging for your services in any way, get liability and indemnity insurance to cover yourself, just in case the couple do not like the photographs, or in the event, however unlikely, of something going wrong.

Pricing

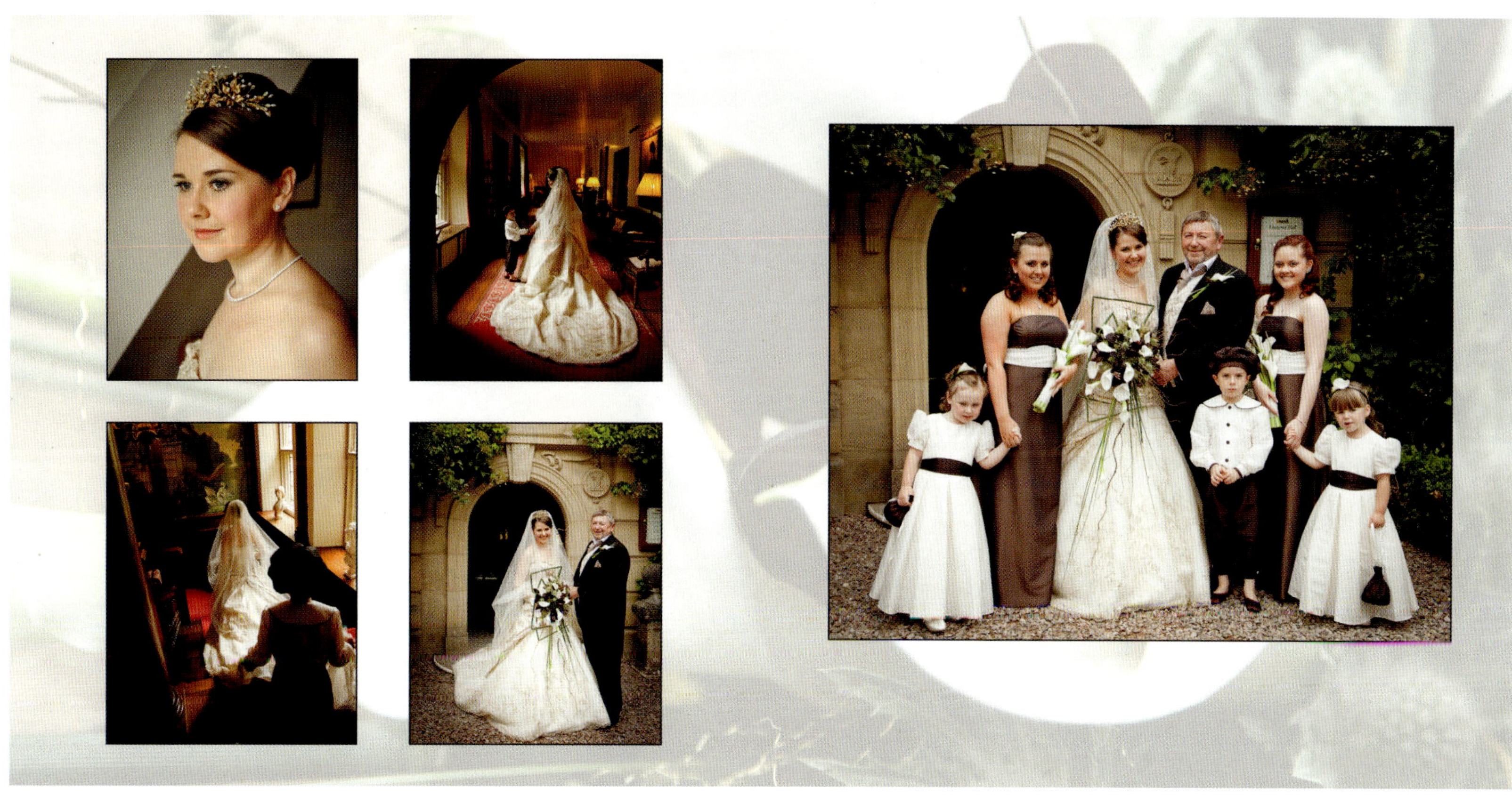

Now we look at the trickiest question of all: how much do I charge? The easiest way to decide how much to charge is to work out how much you are worth, which means starting with calculating how much one day of your time is worth. If you are shooting weddings as an additional income, it's quite easy to work this out, because you know how much you get paid each day in your main job.

Day rate

The amount a photographer charges will, of course, differ depending on their circumstances and experiences, as well as their levels of confidence, location and the brand they have built. If I were just starting out I would get at least two or three weddings under my belt to build the relevant basic wedding knowledge, my confidence, and a portfolio to show potential new clients. Even if you are working for costs alone, this experience is valuable to you, as well as a balanced risk for the bride and groom to take because they do not have to pay you.

Once you have your basic skills you will probably still want to choose a day rate, to cover the time from shooting at the bride's home to the first dance. This price will be based on what you think you are worth and what someone is willing to pay you—I would base this on a rate of three to four times your main job salary.

When you become a full-time wedding photographer, you will need to base your charges on the amount you want to earn each year divided by how many weddings you are going to be able to shoot. So if you want to earn $50,000 per annum, then you will need to turn over between $120-150,000 to cover running costs, tax, and so on. So, basically you would need to cover 50 weddings at $2,500 each to make the business work.

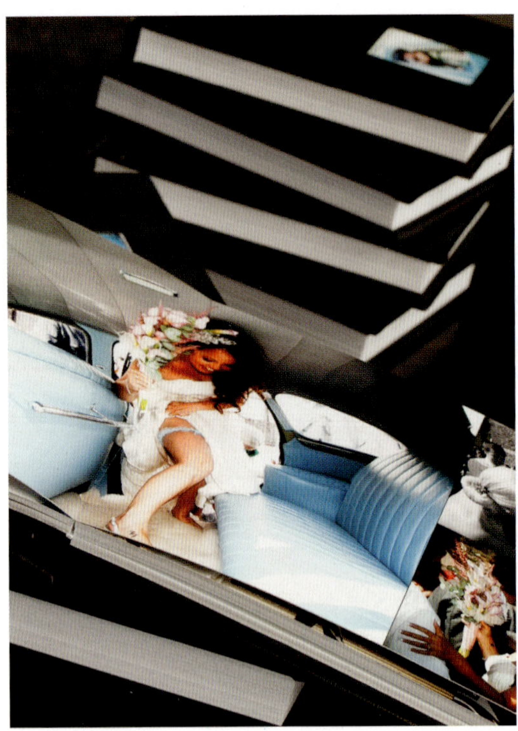

Above: Because of the size and weight, a coffee-table book allows a bride and groom to have hundreds of images in their album, if they so wish. Even though the product costs us the least, it is our most popular type of album. It is also possible to buy duplicate coffee-table albums in different sizes, allowing us to offer additional books for parents, bridesmaids, friends, and so on, as part of a whole wedding package.

Albums

Albums come in many shapes and sizes as well as costs, so make sure that you do not offer an album that is outside your profit range or your client's price bracket. For budget weddings, including an album of any shape or size will eat away at any profit for you, so you might have to opt for a press-printed book, which looks and feels like a coffee-table book. These albums are contemporary in design and naturally match the style of a more modern wedding. In fact, when these albums first became available in early 2000, they were the most expensive to buy and the most expensive to sell because of individual production costs.

Traditional albums tend to be based on prints that have a front mount and are then stuck on to a page. These can still be purchased at realistic prices, but they are becoming less sought after by couples because of the old-fashioned styling.

A digital album is a presentation in which the print is laid flat across the page or double-page spread. The layout can be designed using software such as Adobe Photoshop. However, specialist companies offer free software design options that are simple to use and can create superb-looking album layouts.

When pricing albums, remember it is best to multiply the supplier's price by at least three or four times to cover design time and a profit margin.

Reprints

Extra print orders are not just in the form of loose prints, even though that's what most of my guests buy. It is a good idea to set up an online reprint sales web site using an "e-commerce" web service. For instance, I sell reprints online using my SmugMug web site, which acts as my sales environment for weddings as well as a way to show samples, and it also provides me with an offsite storage solution. Family and guests can purchase anything from prints to wall art, previewing their selection before buying it through a simple purchase system. The benefit of the SmugMug website is that it allows me to set a price for each individual product, or to add a global percentage mark-up across a range of products.

When pricing prints, remember that it is not about how much they cost you, but how much you feel they are worth to the purchaser.

Disc of images

Selling a disc of images is not like selling the negatives years ago, because today, even if you sell a disc to your client, the guests can still buy the images from you directly—you are not giving away

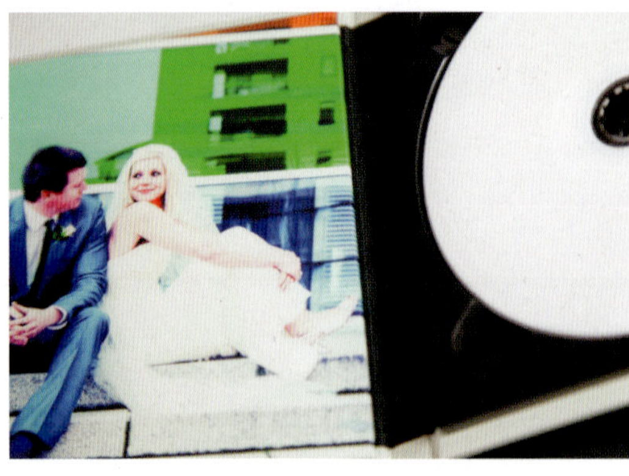

Above: To add value to a CD of images, as well as to protect the disc, use a special, custom-wrap cover.

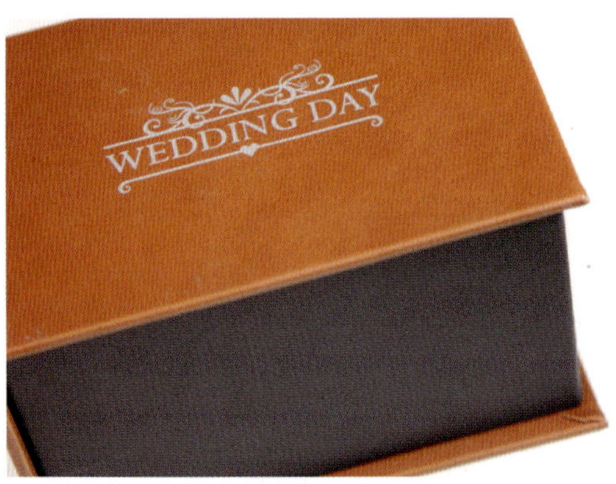

Above: If clients want just loose prints instead of an album, present them in a customized print box such as this one from Loxley Colour, which can be fully print-wrapped, and which acts as an image safe.

your reproduction rights. Most of the couples who buy a disc of the images—as a supplement to the overall package—will still want you to sell to their guests, because this takes all the hard work out of it for them, and avoids the problem of guests ordering images but never paying for them.

So how much should you charge for a disc? I charge by the image (for instance, $30 per image), but the more images I supply, the more I reduce the price per image. Once a couple has purchased a package from me, I charge about $1,200 for a basic disc, which would include 100 images.

Scouting the Venues

If you have not been to a certain location or venue before, always visit it in the weeks leading up to the event. This is so that you can get a first-hand feel for the atmosphere, style, and layout of the place. This can be difficult to do in some churches because of security, but it is still worth visiting, even if you only see the outside location and nothing else.

If you intend to shoot at a location stop somewhere between the church and the reception after the wedding ceremony, try to choose somewhere with a dramatic background or a classic feel. This might mean spending just a few minutes shooting in the streets if working in a town, underneath a bridge, or by a barn or garage door if it has a dramatic texture and design. Even walls covered in graffiti can look amazing in the background with the right kind of couple and style of wedding. If you have no other options than just another park, then you have to decide if it is worth making a stop after all.

I prefer locations that offer options such as wet weather cover, an alternative backdrop, architecture, space for composition, and even sculptures—it is amazing what you can discover when you start to look around. You can consider anything as a backdrop to the bride and groom pictures, but it is important to be sympathetic to the style of the wedding, as well as remember how much of a diversion the location will be from the ideal route to the reception.

Good lighting is obviously a priority, as this alone will provide an edge to the images before you need to use supplementary light such as flash, so bear this in mind when choosing a location. I work very fast as time is never on my side, so when I am shooting the couple I want to minimize how much time I spend on technical setup, rather concentrating on them and their expressions—the whole day is really about their relationship.

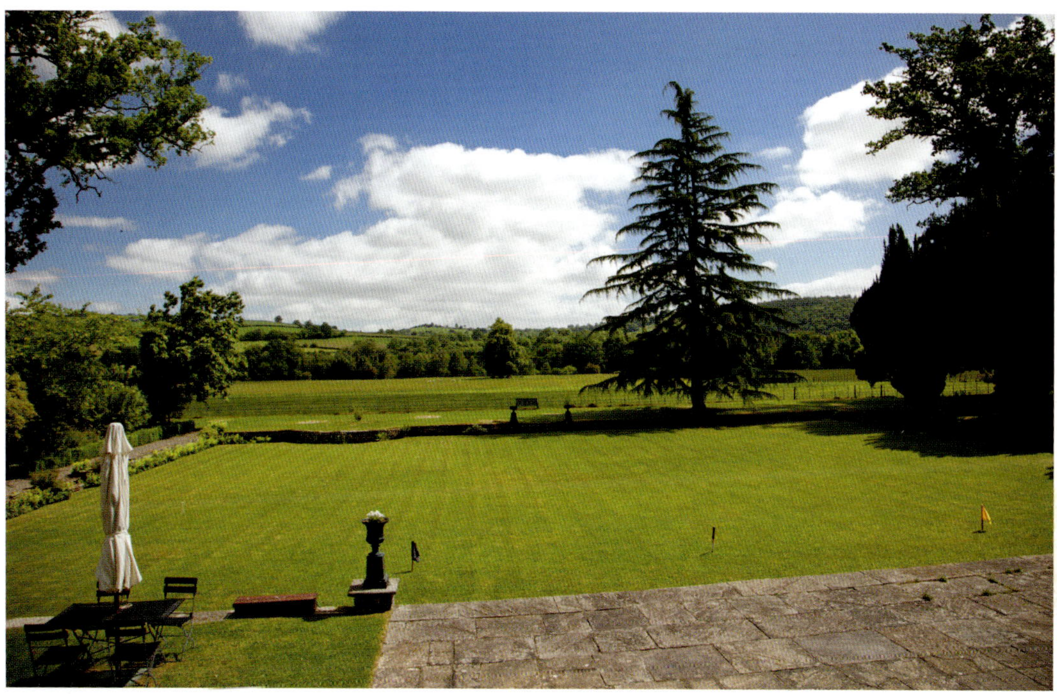

Above: Just because it looks good, it does not necessarily mean that it is a great location. Open, light locations are good for a couple in the scene, but bad for any close-up shots because the direction of light coming from above creates ugly shadows in the eyes.

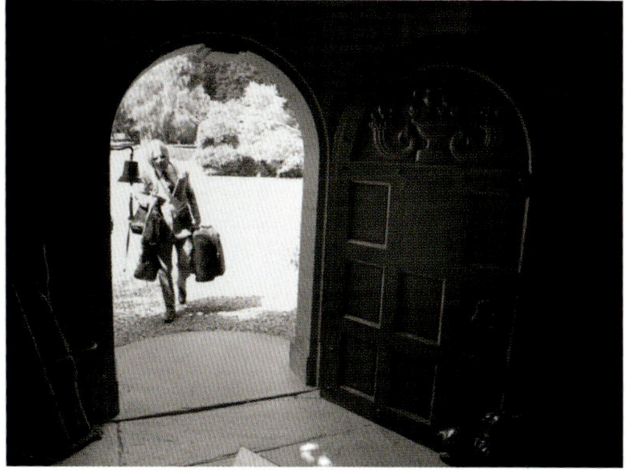

Above: Using an opening or a gap between buildings or foliage will reduce some of the light from above, and will help to make sure the light has some direction.

Tip

If I am going to be shooting at a new reception venue, I will try to meet the person in charge of at the venue when I visit. This is so I can get to know that person, understand their plans for the day, and make sure that my photography will fit in with those plans.

Setting the Style

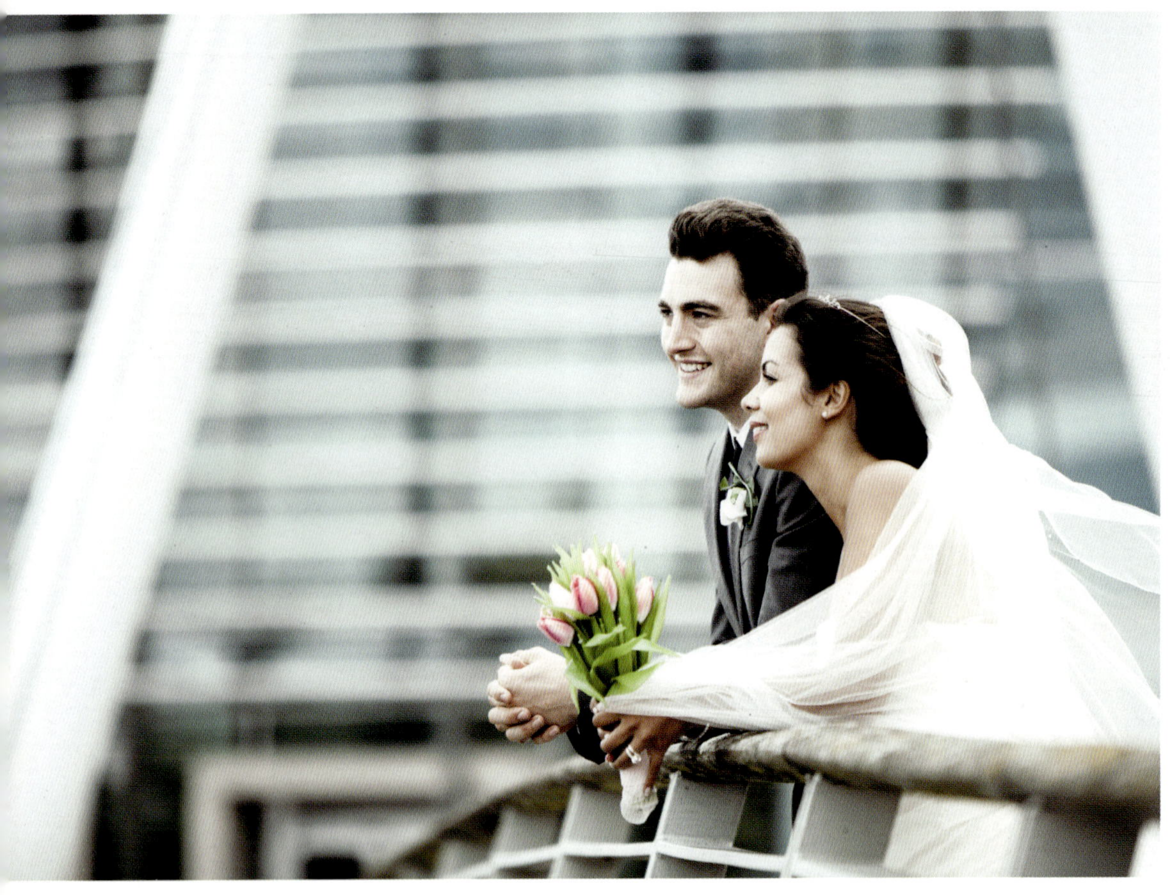

Above: Understanding and delivering the style and atmosphere preferred by the bride and groom is vital to successful wedding photography.

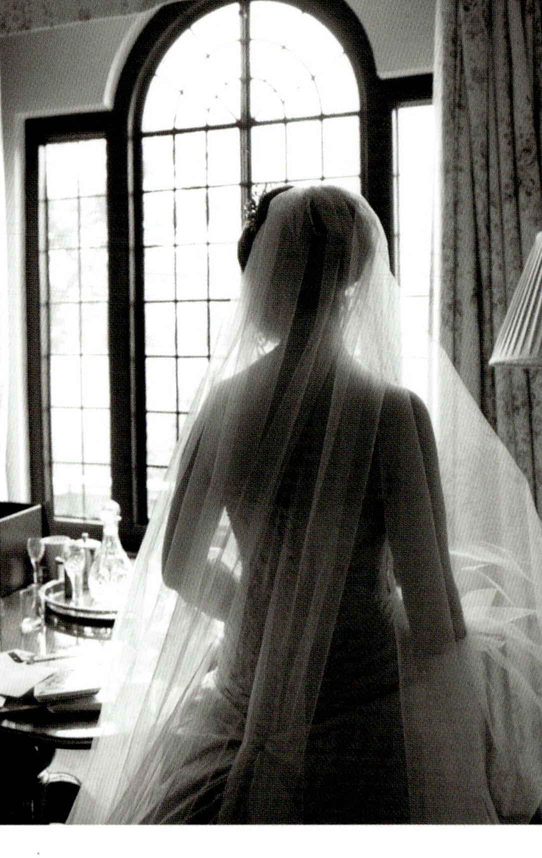

Above: When possible, stand back and observe the scene, waiting for pictures to happen by anticipating the action and sometimes even instigating it.

Each wedding will always have some sort of style, from basic or minimal, to over-the-top, or even teetering on the edge of tacky, but we are just the photographers who are paid to record the people, the objects, and the places.

When couples start to talk about their wedding day with you, ask them to tear out pages from wedding magazines or save a variety of images from the Internet that they both like and hate. Today, thanks to Google and social media sites such as Pinterest, a huge number of images are available to help your couple decide on a "look" for the photography. I have been shown an incredible range of images, including beach shots and castles when neither will be within a 100-mile radius of the wedding location. However, the aim of the exercise is not to find exact images to copy, but to get a feeling for their preferences, such as the emotions or atmosphere evoked by the images.

After discussing what the couple want, then try to interpret photographically what they have requested on the day. Without question, the photography of the bride and groom should match their requests as precisely as possible, as you know the location and so should be able to control many aspects of the scene on the day.

It is important to remember to observe each wedding from a distance and to take care not to shoot the same images time after time. All photographers have a workflow and their own particular style, but I believe that it is our job to record and present the wedding day as if it

Right: When you are struggling to capture the wedding's style and feel, concentrate on the details, as these will often reveal the elements that make up the day's look and feel.

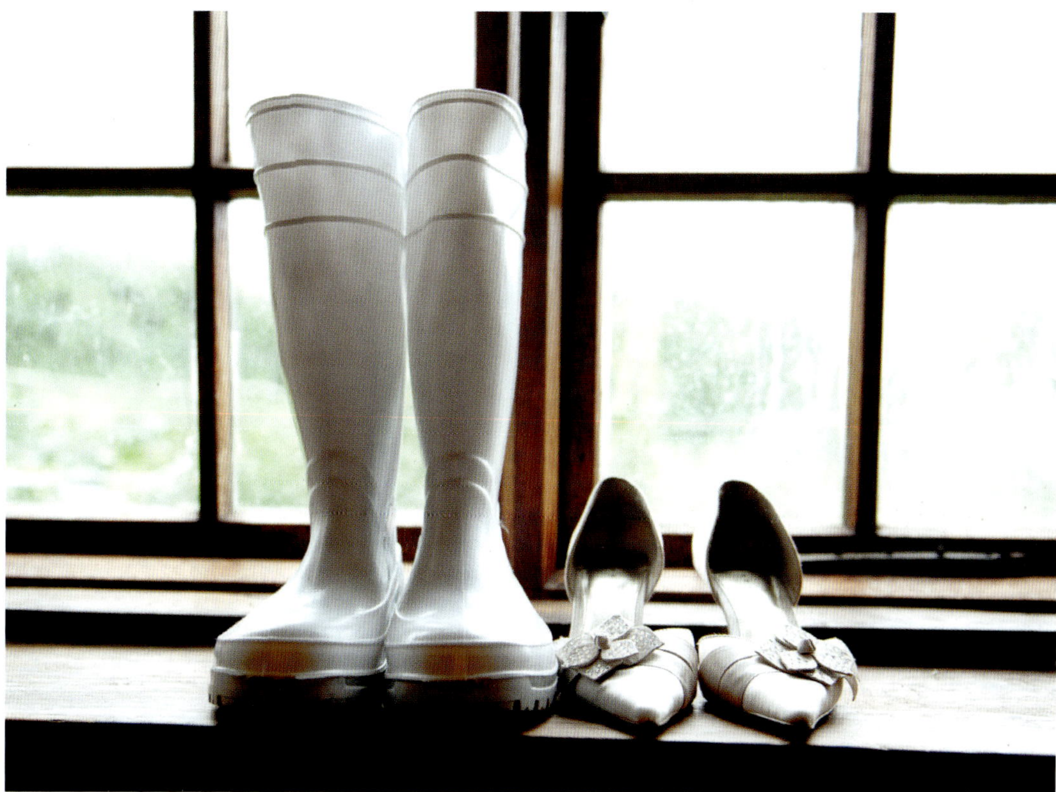

were a book or a play, scene by scene, chapter by chapter, including all the highs and lows as reflected in the emotions and expressions of the couple, friends, family, and guests.

The one thing we can never guarantee is the reactions of the guests on the day. Some of the best planned and themed weddings I have shot have been the ones that just lack that "something" to get everyone enthused, animated, and interacting with each other. For the photographer, this can be hard to cope with at times, especially if the couple is looking for candid shots of the day—there are only so many times you can shoot the same guests doing nothing. So be aware that at some point you may have to switch your style of photography to get a good variety of pictures.

Tip

Try and stand apart from the action and observe the scene, absorbing a little of the atmosphere so you can record it. We can get too close to the event and end up with the "same-old, same-old" shots, instead of original ones from a unique perspective.

Right: A wedding is all about the way the guests and key subjects interact with each other, and capturing those candid moments is as important as taking the perfect couple shot.

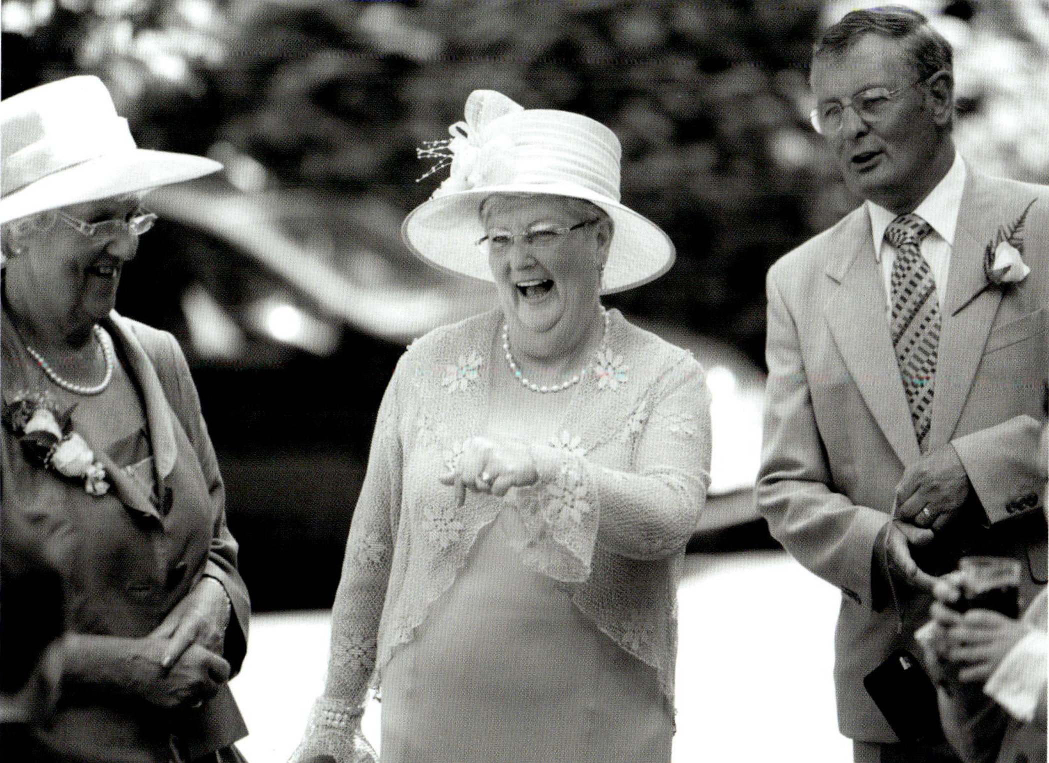

Classic Wedding

A classic, or formal wedding is, in some way, the bride's search for perfection. If you think about this too much and try to apply this to your photography it can scare you, but don't let it, since every wedding will seem perfect to the couple, and all we can do is our best.

Instead, plan ahead by breaking down the wedding into each section that needs to be shot—this helps to avoid the trap of becoming overwhelmed by thinking about the whole day. You can divide the classic wedding day into four sections: posing, lighting, formal portraits, and timing. This will help you to concentrate on each part at a time and then bring them all together at some point in your forward planning, which can of course be mimicked on a real wedding day.

Advance planning

One of the problems with more formal wedding photography is that it can take slightly longer to perfect each shot, especially to get the pose and use of light right. Most wedding couples fear formal wedding photography, because formal photographs can look stiff and the expressions lacking in life. This is usually due to the photographer taking too much time over the finer details, missing out on capturing the moment of the day as they fuss with little distractions in the search for the perfect shot.

The secret to formal wedding photography is to use it as a starting point. With each new setup or location, you should decide on the variety of images you are going to take before posing the couple. Also decide on what part the formal selection will play in their overall collection of images. By making these decisions before starting, you will be able to select the right location with the lighting and backdrop that suit the couple and the style.

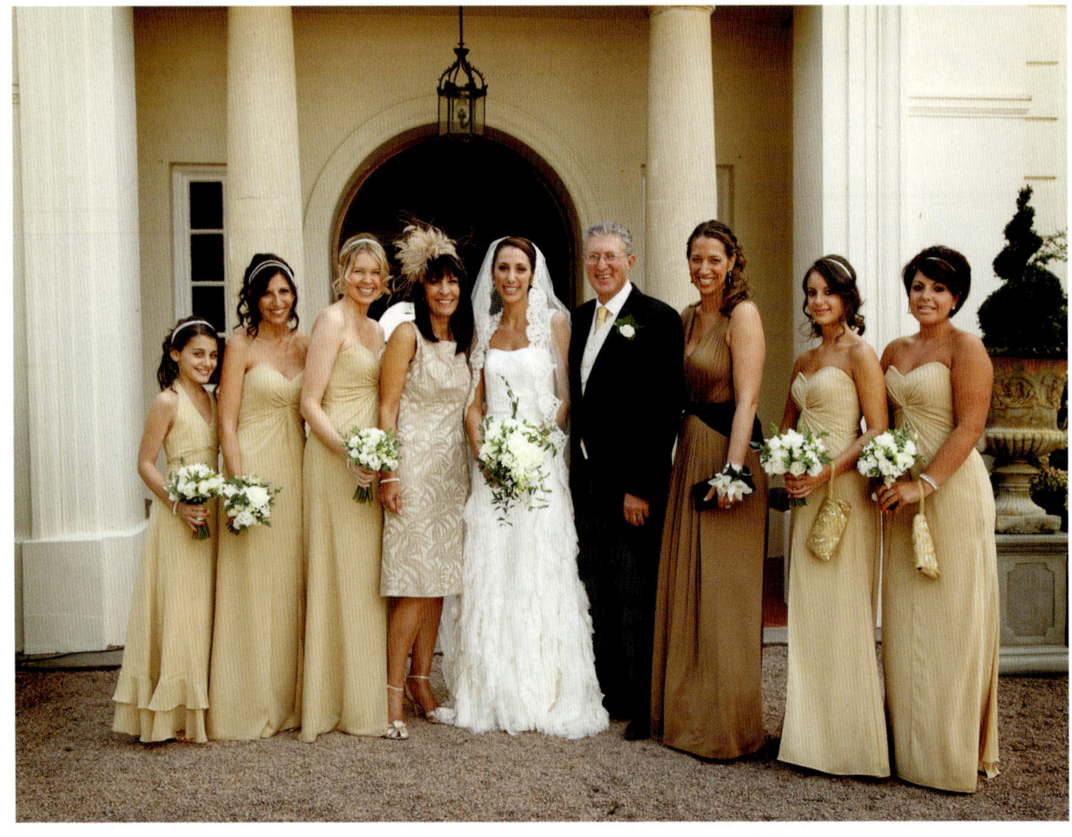

Posing

Posing your subjects for a classic wedding is not just about how they stand and where they position their feet and hands, but also about the importance of etiquette in clothing and how or where to position each subject. For instance, bear in mind that it is important to show a shirt cuff beneath a man's jacket sleeve, because if the cuff is missing it will later look as though the hand has been added in postproduction.

Essentially, formal posing is about making your subjects look balanced, and relaxed, but at the same time "finished," almost like a mannequin with a smile. If you've done your job well, everything will look natural and animated, but get it wrong and

Above: The standard, classic wedding groups are quick to set up and are easily changed by pulling people in and out of them; this creates a variety of simple groups very quickly, useful when time is not on your side and the bride is ready to leave for the ceremony.

Right: Even though classic wedding photography is sometimes over-posed, careful positioning of some groups can result in great interaction between the subjects.

the whole image will always look falsely posed.

Formal photography, when done well, can be classical and timeless. This requires all of the elements—pose, light, and backdrop—to be combined well, so don't be afraid to use formal photography as part of a wider repertoire.

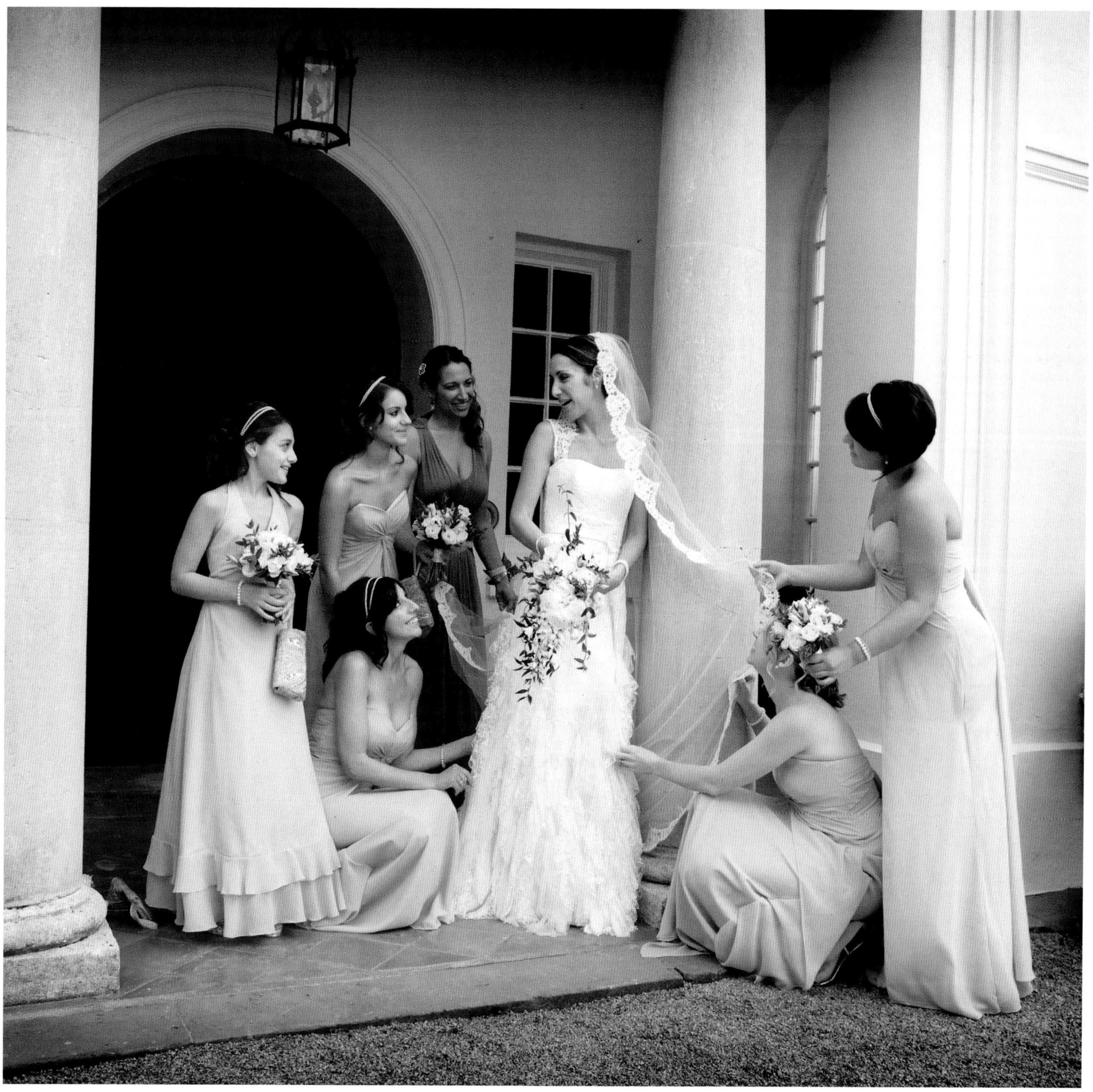

Lighting

There are two main sources of light at a classic wedding: the natural light in the scene, and flash to fill in lighting as and when necessary.

Lighting should always be used to be sympathetic to both the scene and to the subject. The light should have a direction, which helps to make the subject look thinner by creating shadow. Lighting that comes from either the 5 or 7 o'clock position will be the most flattering for couples and small groups, but it is better to have flatter lighting for larger groups. It is always better to position groups of people with their backs to the sun. This helps to separate them from the background and improves their expressions in bright sunlight, as direct sun in their faces will make them squint.

Flash is mainly used to light up shadow areas, such as under ladies' hats, but it can also be used to create all the light in the scene, especially at winter weddings where the natural light is available for such a short time.

Formal portraits

Formal portraits (or "formals") don't necessarily mean photographs of the bride and groom, or the groups, but more what is expected by the couple. Shots like the signing of the registers, the bride and her father in the car, the couple at the church door, and the aisle shot all fit into the this category, and will be determined in advance during your pre-wedding chat with the couple.

When shooting formal groups, concentrate on showing everyone in their best possible light. Turn each subject slightly to the middle to help condense the group, as well as thin the subjects. A group of people in a line always feels formal, but hiding guests behind each other is just lazy. So instead

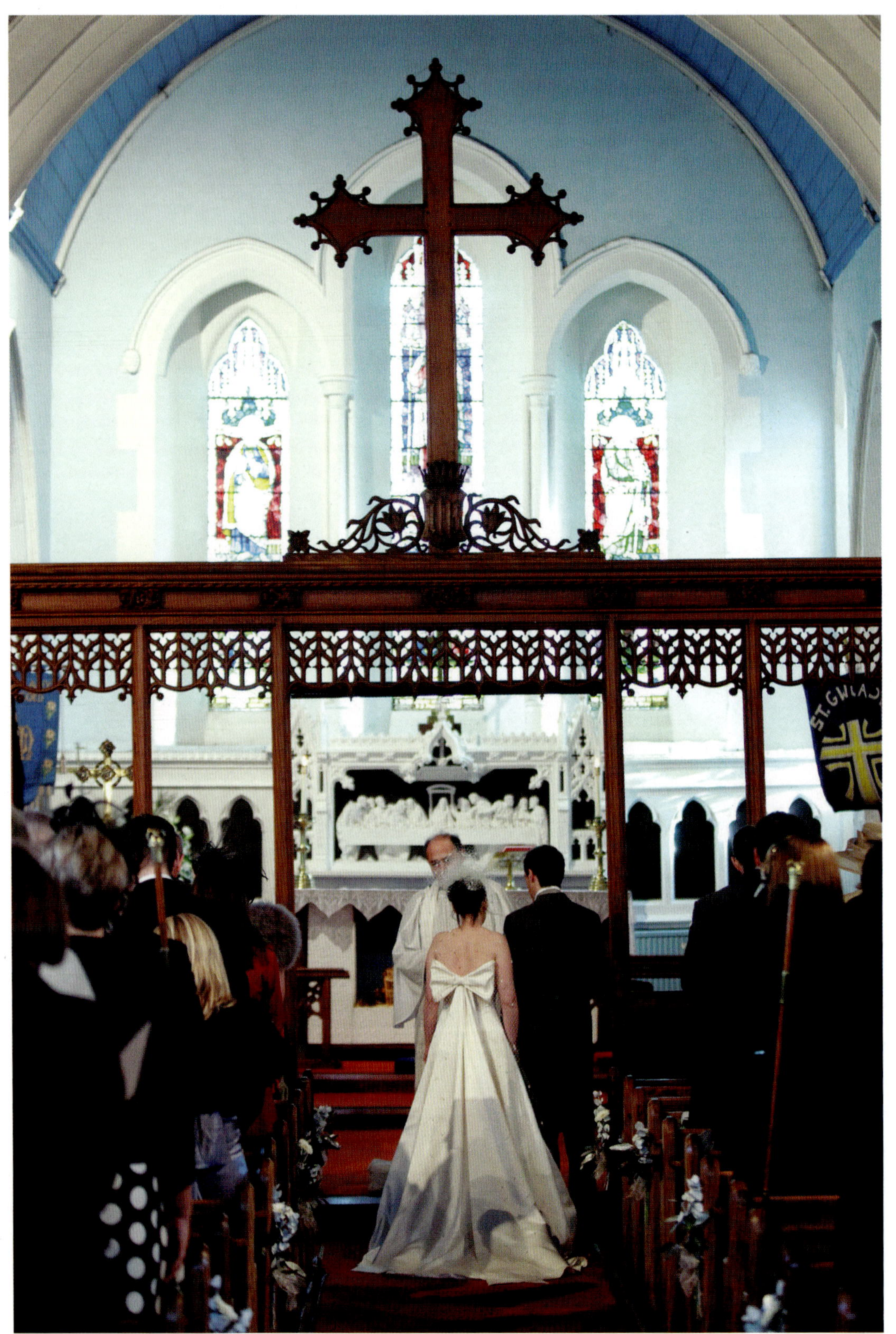

Right: There may be restrictions on what you can and cannot shoot during the ceremony—this all depends on the venue and its rules. If you can, try to shoot without using flash or moving around too much, as this way you can take a few photographs of the ceremony without being noticed.

stagger large groups with the ladies in a line and with the men either in front of them kneeling down or standing up behind them.

Formal groups are easier to arrange and quicker to shoot—this is because you can use your agreed list of who to shoot to create a workflow on the day, keeping the main subjects together and adding and subtracting subjects with the minimum of fuss and inconvenience to the guests.

Timing

Taking control of the wedding is something that some photographers seem scared to do, possibly because they don't like to call out names or draw attention to themselves, or because they think the guests will not listen. For a classic wedding, though, this has to be done by someone, and it may as well be the photographer.

Time is never on our side at a wedding—we are always waiting for someone or being prompted by someone else—but at least with a formal wedding plan there is a schedule that must be met. The photographer does always have the option of adjusting the times to make sure that the shoot list is completed, but remember that this can really upset the other professionals servicing the wedding, including the chef and the vicar, so it is best to keep to the plan. I always like my brides to go into the ceremony as near as possible to the agreed time, as I don't want to have any of the blame for everything running late—especially with the wedding meal, as it can be quickly spoilt if delayed.

If I were looking for three more words to sum up the formal, classic wedding they would be: structure, perfection, and expression. Put these together with my four sections and you have the flavor of the classic wedding: a structure to everything in the day, a perfection in pose and lighting, combined with the expressions of your subjects to match the mood.

Right: Windows provide a fundamental ingredient of my classic wedding style, as the directional light from a window creates a simple, elegant, and almost timeless image.

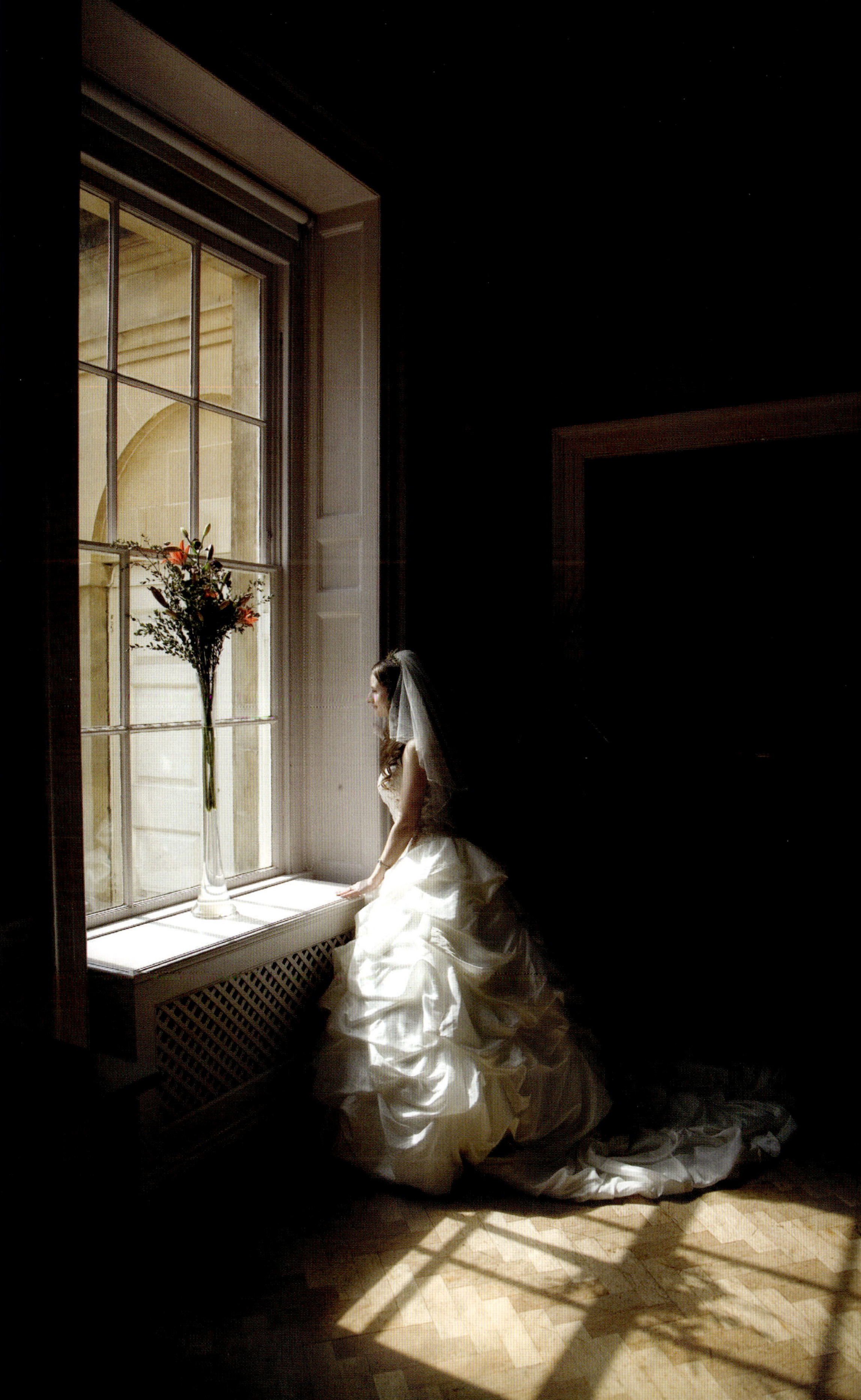

Fun & Fashionable Wedding

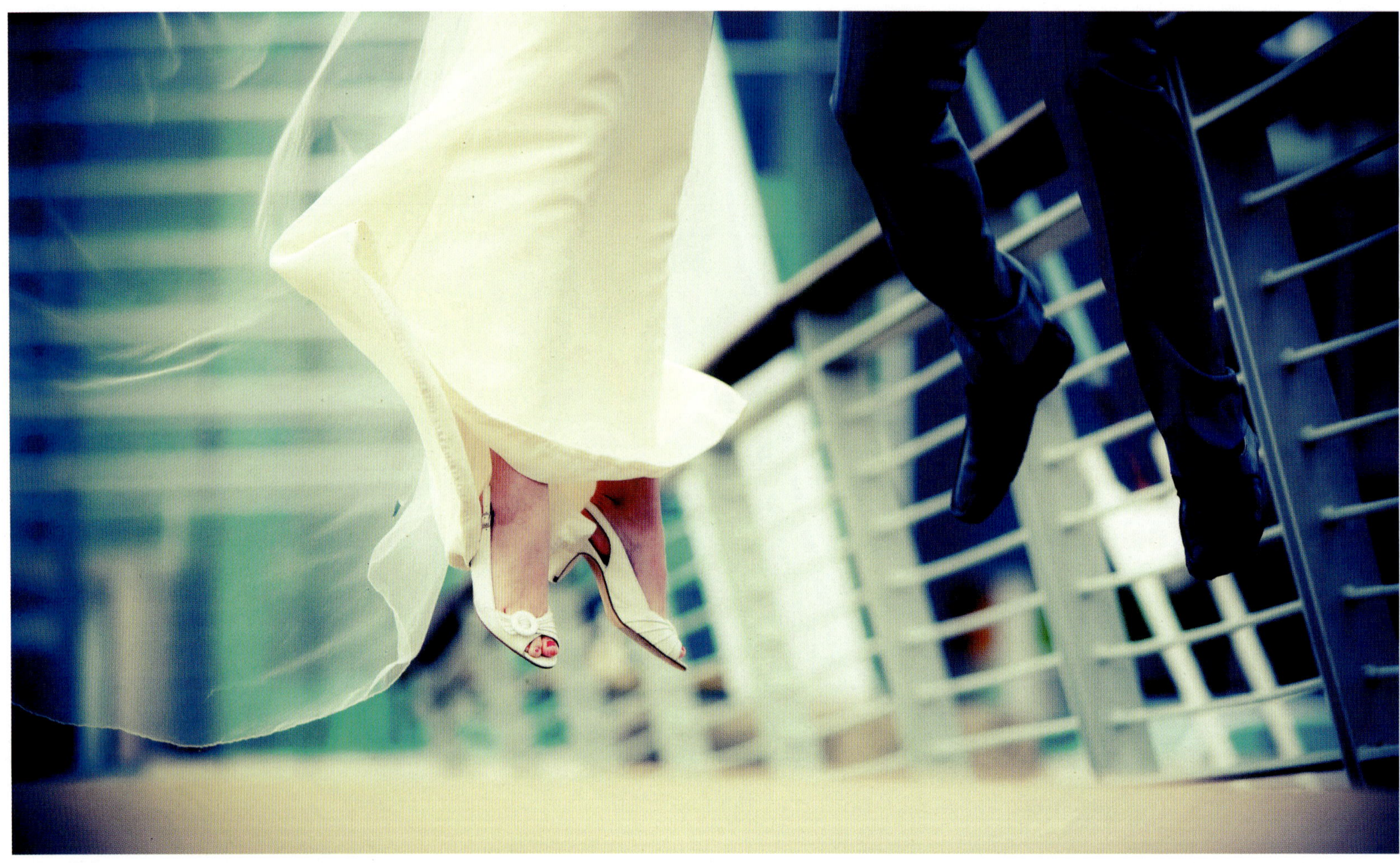

The fun and fashionable wedding style is probably the most sought after at the moment, as the couple often feel this provides the best of both worlds, mixing the formal poses with a "funky" fashion feel, with the images often adjusted with retro coloring in postproduction.

It is best to view this style of wedding photography as two separate styles: the fun and the fashion. The two are slightly different and, if mixed incorrectly, they can look cheesy or even tacky, especially if subjects' expressions are all wrong for the poses.

Fun

You may think that couples would naturally have fun on their wedding day, but they can often struggle to let their real selves come out because of stress and nerves. This does not just apply to the bride and groom by any means, as it can sometimes be true for the whole wedding party— even the biggest and liveliest of characters can be "toned down" on the day. It is the photographer's job to help everyone relax and make the most out of the occasion.

Above: Photography is not always about rules. Remember to play with camera angles and lighting effects. This image of the bride and groom jumping for joy gets mixed reactions, especially with cross-processing in postproduction, but it is still fun to shoot, and it looks great hung on a wall.

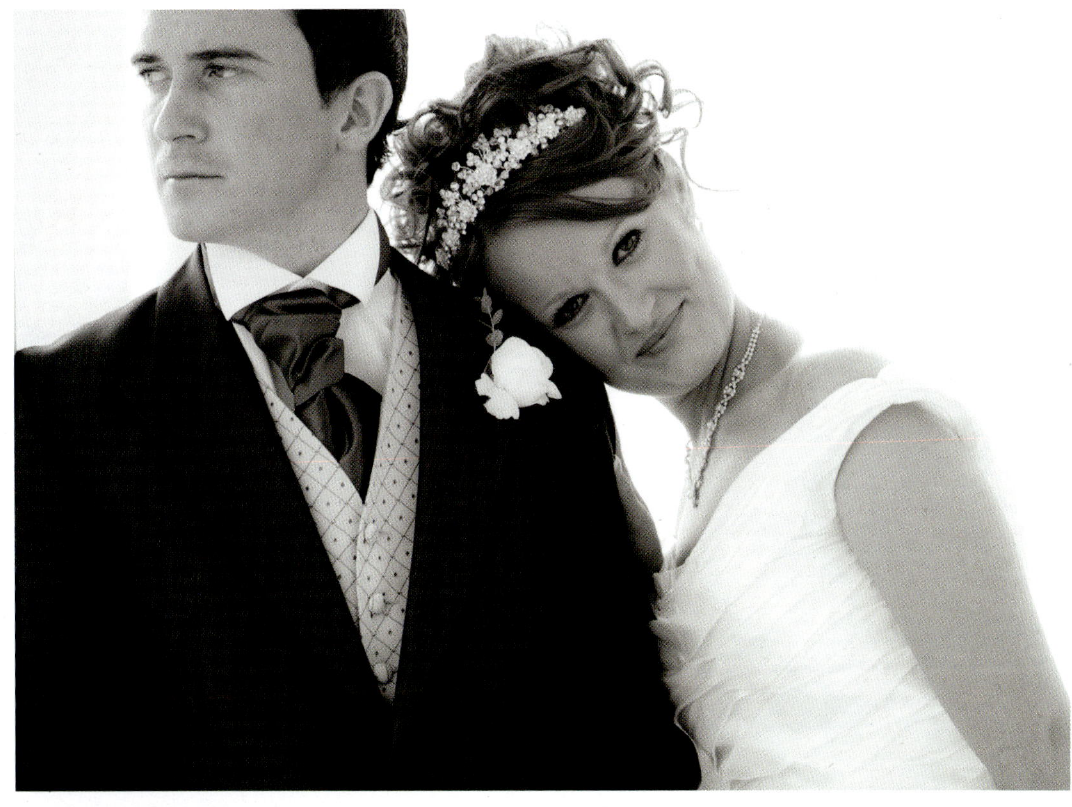

Setting up the group photographs can provide a chance of release, and friendly banter with the couple and guests often works as a distraction, and is sometimes enough to break the ice. I don't mind being the butt of a joke if it works, but you may need to make something happen or the guests will be stiff and unengaged, and there will be no fun while you shoot—which means you need to change the style of photography quickly.

Often it is easier to achieve the expressions you need from the bride and groom when they are on their own with you. They can become a little embarrassed about being the center of attention when they're put with larger groups—in these circumstances I separate the couple from the guests as soon as possible.

Sometimes, if you are lucky, there will be a few characters who will get the party started all by themselves, and hanging around with them will give you the opportunities to shoot a variety of fun images as they interact with the other guests. For these fun and candid shots, I mainly use two lenses: a 70–200mm zoom to get in close from a distance, and a 24mm wide-angle to capture all the action.

Tip

You will have to shoot a lot more images with a fun wedding than any other style, in order to capture the event as it unfolds. However, remember it is always best to edit your images ruthlessly, so that you show only the very best selection in the proofs.

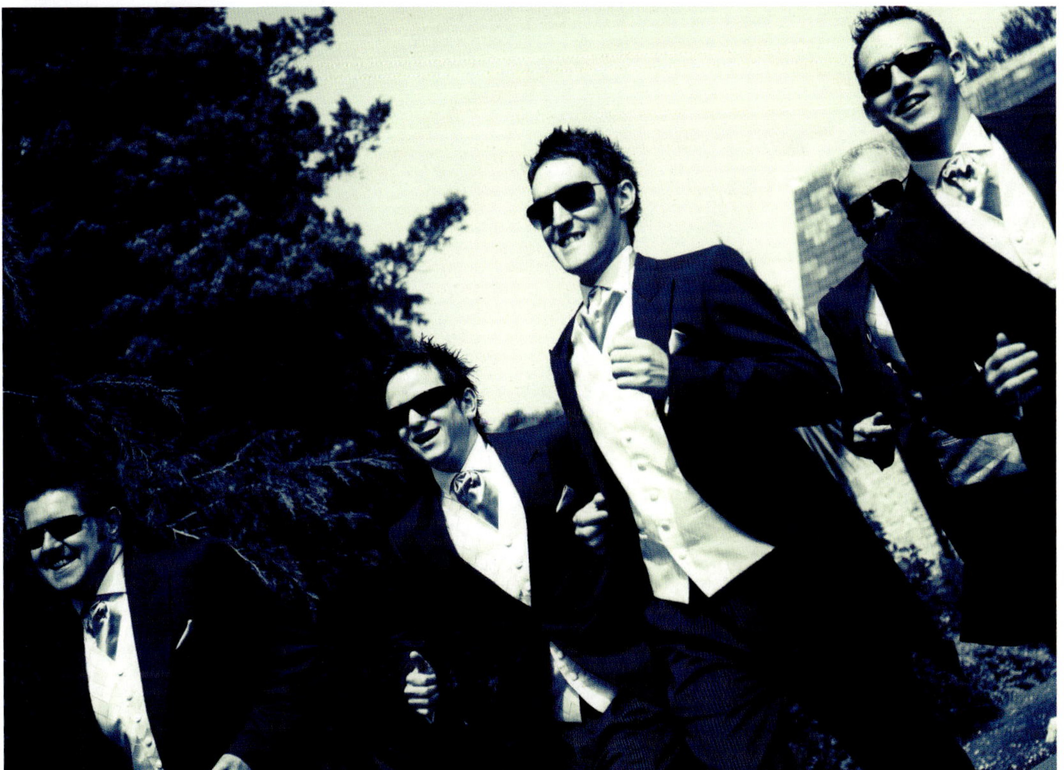

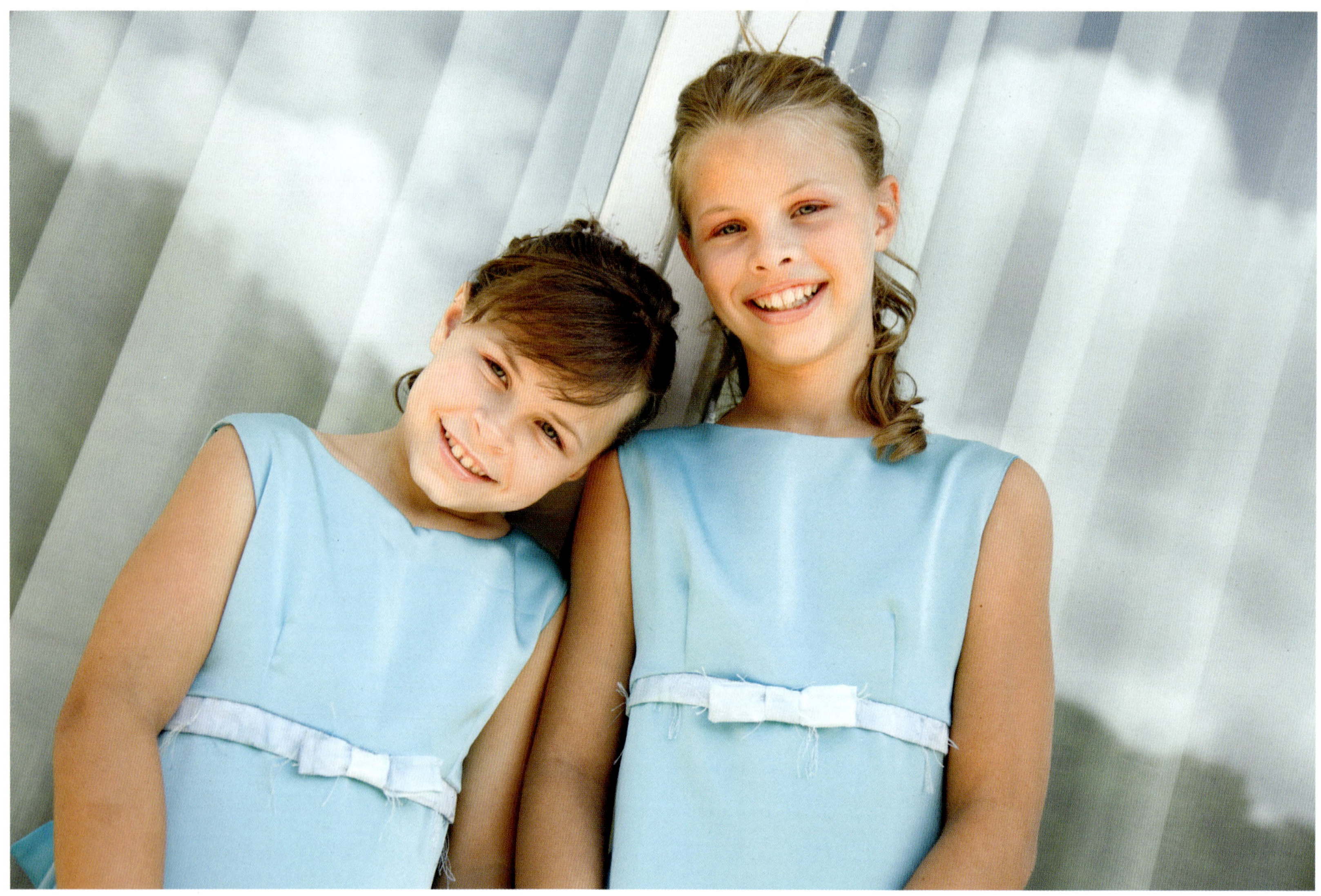

Fashionable

Weddings are becoming more and more quirky, with the couples to match at times, so giving the images a fashionable edge is not hard to achieve and, with some editing in postproduction, the images can take on a completely different look.

To add a bit of fashion edge to a wedding, I first try to break the classic rules of posing and composition, as these changes alone will make the images stand out from others. Instead of posing the couple very close, with no gaps visible between them, I will deliberately add a space, so they are almost reaching out to each other. Straightening the subjects' limbs creates new angles and lines in the pictures, with a fashion magazine look.

The secret is to break the rules when you need to in order to create a difference in the images. For instance, you can add natural sun flare on the lens for a few shots, which creates a retro and degraded coloring to your images. You can also try animating the bride and groom in awkward, exaggerated positions, again to jolt the viewer a little.

Another one of the easiest ways to create the right look to fashionable wedding images is to use very dramatic backgrounds. I love using graffiti walls and metal doors or large posters for an instant wow factor. If you are then able to add further drama by animating the couple, your pictures will jump off the page.

One of the biggest problems when discussing wedding styles with couples is that they only tend to ask for whatever you show them in your display albums. So if you only ever show your potential clients safe, classy images, you will only be commissioned for safe, classy weddings. This is a common problem when starting out as a photographer, and I also thought initially that

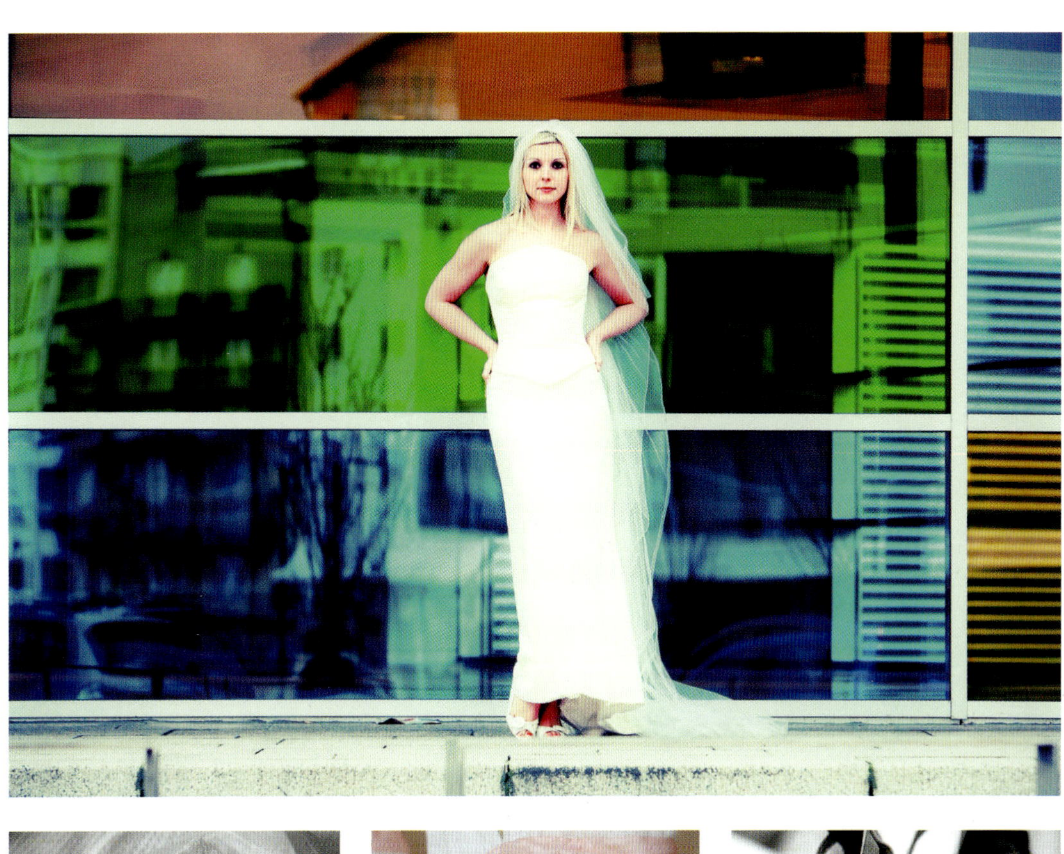

was what wedding photographers should offer—the same as everyone else. However, thankfully, because of my young age when I began shooting weddings, I attracted like-minded couples, who also wanted something a little different. Even if we could not shoot different images on the wedding day—because the parents were paying and wanted to see traditional images—I often took the couples out after the ceremonies and photographed them on beaches, castle ruins, city centers, and anywhere else nearby to provide different backdrops and colors.

If you're really stuck, and are rarely able to persuade couples to try something different, then book a few models for a day's shooting to generate some sample images. Whatever you do, make sure you plan and research your wedding shoots, and analyze them afterwards, to help you create images that will not only inspire you, but will also inspire future clients.

Never be afraid to undertake a bit of extra postproduction editing to your fashionable images, as the creative in you will demand that you push your images beyond the basics to make them stand out in a crowd. Personally, I do prefer to make the difference with the camera at the time, if possible. I use special color and contrast settings in-camera to create the kind of effects I'm looking for, even though the in-camera settings only affect the JPEG file and not the Raw file. This way, the image on the back of my camera will help me to preview the look I'm after, and it will also help to show what I'm shooting to anyone on the day.

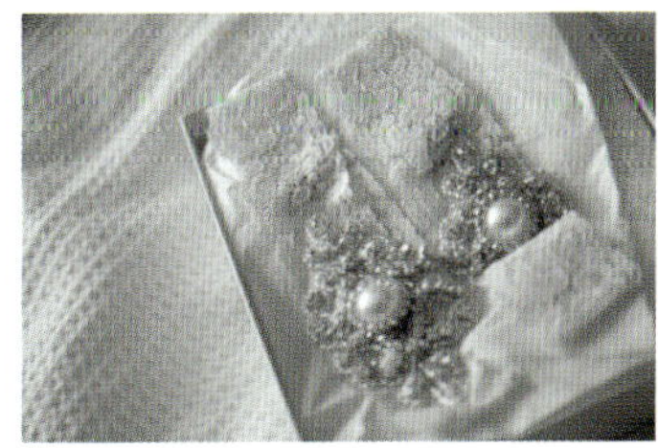
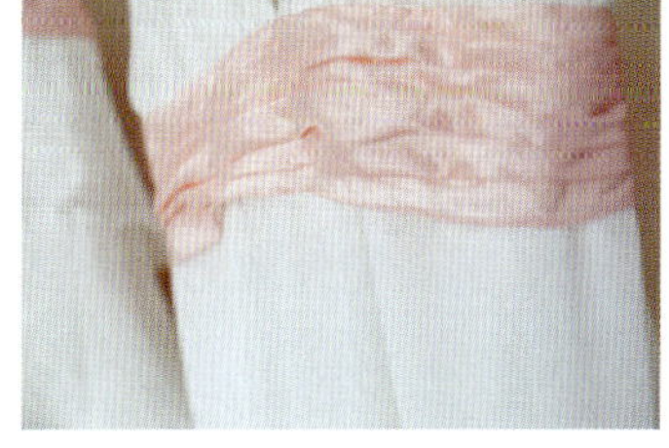
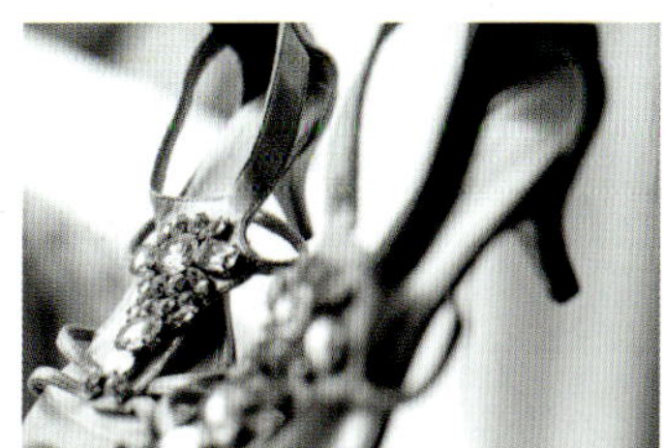
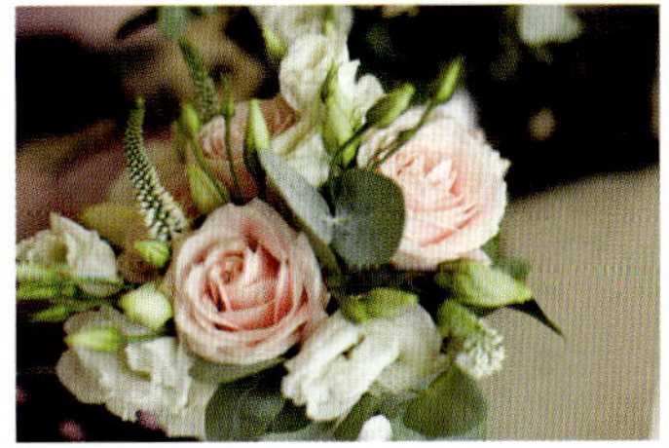
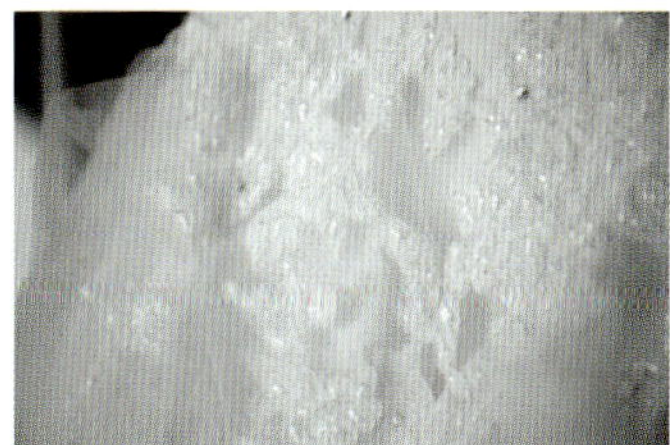
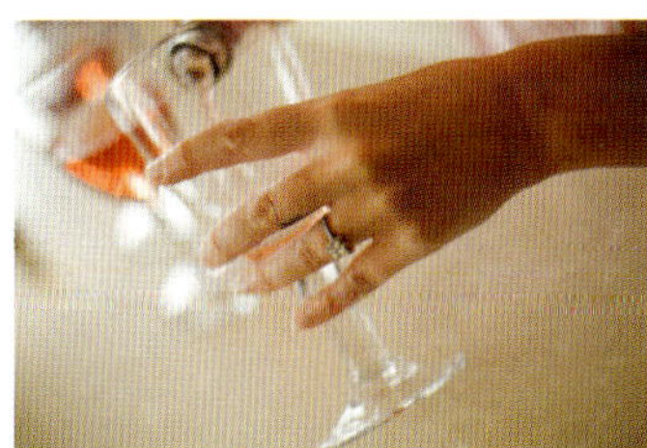

Tip

Don't be afraid to book a model to practice with, and to help you develop a style. Clients often booked me to shoot their weddings because I offered something a little different—which often just began as fashion shoot concepts.

Above: Use detail shots to form several themed spreads in the finished album, as they can emphasize the colors and elements that gave the fashionable theme to the day.

Relaxed & Informal Wedding

This style mixes the classic and photojournalistic styles to create a more relaxed and informal wedding, but still provides a structure to the whole day. The best way to shoot it is to act a little like a guest, interacting with others, while continuing to be an observer. This means that the posing of the groups is more informal, allowing you to capture the guests chatting. At the same time, you'll need to be able to act quickly and ask guests to look towards the camera for simple group shots.

For many photographers, this is as close as they get to true reportage wedding photography, because they still have to get the shots that were agreed in advance of certain people, if not all the guests, attending the wedding. This is the main benefit of this style: the photographer has a structure to work with, but is also able to stand back and observe, and shoot natural, informal images of the day.

The disadvantage of this style is that the photographer has much less input on the day, and so the shots of the couple will not be as perfect as they might want them to be—it is therefore absolutely essential that you make sure the bride and groom understand this. This means that the placement of the dress, the backgrounds, and the expressions of the couple and the guests will not be so carefully composed. As long as the couple understand this, and it is what they want, then you can have some fun shooting.

If you are worried about missing the shot because you are in the wrong place at the right time, you will have to think about bringing along a second photographer to help you cover the event. If this is the case you must both shoot in a similar way, or the styles of the images will conflict.

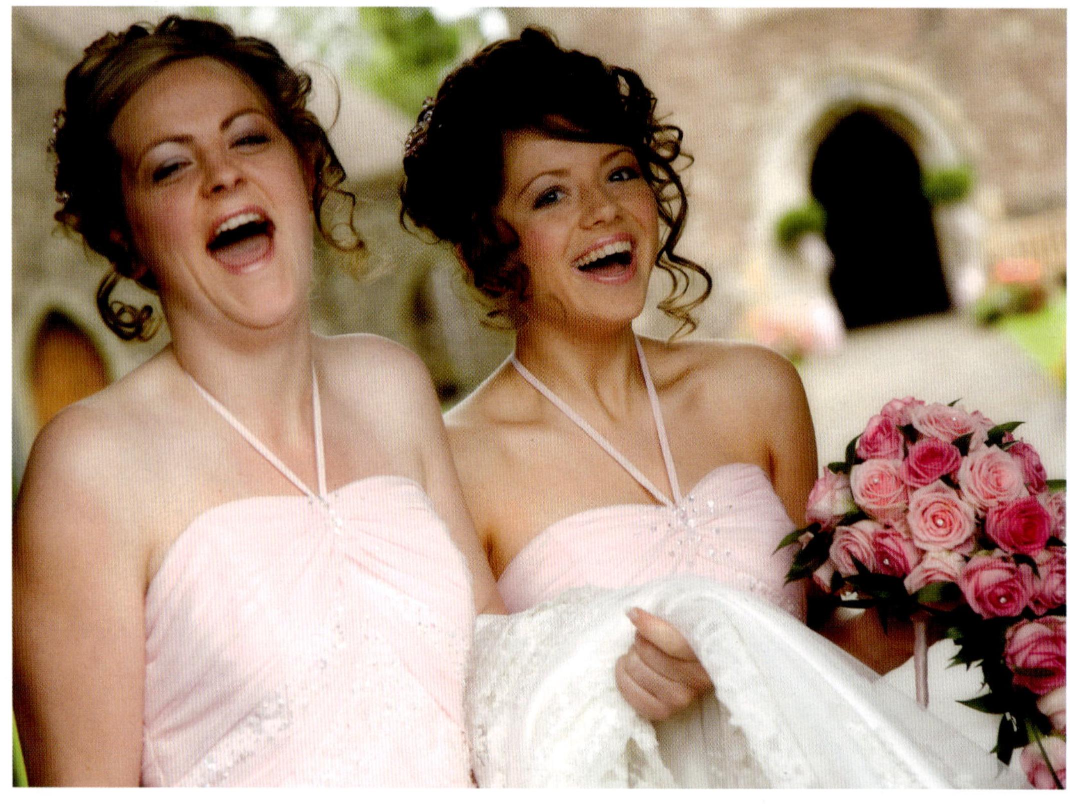

Above: Even though you might be shooting in a more relaxed style, it does not mean you cannot interact with the subjects to get the right expressions—after all it is all about the expressions, as they are what sell the images and show your subjects' true characters.

Tips

On some occasions it can be acceptable for the photographer to appear like a guest with a professional camera, and be willing to take control if necessary to capture the special people and events of the day.

Remember that, after the event, it is essential to edit your images ruthlessly. The couple do not need to see everything—you should only ever show them the very best expressions, the best group shots, and the best couple images, or it will look to them as though they have paid for a whole load of snapshots.

Right: Shooting relaxed couple pictures can be difficult, especially when trying to pose the subjects while avoiding awkward hand and limb positions.

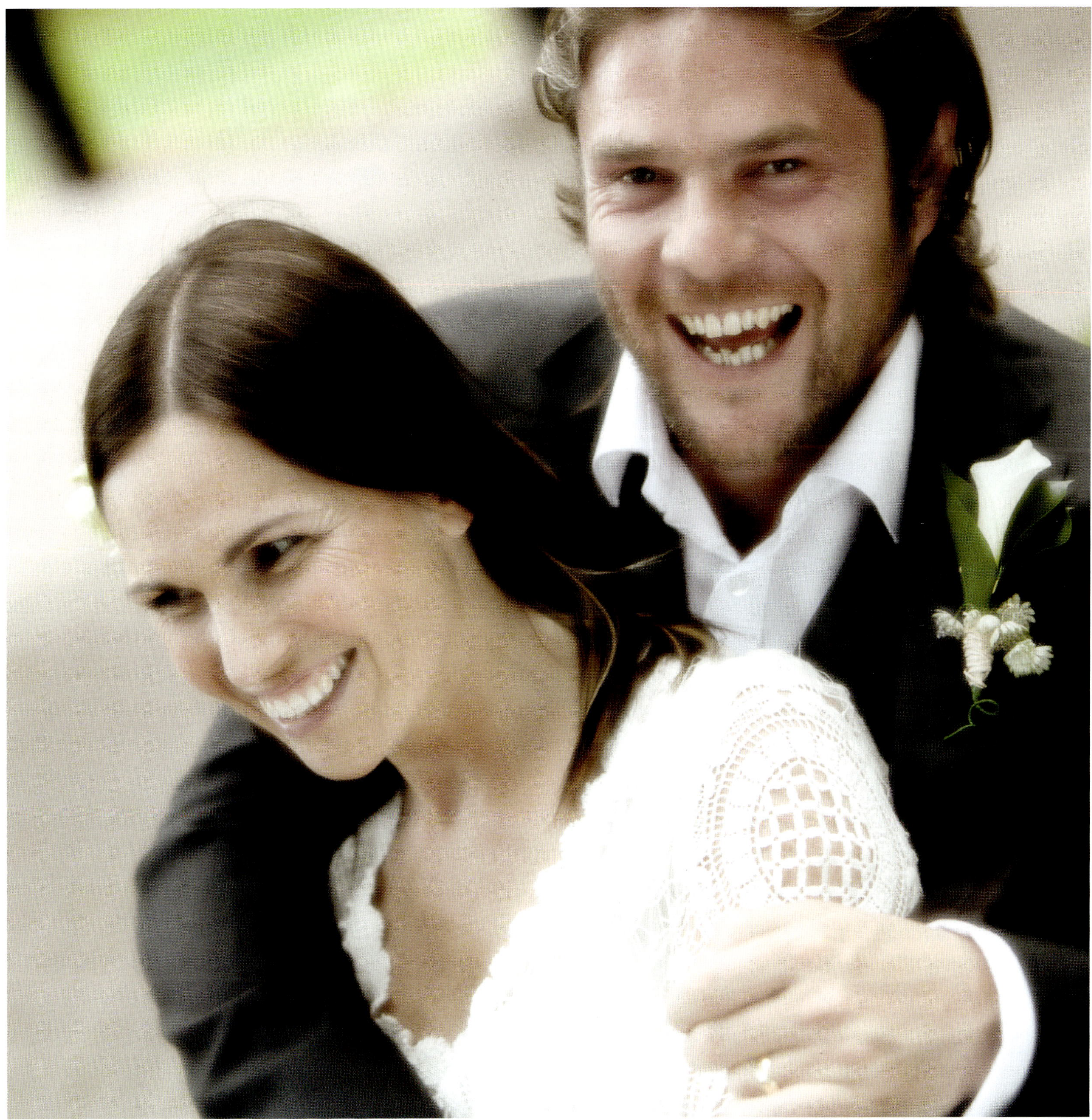

Photojournalistic Wedding

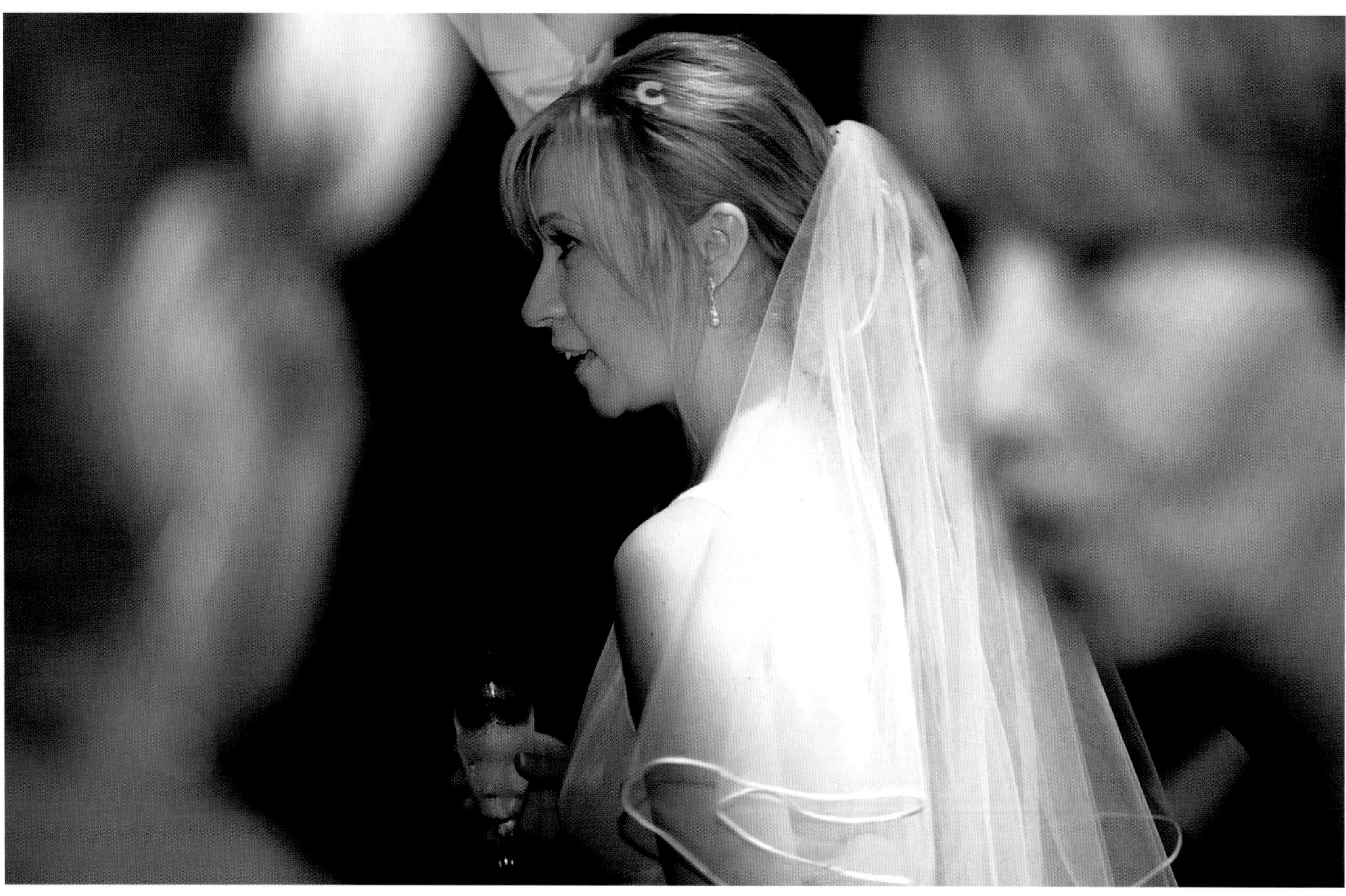

True photojournalism is a specific skill and is one that many photographers cannot master. Providing totally candid coverage of a wedding means shooting thousands of images on the day to produce between 300 and 400 pictures—usually the bride and groom actually see only about 10–15% of what is shot.

Personally, I prefer to shoot this way, but it is actually the style I use the least, as most weddings need the photographer to interact with the guests in order to ensure that certain groups, family members, and guests are photographed—and, of course, this breaks with the true fly-on-the-wall approach.

The closest many photographers get to this type of coverage is when they are employed as a second shooter at a wedding to support the principal photographer. A photojournalist is more like a sniper, prepared to shoot the picture at any moment, relying on their instincts to know who to

Above: The fly-on-the-wall approach and black and white finish of a photojournalistic wedding can be enjoyable to shoot and review, but makes interaction with the guests for set shots difficult.

watch and how the events are about to unfold.

It is also essential that the series of images are linked together by a "story." It requires powers of observation and instinct to shoot a set of images

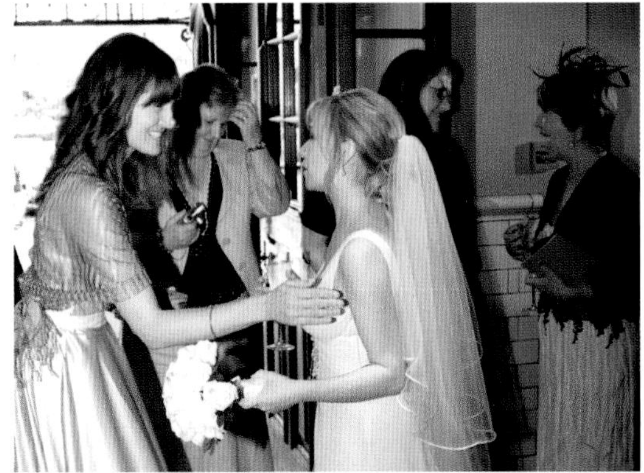 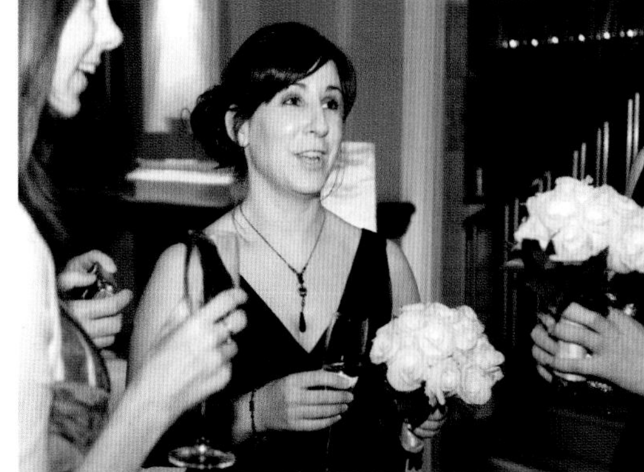 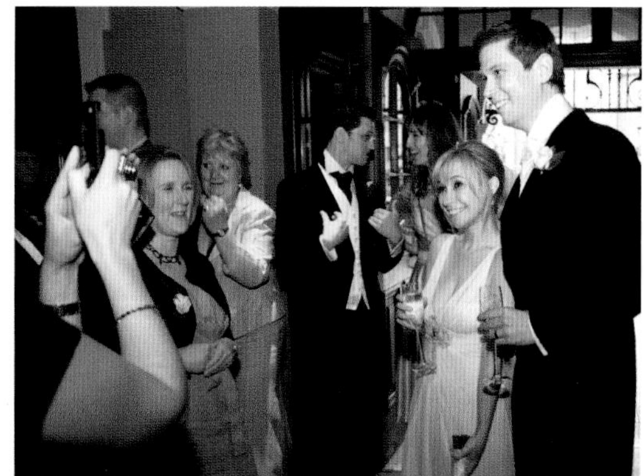

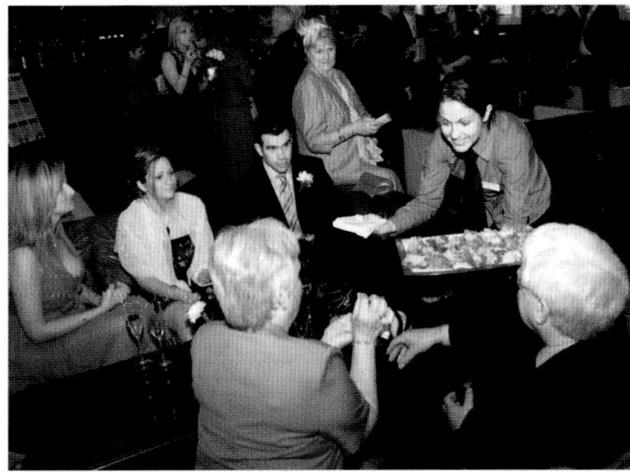 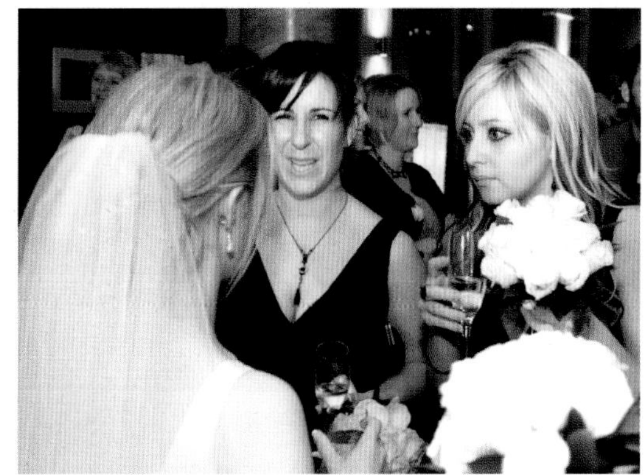 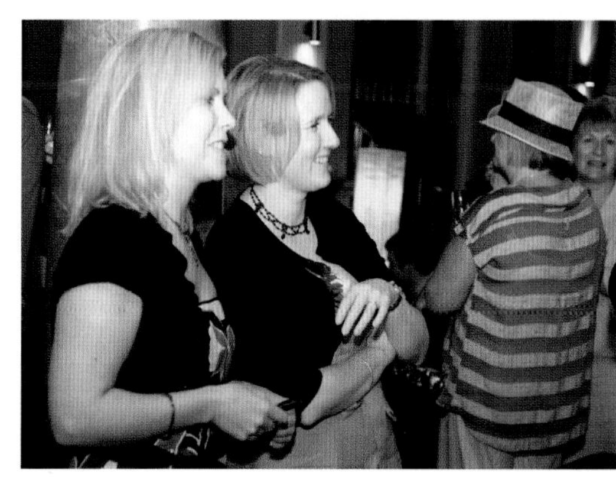

that focuses on the people, their emotions and intimate moments, as well as capturing the scene and the events of the day in such a way that no words are needed to explain what is going on.

The reportage style of photography, if you are a purist, tends to use black and white. However, we all have our own approach, so you can mix mono and color images if it suits your style and the style of the wedding—this has become more common again since the arrival of the DSLR. Coffee-table albums are perfect for showing off this type of coverage at its best, as they provide a simplified, storybook-style presentation, and allow the black and white images to stand out against pure white pages with no or little postproduction editing.

On the technical front, a prime lens— wide or telephoto—is the first choice of most photojournalists, as it helps to throw the background out of focus at f/2.8 or below, enabling them to emphasize the subject. However, a long lens is essential for shooting expressions close-up, and many photographers opt for a 70–200mm lens for their second most-used lens at a wedding.

Flash is not normally used in reportage photography. Instead, you need to rely on fast ISO settings, slow shutter speeds, and wide apertures to get the shot—grain or noise only adds to the "real life" look of the images. When only using the ambient light in a scene, it is important to concentrate on areas with a good contrast of light, even if it is in a dark location. This will help the images "pop" off the page with intense blacks, and pure whites.

Above: A series of candid, fly-on-the-wall shots, usually in gritty black and white, can give a real sense of the day as it unfolds, capturing the action and interaction between guests and, when seen together, resemble a filmstrip.

Tip

Use very wide-angle and long telephoto lenses, all nearly wide open at large apertures, to throw the backgrounds out of focus.

Pre-Wedding Shoot

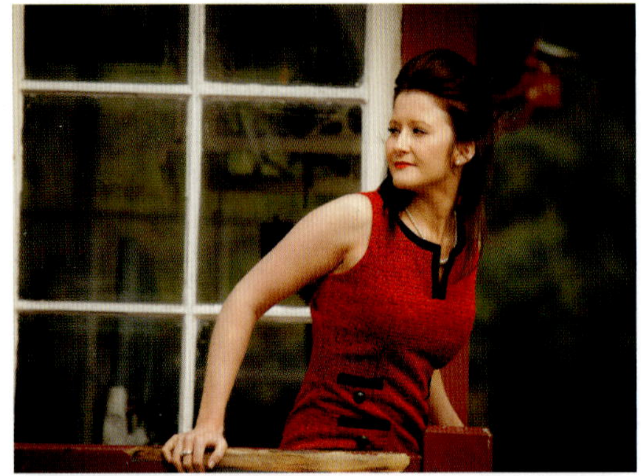

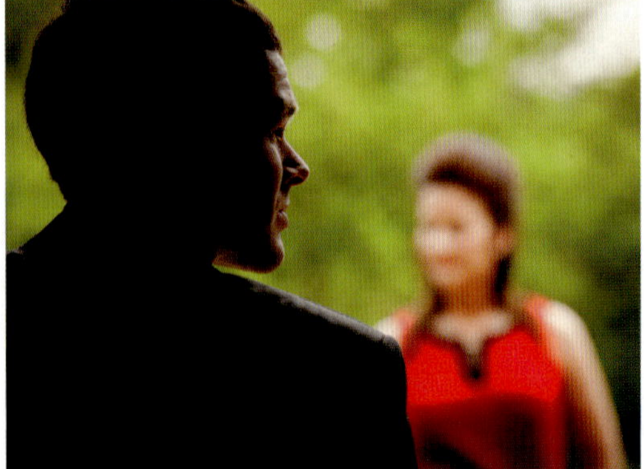

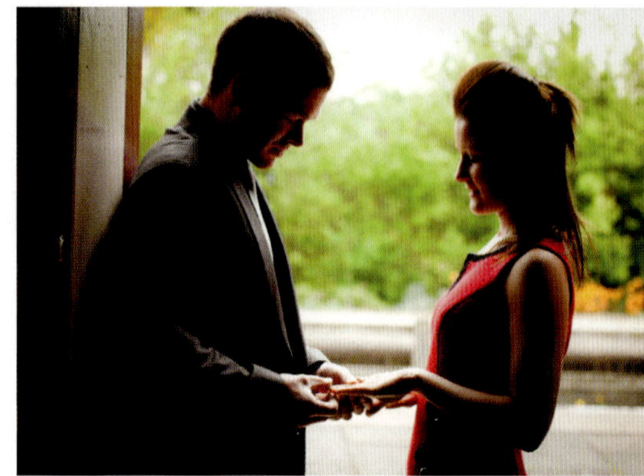

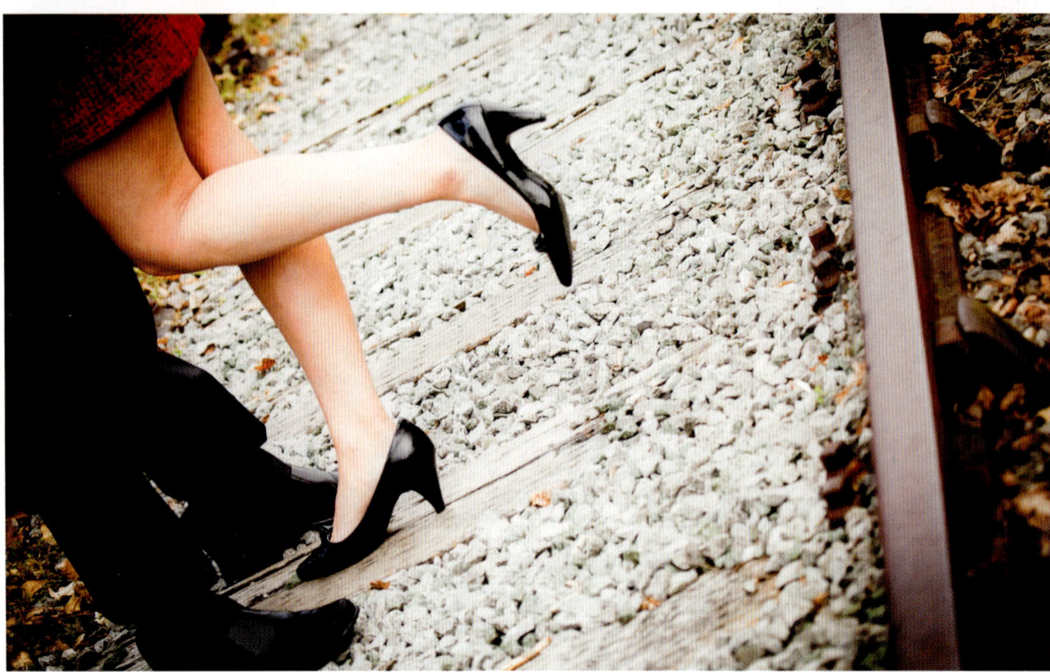

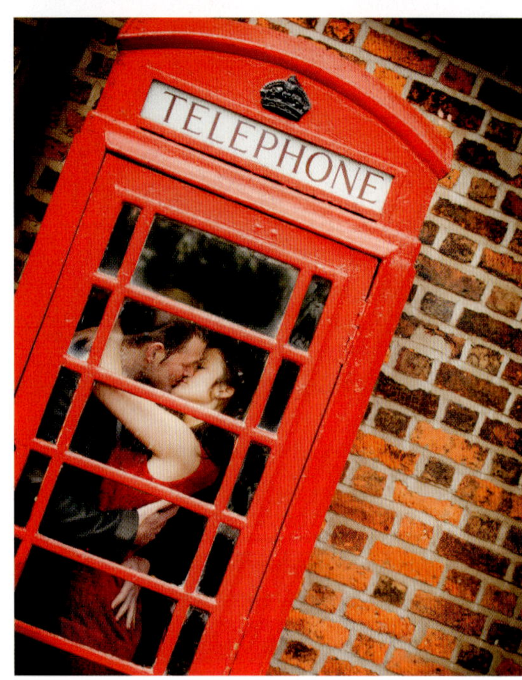

The pre-wedding or engagement shoot is one of the most important events, as it gives the photographer time to get to know the couple. This session is not only a good training exercise for both parties, but also a perfect way to add to your income as well as your portfolio—in fact, engagement portraits can be a viable business in their own right.

Make this shoot fun and most importantly relaxed, as you want to build your couple's confidence and not kill it. A few hours of fun on location with a couple before the wedding can really make a difference to your images on the day, as the couple will have more confidence in you by that stage and know that everything you are doing is to make them feel and look good. But remember that if you make them feel uncomfortable or bored during this shoot, you will have the reverse effect. Think of this session as a fun and funky fashion shoot, with your couple as the models. Choose a location that is dramatic, or somewhere that is special to the couple, and the experience will be amazing for you and for them.

Always try and build a story into your shoots, but don't tell the couple this, of course. The story helps to provide a flow to the range of images and physical animation of the couple, as well as a flow that progresses from one location to another. The series of images will include shots of the couple

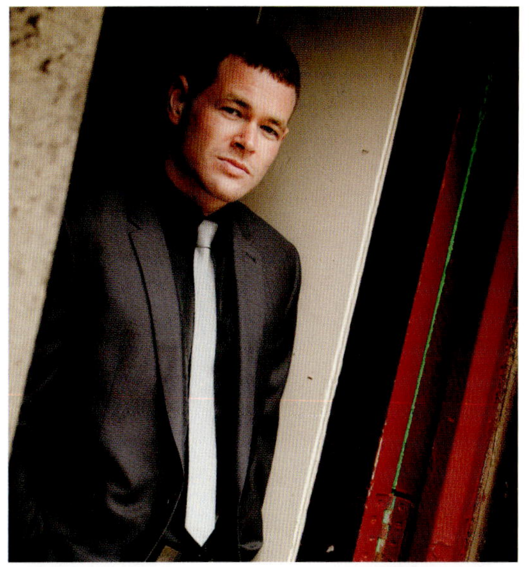

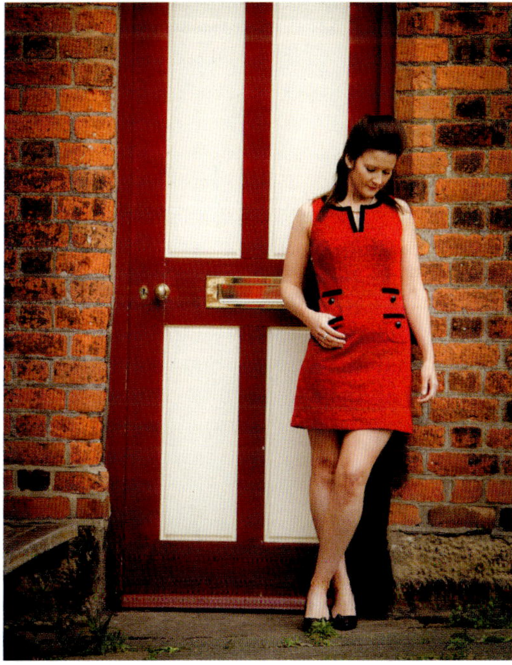

together as well as individual portraits of them in the scene and close-up. Variety is key to any session, so shoot with a variety of different crops, but also with dramatically different compositions, including more and less of the background. If you do this well, the couple—and their family—will not be able to resist purchasing them all in an album or montage collection.

Posing is obviously important, so you should explain to the couple during the session why you are getting them to animate their bodies in a certain way. By telling the couple that you're choosing certain foot positions to provide balance, and body turns to make them look slim, as well as head tilts to soften their poses, and hand positions to complement their stance, they will quickly understand what you're doing and the difference it all makes to the finished image.

All images: Engagement shoots should be relaxed and fun, and provide some shots of the couple with great expressions. At the same time, you should be able to rehearse potential poses and solve any body or facial issues the couple may be worried about.

The Wedding Day

There are some key elements that you need to know about weddings to ensure that the day runs smoothly, and there are some aspects you don't need to concern yourself with at all. One of your main considerations is to remember that time is precious on the day and you can only do as much as you plan for.

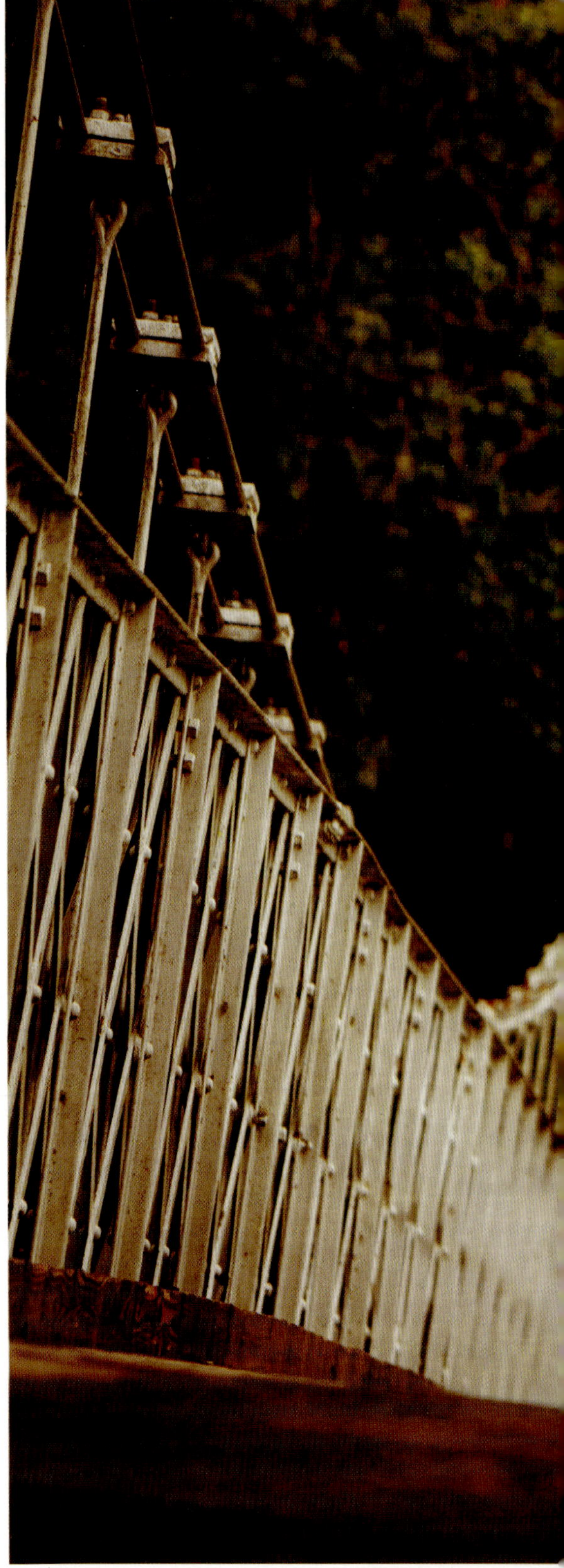

Right: Most wedding days follow a similar format. Once you have mastered this you will be making the most of your time with all the guests, particularly the happy couple.

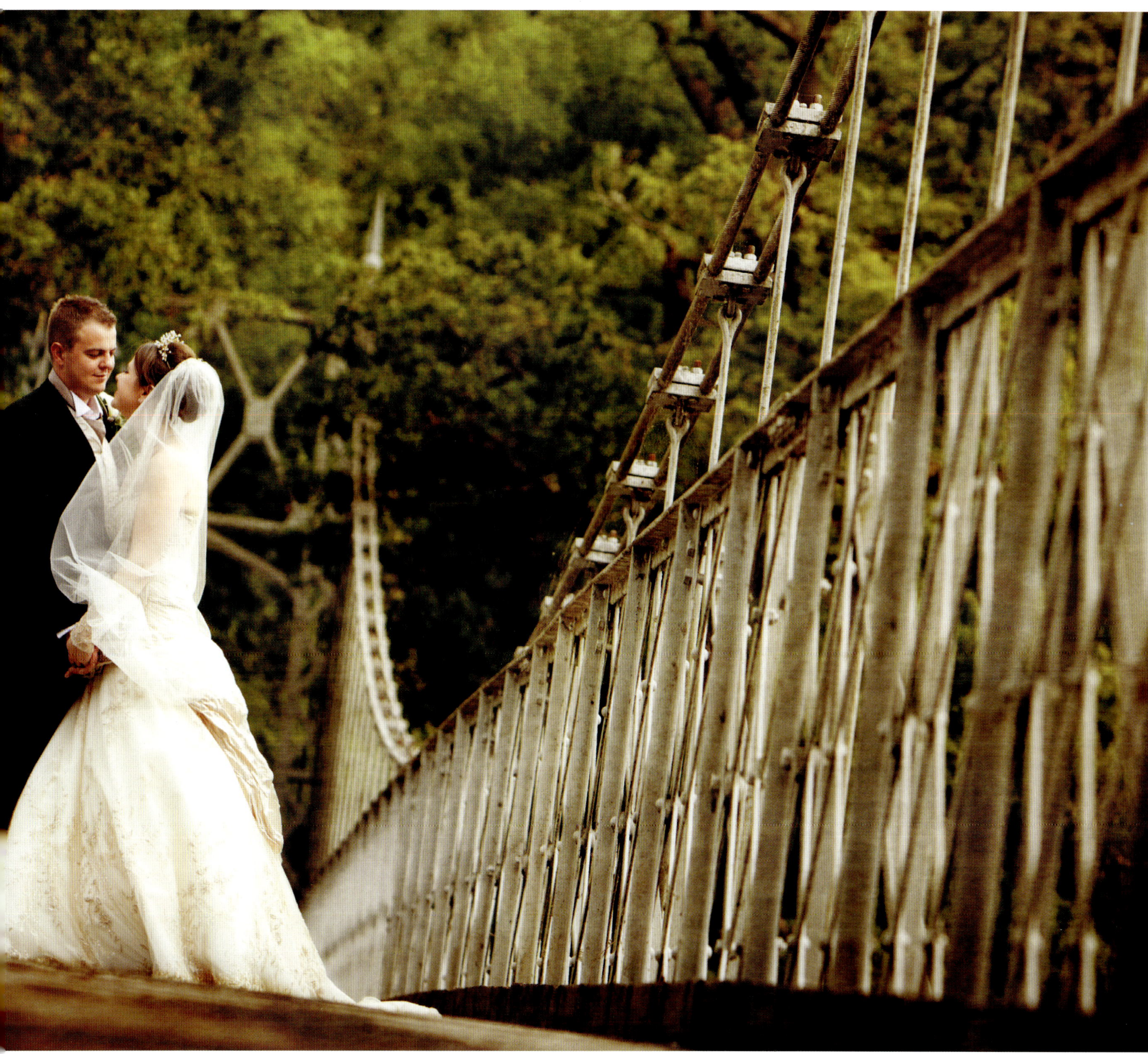

Shooting List

There are certain shots that the couple will ask you to provide. Over the following pages I have therefore provided a shooting list of the 48 shots you will usually be asked to provide, in the order in which they'll most likely be shot.

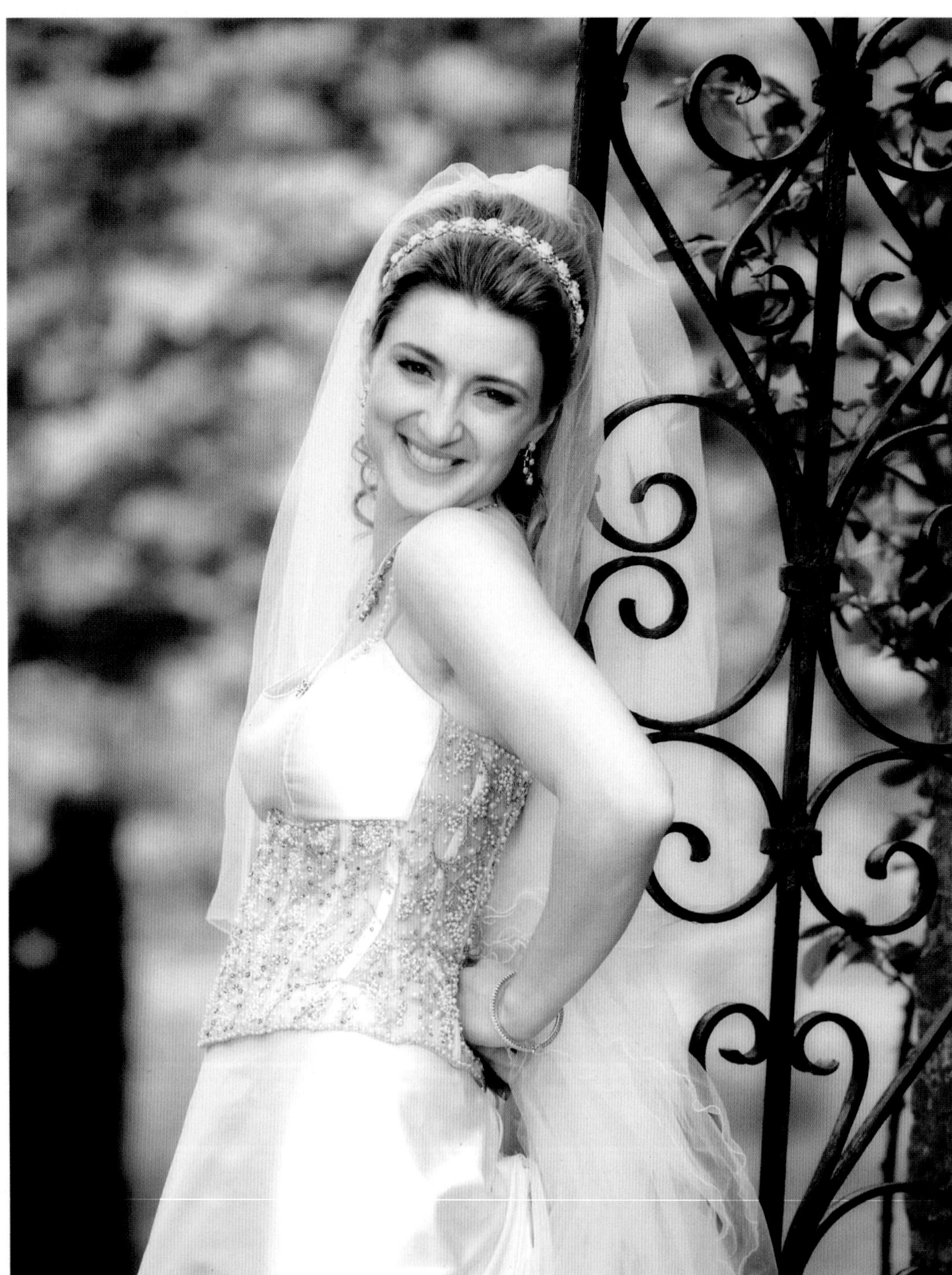

Right: Keep your kit to a minimum and know it inside and out. This means you will give yourself more time shooting fresh and dynamic images, and less time working the technology.

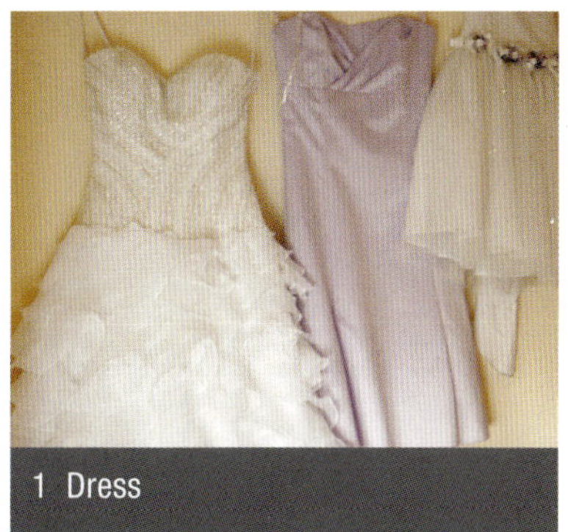

1 Dress

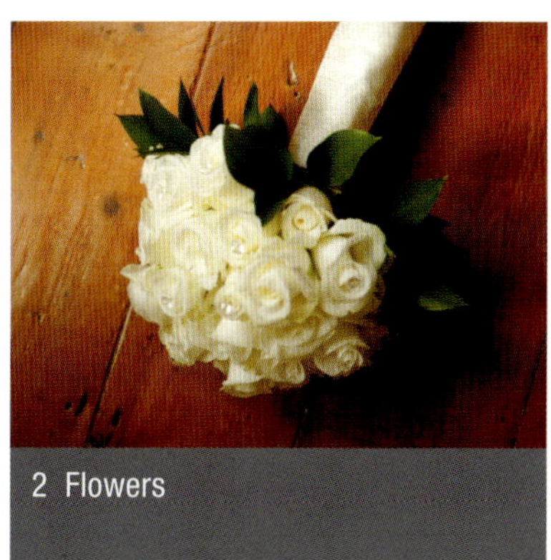

2 Flowers

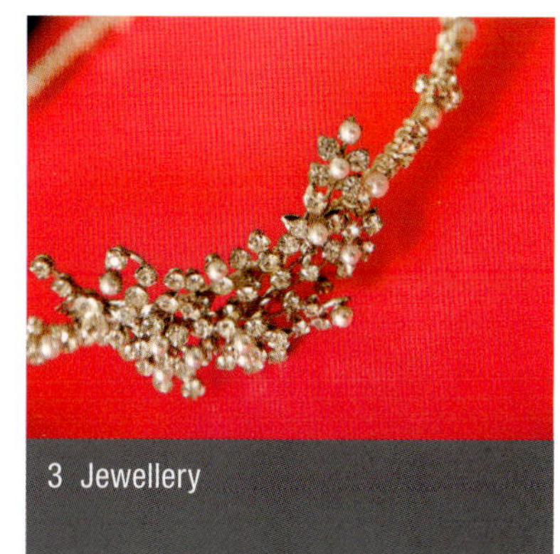

3 Jewellery

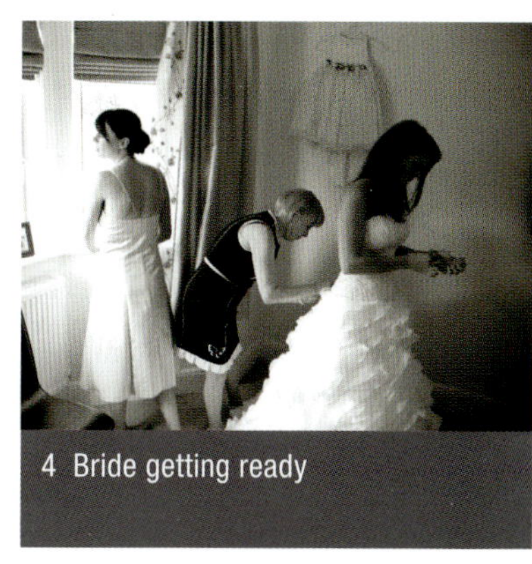

4 Bride getting ready

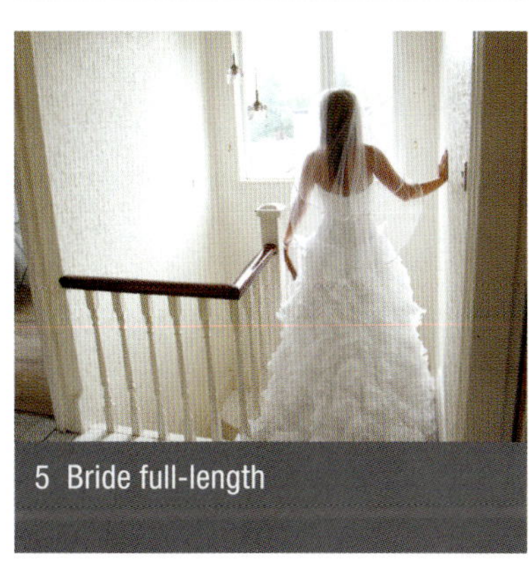

5 Bride full-length

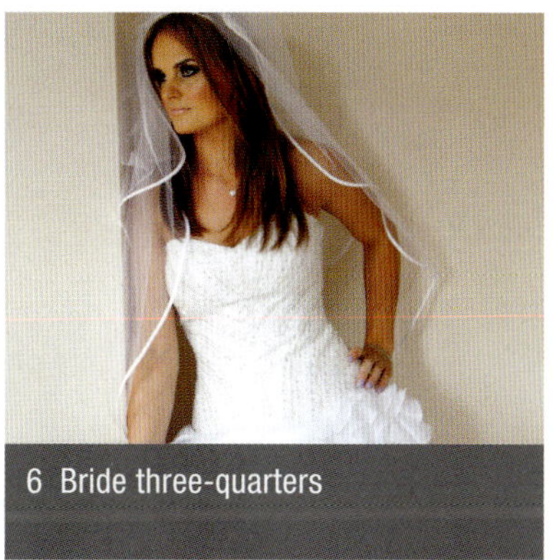

6 Bride three-quarters

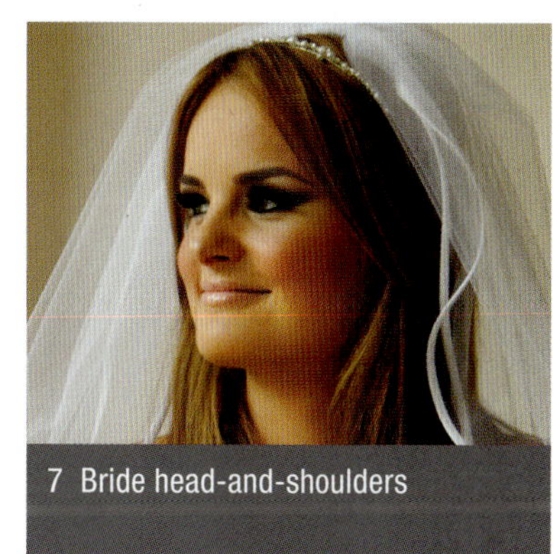

7 Bride head-and-shoulders

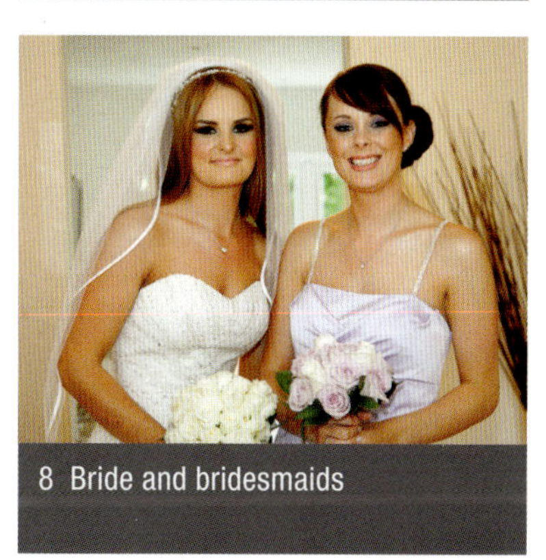

8 Bride and bridesmaids

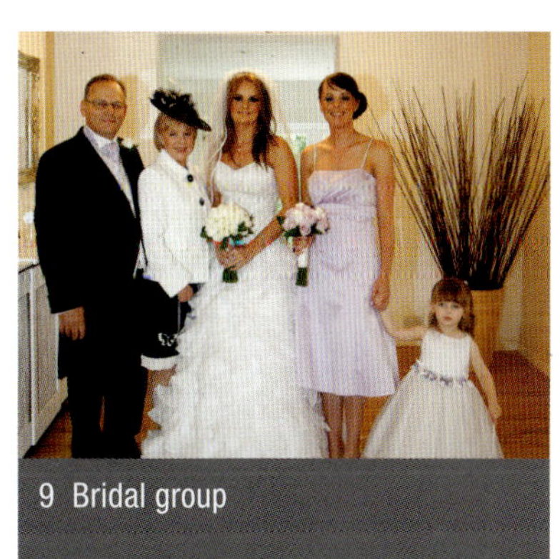

9 Bridal group

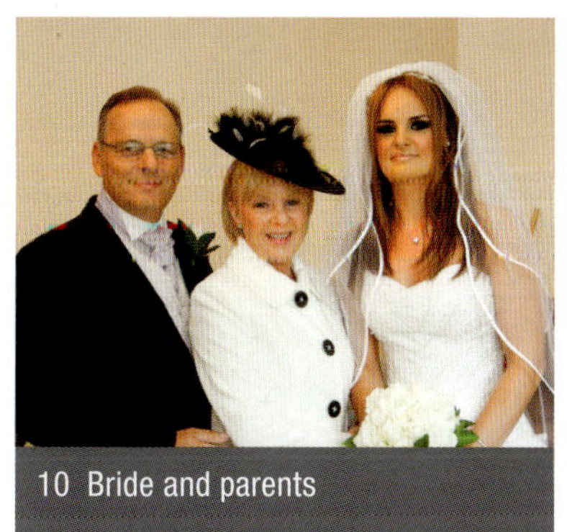

10 Bride and parents

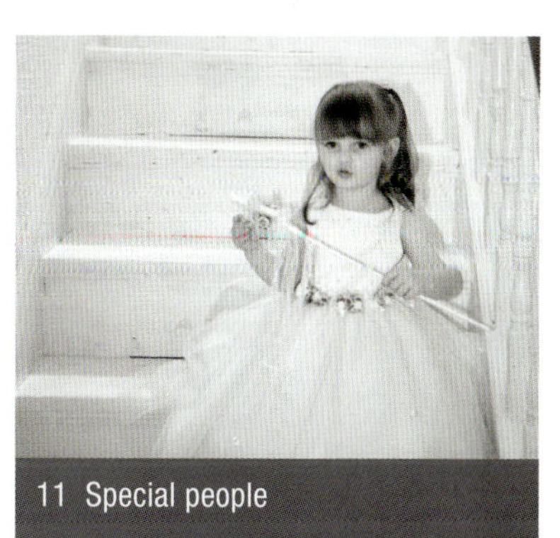

11 Special people

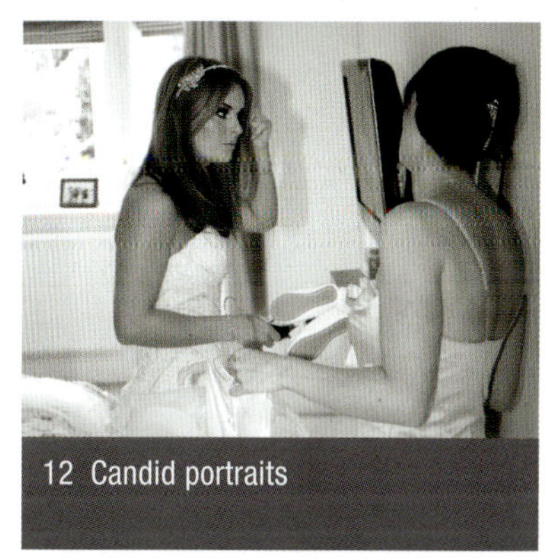

12 Candid portraits

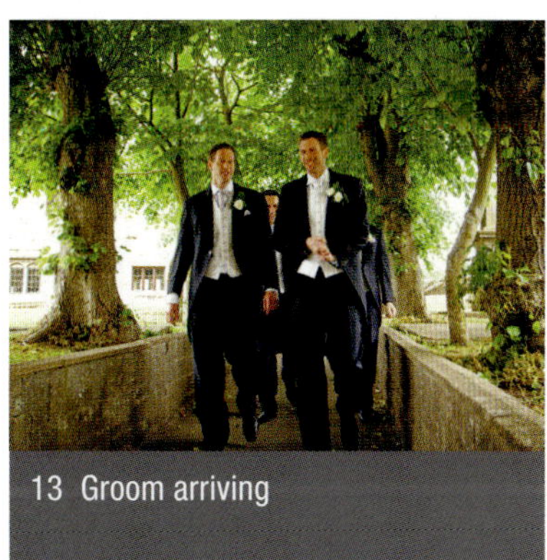

13 Groom arriving

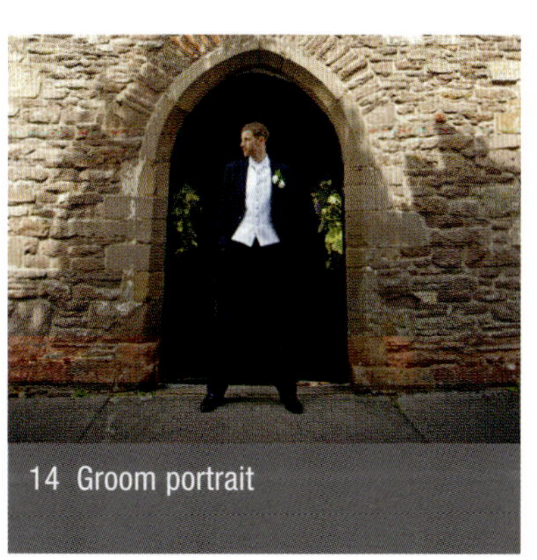

14 Groom portrait

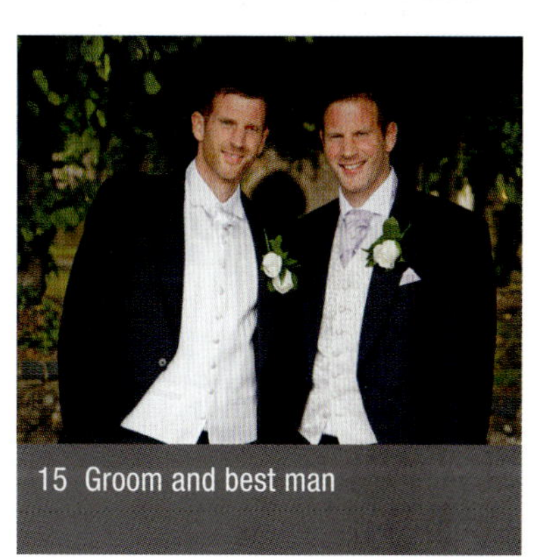

15 Groom and best man

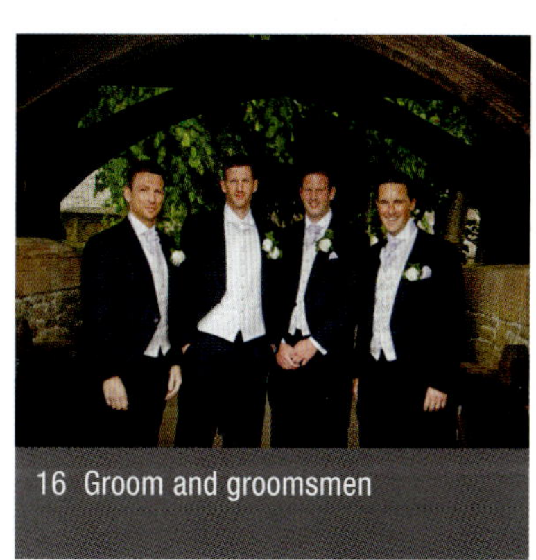

16 Groom and groomsmen

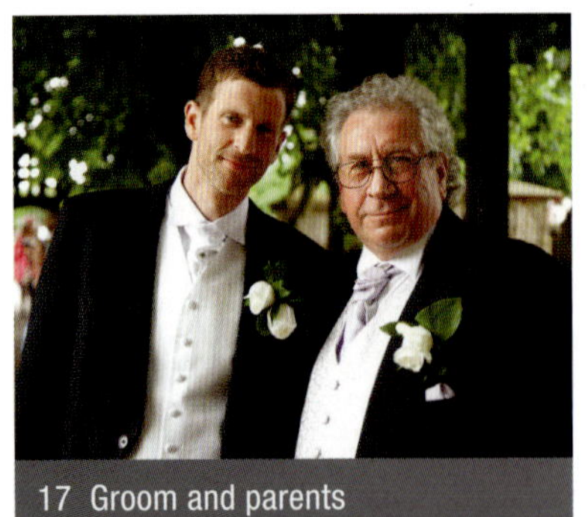

17 Groom and parents

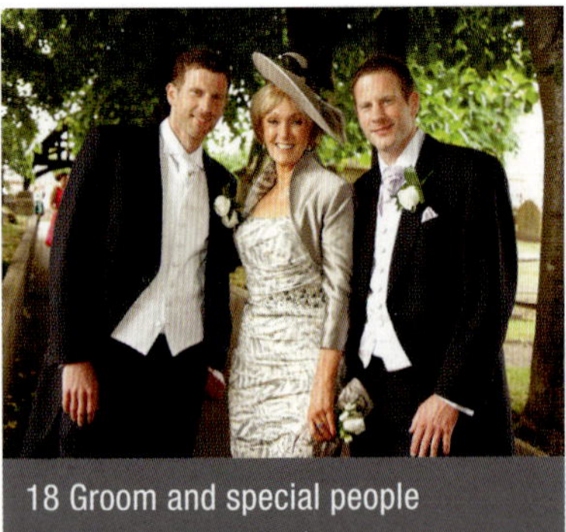

18 Groom and special people

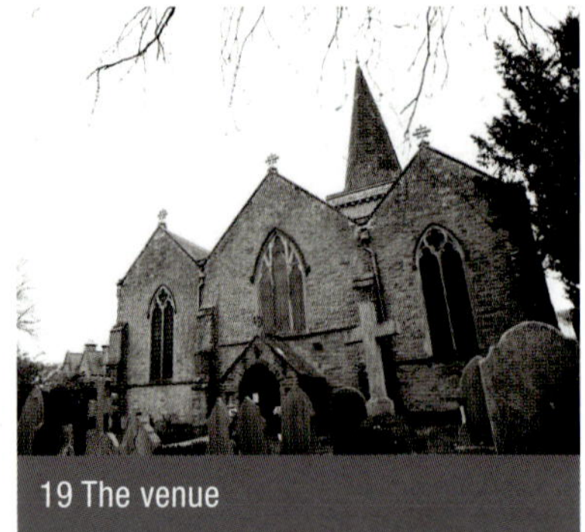

19 The venue

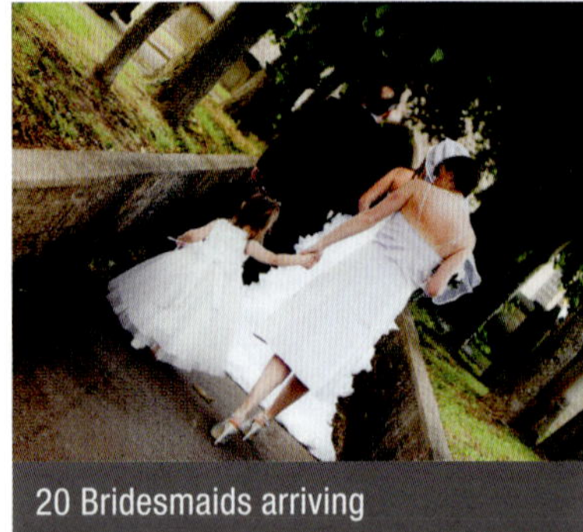

20 Bridesmaids arriving

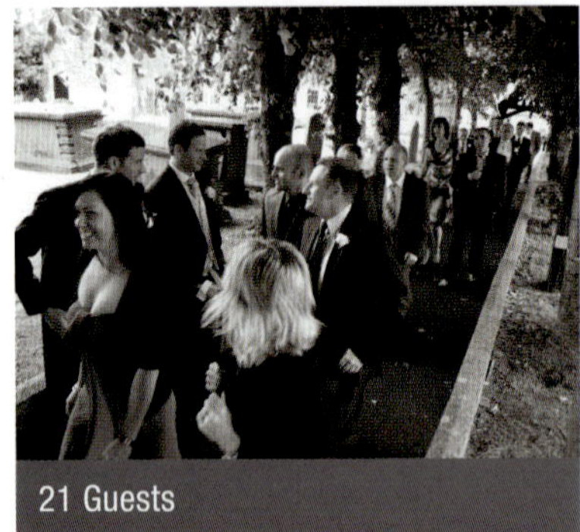

21 Guests

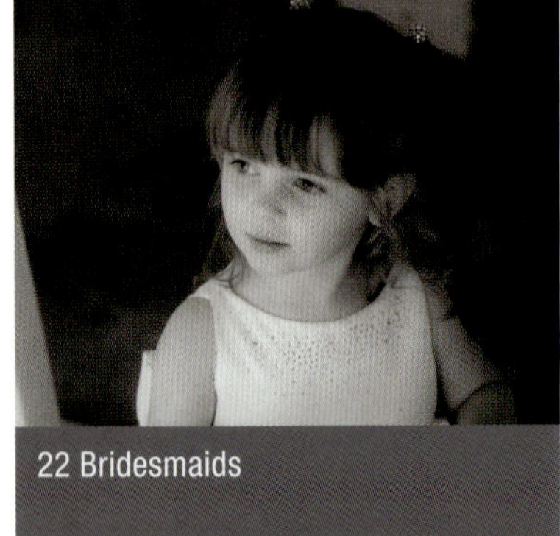

22 Bridesmaids

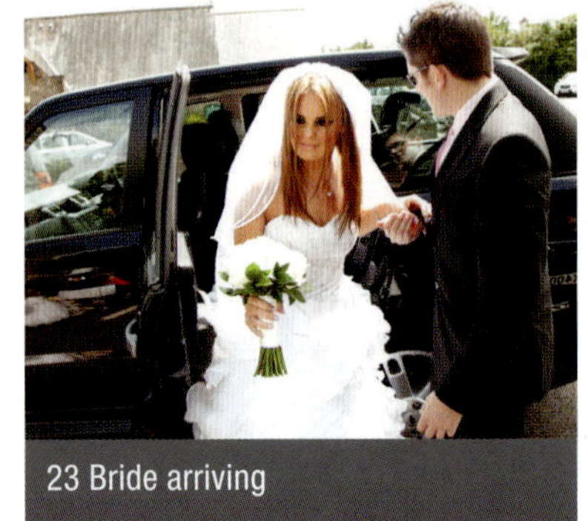

23 Bride arriving

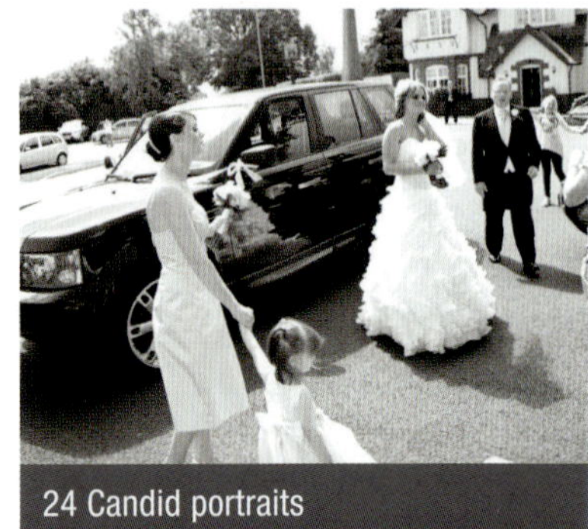

24 Candid portraits

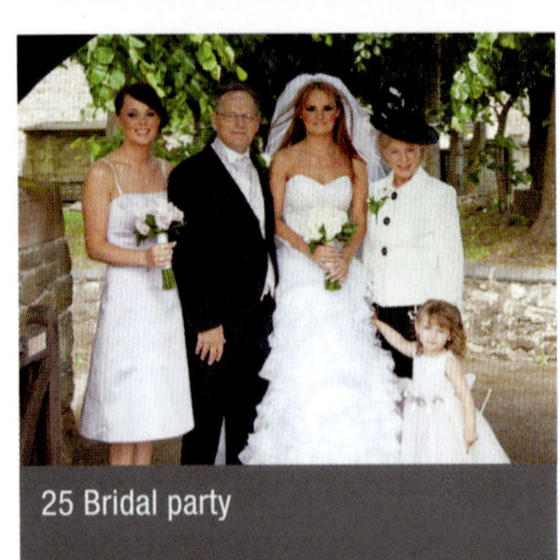

25 Bridal party

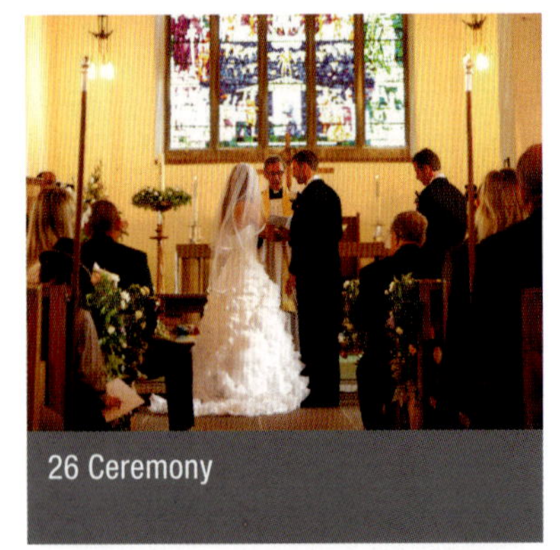

26 Ceremony

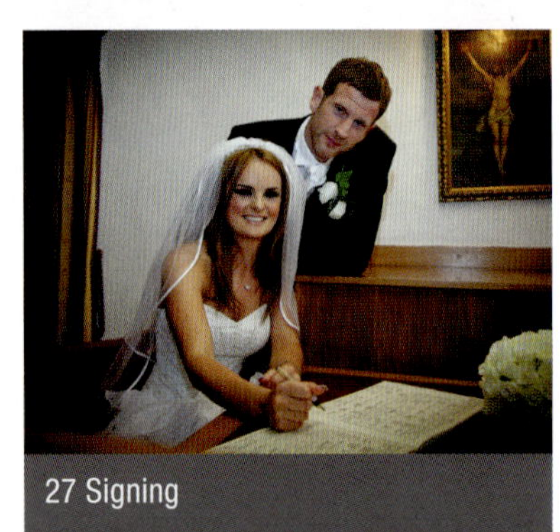

27 Signing

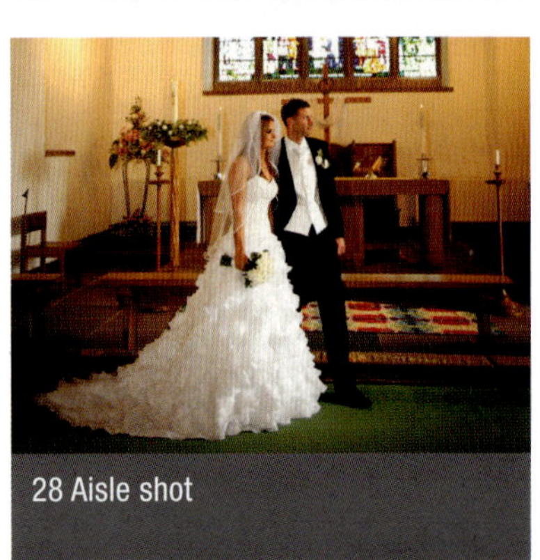

28 Aisle shot

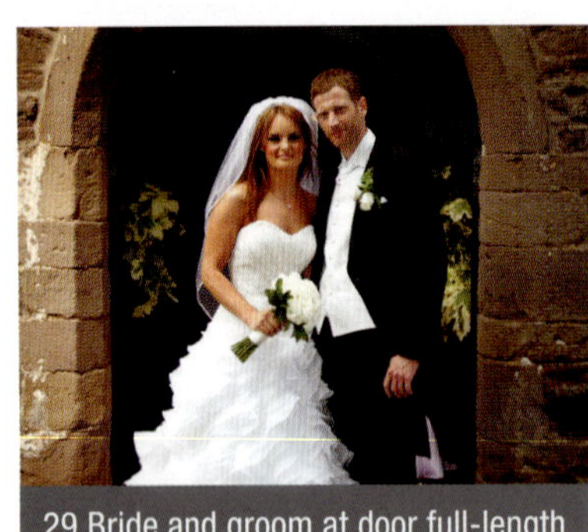

29 Bride and groom at door full-length

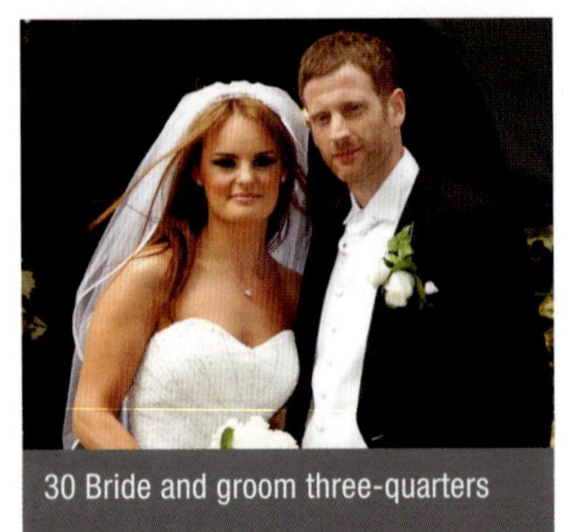

30 Bride and groom three-quarters

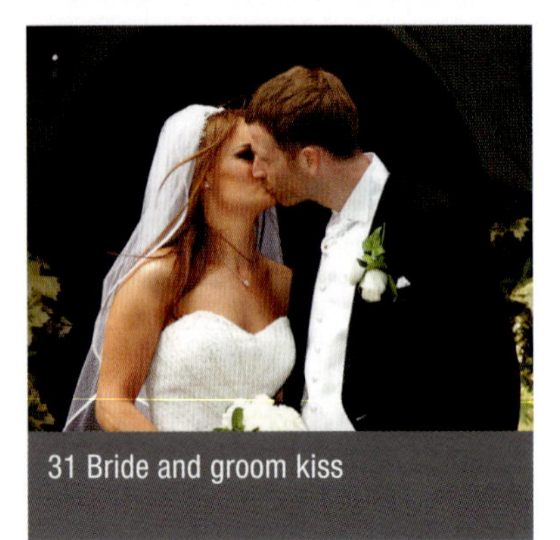

31 Bride and groom kiss

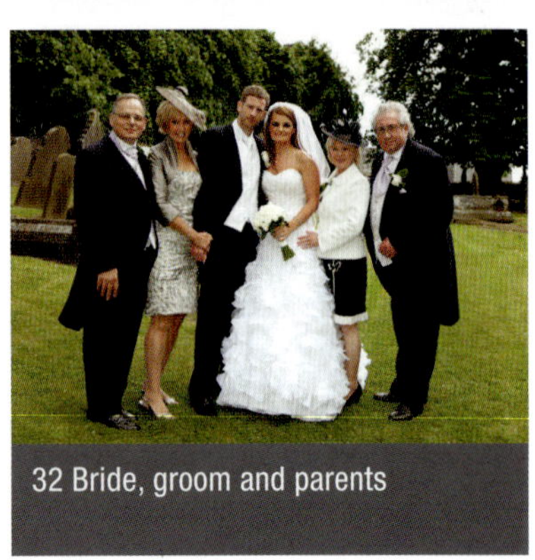

32 Bride, groom and parents

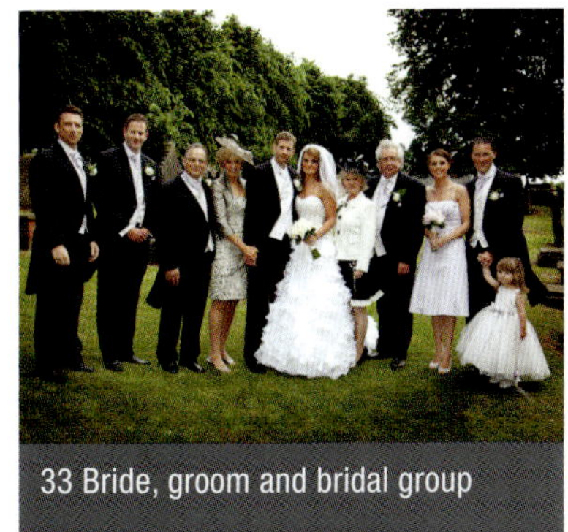

33 Bride, groom and bridal group

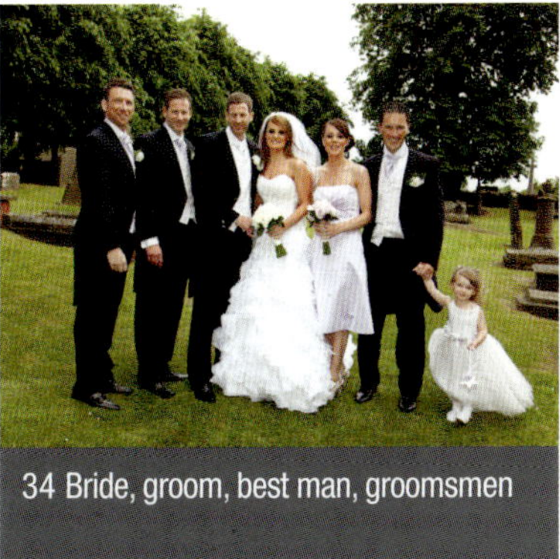

34 Bride, groom, best man, groomsmen

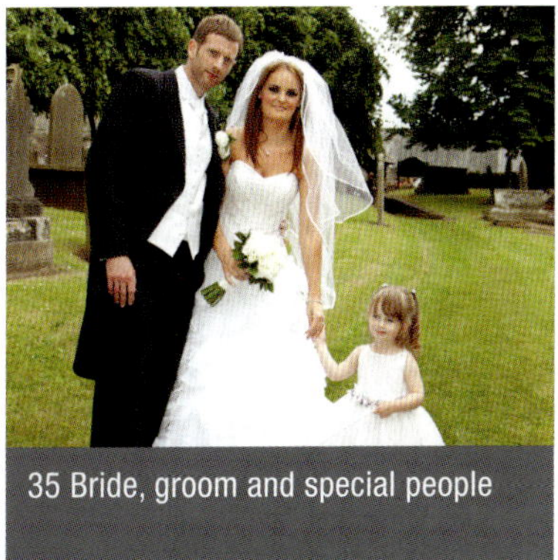

35 Bride, groom and special people

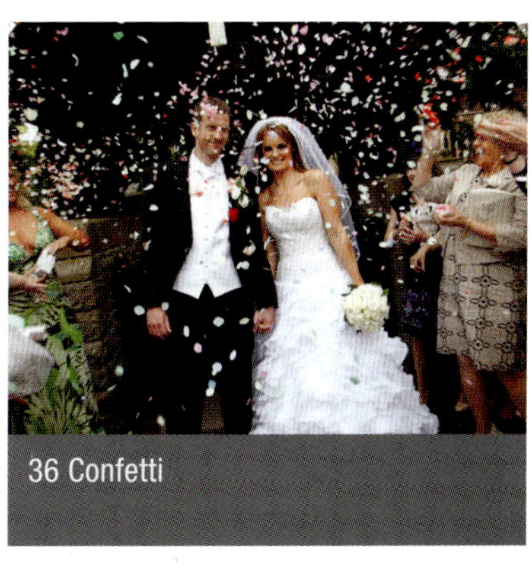

36 Confetti

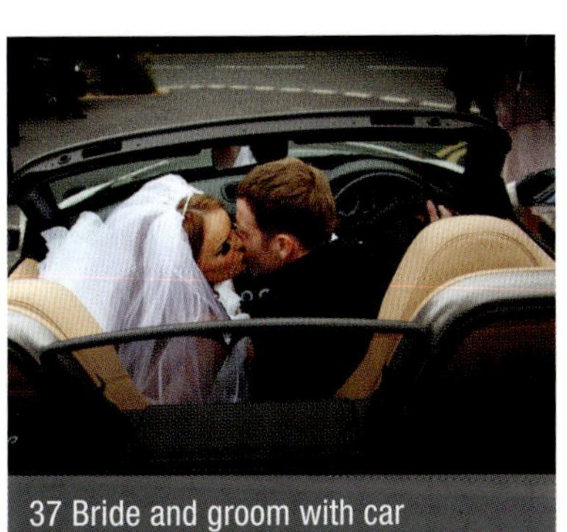

37 Bride and groom with car

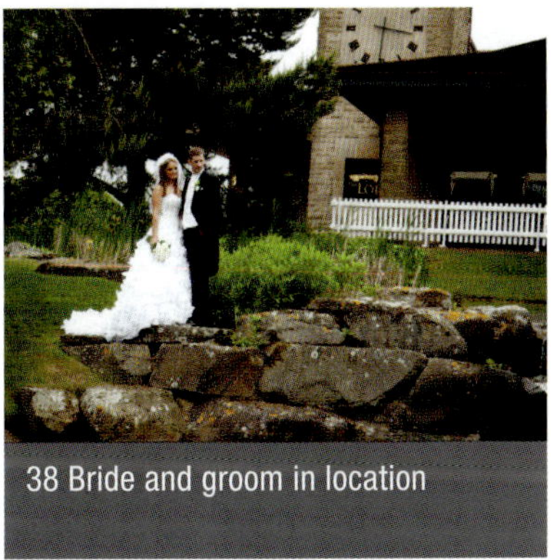

38 Bride and groom in location

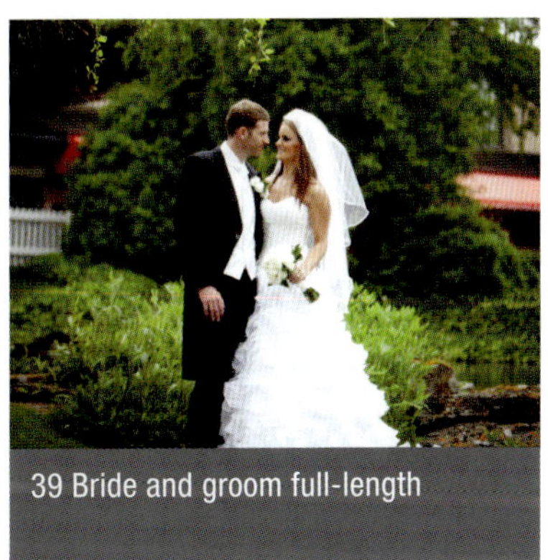

39 Bride and groom full-length

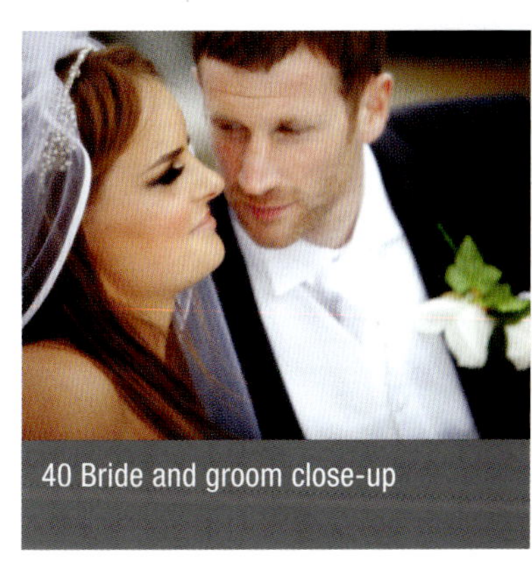

40 Bride and groom close-up

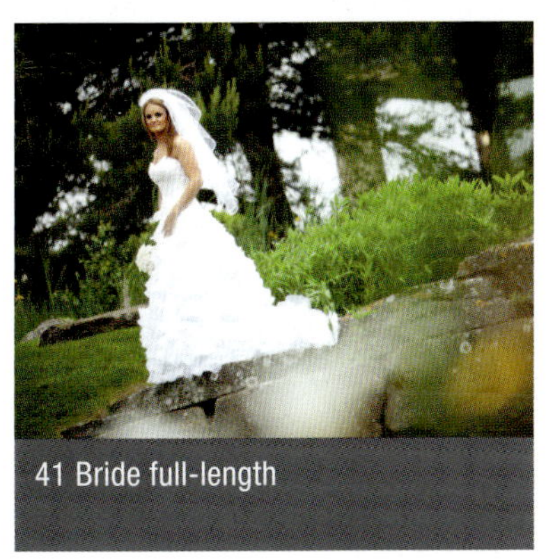

41 Bride full-length

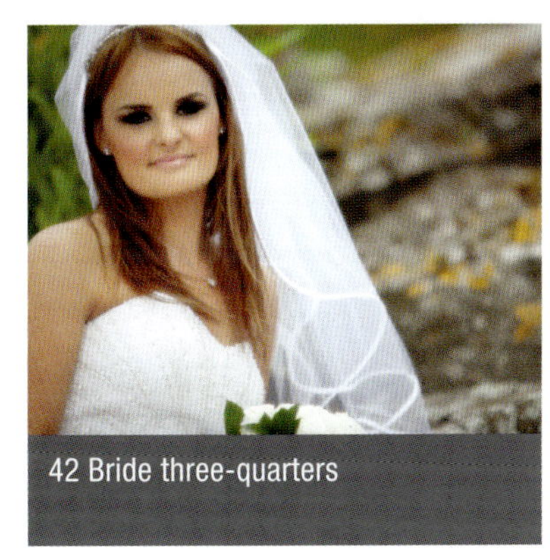

42 Bride three-quarters

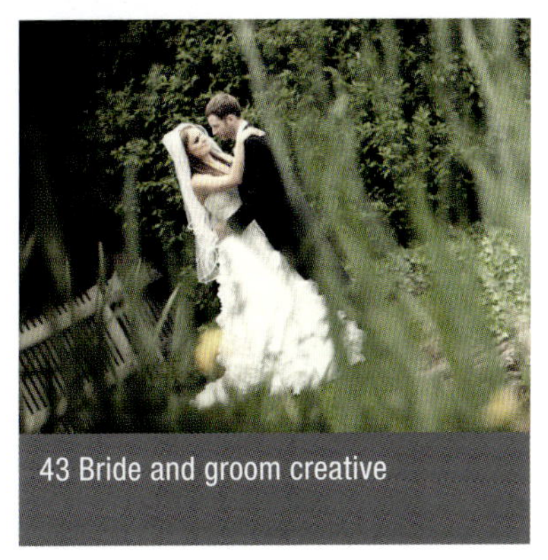

43 Bride and groom creative

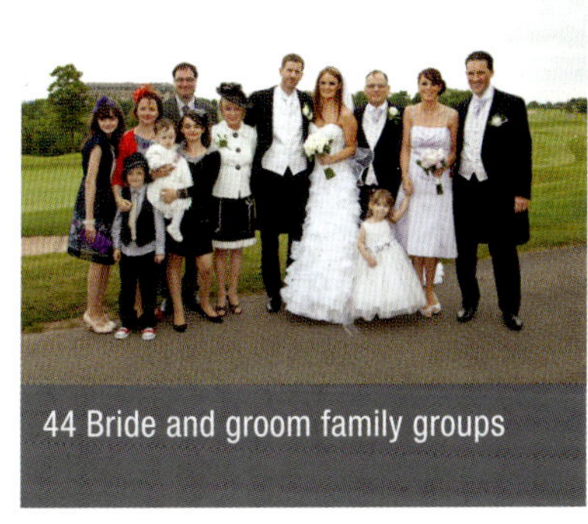

44 Bride and groom family groups

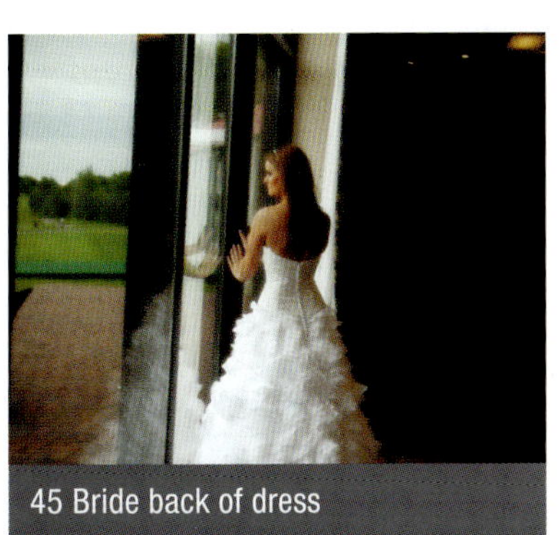

45 Bride back of dress

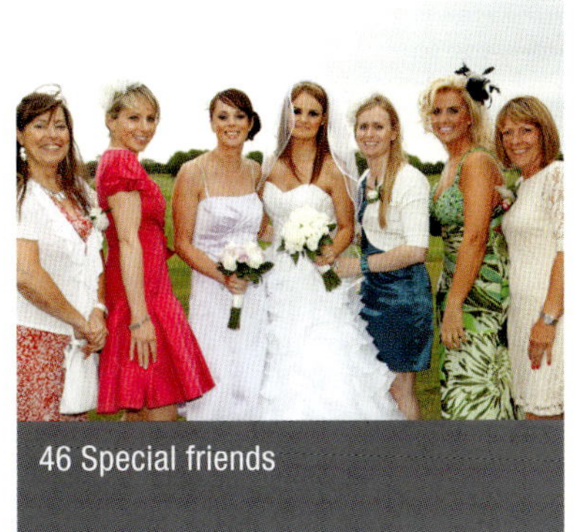

46 Special friends

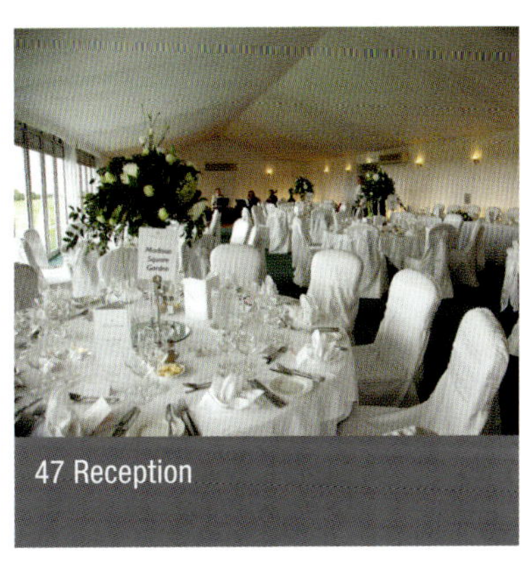

47 Reception

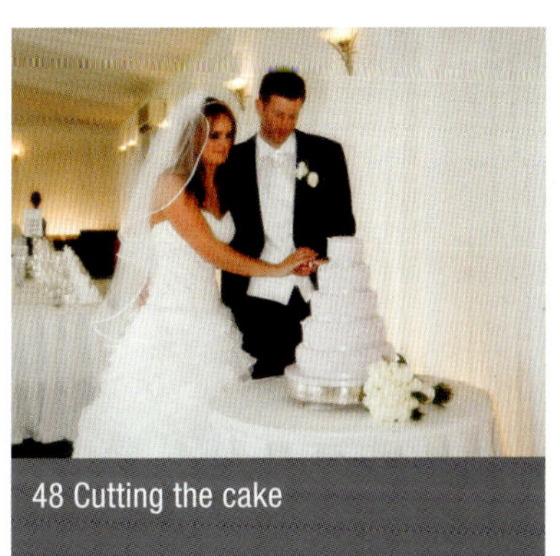

48 Cutting the cake

Key Moments

10.00 Atmosphere

When you first arrive at the bride's house, or wherever she is getting ready, you will more often than not find that already nothing is running to time, and the bridal party is still in hair and makeup. In fact, this is a good thing as it lends itself to some great candid moments.

Capturing the atmosphere is a great way to start the day off. Stand back, watch, and shoot the scene, all the time looking for interesting elements such as flowers arriving, champagne being opened, bridesmaids having tantrums, as well as all the fun and the laughter that always happens at this time.

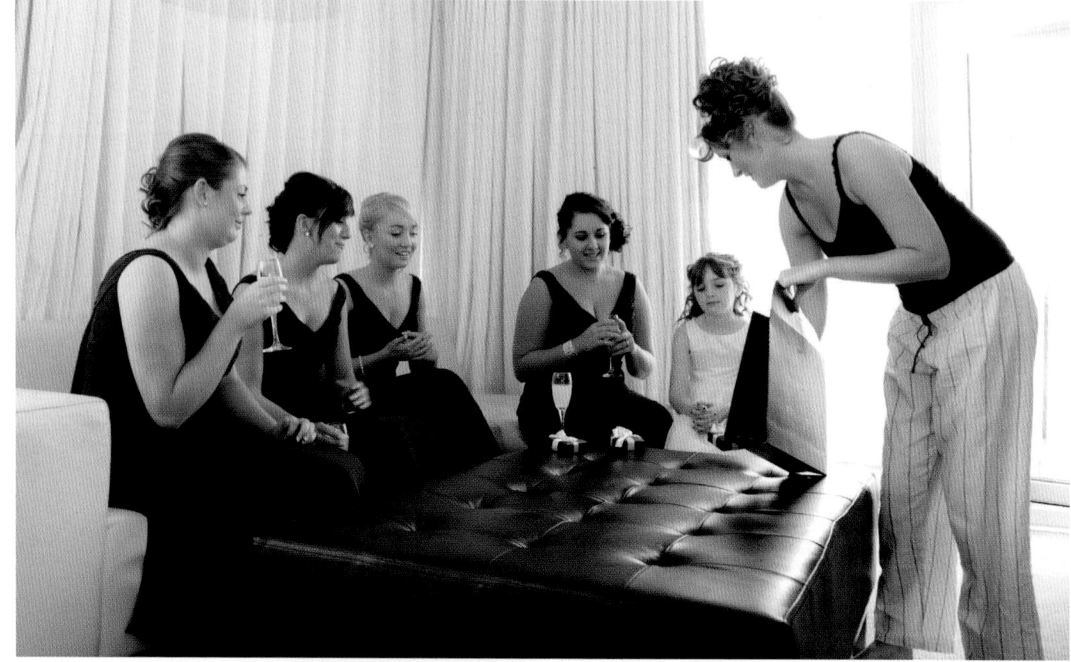

Right: It is traditional for a bride to present her bridesmaids with a token of thanks, which is often jewelry to wear at the wedding. The presentation makes a nice series of images in the album.

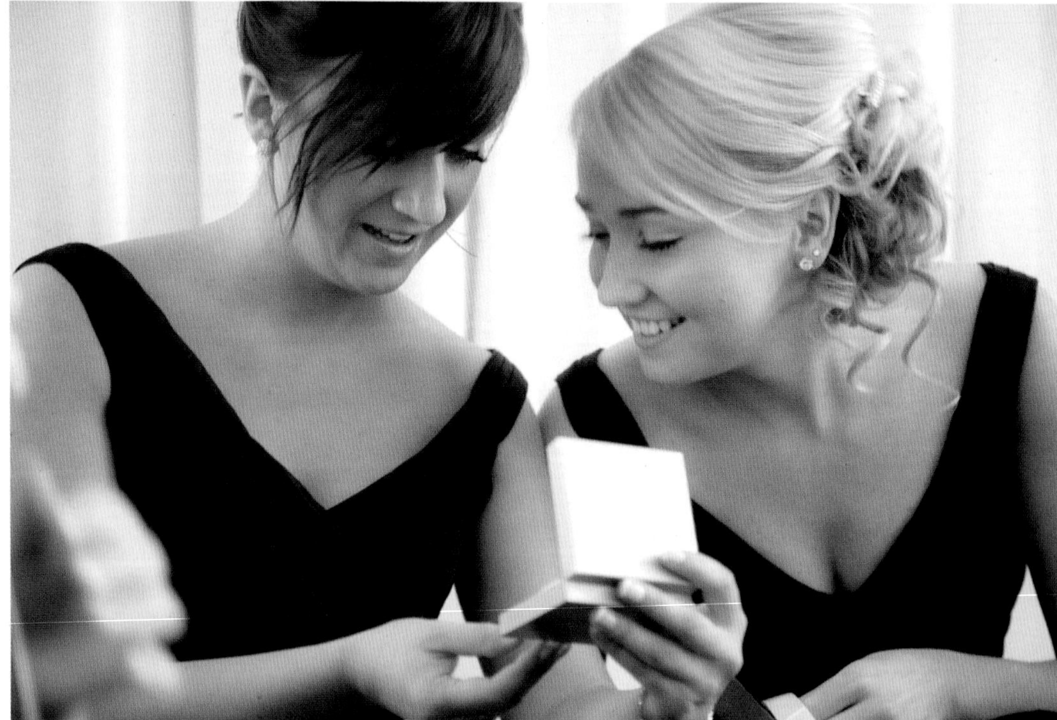

Tip

Use a wide-angle lens to show the scene and a medium telephoto lens, or even a standard 50mm lens, for detail shots with shallow depth of field.

10.15 Details

Filling time is something that happens quite a lot at this stage of the wedding preparation. Shooting a variety of details will not only keep you busy, but will also provide a good range of images for the album to show off all the thought and planning that go into making the day special.

Objects for you to look out for include: flowers, shoes, jewelry, cards, dresses, favors, presents, makeup, perfume, speeches, orders of service, invitations, reply cards, as well as any gift that might be from the parents or groom.

Right: A wardrobe or rail is usually a good place to hang the dress so that it can be displayed at full length, but always look for some natural light from a window to illuminate it and show its texture and details. Failing that, bounce flash off a wall or mirror.

Far right: Shooting the bottle of perfume that the bride will be wearing, as well as the manicure and engagement ring, is a great way to combine several important details. Use backlighting to shine through the liquid and create a simple advertising-style shot.

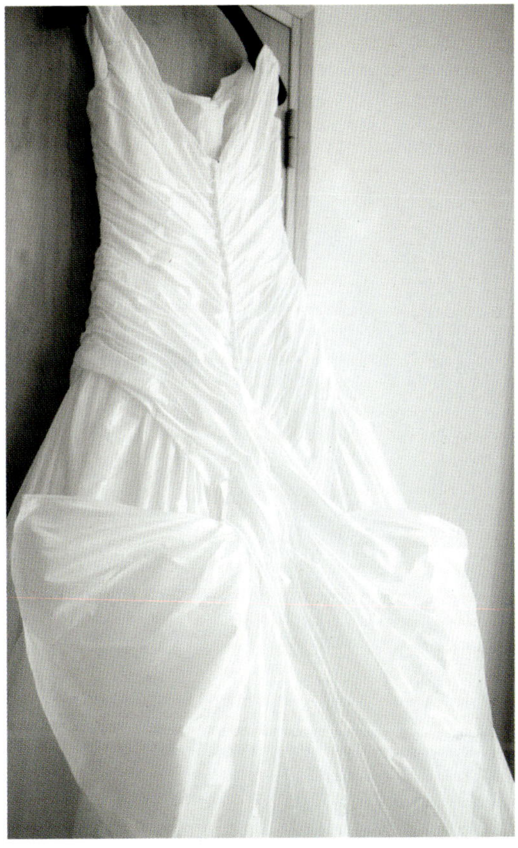

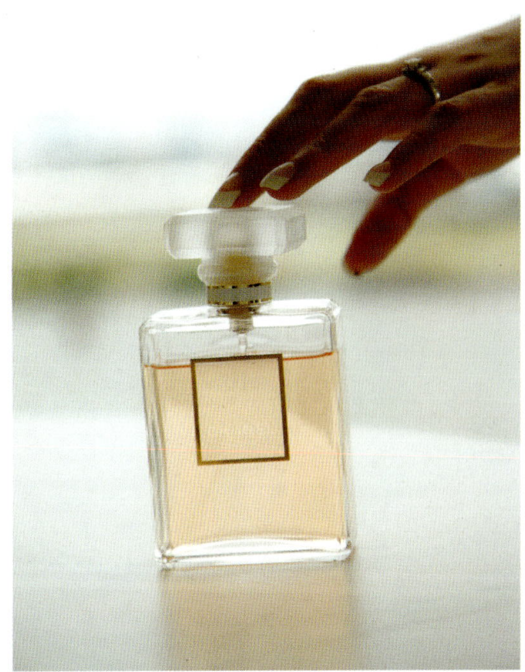

Right: Try to not just repeat the same shot wedding after wedding. Here I used the background scene in the distance as a secondary point of interest, while keeping the focus on the shoes.

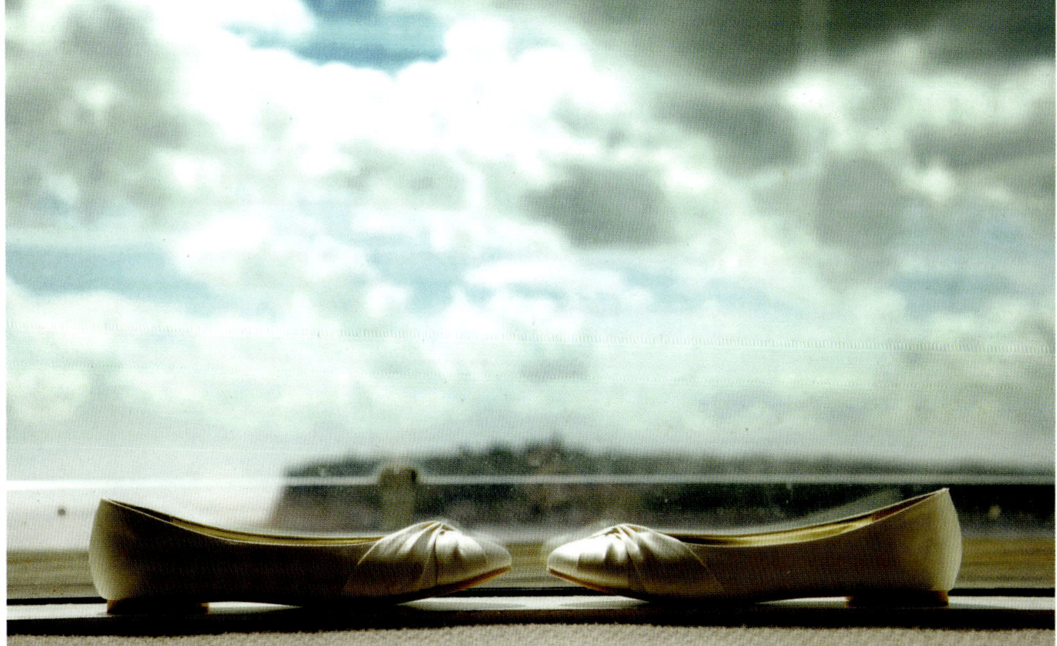

10.30 Getting ready

It is usually a good idea to arrive at the ceremony location about 30–45 minutes before the start of the wedding service, so your preferred time to leave for the church must be discussed with the couple beforehand—then remind the party on the morning, and keep it in your mind all the time! Never be afraid to give the wedding party a little verbal nudge, but don't get hung up on it or you will start to irritate them a little—remember that it is the bride's day, not yours.

If you have not shot the wedding dress by itself by now it is probably going to be too late, so use the final preparations to shoot fastening the dress, finessing jewelry, and other details to set the scene—simple shots of the hair, dress details, and portraits and expressions of the family and wedding party. Try to opt for shots other than the basics, searching them out all the time—for instance, shooting through doorways and using mirrors to frame an image. Remember, as soon as you feel you have the shots you need, leave the room and search for other interesting subjects and details, including the bridesmaids, or even the family pet!

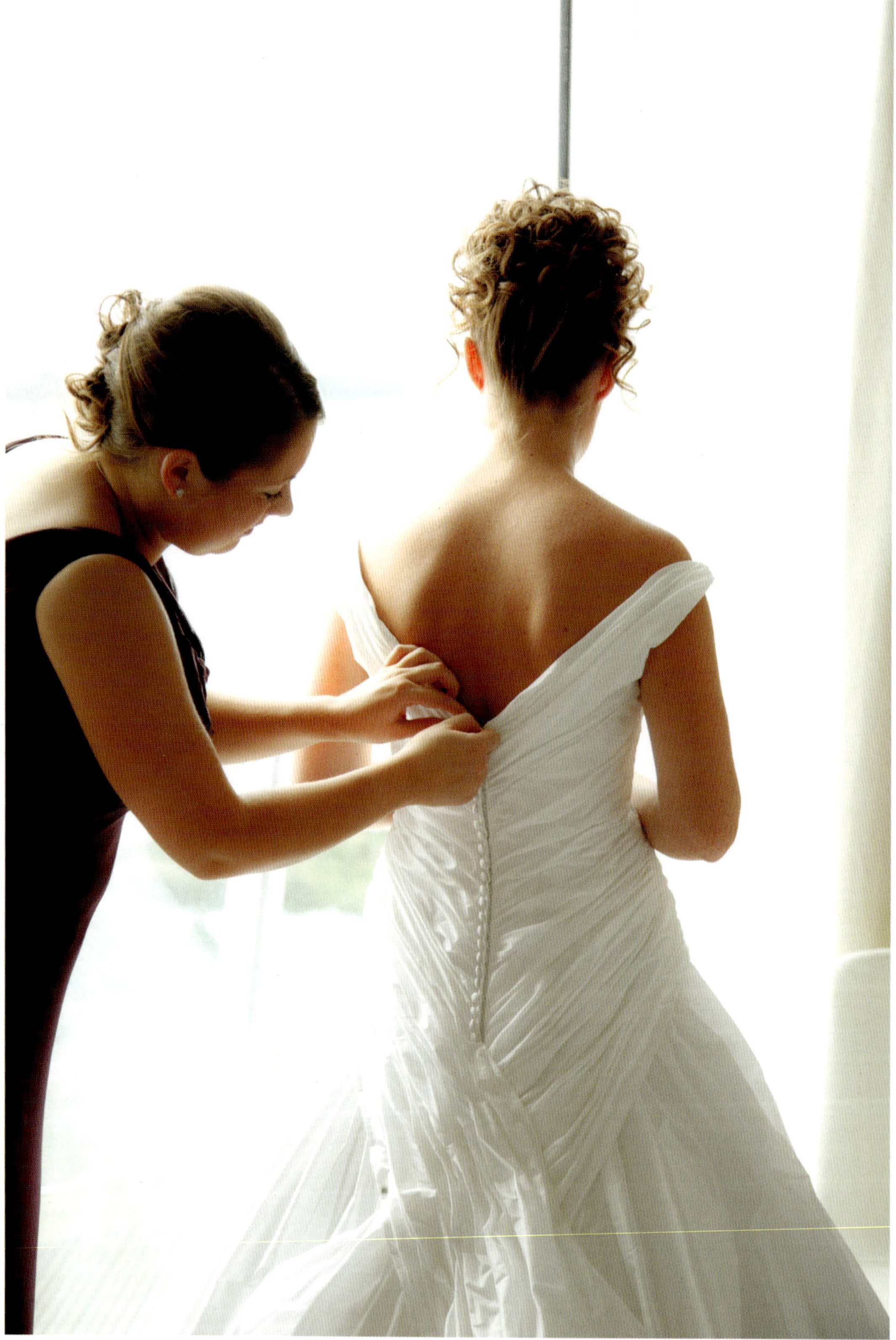

Right: A shot of the bride having her dress fastened is an ideal detail to capture her getting ready.

10.50 Bridal portraits

If all is going to plan, the bride will be ready first. If not, shoot the bridesmaids if they are ready, as the more images you can tick off your shoot list early on in the day, the more time you will gain for later. Decide in advance where to photograph the bride, usually in the room with the biggest window and a nice backdrop. A big, bright room will allow you to use just natural light in the image, whereas a small, dark room may need some bounce flash for the less dramatic images that will sell well.

Remember that time is not going to be on your side from here on, as there will probably be lots of small, intimate family groups, as well as the bridesmaids to contend with, so be as efficient and in control of your time and subjects as possible to maximize your workflow. Most of these images will be shot using the 24–105mm lens, as it's perfect as both a telephoto and wide-angle for small rooms and family groups.

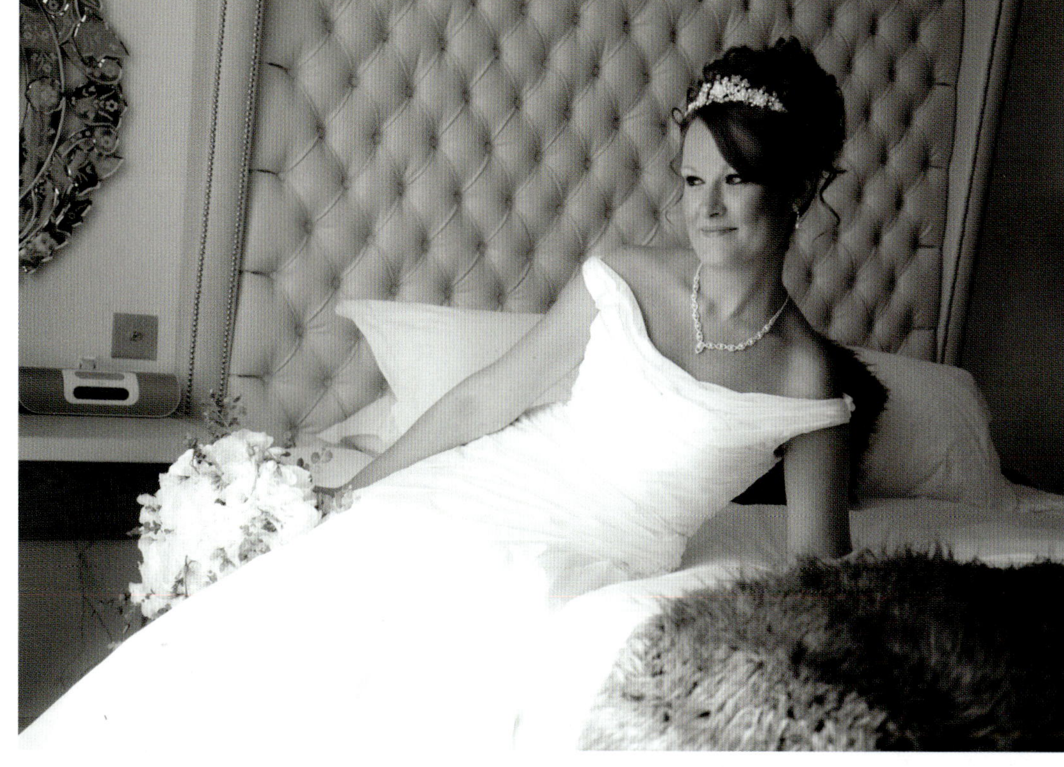

Top right: Shooting variety is key, so as well as the simple three-quarter shot by the window, I also shoot the bride sitting on the bed, to add not only variety, but also a different quality of light.

Right: In a small room a full length image can be difficult to shoot, especially if you want to use a specific window, as in this image. To avoid using any flash ask the bride to look towards the light source—this avoids a bleached out window due to exposure, as well as flat lighting on the face if she looked at the camera.

Far right: To complete the series of images, always shoot a variety of headshots, one looking at camera, one looking down, and one looking away. Not only does this type of flow give variety, but it also safeguards against blinks and unflattering expressions.

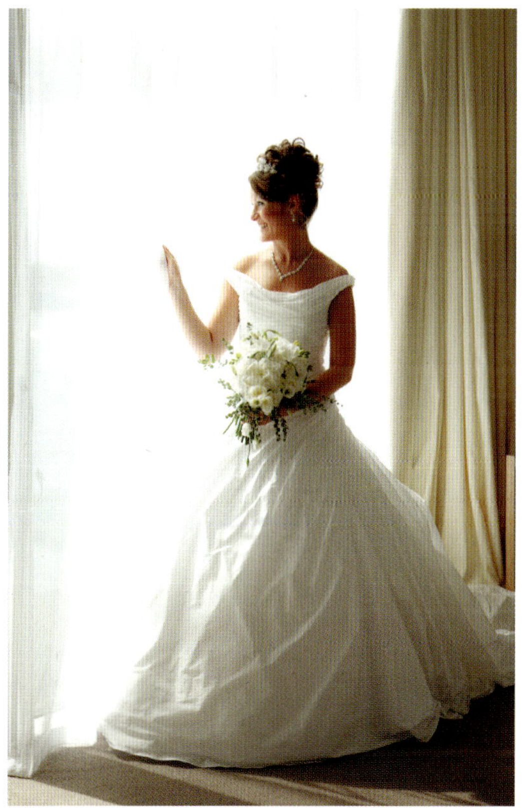

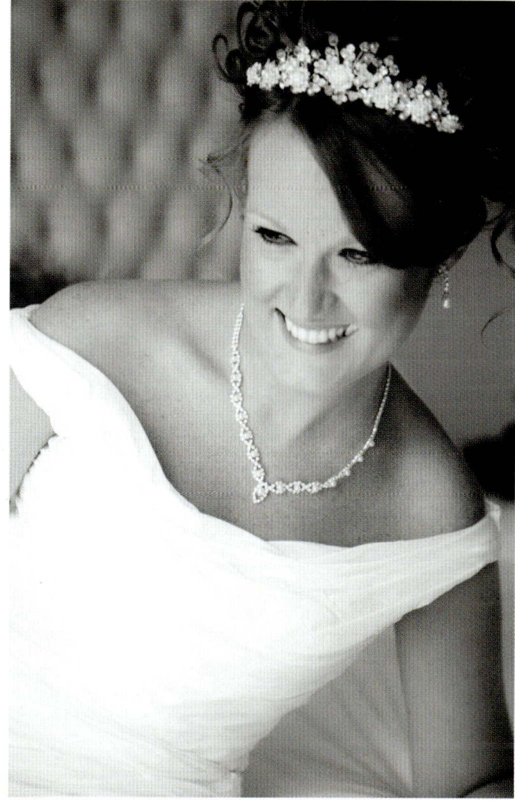

11.00 Bride & bridesmaids

By shooting some of the bridal groups at the
house, especially if it has a nice interior or gardens,
you can really save yourself a lot of time later on,
as well as adding an extra selection to choose
from. The other benefit of shooting some of the
bride and bridesmaids shots at this time is to make
sure that they are all immaculate. This is especially
important when little bridesmaids are involved, as
they soon become fed up with hanging around,
or get overexcited and start to rebel, removing
their headdresses, having tantrums, and generally
getting the house in a state of chaos.

Use as much natural light as you can, which
warms the scene and is quicker than fiddling with
flash anyway. By positioning yourself near a big
window and shooting back into the room, a little
of each subject will be evenly illuminated, allowing
you to concentrate on pose and expression. The
flash unit might have to be switched on at this
stage to fill in the shadow detail as the group
gets bigger and bigger. I usually use the flash
in the bounce position and set at TTL -2/3 or
-1 exposure compensation, depending on the
ambient light in the scene.

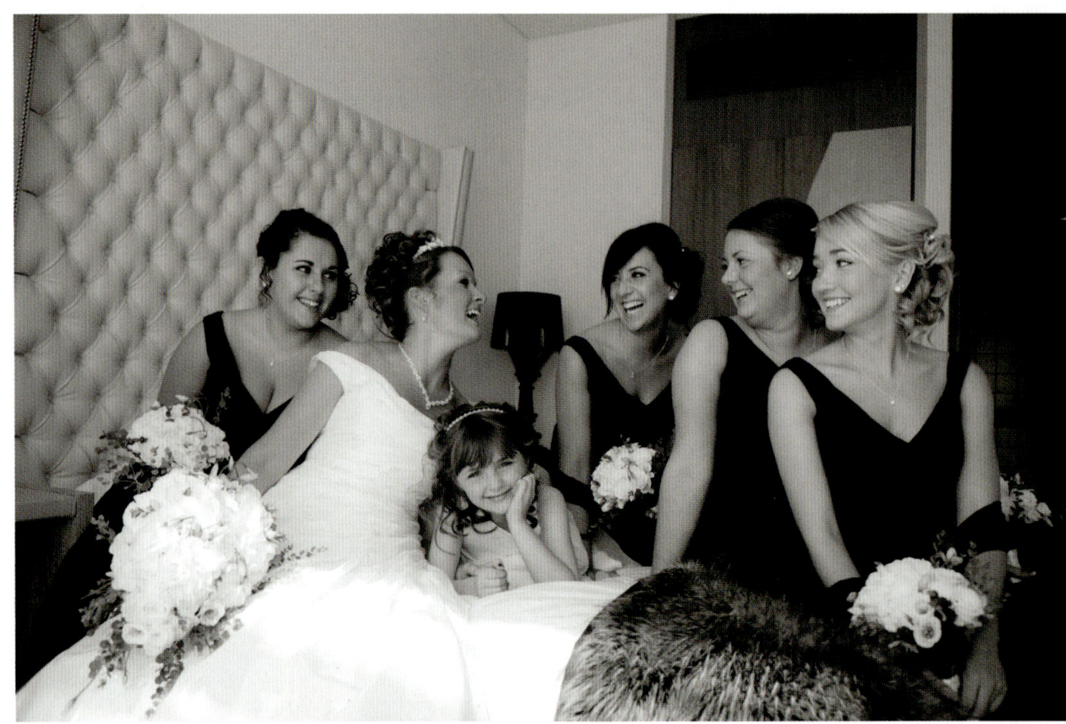

Above: Always try to shoot a few images of the
girls together at home, as it can start the fun
banter. Shooting a variety of images at this stage
will be useful, as the bridesmaids may have had
enough photography later on, and it will get harder
to convince them to pose for a few more shots.

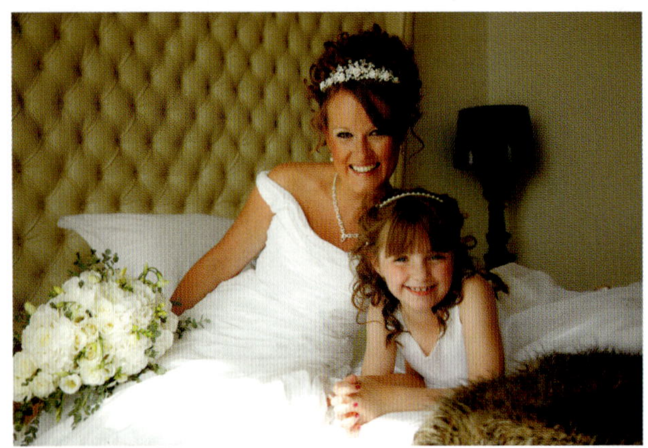

Left: Shoot the bride with each of her
bridesmaids if possible, as it is a special memory
for each of them, plus it's great for sales.

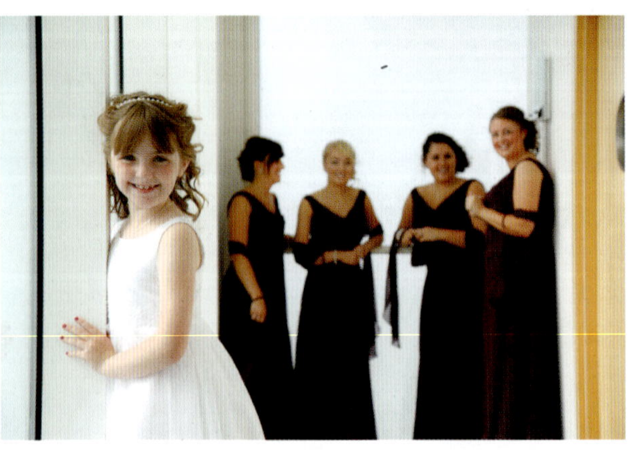

Left: If you can use the natural light on your
subjects as well as the scene, you will be able
to shoot more varied images more quickly. For
this series of images each bridesmaid was
picked out in turn and featured in a slightly
different way, using the rest of the girls as
added interest in the background.

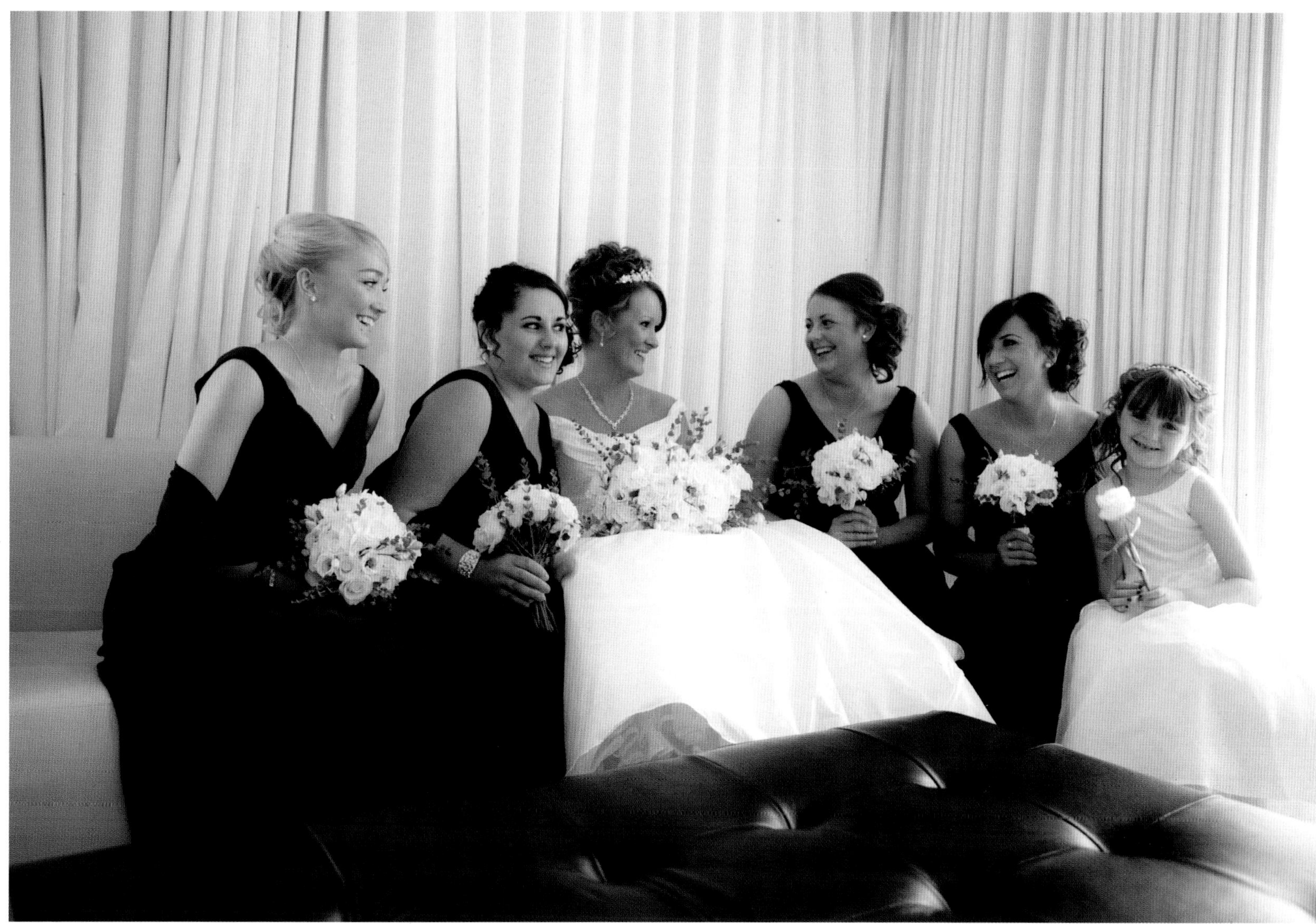

11.05 Bridal groups

Using the same quality and direction of light that you have just used to photograph the bride and the bridesmaids' portraits, you can now add more and more people into the group, without having to change location—unless, of course, there are a lot of family and bridesmaids to be included.

I prefer to use great backgrounds with the best light and, if possible, I shoot all the groups in the same location. However, if there is a reverse angle, I will try and add some changes of location for variety, but it all depends on how much time we have.

You may hate posing groups, but once you get into a flow—using a list of requested images to call people in and out of the shot—the time will fly by with very little stress.

Tip

Use natural light wherever possible, with flash to lighten the shadow areas. Only use flash for lighting the whole scene, dominating the ambient lighting, if you have no other choice.

Above: When I am shooting groups I tend to use a touch of fill-in flash to brighten the faces, but only when the subjects are looking at the camera, as I need to correct the lighting on the face. In this image, because of the high-key scene, I used a touch of fill-in flash when the subjects were looking away, as I felt darker faces would look odd in the very light room and background.

11.15 Leaving the house

Just before you leave the house, check your shoot list and make sure you have completed all that was required. It is so important that you get what you went to shoot, otherwise you will be kicking yourself on the way to the ceremony. Even if the bride has not asked for parent groups I always shoot them anyway, as they are good sellers and act as a backup to the parent shots later in the day.

I usually ask as I leave if the party needs me to take anything to the venue for them, as from time to time they realize they have forgotten to send ahead buttonholes or the order of service, and it's a nice touch to help them out on their big day.

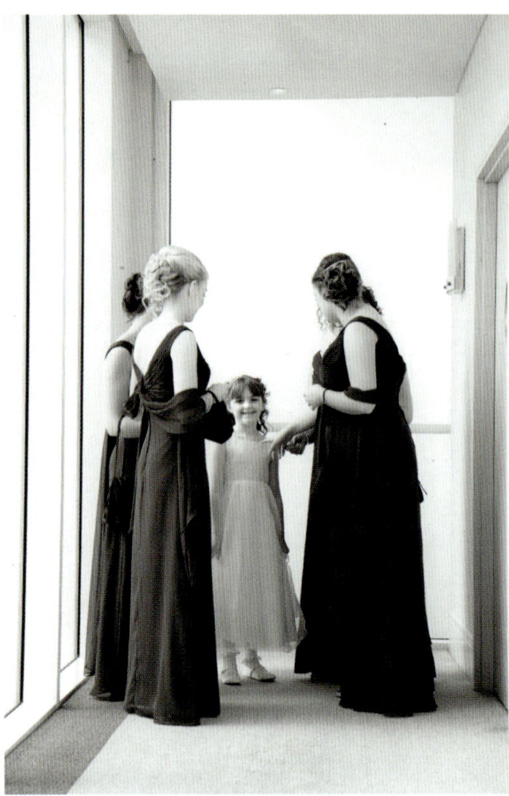

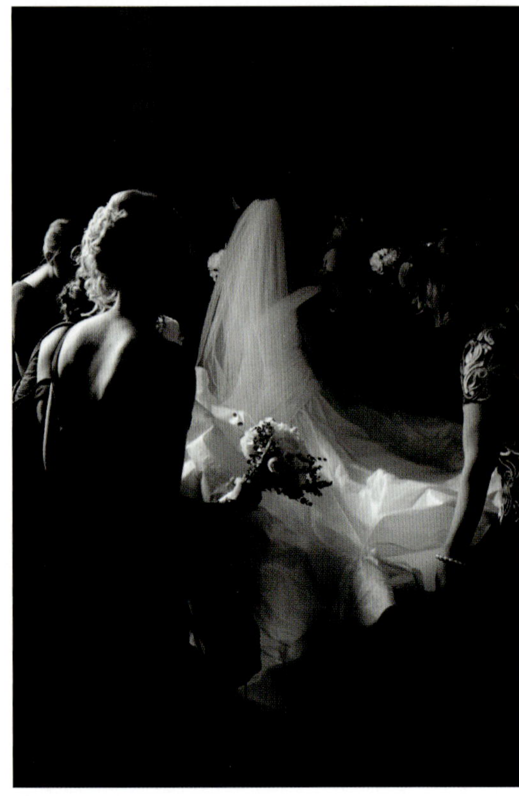

Above left & right: More often than not you'll find yourself leaving 30–40 minutes before the bridal party, but sometimes you can shoot images that look like they are leaving or making their final preparations.

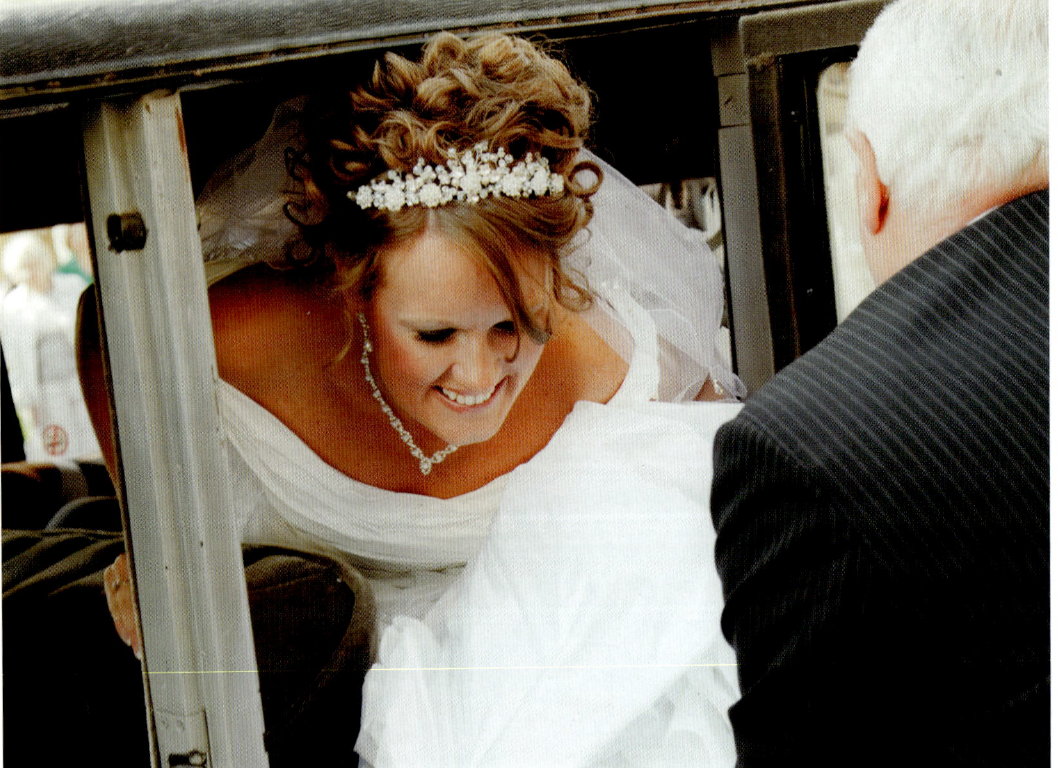

Left: If you are following the bride's car to the venue, or using a second photographer to complete the at-home shots, try to shoot some traveling images through the car windscreen. A perfect time to do this is when the cars have stopped at traffic lights, as the slight delay between the bride's car and your own leaving the lights can create some interesting images.

Tip

Have all your kit ready and packed to go, because as soon as the last shot is done you need to leave, and leave fast. Have the right lens on your camera before you leave the house, so if you are in a rush at the other end, you can get out of the car and shoot straight away.

11.30 Church & arrivals

As soon as you arrive at the church, which is usually 5 or 10 minutes late because of delays at the house, go in search of the groom and his family—these shots are as important as the pictures of the bride and her family.

On my way to find everyone I need, I usually shoot a variety of images, including some details and a few candid guest shots. It is amazing what you can shoot en route, and the more weddings you do the more alert to possible images you become, spotting pictures everywhere. However, I am always aware of the ticking clock—30 minutes to go and there is still so much to shoot.

Right: While waiting for the groom and his family, I start my candid guest images, usually using the 70–200mm zoom to get in close from a distance. The long lens allows me to concentrate on a specific person, picking them out from the crowd. Turning these images to black and white for online sales works best for reorders, especially with shots of teenagers, couples, and older people.

Right: By the time you arrive at the church, there are usually a few people already waiting to go in, especially on sunny days. This is a great opportunity to grab a scene shot, which is often used as a background image in an album design.

Far right: Look for the groom as soon as you arrive, and this can lead to a variety of images—in this case he and his groomsmen were in charge of lighting the candles in the church. So I used some off-camera flash to create more drama in the scene, and give a more three dimensional sun-kissed effect on the side of the groom.

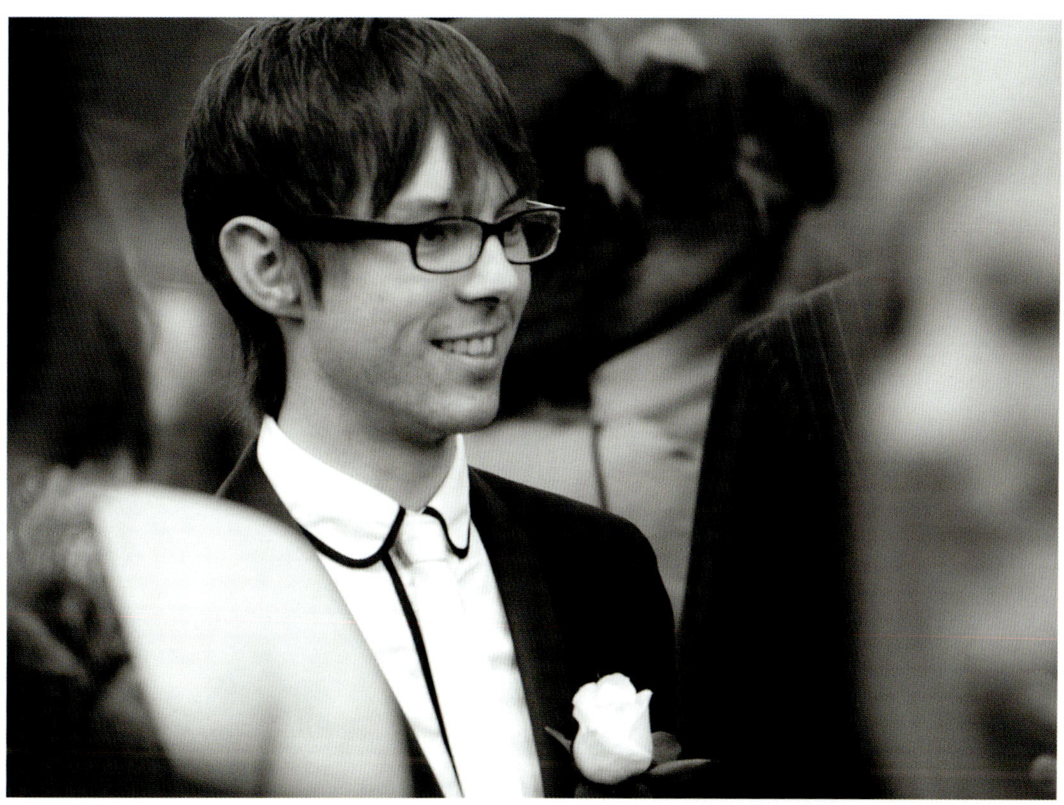

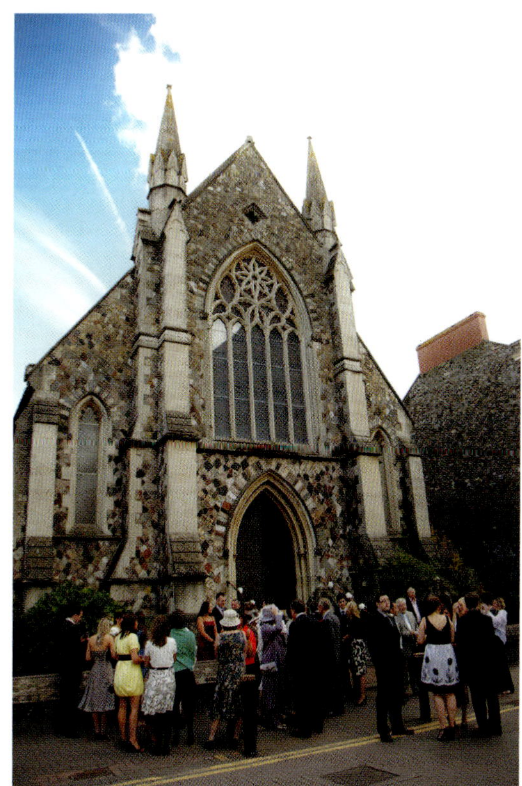

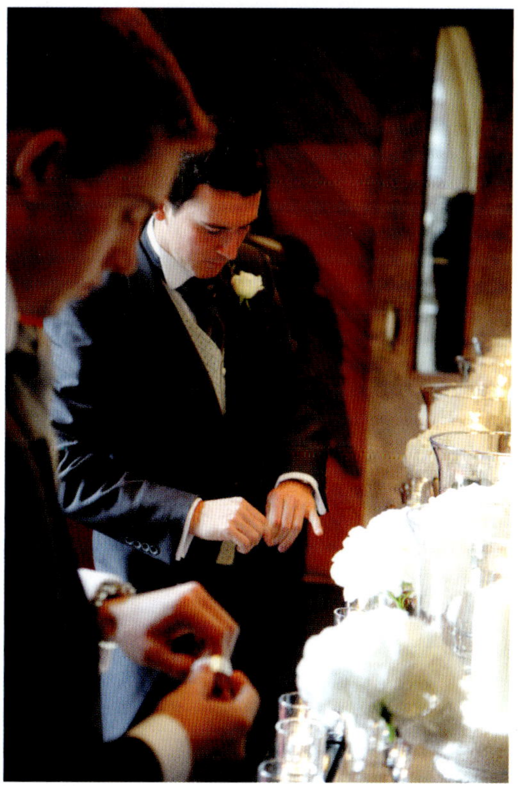

11.35 Groom arrives

It is too easy to forget about the images of the groom and his groomsmen, especially if you are running late, but get them done you must—they are a vital part of the story of the wedding day.

Even if the groom and his best man have gone into the ceremony room, you'll usually be able to steal them away again for 10 minutes, just to get the basic shots done. Remember that most brides arrive a little late, so a few extra minutes is enough to shoot the groom and his boys, with a chance to show off their characters.

On your list of images to shoot will usually be: the groom; the groom and best man; the groom, best man, and groomsmen; and perhaps the groom and his brother(s), if they are a part of the group. In addition to this, try to get the party started and encourage the guys to have a bit of a laugh, one way or another.

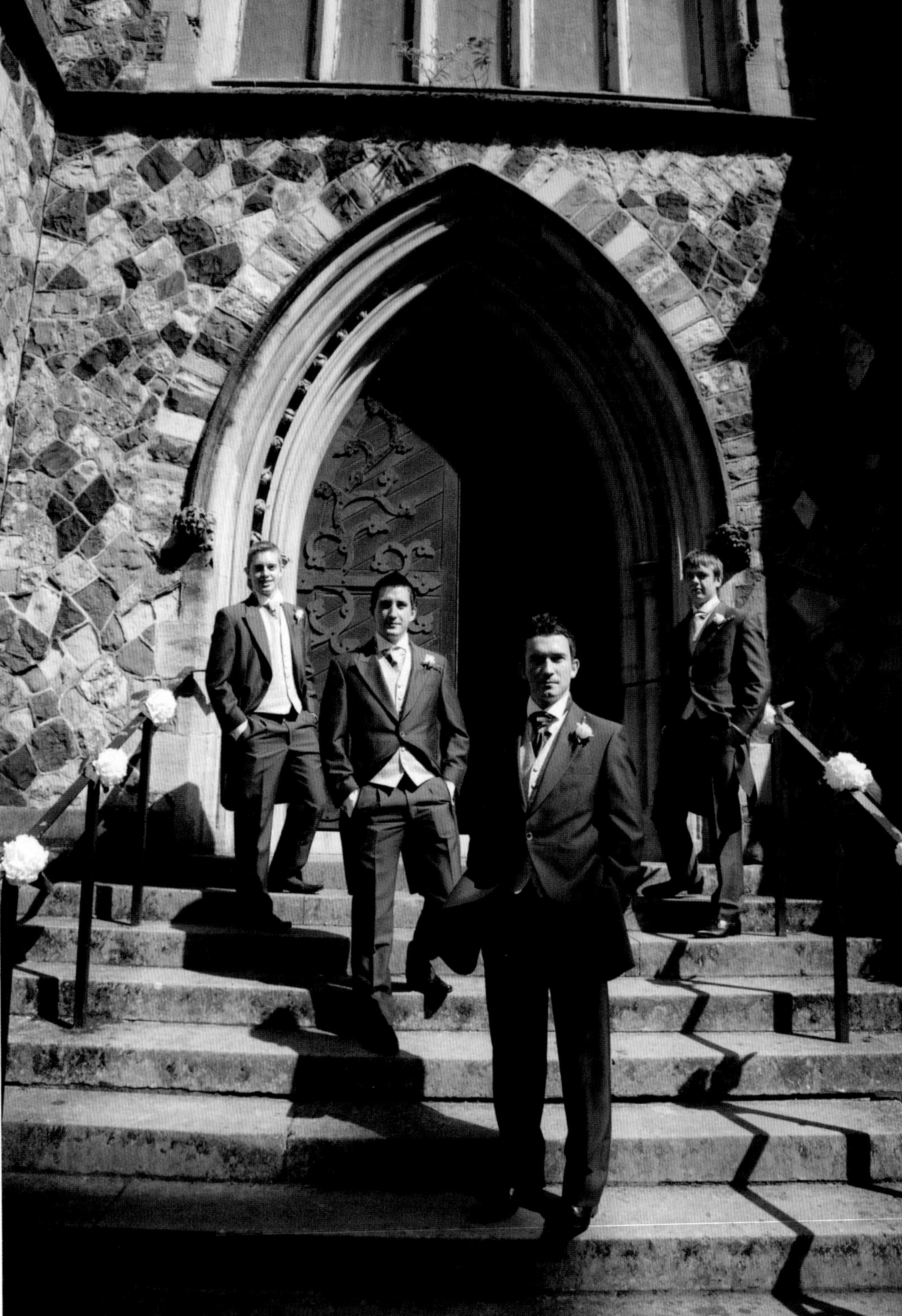

Right: In addition to the basic line-up shot, add a little variety to the groom and groomsmen shoot—after all, you made all the effort with the bride, so why not with the groom?

Tip

Ask the groom to make sure all his boys have sunglasses, especially in sunny climates, to make the image look like a scene from a movie.

11.45 Groom's family arrives

As a father of two sons, I know the importance of making a fuss of the groom's parents and family, as they can so easily be forgotten on a wedding day. By shooting the groom's close family before the ceremony, you'll have backup images of the family but, more importantly, images of the groom and his family without his wife-to-be in the shot, just as you shot for the bride and her family.

Try to encourage the bride and groom to include all immediate family in their shoot list, including parents, brothers, sisters, and grandparents in a variety of combinations. This ensures a good mix of images for the album, but the parents are the essential images, and everything else can be done later.

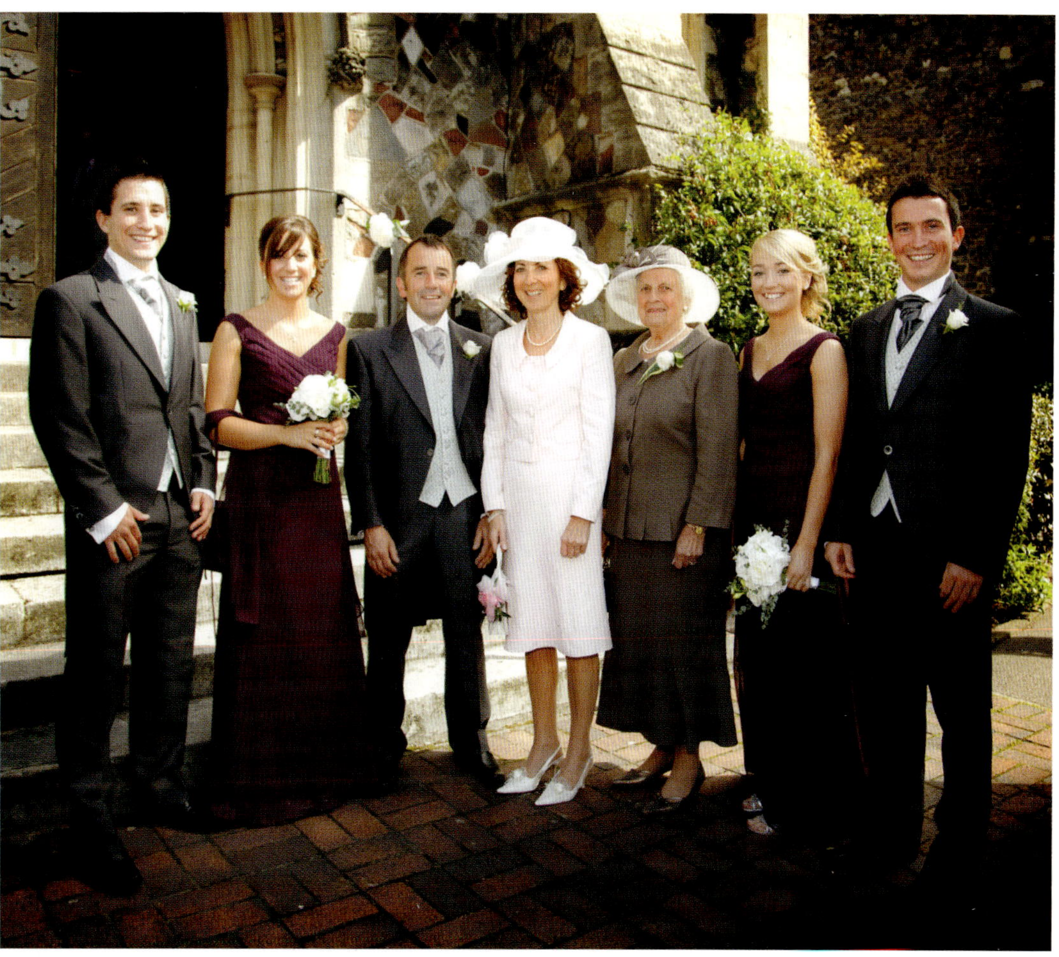

Right: There's usually at least one family member who arrives a little late, but even if you have already shot the family groups, try to get them shot, as it will save time later in the day.

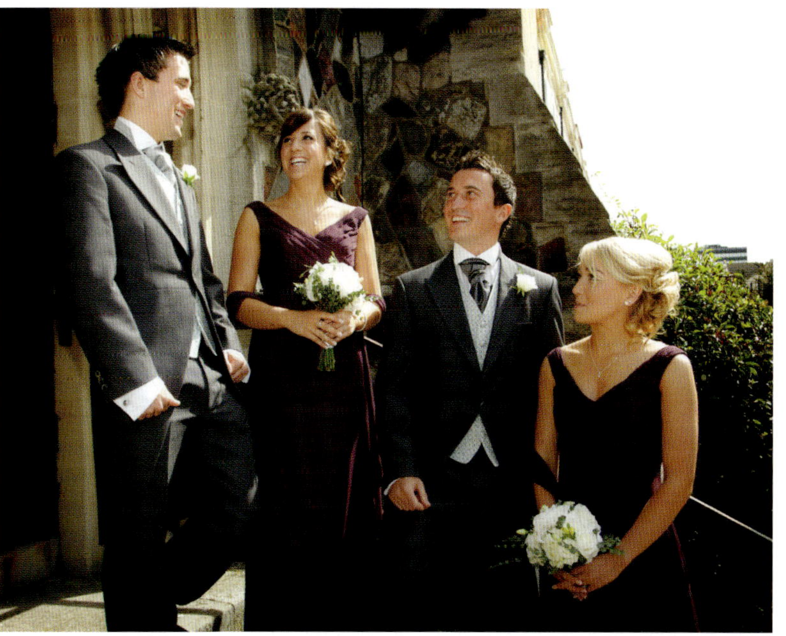

Right: Once again, as well as for the usual line-up shot, try and bring variety to even the simplest of groups, especially if you have the time.

Tip

If time is not on your side, use the best man or the groom's brother to run and fetch the close family, as this will give you more time to shoot with the groom.

11.55 Bride arrives

There is usually time for a breather between
shooting the groom and his party, and the bride
and the bridal party arriving, as most of the time
the bride will be running late. This is a good time
to check your camera kit as well, and to quickly
review your images so far. It is also a good time
to check your shoot list, ticking off the requested
shots that you have done and adding the ones
that have not been shot to the end of the list. This
checking of group shots will help you to relax a
little, knowing that you have managed your time by
completing many images before the ceremony.

Try to make sure you know which way the
brides cars will arrive—there is nothing worse
than looking the wrong way or being at the
wrong gate. I look to shoot a few images of the
scene, and then the rest will be close-up images,
concentrating on the expressions of the subjects
as well as any interesting details. Shooting
through a car window can be difficult because of
reflections, so try to see how bad the reflections
are on a nearby vehicle beforehand. This is also a
good time to get an exposure reading of the inside
of the car.

Right: The bride's arrival is a big event and during the
3–5-minute window you get as she prepares to go into
the ceremony, there is a lot to shoot—everything from the
bride and her father in the car, exiting the car, the basic
groups, and, of course, the procession to the church door.

Tip

I usually resort to fill-in flash for the groups,
to help correct any harsh shadows on faces,
or to increase the contrast when the subjects
are backlit.

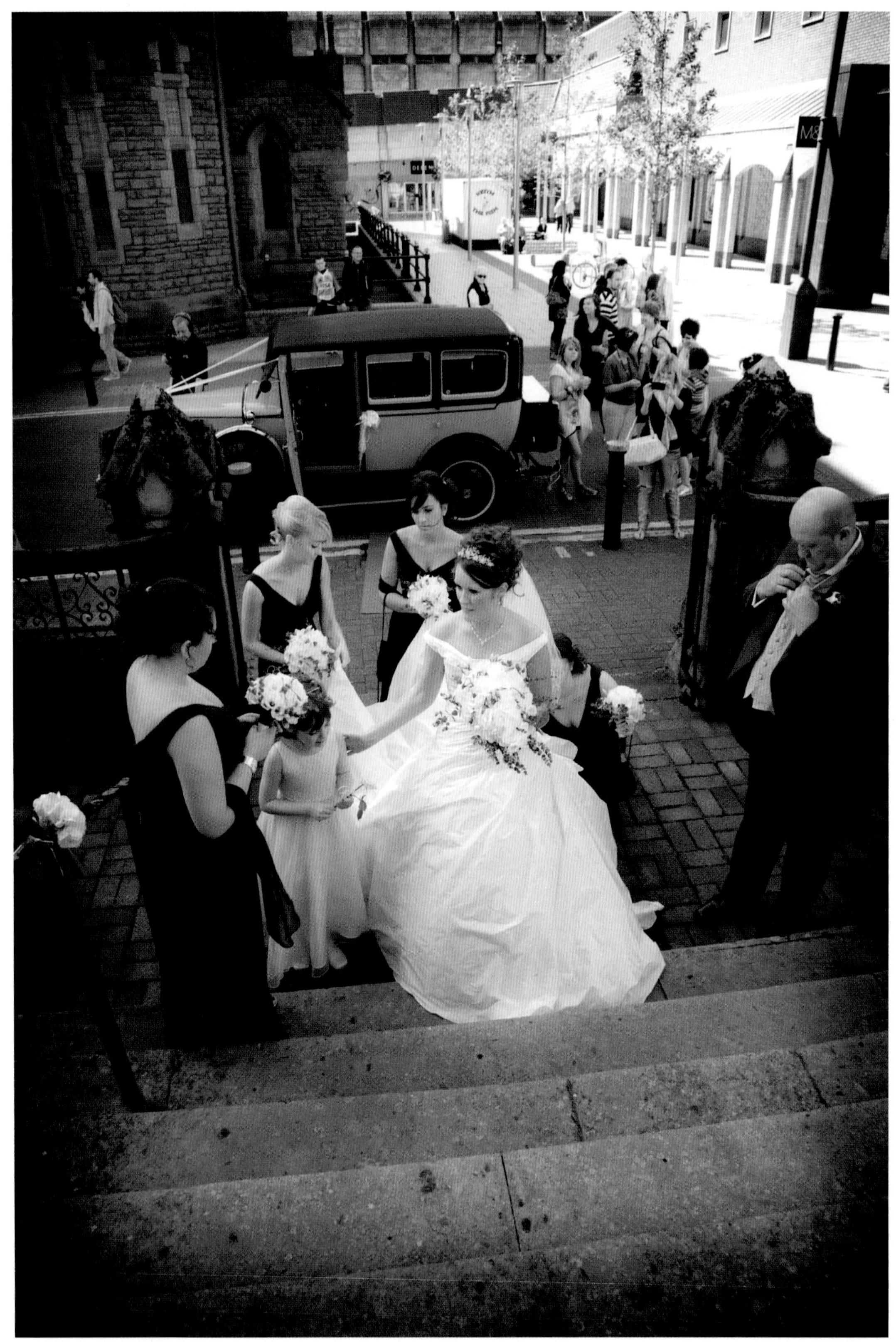

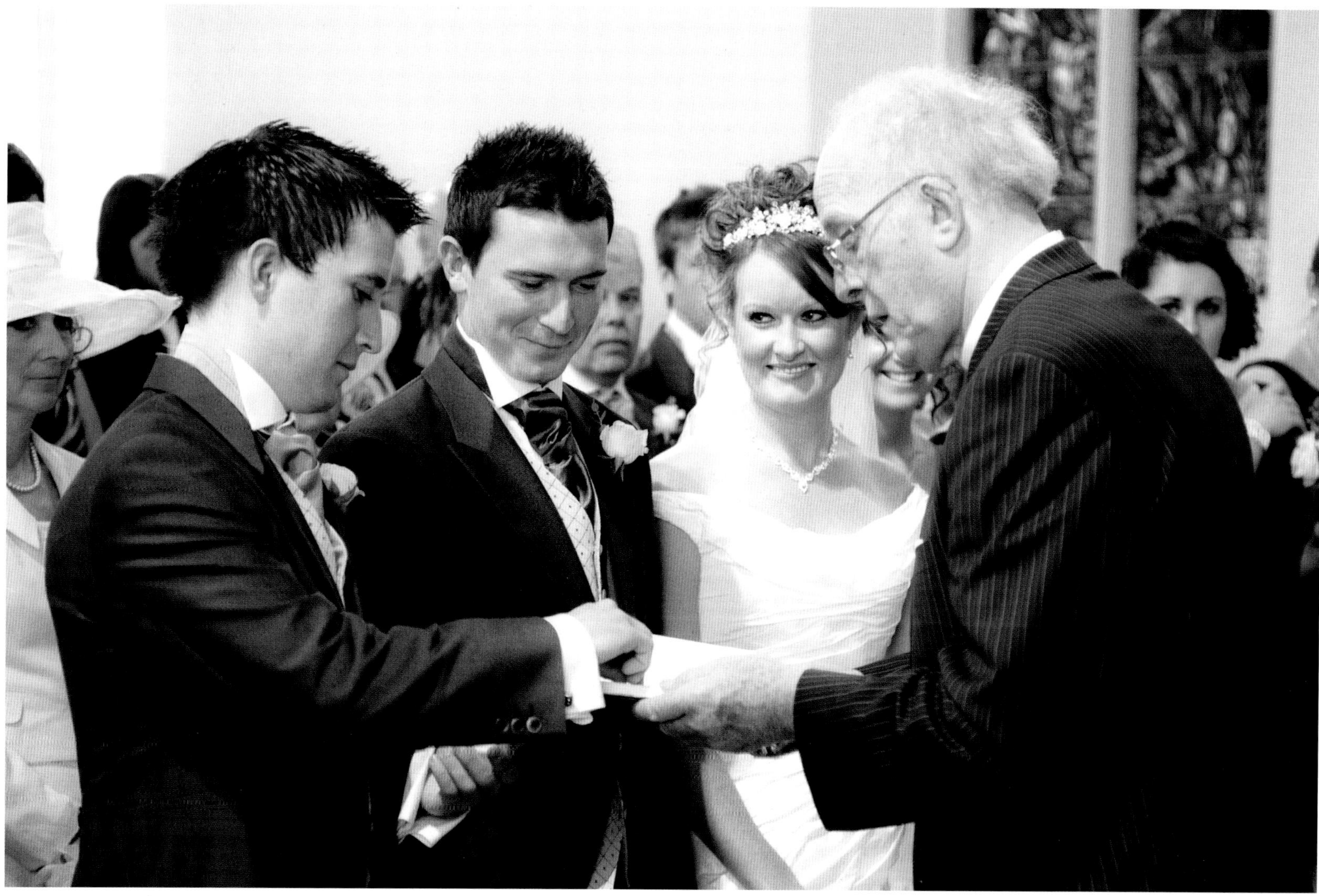

12.00 Ceremony

There are several key things to shoot during the ceremony, depending on the type of service and religion, so make sure you get some advice before the day. It is a good idea to ask for help from someone who can prompt you at Jewish, Greek, or Hindu weddings, for instance, if you're unfamiliar with the ceremonies.

The starting point is when the bridal party procession enters the church or ceremony—a shot from the back to show the back of the wedding dress is essential, especially if the dress has a long train. If you are using a second shooter at the wedding, decide on who is going to take which images on the shoot list to ensure there is no misunderstanding and no images are missed.

A fast lens and high ISO are the best choice when working in locations such as churches, especially if you are not allowed to use flash during the service. Even if you are told you cannot shoot during the service, try to get some discreet images from the back. If nothing else, try to shoot the exchange of rings and the first kiss, even if you are at the back of the room.

Above: If you are allowed to shoot the exchange of the rings, don't miss it—if the venue is too dark, use a little fill-in flash to lift the shadow detail. Modern DSLR cameras have a great range in usable ISO settings, so as long as your lens is not too slow, then you should be able to capture anything, even in extreme lighting.

Tip

If in doubt, remember to ask—it is much better to ask a silly question than to miss vital shots.

12.45 Registers

The signing of any registers or documents will draw the official part of the ceremony to a close, and the preparation for the signing and the time following it will offer chances to shoot a variety of candid images as well as the signing shots.

I try and shoot all of the candid images with no flash, as I like to become a "fly on the wall" as much as I can. This produces truly observational pictures, capturing the intimate moments when the parents greet the newly married couple and talk afterwards.

For the formal image, I resort to my camera with the 24–105mm lens—with a flash unit on the hotshoe in TTL mode to provide all the light on the subjects. Usually a setting of 400 ISO, 1/30 sec. at f/4 or f/5.6 will provide the flash for the image of the couple and group, with the natural ambient light showing enough detail in the room.

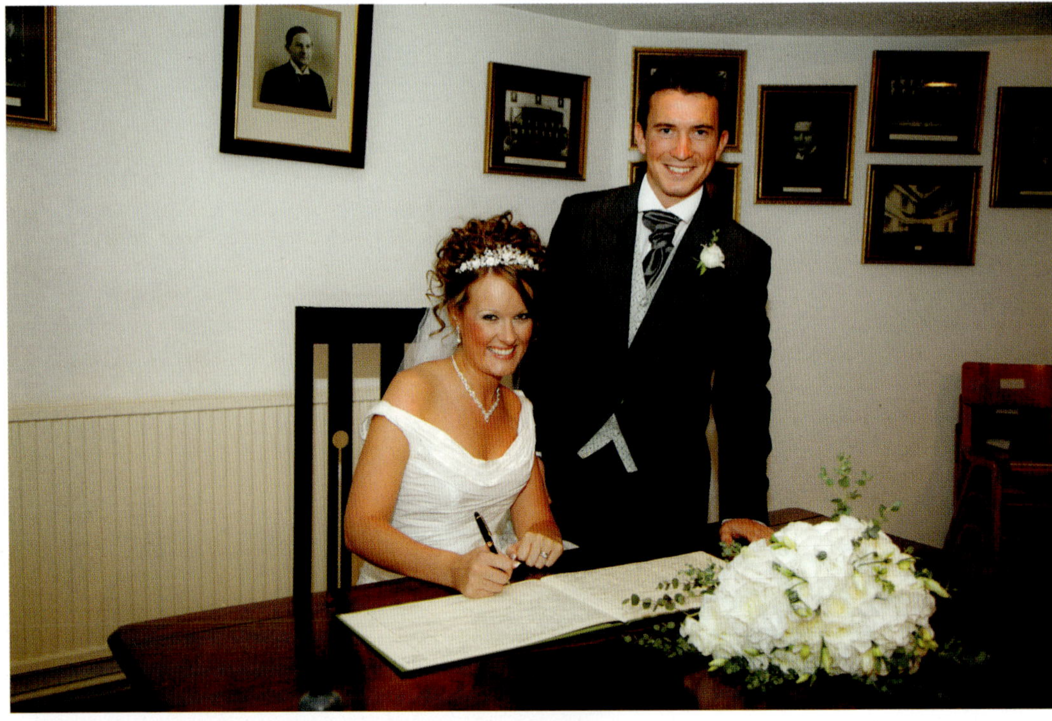

Above: During the actual signing of the registers, I take a variety of scene and close-up images using just the ambient light. However, when it comes to the posed image, I once again resort to bounce flash in TTL mode using a setting of 400 ISO, 1/60 sec. at f/4. This allows some of the ambient room light to act as a fill-in for the scene, and the flash to illuminate the subjects fully.

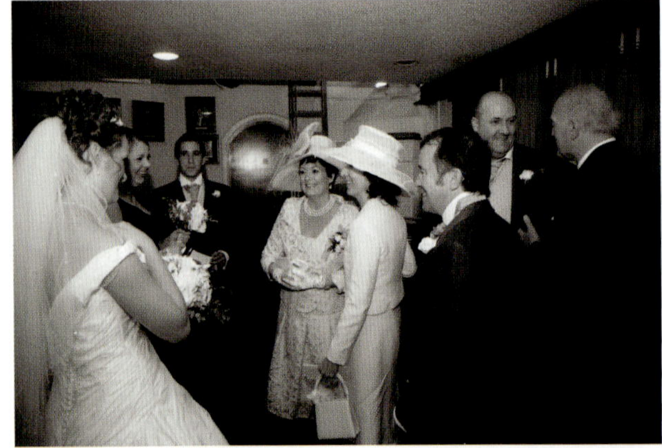

Right: As soon as the bridal party enters the vestry, a side room used for signing the registers, there will be reactions.

At this point always concentrate on the first contact between the parents and the couple after the ceremony, as their reactions can be the most emotional of the whole day.

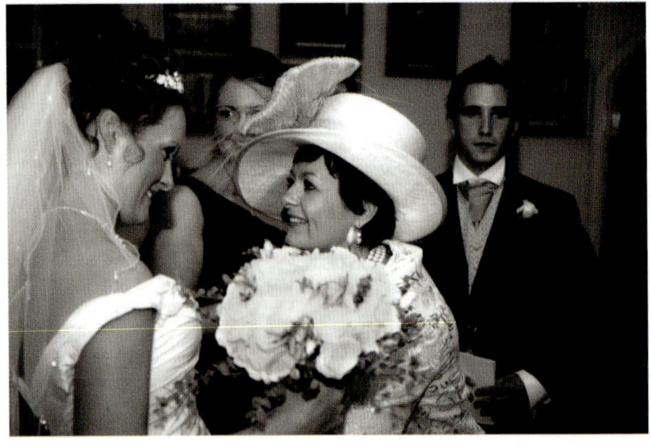

Left: These small, intimate side rooms can be either full of natural light or have none at all, and in this case it was none. There were no windows in the room, so it was essential to add some bounce flash to light the scene. When shooting with pure bounce flash, try to just shoot horizontal images, so any shadows from the flash go directly behind the subjects.

12.55 Aisle

Photographing the couple as they walk up the aisle at the end of the ceremony is an essential shot—try using a flash unit on the camera to freeze the motion a little as they walk towards you. Different photographers shoot this in different ways: some like to stop the couple at some point up the aisle, which is not a bad idea when you are getting started, but for a more naturally animated image shoot them as they walk towards the camera.

To avoid motion blur, do two things. Firstly, always shoot with the flash in second-curtain sync mode. This fires the flash at the end of the exposure, helping to avoid motion freeze, as the flash fires to gain the exposure just before the shutter closes, creating a "clean" subject. Secondly, walk backwards as the couple walk toward you. This tracking method works well, especially if they are walking fast—just avoid walking into anything behind you! I have heard of so many photographers falling over their own bag or bumping into the christening font.

Another thing to do is to darken the guests on the side aisles so the bride and groom are emphasized. To do this, shoot a slightly wider shot but with your flash set on zoom to the full 105mm—this concentrates the beam of light into the middle of the frame, creating a spotlight effect that I call "funneling."

Right: For a naturally animated image, shoot the couple as they are walking towards you, rather than asking them to stop completely.

Tip

Try and shoot the image at a moment when the couple are no longer moving—there is a point when the body weight moves onto the ball of the foot, creating a static pose for a fraction of a second.

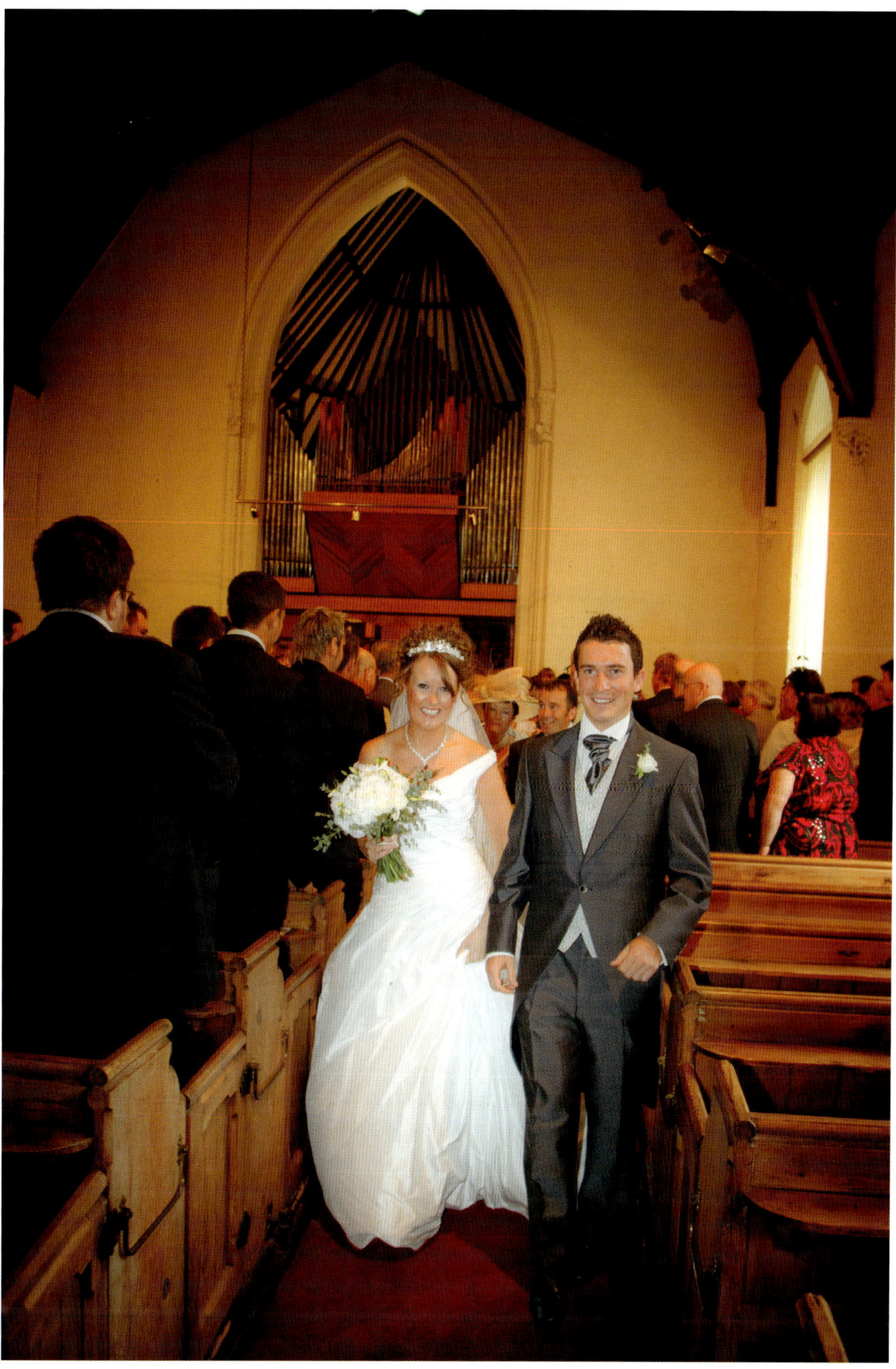

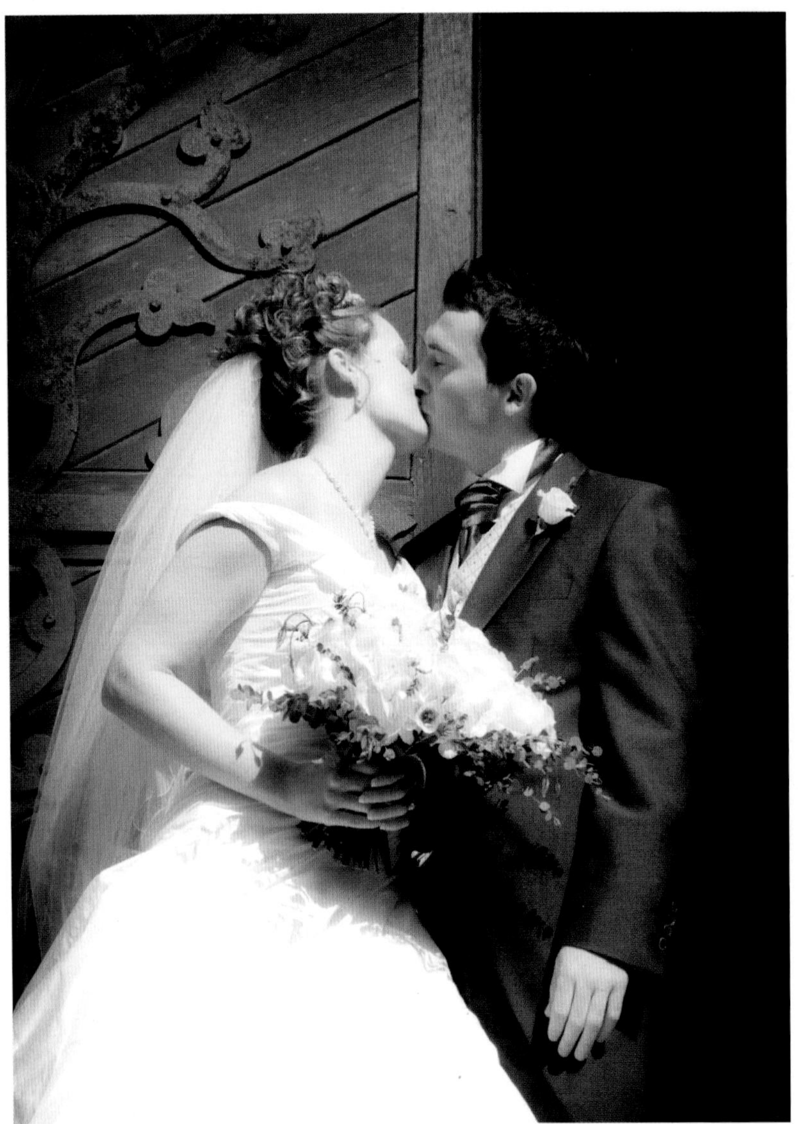

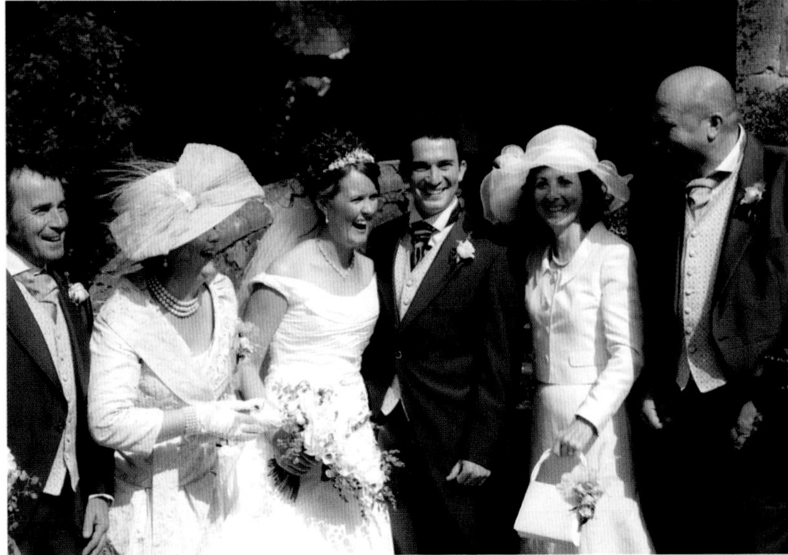

Above: The groups are posed so the couple are in the middle with the mothers next to their own child and the fathers swapped—this is a UK tradition, which helps if parents are divorced. After the staged group, follow up with a candid-looking image. Even though it has been set up, ask the group to look towards the bride and groom and just gossip, which will result in some great expressions.

Left: The photographs taken at the church door can be some of the bestselling images of the whole wedding. Unfortunately, the door is often bathed in sunlight, making it difficult to achieve great images. A touch of fill-in flash will help lift the shadow details but, when all else fails, you can always rely on the kiss to get you out of trouble—as the couple look at each other and away from the camera, the sharp lighting becomes less important.

13.00 Bridal party leaves

Following a few quick shots at the church door or venue—which still provide some of the images that sell the most to friends and family—move the couple and the bridal party to one side. This enables the guests to leave the building, instead of being trapped inside. Shooting the bridal party to one side also allows you to gather the important people at the wedding—the parents, best man, groomsmen, and bridesmaids—and quickly shoot a series of either candid or formal portraits. The most important thing, though, is gathering them and keeping them away from the doorway until it's clear.

More often than not, I will repeat the same groups later in the day with a better background, but I photograph them now to get some early shots for variety and to control the movement of people. Once outside the church or venue, the wedding party can become a little like sheep let out of a pen—they wander around with no real purpose, sometimes getting lost—so a little control helps them know what to do, as well as helping you to complete some of the shooting list.

Tip

Watch the weather—if it looks like rain, and the reception location is not very good inside or if it is difficult to shoot in, get on with photographing all the groups, just in case.

1.05 Candid portraits

Once the few formal images of the bridal party have been shot, and most of the guests from inside the church have been cleared, then you can release the couple and party and start to interact with the guests.

This next 10 to 15 minutes is a perfect time to step back and start to shoot some candid photographs, as it's the first time the guests get to interact with the couple after the ceremony, and this usually results in a lot of great expressions and animation from everyone. I take these shots with either a 70–200mm zoom set at f/2.8, or a 50mm prime also set at f/2.8.

If there is a large area around the venue, you can usually take several steps back and shoot from a distance with the zoom lens at 200mm. This forces the background out of focus and emphasizes the main subjects. If you are working in a small area, or if the guests are packed tightly, you'll need to get into the crowd, otherwise you'll just shoot the same few faces all the time. Again, use an aperture of f/2.8 to separate your subjects from the background and the other guests.

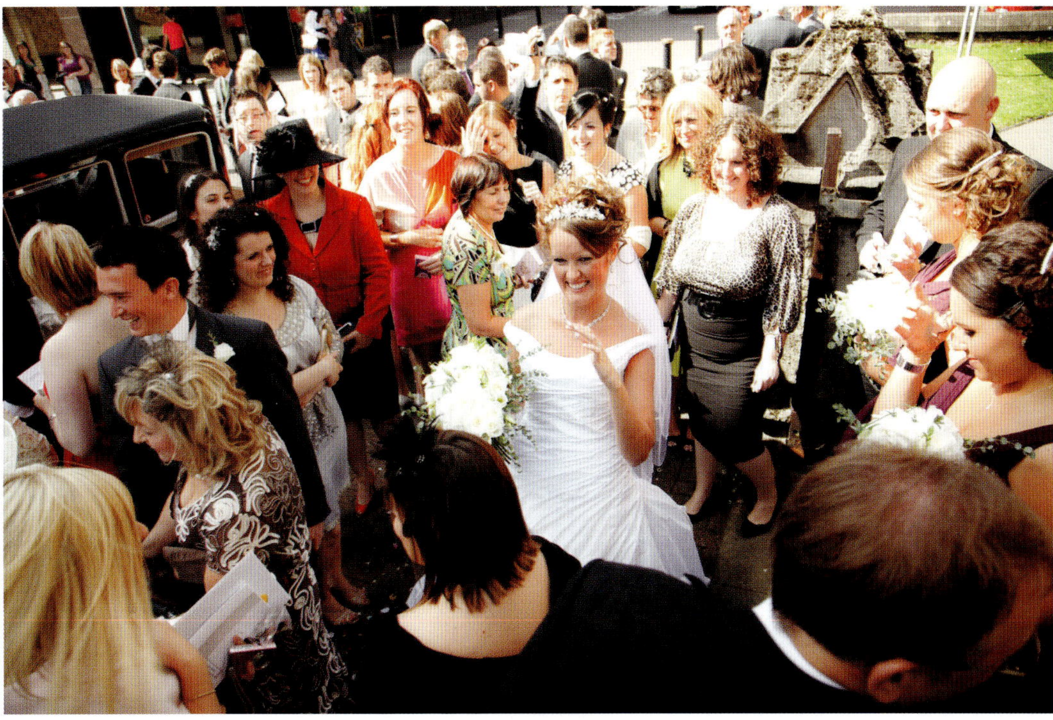

Above: If I could have eyes in the back of my head it would make this part of the wedding a lot easier, but I love the buzz and the excitement of all the guest reactions. Even with all the distractions, the bride and groom are still conscious of the photographer being around, and you can sometimes catch their eyes at the right time for some great candid portraits.

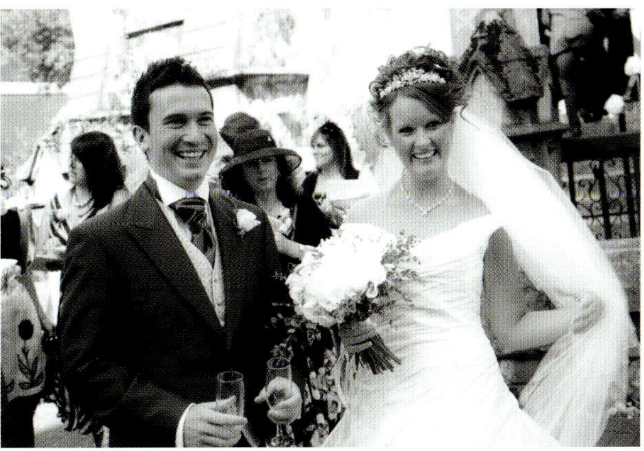

Right: You'll find it hard to stay away from the couple, as you are always aware of their interactions with the guests and with each other. However, keep moving and allow your focus to move quickly from one person or object another—this is the key to capturing variety when you are shooting alone.

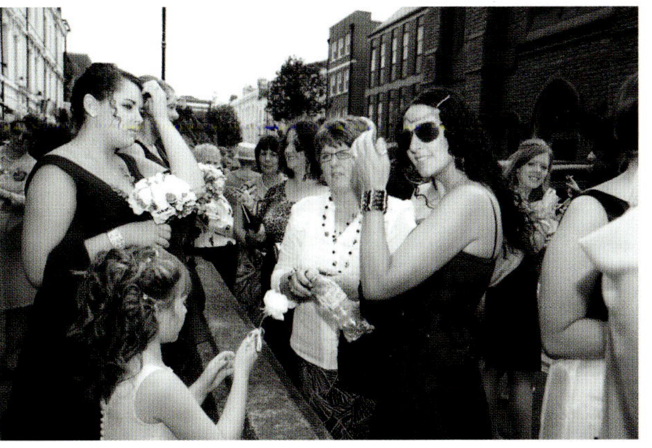

Left: During the next 5 to 10 minutes, concentrate on the couple in the scene, as well as the guests' reactions to seeing them for the first time after the ceremony. Remember, however, that it is also good practice to give the couple some space for a little while, to allow them to focus on meeting their friends and family.

Tip

Try shooting through some of the guests and picking out someone behind them with shallow depth of field, as this adds a three-dimensional effect to your shots.

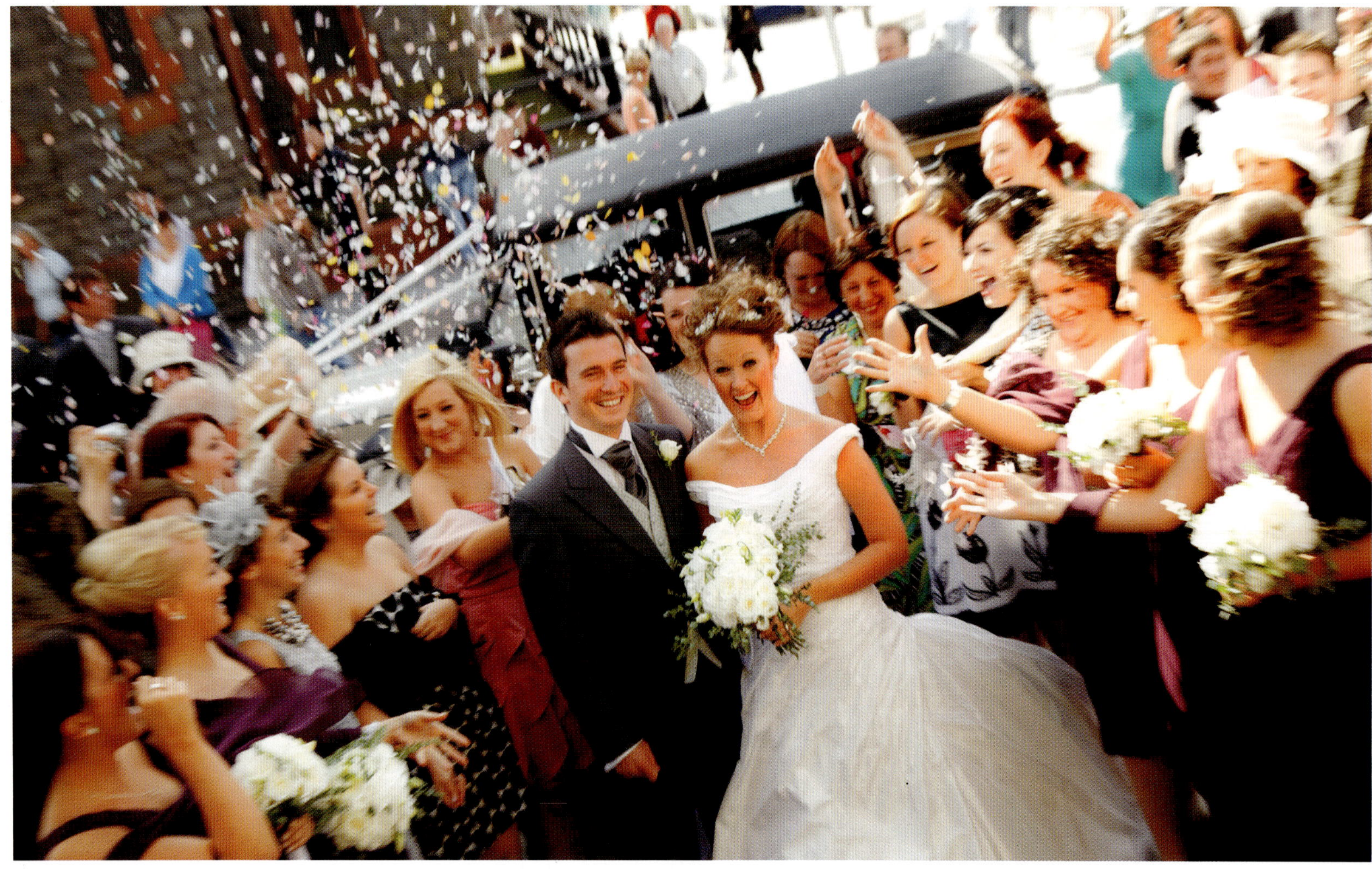

1.15 Confetti

Control is key for the confetti shot, otherwise people will just throw it when they want, and you end up with no image at all, or with very little confetti left to make a great shot. Quite often, one person tries to orchestrate the confetti-throwing before you are ready, so if you spot someone who looks as though they are about to do this, quickly approach them to curb their enthusiasm.

You might prefer to position yourself so that the guests surround the couple from behind and to the sides, which avoids the couple being bombarded in their faces with the confetti, and makes it difficult to get a good shot. Then ask for a count of three, before the guests discharge the confetti with invigorated enthusiasm at the same time.

If confetti is not allowed at the venue, a lot of couples organize an alternative, such as flower petals or bubbles, and these can also make great pictures—a shot with bubbles can be especially effective when the bubbles are backlit.

Above: Always orchestrate the confetti-throwing, otherwise the guests will run out before you can get the shot. Take control and gather everyone with confetti, then agree a count to three. The resulting explosion will create a series of fun images of the couple and their guests. Always check how many shots are left on your card beforehand to make sure you don't run out in the middle of the shot—there is no dress rehearsal.

Tip

Switch off your flash if possible—with it, the confetti will cause spot-like shadows on the faces of the couple.

1.30 Couple on location

I like to stop off with the couple en route to the reception venue if possible, because this gives me time alone with them, and serves as a breather for them, as often they have been surrounded by people for what can seem like days.

Seek out locations that have more than one look, by which I mean a variety of different-looking backgrounds, even if the light is only perfect in one. The secret to using your limited time with the couple wisely is to walk less and shoot more. By simply walking around them, using a shallow depth of field, you can often shoot the necessary images in the minimum amount of time.

It still frustrates me, though, that most couples today want to minimize their time away from the guests even more, cutting down the creative time the photographer can spend with them. However, I am fully aware that this is not a fashion shoot—it is their day, after all—and you won't get the best shots if they're not enjoying the experience.

Most couples will be happy with about 48 shots, as long as you shoot a good variety. The must-do shots will be: full-length images, three-quarters and head-and-shoulder portraits, and individuals too. Remember throughout that, as a couple, they want to look immaculate and thinner than in real life. If you can persuade the couple to spend another 20 minutes with you, though, it will make a huge difference to the number and variety of shots you can take for them.

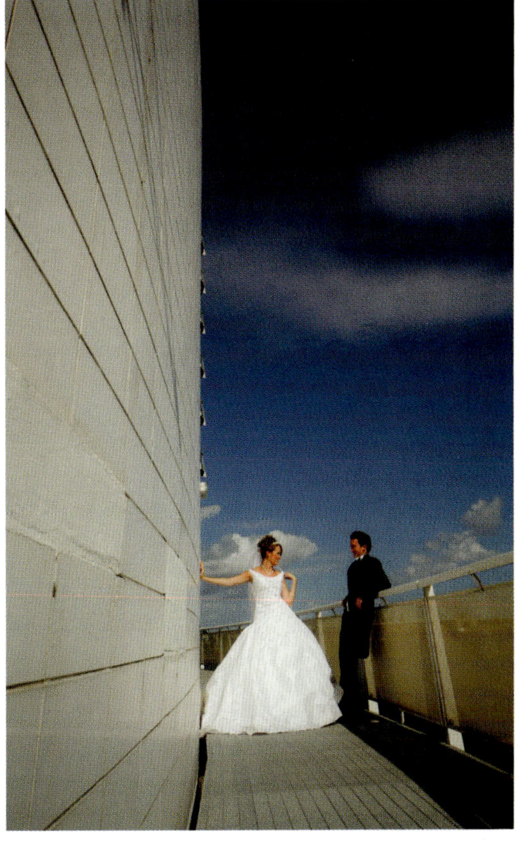

Left: Shooting the couple wide-angle, showing the surroundings, helps to set the stage for the day. Never be afraid to shoot your subjects small in the landscape, as long as there is a creative reason apart from the variety. Negative space can be very dramatic and these images are great used as backgrounds in album design.

Below: The more time you can persuade the couple to spend with you the better, so you can become more creative in your posing and composition.

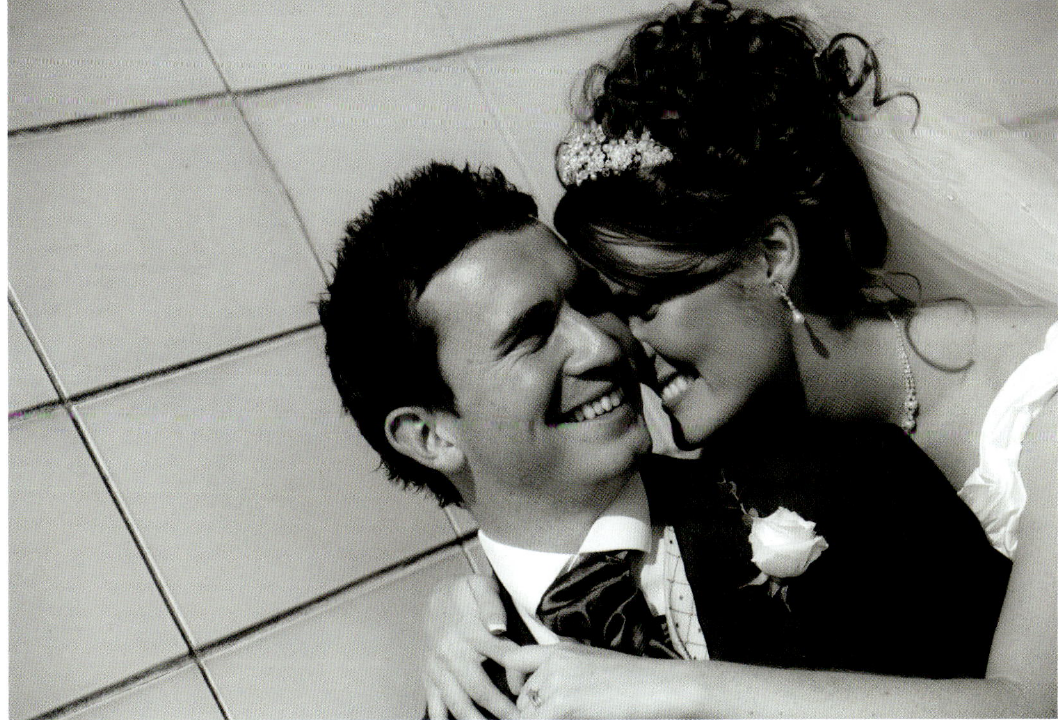

2.00 Arriving at the reception

If you have not done so already, this is where you make sure you get some shots of the couple with their transport for the day, including the car arriving at the reception. Once again, if you have planned what you are going to do when you arrive at the reception, including preparing your camera before you left the bride-and-groom shoot, you can leave your car and start shooting straight away.

Other shots you need to be sure of taking here are of the candid moments, as the couple arrive back into the throng of the guests, again watching out for any big characters and emotions, as well as funny moments.

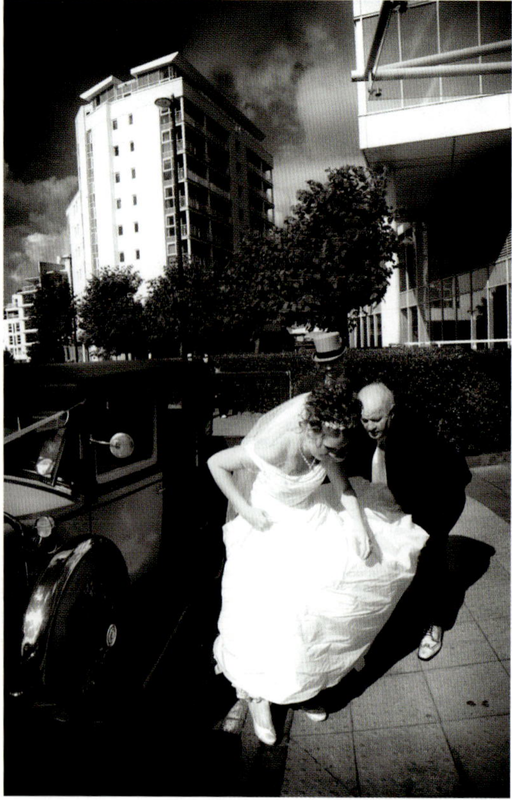

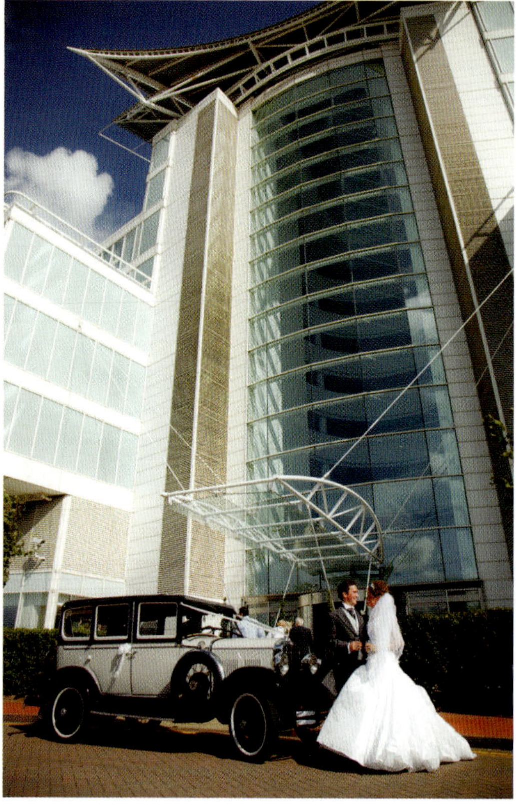

Above right: When the couple arrive at the reception venue you might be greeted by a doorman or function manager, but the chauffeur will usually still help the bride out of the car. You need to anticipate where he is going to stand, which is usually with one hand on an open door. When you have a clear view, look to shoot a candid moment of the bride re-adjusting her dress, as well as any funny moments or glances.

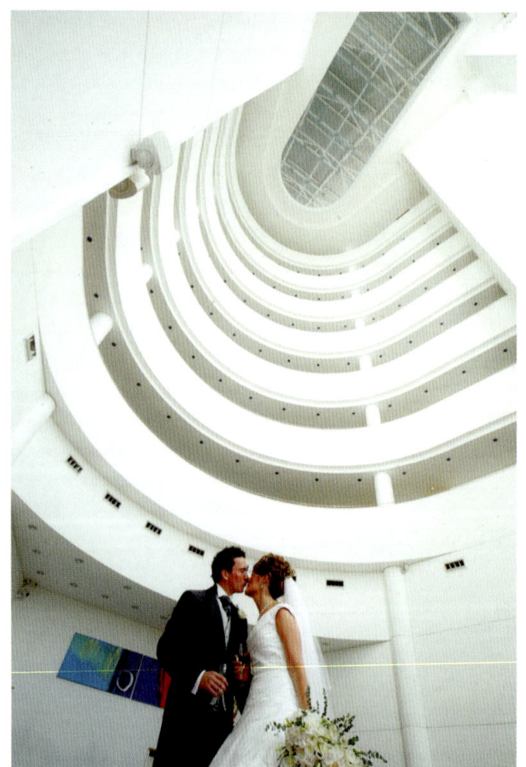

Above: The final shots with the car are the next step in the series, and this usually needs some orchestration to ensure the couple are in the right place. This series will include close-up shots of the bride and groom with the car in the background, as well as a shot to show the couple, the car, and the scene—usually with the zoom lens set to its widest end at 24mm.

Left: Because I have a super-wide-angle zoom lens in the bag, I like to use it two or three times during each wedding, otherwise there is little point in carrying it. This was shot at 19mm wide. This forced perspective will stretch the subjects, so be careful how you use it, as well as how often because too many of these images can look tacky.

2.05 Reception drinks

The informality of the drinks reception allows
you to concentrate on shooting purely candid
moments, and allows the couple to spend some
time away from the camera, even though you still
need to photograph them interacting with friends
and family. I shoot the drinks reception in two
basic loops of the groups. During the first, I take
only candid photographs, with no interaction and
no interference. For the second loop, I politely
interrupt the informal groups to quickly capture
relaxed shots of them.

Almost invariably, when shooting the informal
groups, you will encounter the problem of some
groups having their backs to the sun and other
groups facing the sun. I use flash on-camera in
both these instances but in a slightly different way
due to the extreme conditions.

This is why I use only two exposures—one for
shooting against the light and one for shooting
with the light. As I move around, I only need to
change the aperture or the shutter speed. I tend
to just change the shutter speed but there are
always instances, in extreme sunshine, when this
will not work. I set my flash to high-speed sync
mode to enable me to use higher shutter speeds
to cope with the sunlit images. I also let the flash
work in TTL mode, as it cuts the power output
automatically when exposure is achieved. The only
reason to tweak the flash power would be if I want
to use less flash when working against the light,
so in these cases I use an exposure adjustment of
between -1/3 and -1 to make the shots look less
flash-lit.

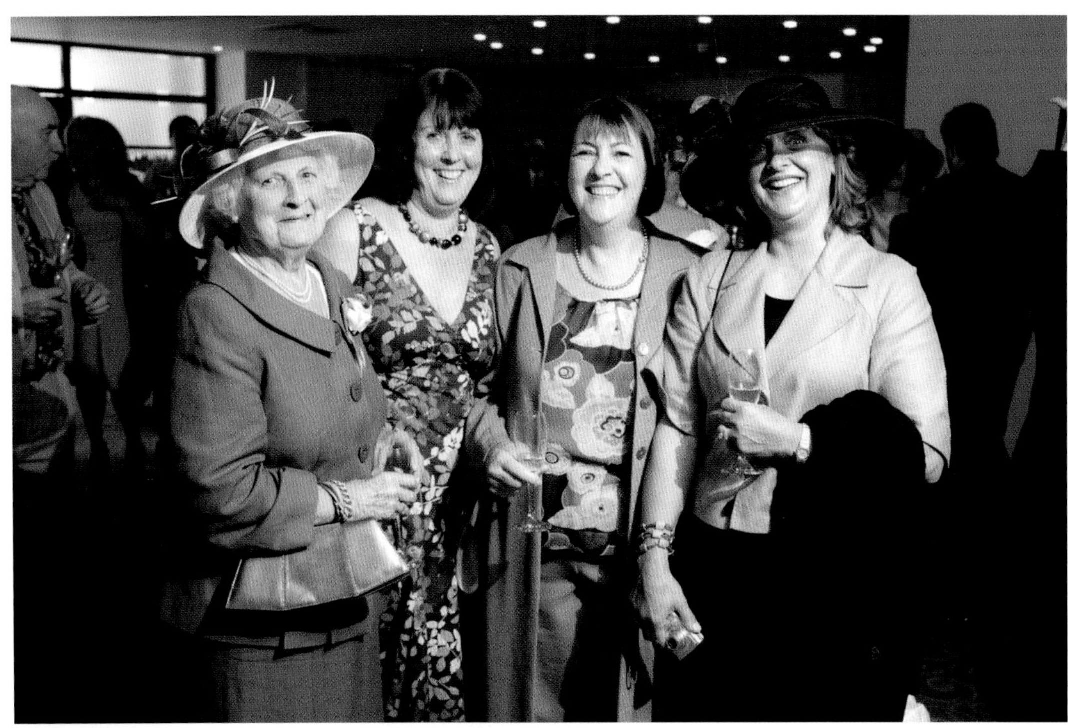

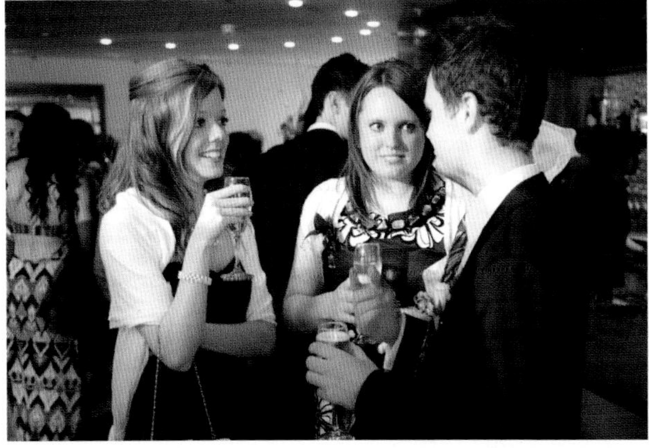

Above & left: I take the flash off-camera to
improve the direction in which its light shines. I
tend to use Quantum flash units when working
with an assistant to provide a round output
of light, and a sunlight-resembling scatter
when fitted with a wide-angle diffuser dome.
The flash output can be controlled from the
camera hotshoe with a Quantum TTL controller,
making every exposure near perfect. The flash
is mounted on the end of an extendable pole to
allow it to be lifted above the guests, avoiding
any unwanted shadows on the subjects.

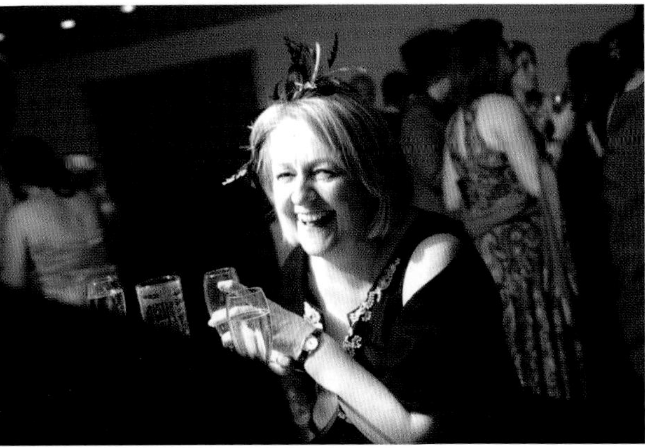

Tip

When working outside, set your flash to high-
speed sync mode to enable you to use shutter
speeds above 1/200 sec., otherwise the camera
will set the shutter speed automatically and you
will end up with overexposed images.

2.15 Reception groups

The formal groups can be the best sellers, so I
never complain about shooting a large variety of
different guest combinations. However I do like to
know what groups the couple want in advance,
as this helps me to manage the time better,
allowing for a few extra groups to be requested
by family and guests on the day.

I usually work through these group portraits by
starting with a core of people, and then adding
to them at the sides and, if necessary, behind
and in front. So, for instance, I will start with the
bride and groom in the middle, then add a parent
on each side, then siblings, grandparents, aunts,
uncles, and cousins.

There will, of course, be special groups, such
as godparents, grandparents, and special family
members, as well. If I know these in advance, I
can work out the best configurations and order
in which to shoot them, avoiding splitting up the
bride and groom at this stage.

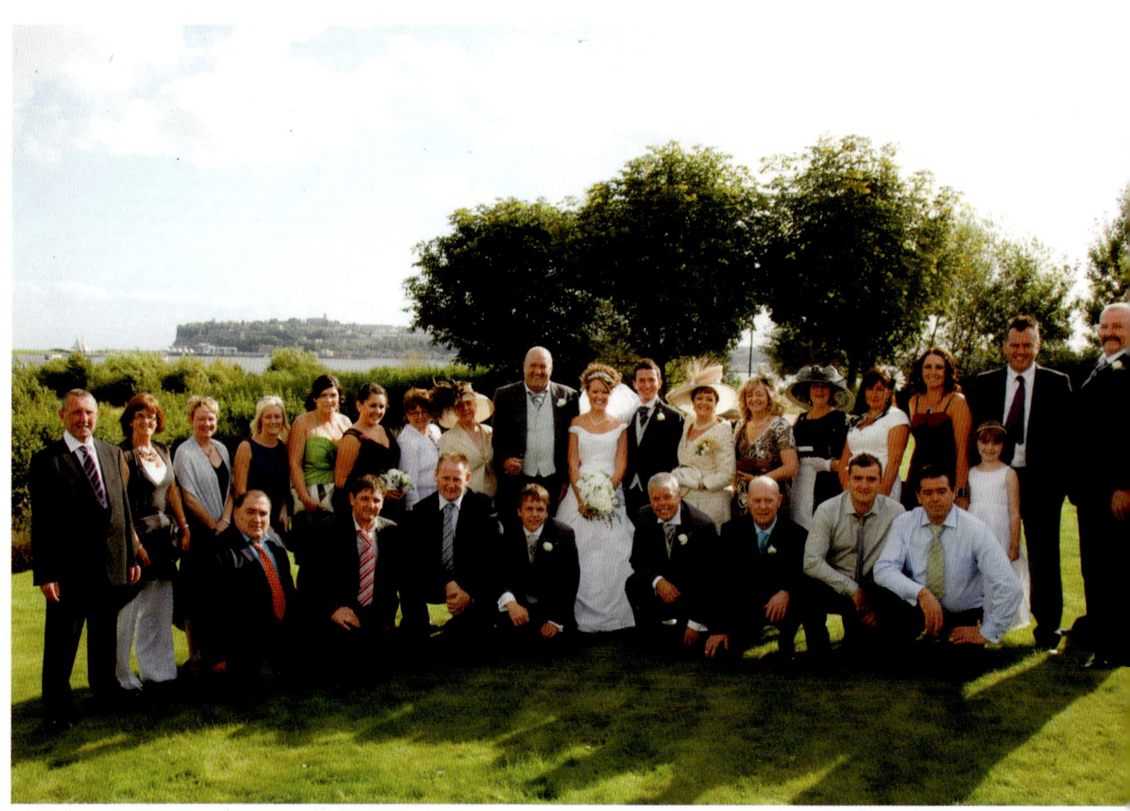

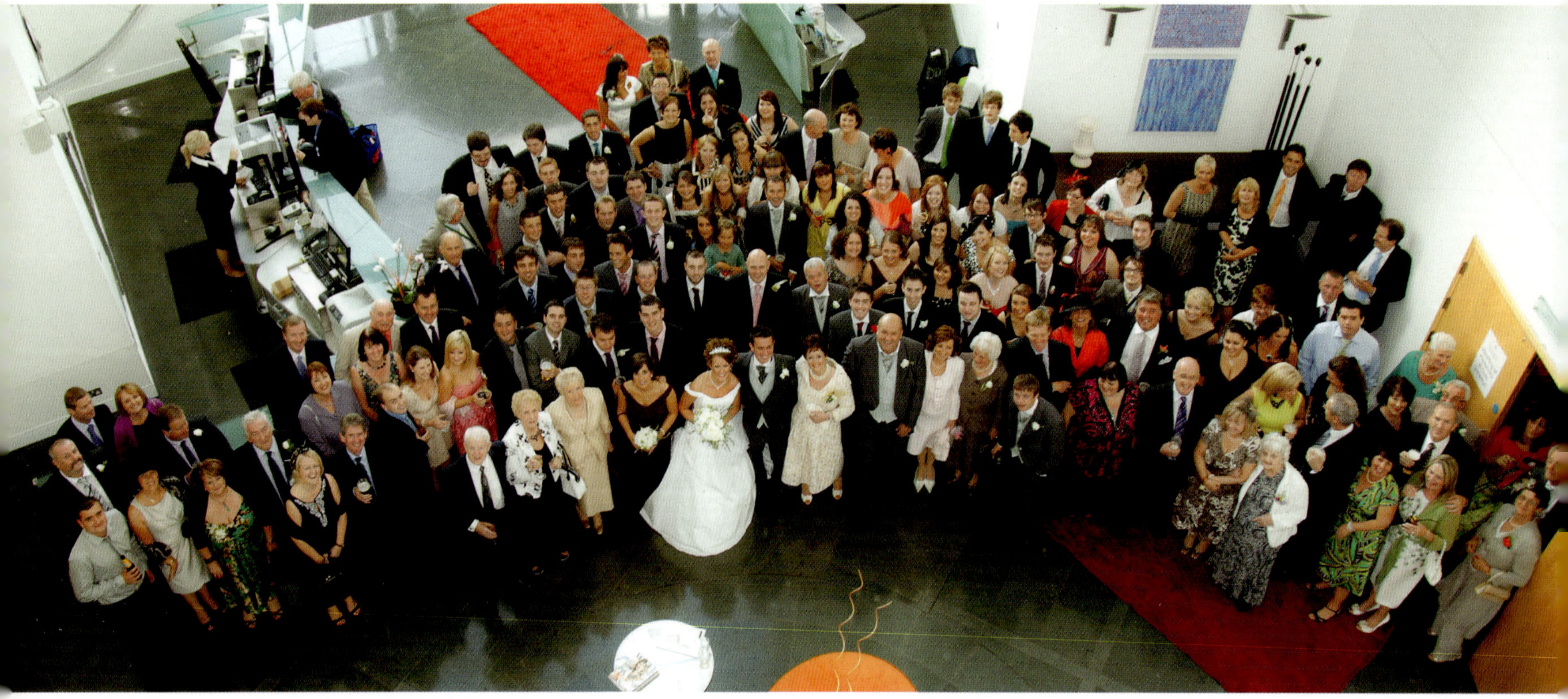

Left: The basic group images are based on the guests being positioned turning slightly inwards, as well as slightly behind each other to lose the inner shoulder. This way, you create a natural horseshoe shape, which will help to keep everyone within the depth of field.

Right: A development from the basic group is to shoot the guests running towards the camera—perfect for friends of the bride and groom, as it adds a little fun for them and you during what seems like a never-ending group list.

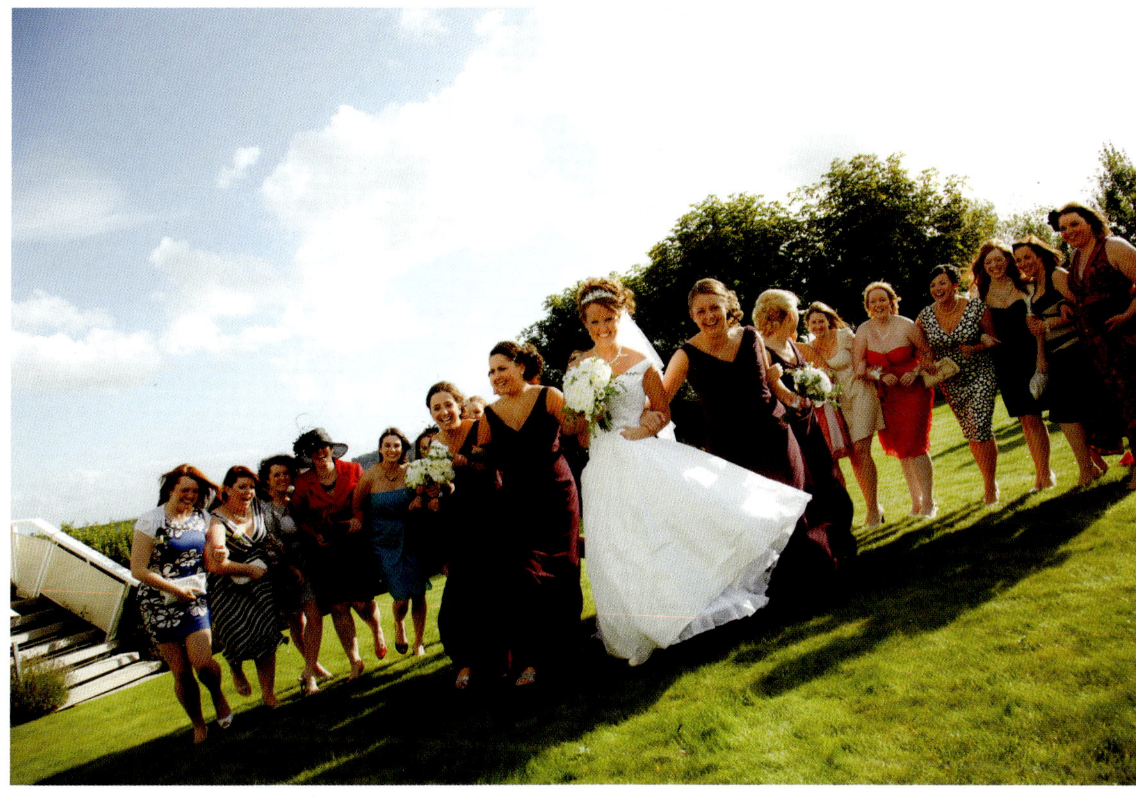

Left: The big group shot is usually my last formal photograph before the guests enter the reception room to eat. I always try and shoot from a high viewpoint, looking down so that everyone is in shot. Exposure is based on the ambient light in the scene, and then full direct flash is added to help fill in the shadows and create brighter faces.

Right: With the groom's friends you will often find that things soon descend into chaos, sometimes with someone's enthusiasm causing them to fall over in front of you.

Tip

Always work from a list when shooting groups at a wedding, and have a spare copy to give to the best man or master of ceremony so they can help you put these groups together.

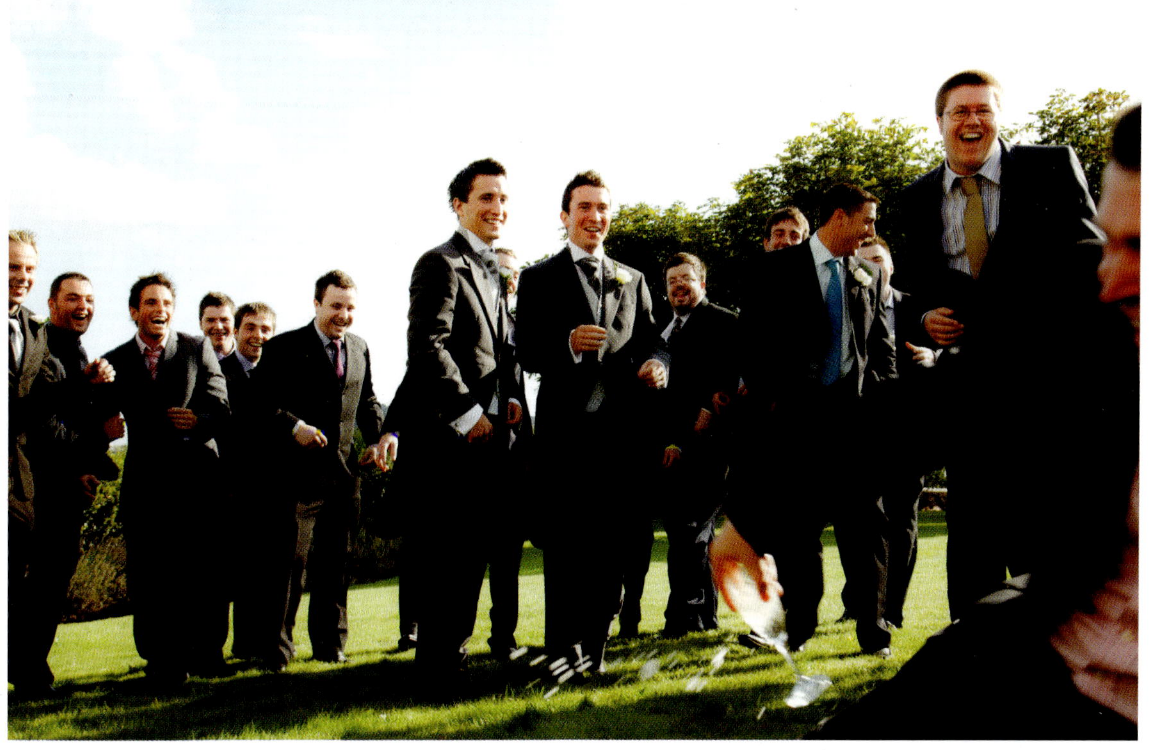

2.30 Cake details

One of the last formal shots, but by no means the least, is the cake-cutting. Even if you are staying all the way through to the first dance, you should mock up the shot in advance to shoot it more candidly later on.

Occasionally there is no official celebration cake, so instead shoot a few more images in the wedding reception room with the bride and groom to capture the scene. If you want a shot where the room is brighter, move the couple away from any windows to enable you to use a slower exposure, with a higher ISO setting or slower shutter speed. Then finish the shot off with a little flash to light the couple with clean light at the desired exposure.

The details are the last images to be shot, and it is essential to get these done before the guests start coming in and reorganizing the tables and the styling. Try to use natural light when shooting close to a window, or flash or LED lighting if there is not enough natural light. Both the flash and LED light will provide a clean, white light that is controllable enough to allow you to still shoot at between f/2.8 and f/4.

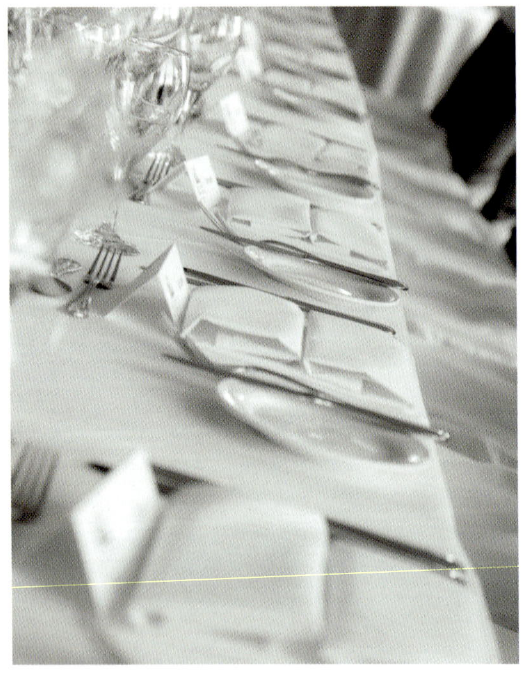

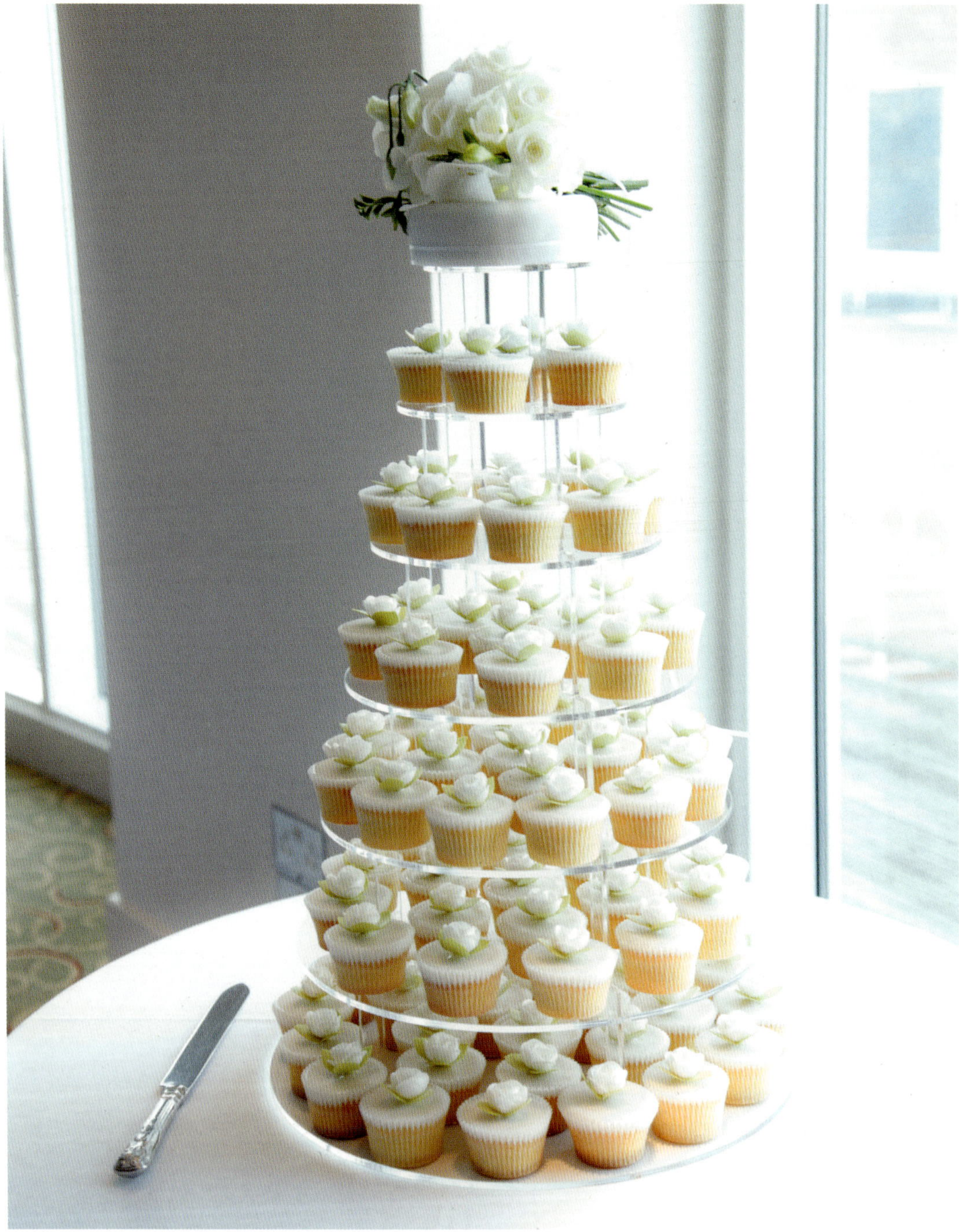

Left: Once again the devil is in the detail, so while the couple are looking around and checking everything, quickly shoot the room details, as well as the room itself. Try and stay as close to a window as possible to make use of the natural light, but if it is too dark you can use either a flash or more often a small LED video light to add accent light to the objects on the tables.

Above: My last shots in the room are of the wedding cake, as well as the bride and groom pretending to cut it. This cake was a little different as it was based on lots of cupcakes, so no cutting shot was possible until later on when they did it live at the end of the speeches.

2.40 Additional couple

If you are on schedule, you can usually steal the couple away from the guests for another 10 minutes of photography around this time. A side room, a conservatory, or a bedroom is a perfect escape and provides a different location to shoot in. This time is stolen while all the guests are being gathered to sit down in the reception function room, so it is essential not to overrun.

Try to use any dramatic locations in these quick sessions to make these images stand apart from anything you have already shot. Sometimes add off-camera flash for more drama, using a simple radio receiver and trigger to fire the flash. Using a flash accessory, such as a honeycomb-type grid, will control the spill of the flash, forcing the light to travel in straight lines and creating a spotlight-like effect.

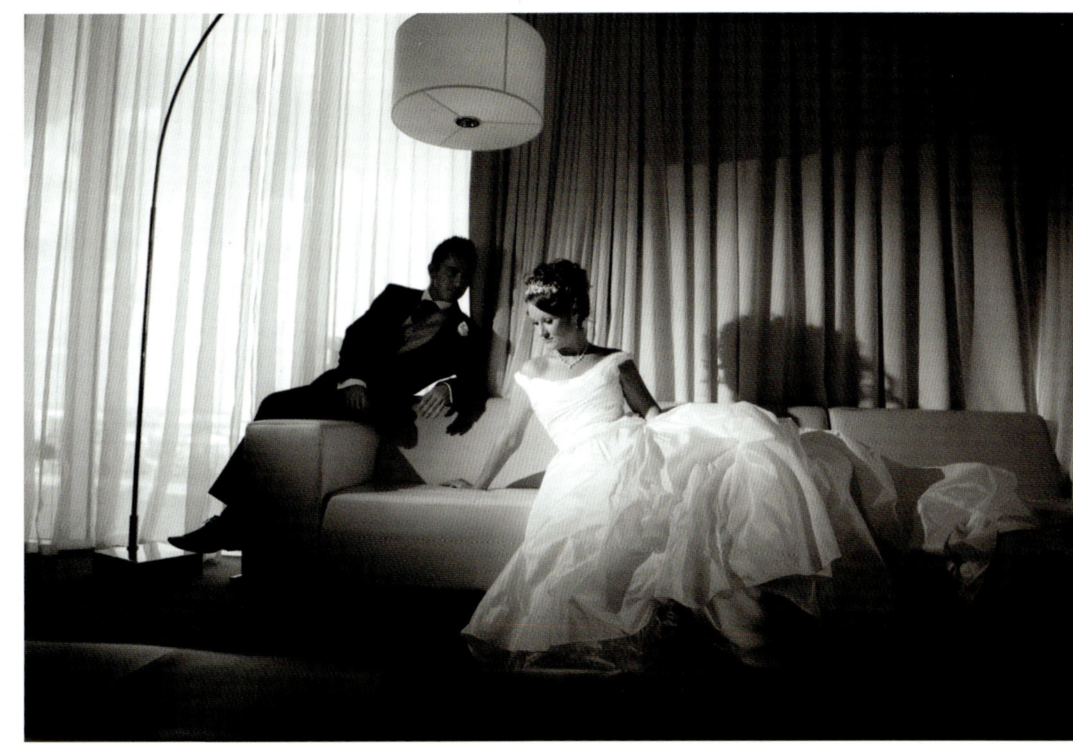

Above: Using a honeycomb grid on the flash controls the light spillage to create a Hollywood-style spotlight on one of the subjects. By dominating the ambient light by only 1 stop, the honeycomb flash will create dramatic lighting every time.

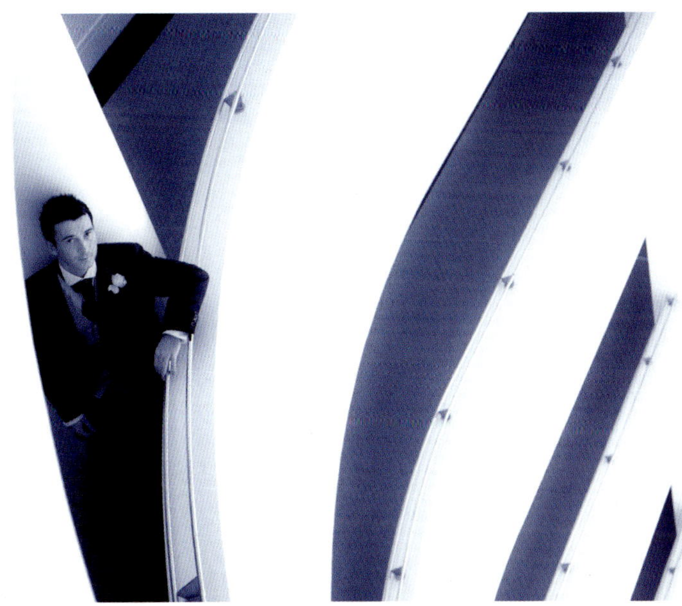

Above: It is always good to show as much of the wedding venue as possible as it is soon forgotten. Afterwards, the only memories that can be shared are the photographs you take, so using different locations or rooms adds variety and extra interest.

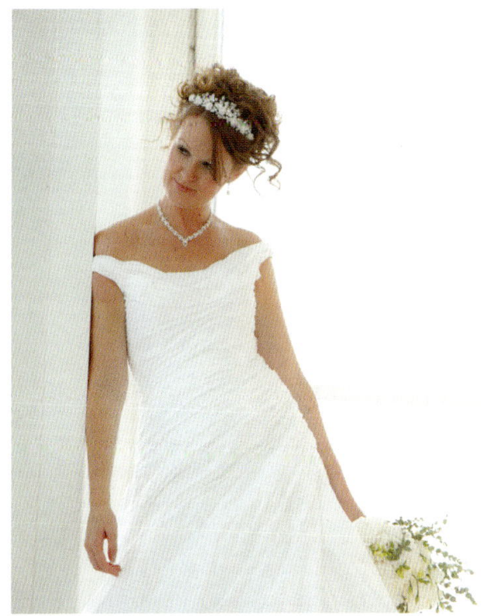

Above: This location, which had frosted glass to the side and behind the bride, helped to create an almost perfect, high-key portrait. The exposure was taken using a handheld meter—set to 18% gray calibration—pointed towards the window from the face.

3.10–4.30 Speeches

Traditionally the speeches take place following the meal, when the mood is lubricated and the guests are content, acting as an end to all the formality of the wedding. However, more and more couples are opting to do the speeches before the meal now.

There are two main lighting techniques and two main lenses I use for the speeches. If I am working in a dark room, with no real contrast in the lighting, I use off-camera flash with on-camera fill-in flash. The off-camera flash acts as a slave to the on-camera master, and is usually on a pole, moved around by my assistant. If I am working alone, I put two flash units on stands, one in each corner behind the main camera. I use the master on the camera to control them and select the flash to fire by using the different flash "groups" as programmed on the camera.

Usually, however, I prefer to shoot with just the ambient light in the room, no matter how little there is, using a very fast lens with an aperture of f/1.4 or f1.8 at a very high ISO and slightly slower shutter speed, if necessary. My preferred shutter speed for speeches is around 1/60 sec. but I can work at a speed of about 1/15 sec., especially if I am using a monopod to support the camera.

Try to be discreet during the speeches, walking around as little as possible and not blocking any guest's view for too long. You can use a 50mm lens or a 70–200mm zoom lens to get the pictures, but it all depends on the room layout and how easy it is to move around the room.

Tip

Look for the key characters being mentioned in the speeches, but don't forget to shoot all of the supporting cast and other guests. A 70–200mm zoom lens will help you to shoot across tables and pick out faces.

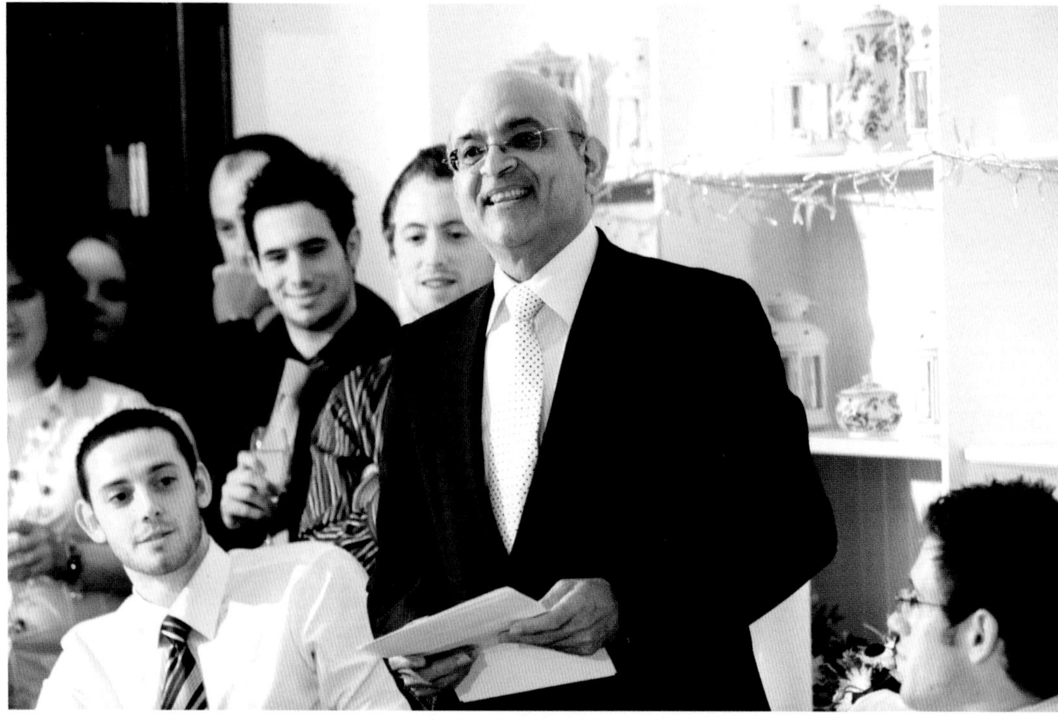

Above: Using off-camera flash to capture the speeches is my preference, as it gives the light a direction, even though it also adds shadows.

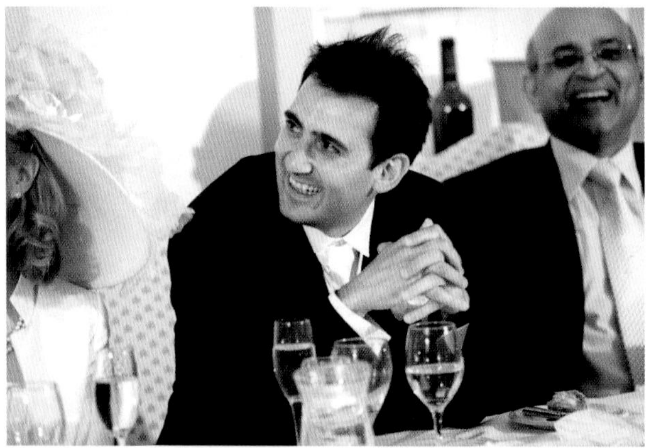

Left: Try to shoot as many guests close up as you can, as well as the people making the speeches, and general shots of the room. By watching the room carefully, you start to pick out the guests with the best facial expressions, so shoot those first, and then watch the others.

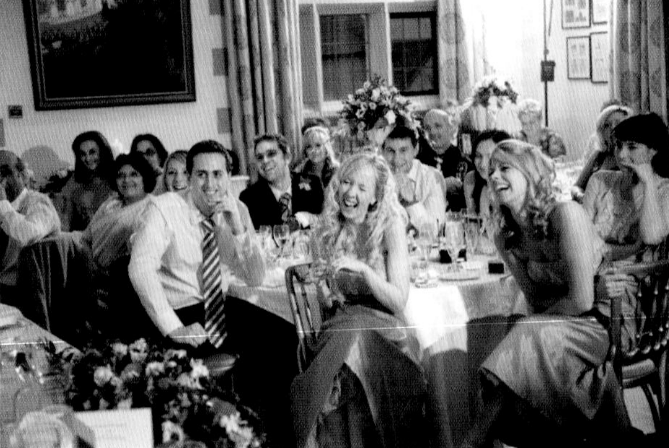

Left: Don't forget to shoot some general shots of the room, including more people in wide-angle shots. This image shows the key players at their own table as well as the applause.

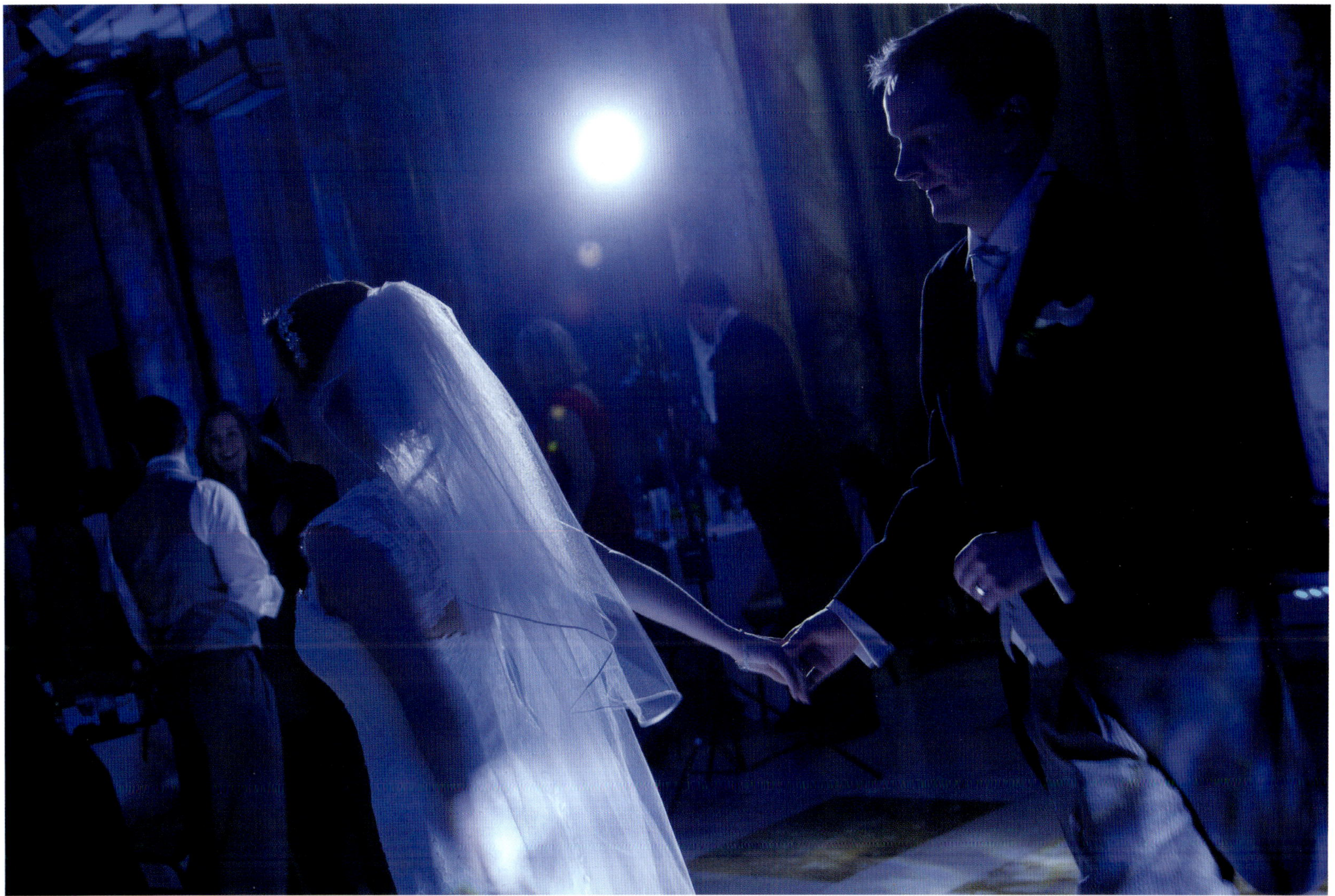

8.00–9.00 First dance

There is often a lot of hanging around while you wait to photograph the first dance, so make sure you have your shots planned, as it's over quickly.

If I can get away with it, I use the room lighting, which at this point tends to be a little more theatrical. Try shooting against colored light from the stage or the band area—even disco lights will produce more creative images than using on-camera flash. I will use some on-camera flash for some of the pictures to light the couple with clean, white light. Also, by using a wide-angle lens with the flash set to zoom, you create a spotlight effect to pick out the couple on the dance floor. A medium-zoom lens is ideal when using flash in this way, as it allows you to zoom in and out from a fixed location, off the dance floor, to get the variety of shots you need.

Above: Shoot a variety of images of the first dance, some with flash and some without. The ones without flash are to capture the scene or atmosphere, while those with flash are to capture the couple. You will normally have to use a high ISO in this situation in order to allow a faster shutter speed to freeze the movement.

Tip

If there is no colored spotlighting in the room, put a flash in the two corners behind the bride and groom, each fitted with a colored gel to create your own dramatic images.

Chapter 6
Postproduction

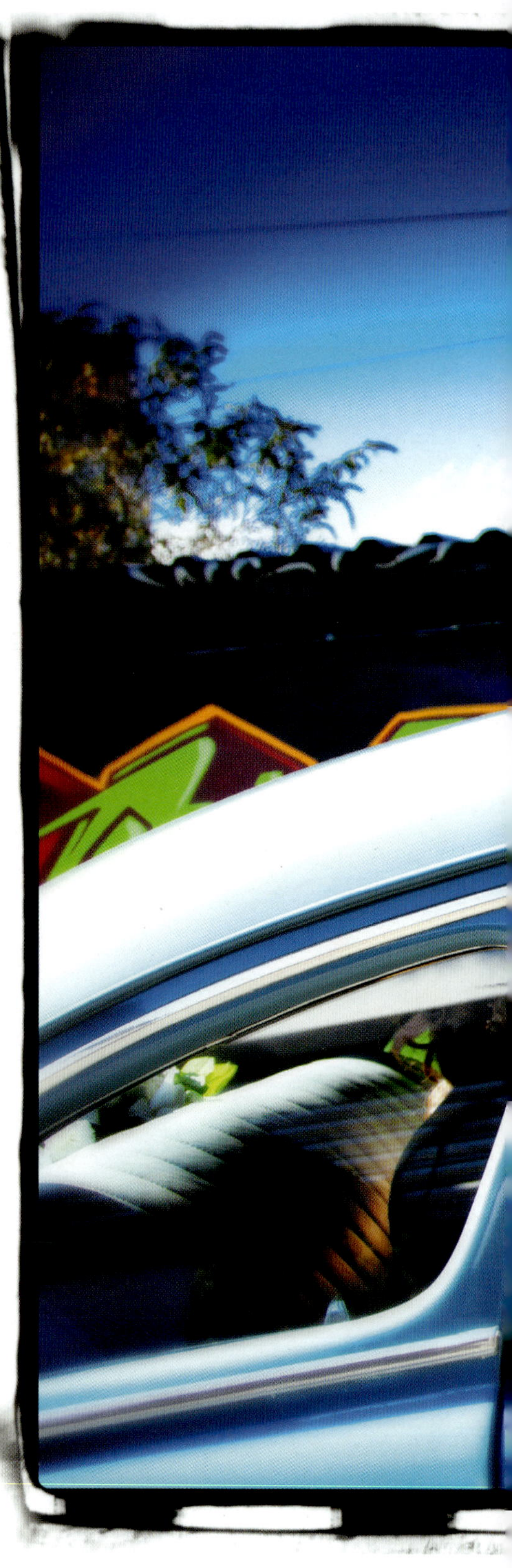

An image always needs to go through manipulation of some sort, including color-balancing and cropping—today this is done by using a photo-editing application. Yet even for a professional photographer, processing the images from a wedding can take days and cause more headaches than anything else. So this chapter covers a processing workflow to create a finished final proof.

Right: Without doubt the real thrill of digital capture and manipulation for the wedding photographer is the chance to add even more creativity to the image, as well as correcting simple flaws with either simple retouching or elaborate changes to contrast and color.

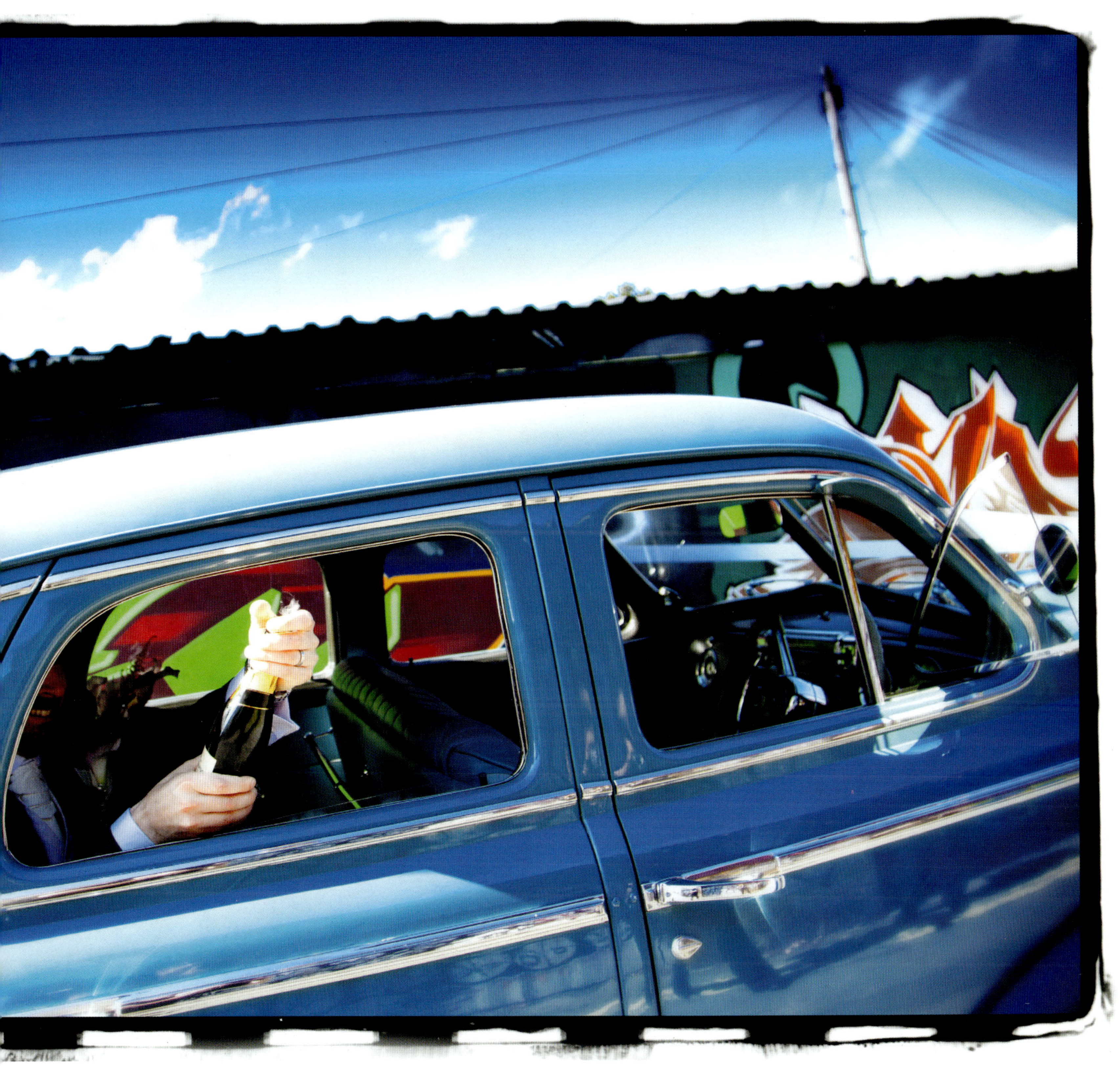

Downloading

A workflow plan for postproduction is essential to make sure you not only complete all the necessary tasks in the least possible time, but also to ensure the security of all your images. I always write out what I need to do on paper first, and then follow it to the letter, but at the same time analyze it to make sure I am not wasting any time on any of the steps.

The first step in the workflow plan is downloading your images. Depending on the number of images you shot at the wedding, and the amount of memory on the cards, you will probably need to download files from between three and six cards.

Downloading the card

For speed and security, I always download each of the cards in turn using a card reader, instead of direct from the camera. This is because downloading from the camera can cause problems, such as the camera battery power draining, the cable from the camera to the computer becoming disconnected, or not all the files downloading. The files also download more quickly from a card reader to the computer than direct from the camera.

Copy each card into a separate folder, within a master folder for the client (e.g. master folder name "03 23 14 Stella & Richard," subfolder names "card 1," "card 2," "card 3," and so on). It is a good idea to rotate the cards during the shoot so that some cards are not used more than others, which prevents any problems from overuse, such as corrupted files. Therefore, at this stage don't worry too much about downloading the images in the order in which they were shot.

Once the first card is downloaded, check that the number of files on the card matches the number of files in the new subfolder on the computer. Also check to make sure there is not a

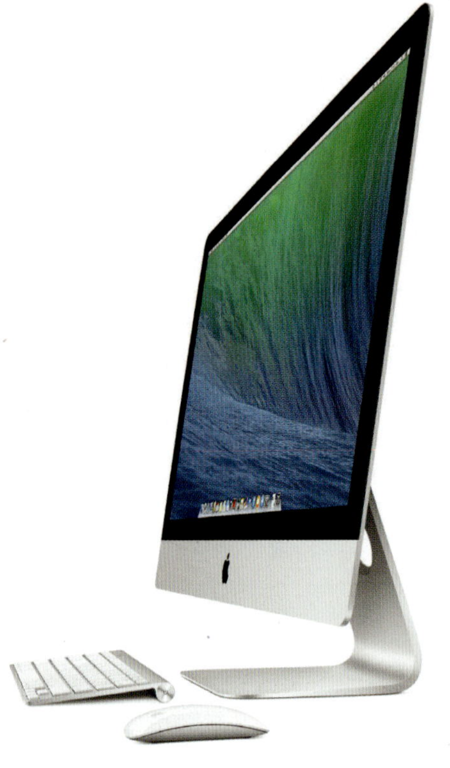

Above: Your home PC is the hub of your electronic workflow. The Apple iMac series, popular with designers and photographers, is a neat combination of monitor and computer system in an ultra-slim chassis.

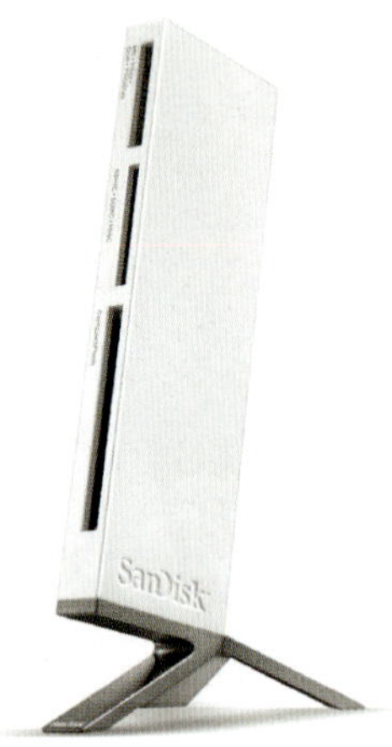

Above: For most sessions a 16GB memory card is sufficient, although some people prefer to use two 8GB cards for security. You will need a card reader, such as this SanDisk ImageMate, if your PC doesn't have one built in.

second folder of images on the card, because the camera creates new folders when a certain image number is reached. Once you've checked, move on to the next card. Occasionally, problems occur with a card and its image files, so downloading each card into a separate subfolder makes it easier to identify any corrupted cards and images.

Downloading one card at a time into a separate subfolder also enables you to start the editing process while the other cards are downloading, speeding up your workflow.

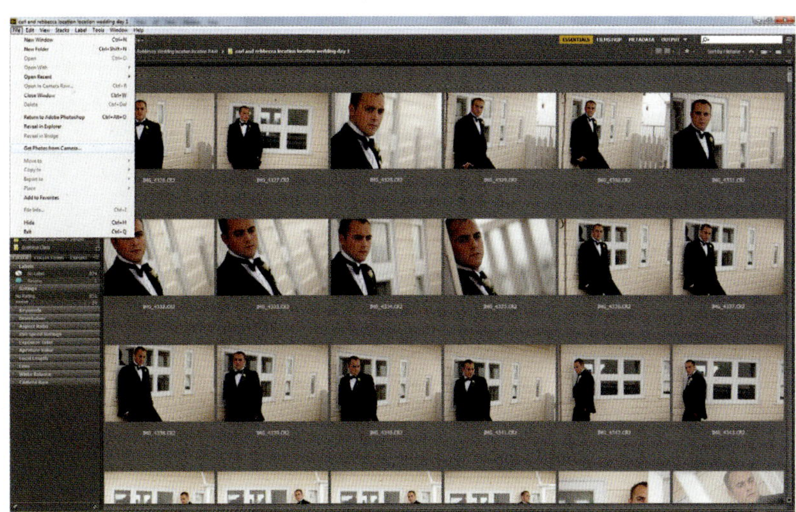

Above: Auto-download software allows you to download images directly from the memory card or camera, providing you with options such as backup and conversion, as well as renaming and duplication.

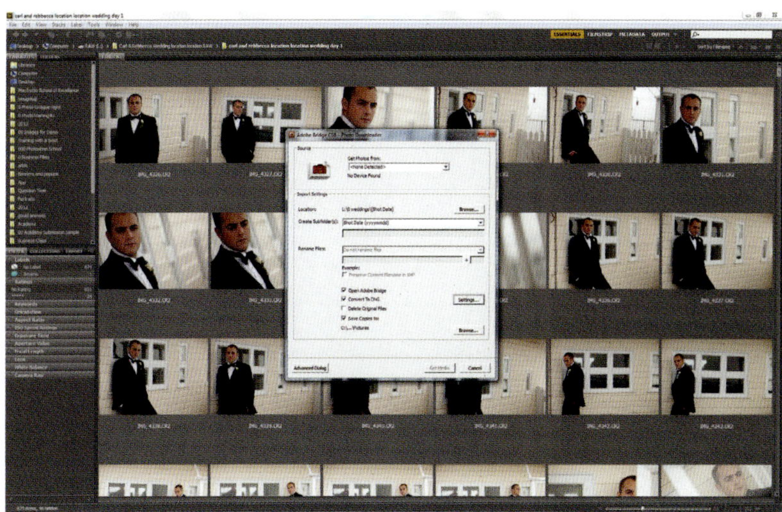

Above: Options to duplicate and convert a file on download can sound like a good idea, but in reality they can slow down the process as well as possibly introduce errors, so if you do use them exercise caution.

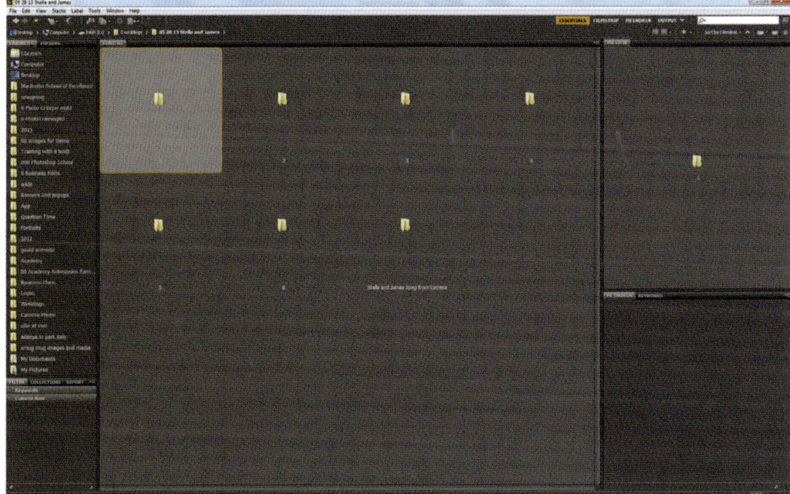

Above: Each memory card is downloaded to its own subfolder within the client master folder to speed up the edit process, as well as to avoid any download errors.

Tip

Card readers are available that read one type of card or several different types of card. It's also possible to buy large card readers with multiple card slots for bulk downloads.

Editing & Backup

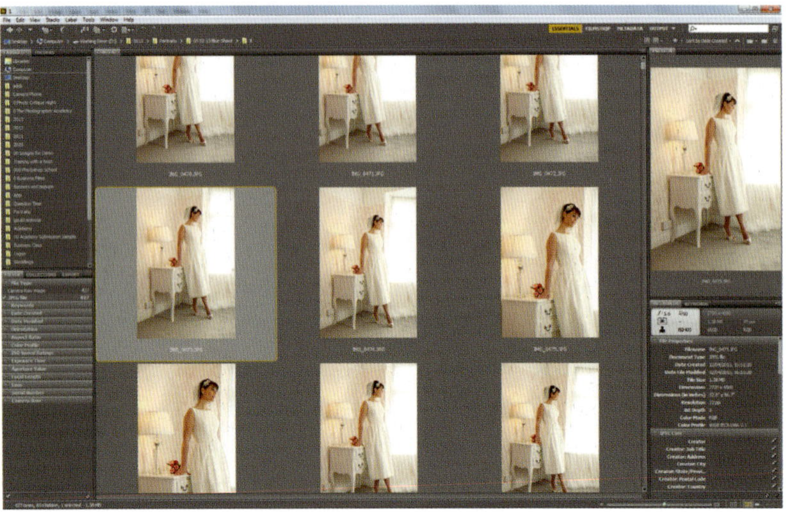

Above: Separating the JPEG files.

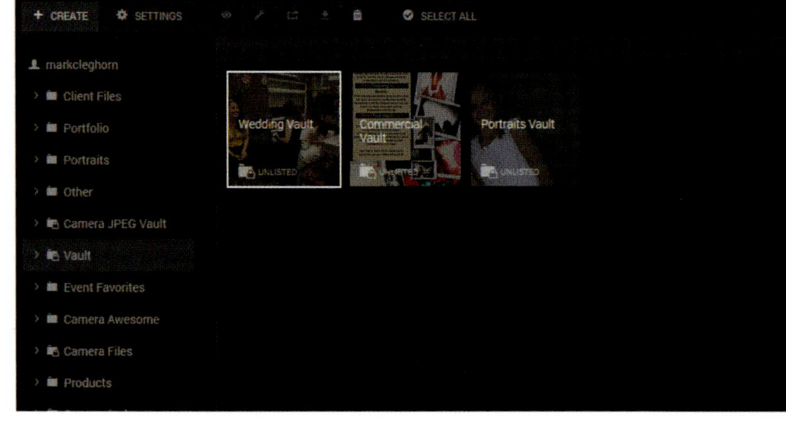

Above: Wedding vault on SmugMug.

You may have shot the best wedding photographs, with lots of variety and creativity, but if you haven't edited your pictures properly, your client will be faced with too much choice and too many similar images, which will mean a bland album selection and a disappointed client.

So you need to be ruthless in editing down your images. Look at all the similar shots and select just one or two—unless you know you want to use a series of images in the album for effect (use this technique sparingly, however). You might think it better to offer your client a range of images to choose from, but this will just lead to confusion and frustration, and slow down the whole process of selecting images for the album.

Remember to have confidence in your own selection and, as I often say, "What the client does not see will not hurt them." There will always be some clients who think they want more images to choose from, because they are paying, and think that quantity is as important as quality. So, in short, choose only the very best images from the shoot, and the client will love them all.

To select the best images, I use Adobe Bridge software, which is free with Adobe Photoshop and one of Adobe's Creative Suite products. I find the layout, image tagging, and slideshow functions provide the fastest way to review hundreds of images in each subfolder in full-screen mode. However, most image editing programs work in a similar way, so you can adapt the following workflow to your own preferred software.

Separating the JPEGs

Once you have opened the first subfolder of images, separate the JPEG files and the Raw files. As the JPEG files are only shot for backup and preview, they are not needed unless you have a corrupted Raw file. I store these JPEGs off-site on the SmugMug web site in a backup wedding folder, for which I pay an annual fee and can store as many JPEG (or MP4) files and folders as I need on the site at no extra cost. I also use the SmugMug web site for wedding image proofing

and sales, as well as my image galleries and details promoting my services.

Selecting JPEG in the bottom left panel in Bridge shows just the JPEG files, which you can then move to a new folder in the master folder called "JPEG from Camera." You do this by selecting all files (CTRL + A in Windows) and then dragging them to the desired folder in the Folders panel in Bridge. Alternatively, you could right-click the mouse to bring up the Options box and select "Move To..." option.

As soon as the JPEGS from one folder have been separated, I upload them to my SmugMug vault folder, completing the first level of off-site backup. Once these files have begun the upload process, I can come back to my folder of images for editing, now only showing the Raw files.

Editing the Raw files

The next step is to choose which images to delete and which ones to keep. You can use the Slideshow option in Bridge (View>Slide Show),

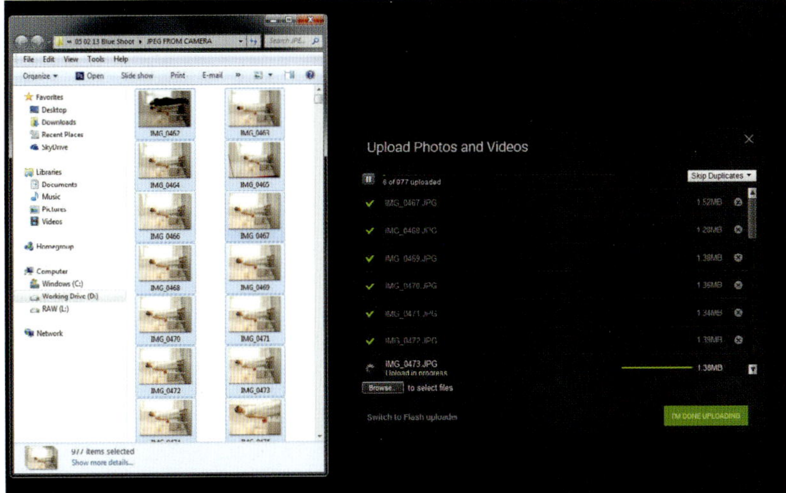

Above: The SmugMug vault drag and drop.

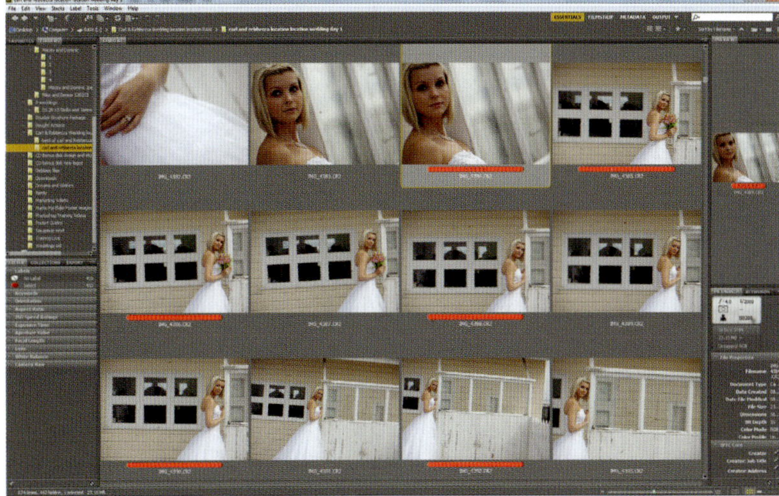

Above: A slideshow from a wedding with red labeling applied.

which allows you to see the images in full-screen mode and gives you the option of zooming in to check fine detail. Then, using the left and right arrows on the keyboard, move through the images, choosing which ones to delete. To mark the images for deletion, I type the number 6, which adds a red label to the file, making it easy to find in the Lightbox viewer. The other reason to use the label option instead of the star rating is that it is quicker and easier to remove the red label by pressing the number 6 again.

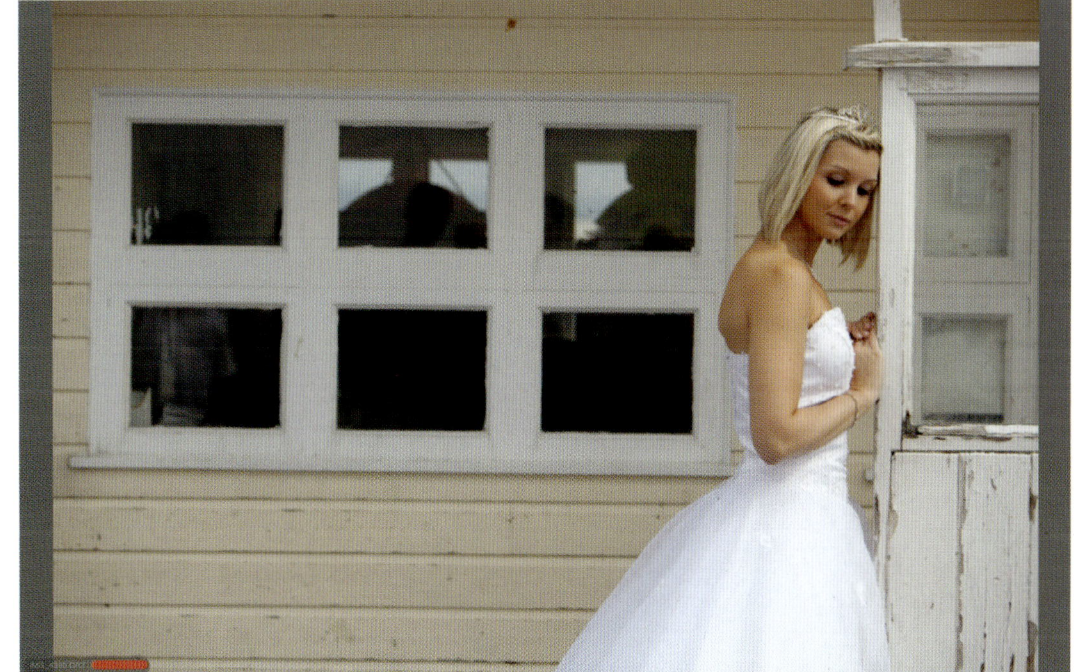

Above: Adobe Bridge allows you to view images at full screen and to zoom in to check fine detail. You can then label images as required.

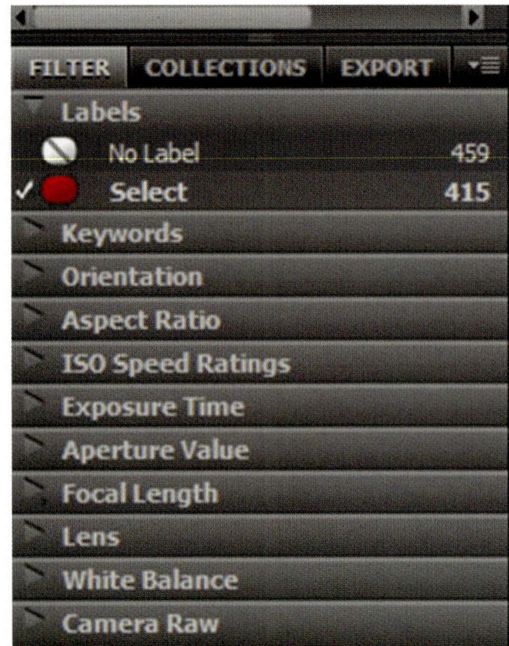

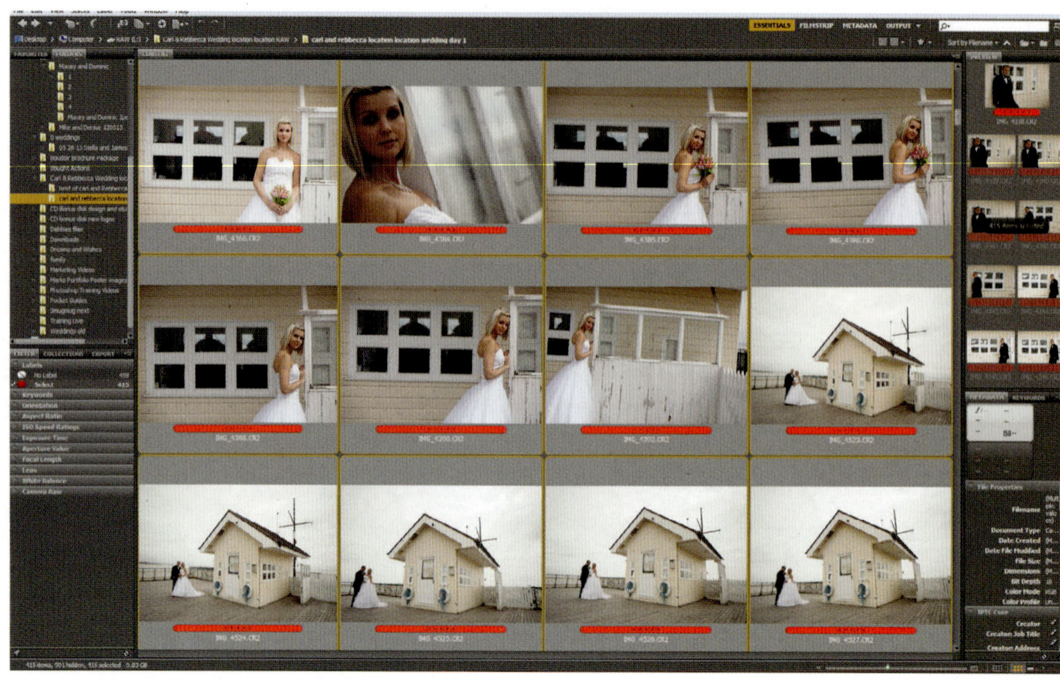

Above: The Filter option in Bridge is a quick way to identify and separate marked files using color labels or star ratings.

Above: Once the red-labeled images are selected, delete them from the computer. If you are in any doubt, though, back them up or process them as corrected JPEG files first.

Once you have selected all the images to be deleted—marked with the red labels—select the Red label option on the Filter panel to only show the red-labeled images. The final step is to select all (CTRL + A), and then hit the Delete key on the keyboard—this will send all these files to the Trash. However, if you're only just starting out as a wedding photographer, it would be a good idea to backup the files to be deleted as well, just to be sure—after all, storage is quite cheap.

An alternative archiving approach is to keep all the Raw files initially, correcting them in exposure and color, processing them as a JPEG files, then backing these up instead, as the JPEG files will be much smaller. You can then confidently delete all the unwanted Raw files.

With this process complete for one card subfolder, simply repeat the above workflow for each additional card—by the time you have finished the edit for one card, another should have finished downloading, so you are never waiting for the computer and you have already begun storing your files off-site. As you become more experienced and proficient, you can adapt your own workflow to suit you.

Picture selection

Choosing which images to keep or delete is a difficult process to master, but it will become easier and quicker the more often you do it. The first thing to look for when deciding which images to delete is to select any unnecessary duplicate shots. Then look for obvious flaws, such as poor exposure, blurred images, or any misfires. Select the shots that are similar, but have only a slight change in expression or camera angle, then compare them quickly, using the left and right arrows, to select the best. After your first run-through, you may find that you still have too many images, so don't be afraid to repeat the process. Sometimes I keep some of the similar image files, process them, and place them in a separate folder, but never show them to the client.

To select the best images, look at the eyes and the expressions of the subjects—these are the main elements that separate the good image from the bad. Make sure that you can see in the subject's eyes how they feel—and exclude any images in which they look bored or tired. Also delete any images with distractions in the background, bad composition, images that are slightly blurred because of camera shake or clients moving, and any awkward or static poses that make them look bored or lifeless. Sometimes your attempts at more creative shots may backfire, especially when introducing motion blur, for instance, so be honest with yourself and delete even those images you may like because they're more creative, but just didn't work.

With all the files from all the cards edited, the Raw files can be moved into one folder ready for sorting, renaming, and then processing. I use the first folder as the new master folder for all the Raw files, and then move all the other files into this folder. Simply drag and drop the files to sort them, making sure that you now keep them in an order so they tell the story of the day—you may perhaps need to use a little artistic licence.

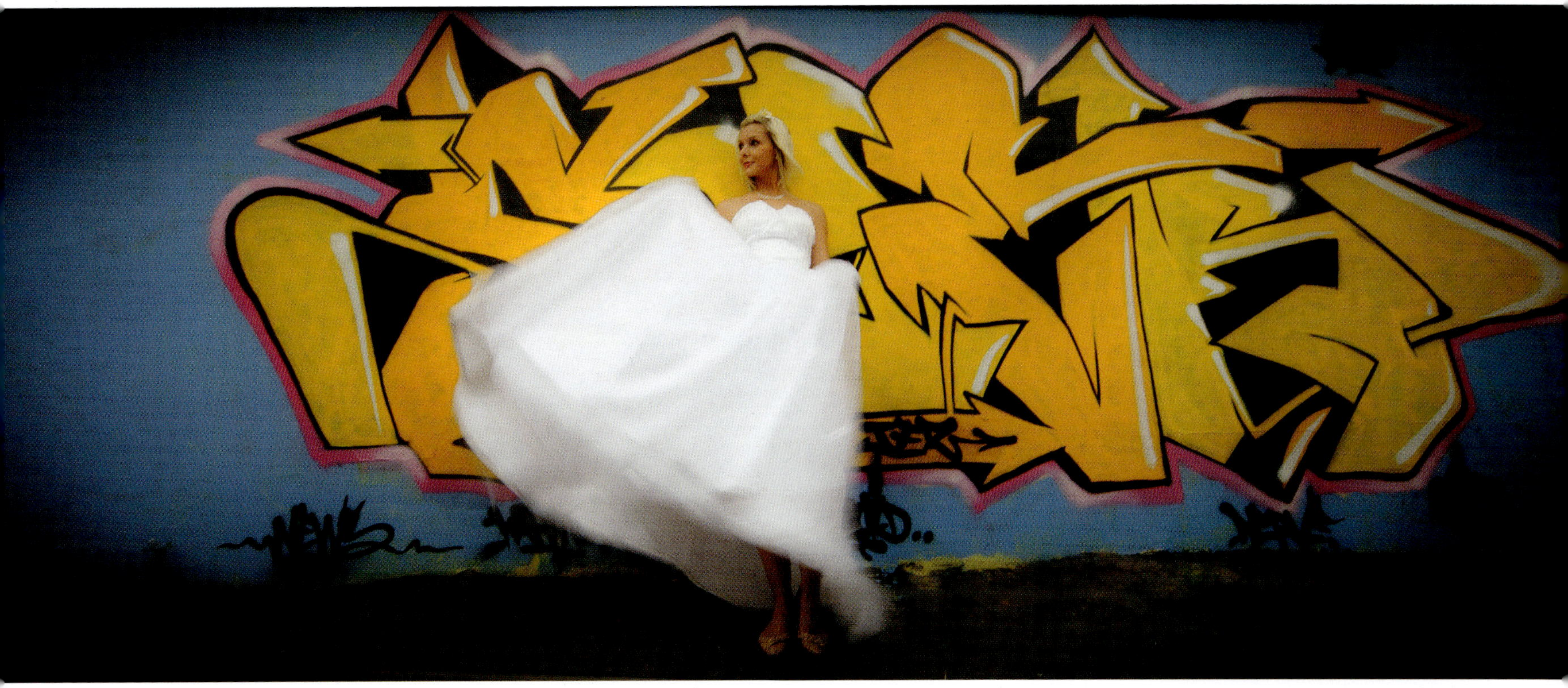

Renaming files

To rename all the images so they run in your preferred chronological order, give them a unique file name that will identify them now and in the future—this avoids mistakes when ordering and selecting them for the album design. I always rename the files after selection, as this will disguise the number of images you are not showing the client from the shoot.

Using Bridge again, rename the files by selecting All Files, and then going to Tools>Batch Rename. I then use a three-digit number followed by an underscore ("_"), followed by the bride and groom's initials, another underscore, then the wedding date in month, date, and year format— for example: "001_KD_092213." This way, each image has a unique file name, and the bride and groom only need to use the first numeric digits to refer to an image.

Above & right: A slow shutter speed was used to allow the bride to move her dress to add motion, but it was essential to keep her face and torso still so she remained sharp. When making the selection, I preferred the first image for its sharpness, but I preferred the second image for the dress and expression. However, the second image is unusable because of the motion blur on her face, so this time a more creative approach didn't quite work, and I deleted both images. But that's photography!

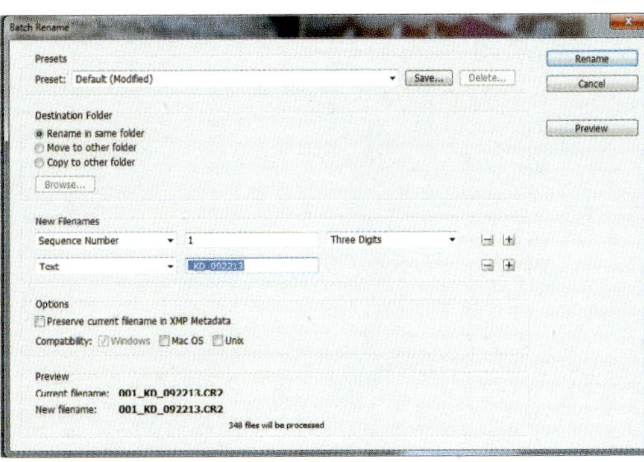

Above: Renaming batch files in Bridge.

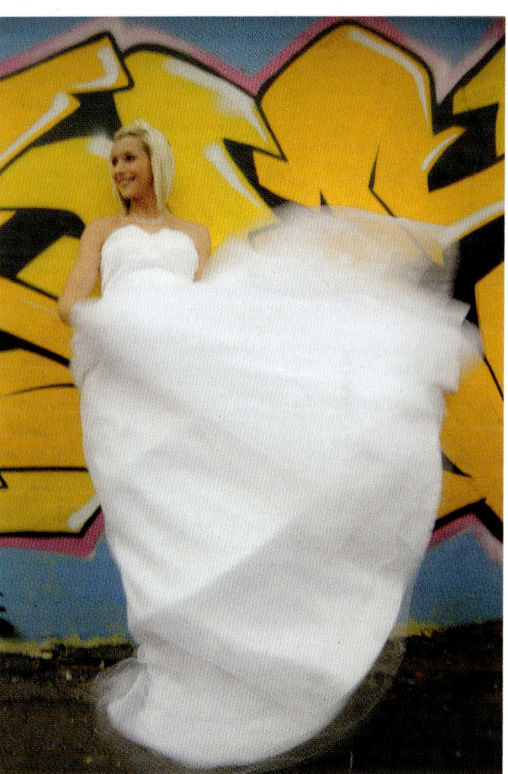

Correcting Images

Even if you are the most technical photographer in the world, I can guarantee that as a wedding photographer—working under real conditions of varying light, color, contrast, and exposure—you will need to do some image correction before showing the pictures to your client.

The benefit of shooting Raw files rather than JPEG on a wedding is that you retain complete control over an image, with all the data being recorded in the files. This means that image detail can be recovered, even if the original shot was slightly under- or overexposed, or taken in difficult or mixed lighting.

Also Raw files can be adjusted in batches very quickly using a Raw processing module such as Adobe Camera Raw (ACR), and they can be edited multiple times without any loss of information, unlike a JPEG file that degrades by removing data every time it is edited. When editing files in ACR, it is always best to open them in small batches, even though you can open them all at once—I choose the home images first, then progress to the church images, and so on, breaking the files up into each part of the day. This makes the process manageable for me and faster for the computer. So once I have selected the first batch of images by pressing Shift and clicking, I can open them up in ACR by selecting File>Open in Camera Raw (CTRL+R).

Adobe Camera Raw window

Looking at the ACR window can be a little daunting at first, but the workflow is easy to understand. Let's look at the ACR window clockwise, from top left.

On the left you will see the image thumbnails:
These are only the images you have selected to bring into the ACR process. The thumbnails can be made bigger or smaller by dragging the bar just to the right of the thumbnails themselves. You can scroll through the multiple images by using the vertical slider. Select one or more images by either Shift-clicking, or Ctrl + Shift-clicking the mouse. You can select all images at the top by pressing the Select All button. You synchronize adjustments from one image to another by hitting the Synchronize button.

On the right-hand side are the Adjustment panels:
These will change depending on which tool you have selected, or by selecting one of the different tab icons. The Histogram panel warns you of detail loss in either the highlight or shadow areas of the image.

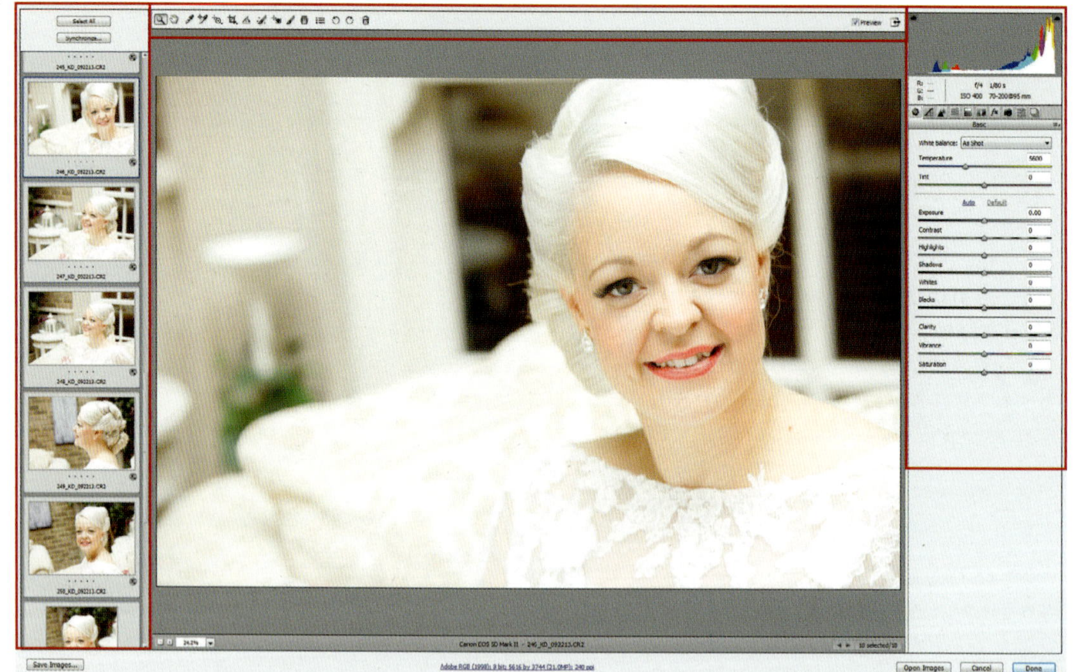

At the top we have the Tool options:

- **Zoom** Double-click to zoom to 100% or click to enlarge; click + Alt shrinks the image.
- **Move** Double-click to show the full image or click to move the image around.
- **Color Picker** Color balance based on clicking something White with detail or Gray.
- **Color Sampler** Sample one or more colors.
- **Target Adjustment** Click and drag left or right on a selected tone in an image to adjust contrast, color, or saturation; select the different options from the icon menu.
- **Crop** Crops to a custom size, a constrained size, or a normal crop, all from the icon menu.
- **Straighten** Drag along one edge of the image to crop and straighten the image.
- **Spot Removal** Removes Camera CCD dust and unwanted items such as spots, litter, and provides basic retouching.
- **Red Eye Removal** Click on the red of the eye.
- **Adjustment Brush** Creative or advanced adjustments based on painting in chosen effect.
- **Gradient Tool** Drag across an image to darken or lighten areas, as well as add color effects.
- **ACR Preferences** Set your ACR preferences.
- **Rotate Left** Corrects image rotation.
- **Rotate Right** Corrects image rotation.
- **Toggle for Delete** Marks an image to be deleted; file is deleted when you exit ACR.
- **Preview** Toggles the effect on and off, as well as any changes you have just made.
- **Full Screen** Makes the ACR window appear in full-screen or small-screen mode.

Basic panel

This is where all the work is done. From basic adjustments to heavy styling, these panels will fix most things and create amazing effects. It is good to note that when holding your mouse on or above a word, the mouse can be used to drag the adjustment left or right—this is called a "Scrubby." Also note that the default setting is for all the sliders to be set to zero. To reset any slider, double-click the "move" icon on the slide bar.

- **White Balance** Options for preset color to match camera modes; there are fewer options when adjusting a JPEG file.
- **Temperature** Sliders to make a manual adjustment in color temperature.
- **Tint** Slightly alters the color in the image.
- **Auto and Default** Options for a quick fix, based on auto-corrections or resets to the ACR default settings.
- **Exposure** Apply a plus or minus amount to correct the exposure.
- **Contrast** Slide to the right to increase contrast, slide to the left to decrease it.
- **Highlights** Slide to the right to burn out detail, slide to the left to recover it.
- **Shadows** Slide to the right blocks more shadow detail, slide to the left opens the shadow areas up.
- **Whites** Slide to the right burns out detail, slide to the left recovers detail.
- **Blacks** Slide to the right blocks more shadow detail, slide to the left opens the shadow areas up; mainly used in correction or for punchy black and white images.
- **Clarity** Slide to the right sharpens the mid-tone, slide to the left makes the tones soften and glow.
- **Vibrancy** Slide to the left increases colors other than skin tones, slide to the left does the reverse.
- **Saturation** Slide to the right increases color saturation all over, slide to the left does the reverse.
- **Tone Curve panel** Adjusts the curve and hence controls detail and contrast.
- **Detail panel** Controls the sharpness of an image as well as the ability to reduce the image noise.
- **HSL/Grayscale panel** Allows you to control the hue, saturation, and luminance within an image and gives you the option to use grayscale color for black and white.
- **Split Toning panel** Quick split tone options by sliding the saturation sliders and then mixing color.
- **Lens Correction panel** Quick-fixes lens characteristics.
- **Effects panel** Grain and Vignette options.
- **Camera Calibration panel** Calibration and correction options.
- **Pre-sets panel** Essential for a faster workflow, but you have to build the Presets first.

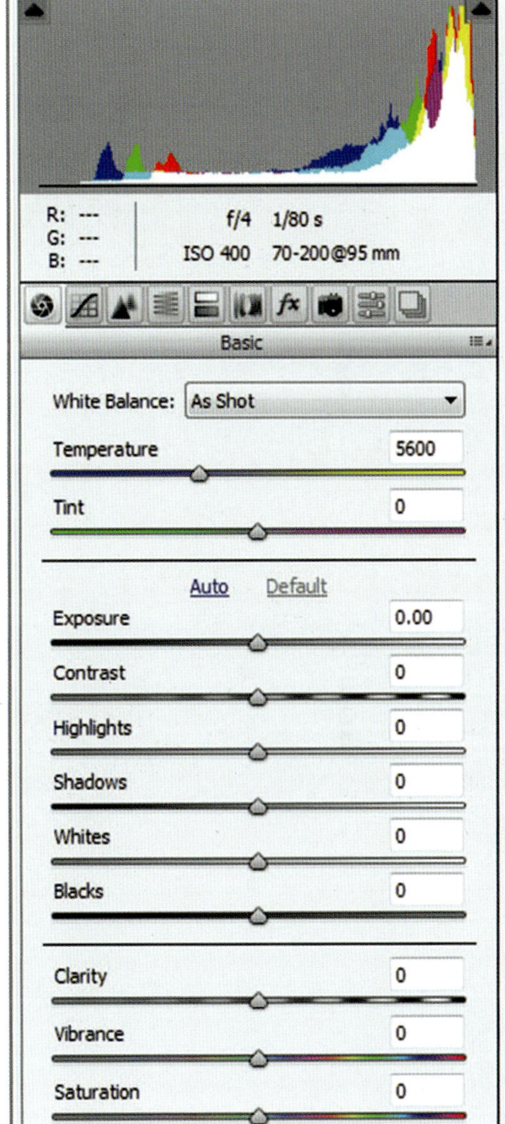

First batch adjustments

Once you have the first batch of images in the ACR window, you can select the first batch shot under similar lighting conditions and adjust them together.

The first adjustment in the workflow is to the Color Balance. This can be adjusted in several ways:

- using the Color Picker tool on the top tool bar
- using the White Balance option on the Basic palette on the right
- or by adjusting the Color Temperature and Tint sliders manually.

Make sure you have a calibrated monitor to ensure your colors are correct. If your monitor is not set up properly you will not be adjusting any color casts correctly.

After color comes Exposure correction. Usually, this means an adjustment between plus or minus 0.25 of a stop. Any more than 0.75 of a stop, and you will need to correct the color and contrast further.

The Contrast is the next tweak. This will really make a difference, often sharpening the image by just rendering the blacks a deeper, blacker black, and the whites a sharper, whiter white.

Highlights and Whites will recover fine detail in the highlight areas. I only tweak Blacks if I need a punchy black and white image, or if I want to give more punch to the blacks without affecting the overall contrast.

Clarity is used to sharpen or soften the midpoint of the image tone, plus helping to sharpen the image, and minus to soften the image. I often adjust the image by setting Clarity to -25 and Sharpening to +90—this creates a soft glow on skin, but sharpens whites for details such as veils and hair.

Finally, in the Basic mode, I reduce the saturation to obtain a more muted color. You can also set this to -100 to create a pleasing monochrome effect, but this is not as good as fully desaturating the colors in the HSL saturation panel—this creates a finer depth and tone to each color.

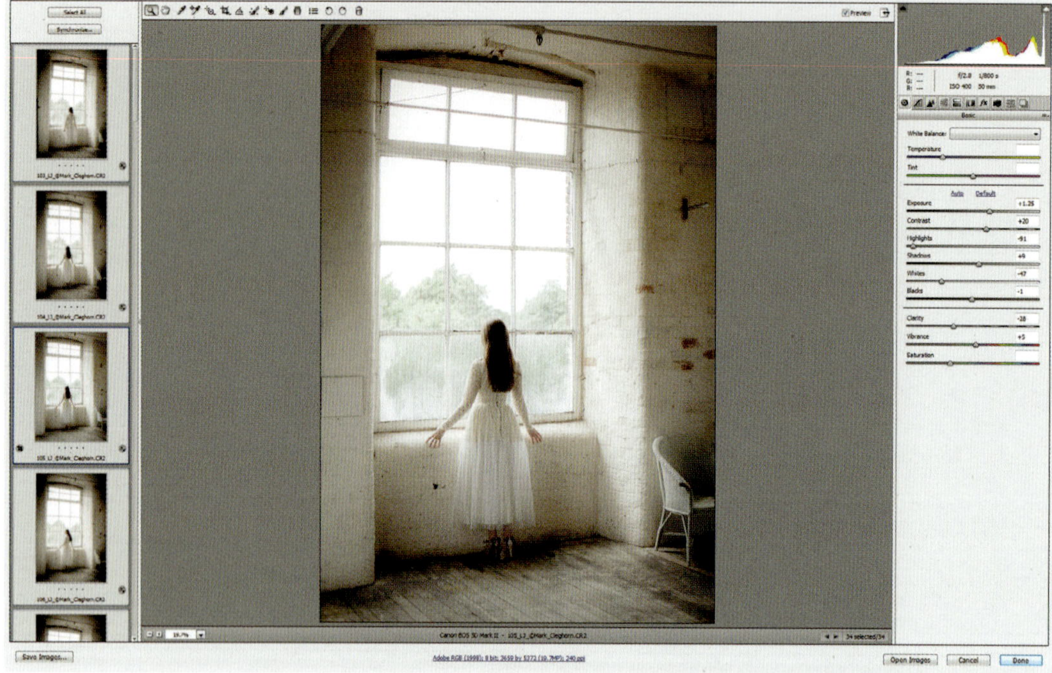

Above: Adobe Camera Raw allows you to adjust Raw or JPEG images either individually or in batches, but most importantly it will save a lot of time compared to using Photoshop for individual adjustments.

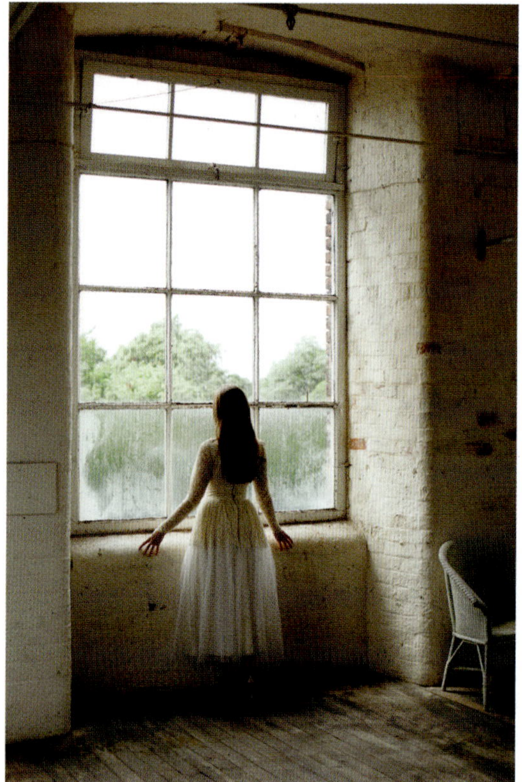

Above: Even if you get the RAW image 95% right in the camera, you will always want to make some adjustments.

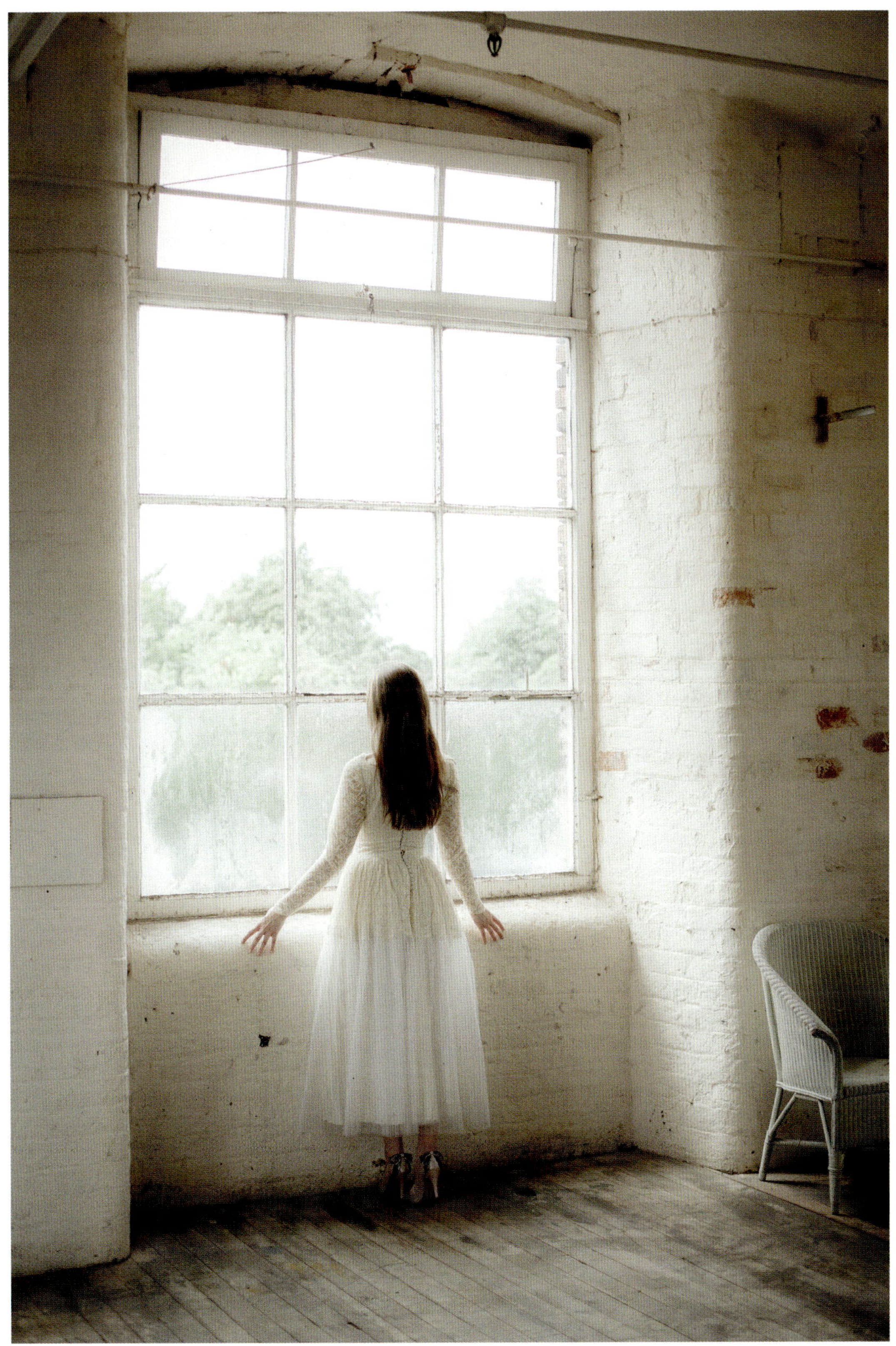

Left: This is the same image with adjustments made—along with 30 other files—to add a more creative finish. Even though the adjustments look extreme, they simply involve adjustment using either the sliders or Presets. Adjustments were as follows:

Exposure +1.25 / Contrast +20 / Highlights -91 / Shadows +9 / Whites -47 / Blacks -1 / Clarity -28 / Vibrancy +5 / Saturation -33 / Sharpening +99 / Vignette -28.

Enhancing Images

In this section I show, step-by-step, how to enhance an image using ACR. Remember that most of these steps can be used across a variety of images, either at the time of initial adjustment, or by selecting more than one file and then synchronizing them.

Black and white

There are many ways to change an image to black and white, but here are three simple ways to do this, as well as how to create the final, finished image.

Saturation

The quickest way to convert an image to black and white is to use the Saturation slider at the bottom of the Basic adjustment panel. Move the slider to the left or type in a value of -100. This will give you a good black and white image, and is a good option if you are in a rush. Remember to use the Contrast and Black sliders for more punch.

Grayscale

The Grayscale option—which is found in the HSL panel—produces a better tonal monochrome image than just by using Saturation, because it allows you to adjust the color sliders to change the color tones in the photograph. For instance, moving the reds and oranges to the right will lighten the skin tones, and moving them to the left will darken them. It will work in the same way with all the color tones. You finally save the image or open it in Photoshop. When you save the image or open the file you will find that it is now in grayscale and not red-green-blue (RGB) format. This is both good and bad: it is good for printing in a magazine or newspaper as the black and white image will have no color cast, but it is bad for a photo print because the image will usually look a little flatter.

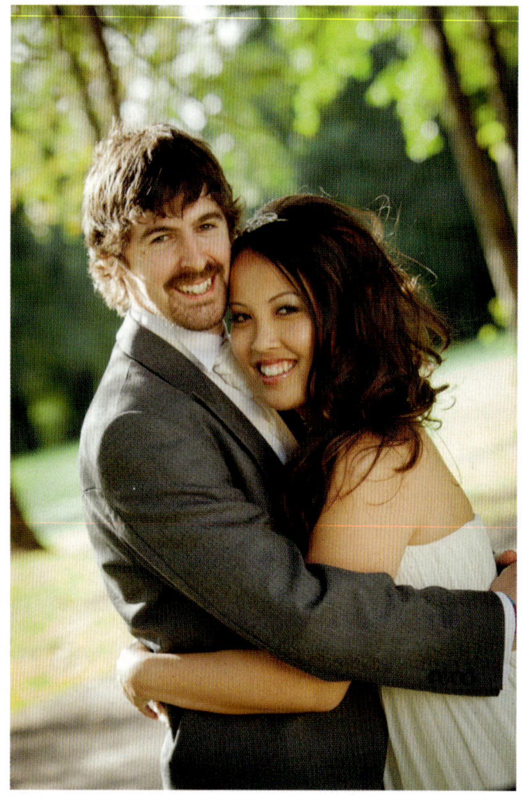

Above: The original image before enhancement.

HSL and luminance

The best way to convert an image to black and white is using the HSL option, but not converting it to grayscale as before. The reason for this is that it will make the finished image contrast "pop" when output for an album or as a photo print.

It is a two-step process. Firstly, reduce all the colors fully using the Saturation slider in the HSL panel. Then select the Luminance panel, and move the color sliders to adjust the tones, making them lighter or darker. This adds to the effect of the finished image, which looks similar to an old black and white print, with different grades of contrast in different parts on the photograph.

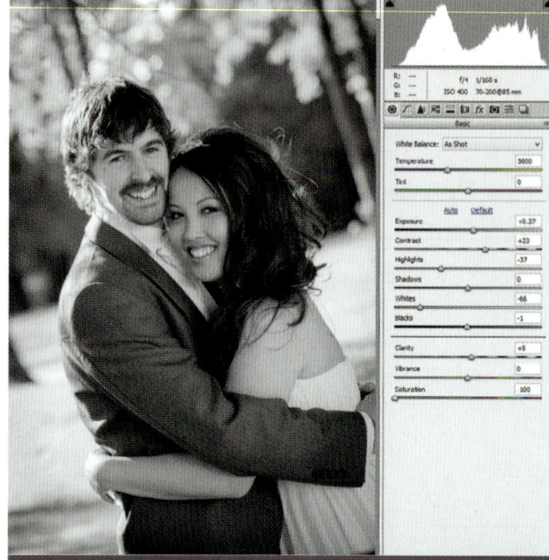

1 Creating a mono image with the Saturation slider

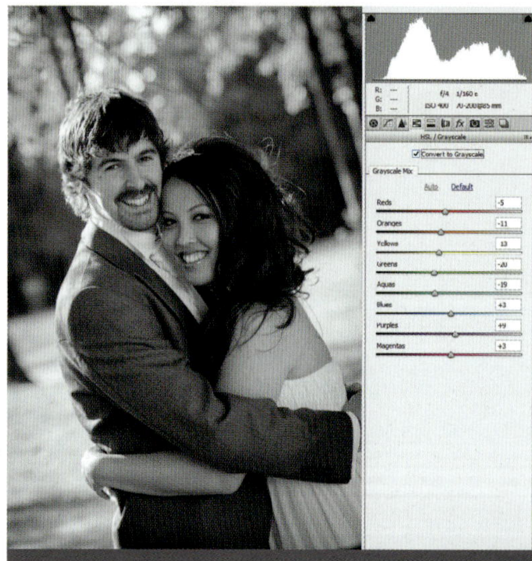

2 Creating a mono image with the Grayscale option in the HSL panel

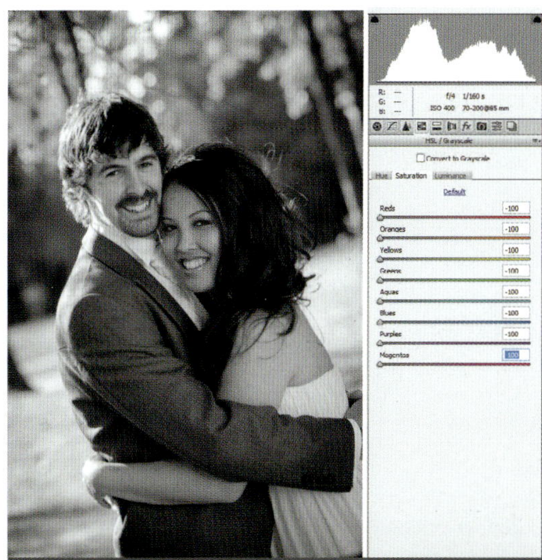

3 Reducing all the colors by moving each slider fully to the left

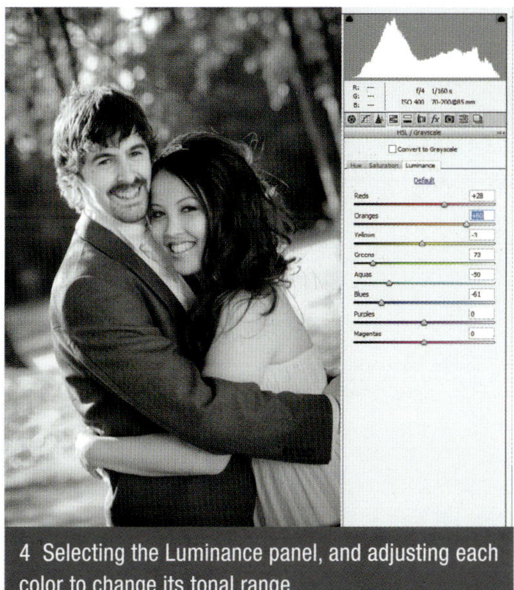

4 Selecting the Luminance panel, and adjusting each color to change its tonal range

Right: The fully finished HSL-converted image has had a final finish of a vignette in FX, as well as an adjustment to the Contrast and Black values in the Basic panel.

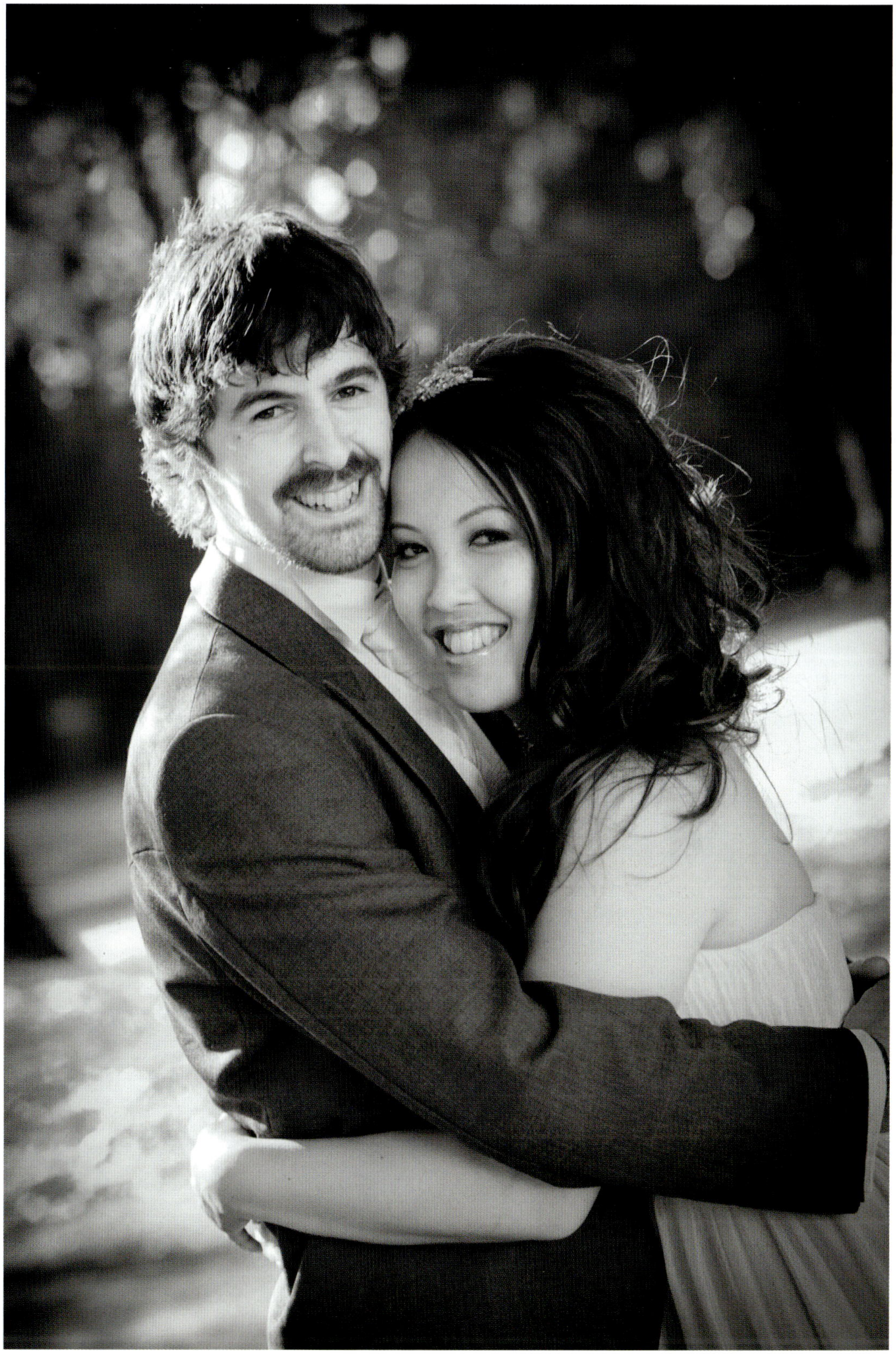

Glow

The problem with shooting with the best lenses has always been the natural sharpness in an image and, when it comes to portraits, this is not always what we want to show a client. This means that softening has become a standard technique. In the days of film, softening was achieved by using a filter, often called a softener, which was attached to the front of the lens. Its job was to give a slight glow, helping to reduce any wrinkles and lines on a client's face. However, this meant that it also softened the whole image, which some believed spoiled the shot.

In ACR, with a digital image, we have the same ability to apply a glow across the whole image by using the Clarity slider. If you move the adjustment slider to the left into the minus range, it causes an overall glow—the more you move the slider to the left, the more you increase the softness. The Clarity slider can also be used in reverse, with the positive values, to sharpen the mid-tones. I usually choose a value from about -25 to -40 at most, but most often I set it at no more than -25, as I want some softening, but not too much. If you want to selectively soften parts of the image, you can use the Clarity slider in the Adjustment brush, and then just pan the areas of the image you want to change.

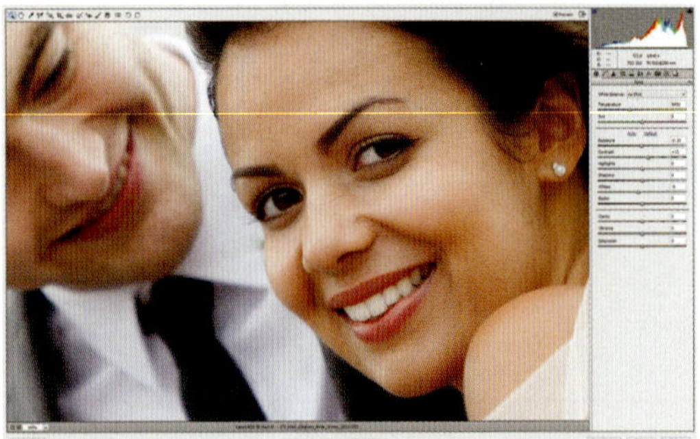

Above: 0 clarity 0

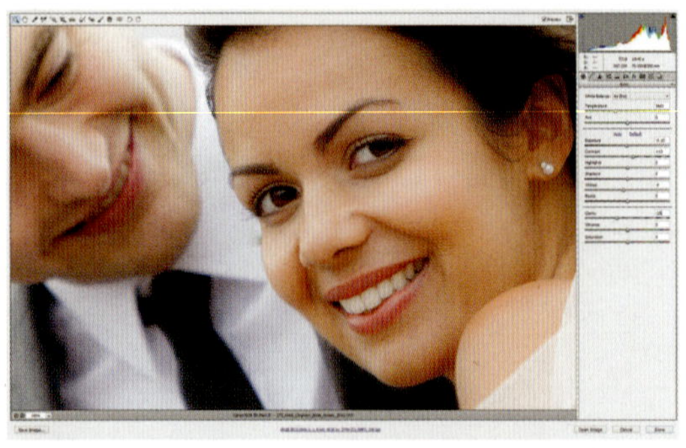

Above: 0 clarity minus 25

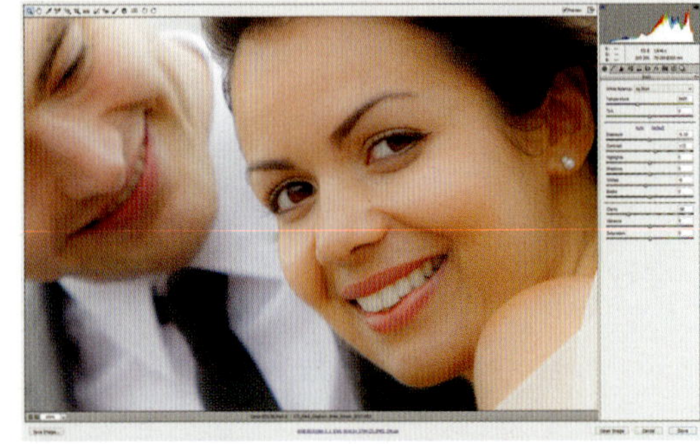

Above: 0 clarity minus 50

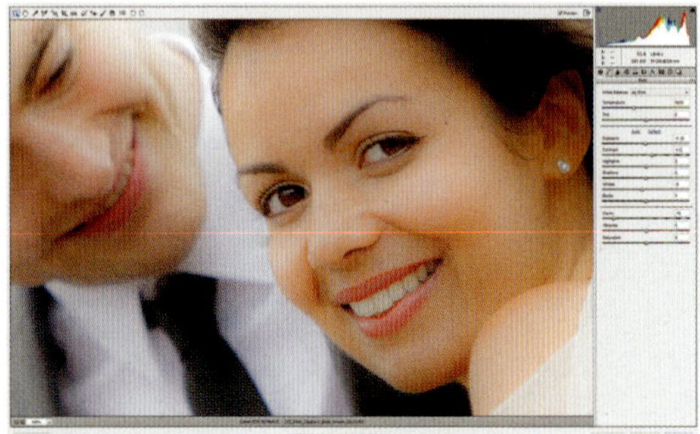

Above: 0 clarity minus 75

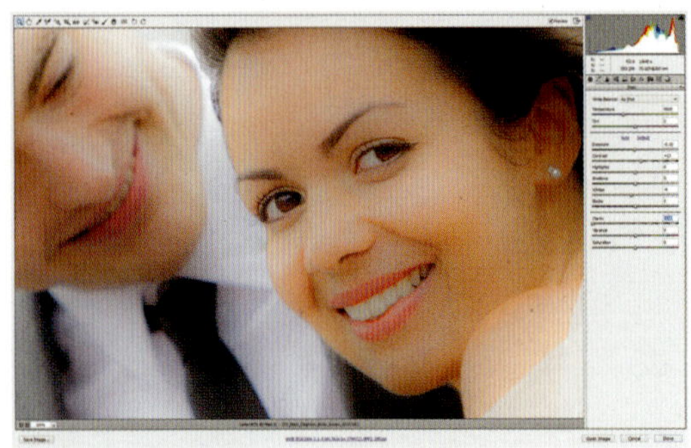

Above: 0 clarity minus 100

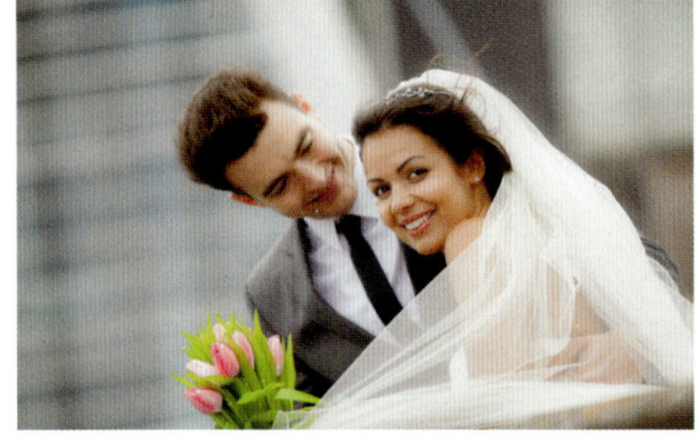

Above: Basic glow at -25

All images: The more you move the Clarity slider to the left, the softer the image will become. The Clarity slider adjusts the mid-tone sharpness, and hence softens the skin detail. Be careful not to reduce the clarity sharpness too much, as the image will start to look unreal.

Soften & sharpen

The one thing you could not do with physical filters—or at least very easily—was to soften the image but still add some sharpness to the highlights, for instance, softening the skin but sharpening the detail in veils. However, adding softening and sharpening at the same time is possible in ACR—as are all of these techniques in Photoshop or other editing programs—but being able to do this at this Raw file stage is very effective, and also saves a lot of time.

To make this change, first set the softness in the Clarity panel, and then click on the Sharpen panel to increase the sharpness a small amount at a time. Move the slider to achieve the desired level of sharpening—which depends on how much you want to sharpen the edges and highlights in the image. I usually move the slider between 70% and 100%.

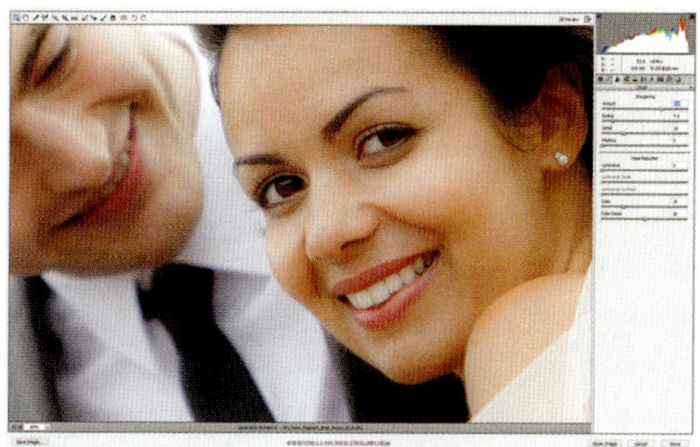

Above: The Sharpen option in ACR brings back some of the sharpness in the highlights that was lost by using the Clarity slider.

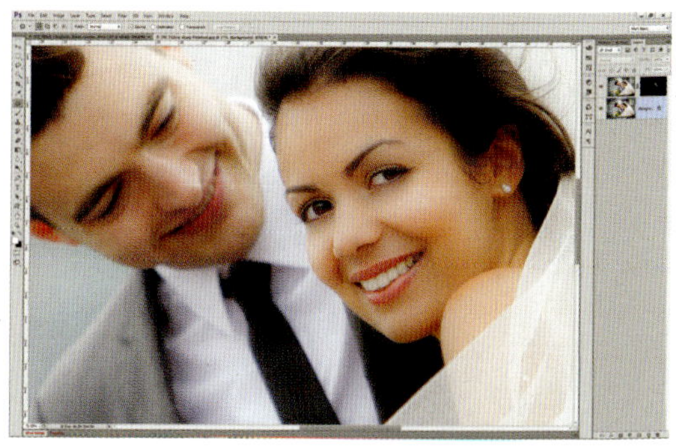

Above: This technique is used to create an image ready for the proof stage. When an image is ordered by the client for either a print or an album, I will also take the image through a quick fix in Photoshop. The final finish usually includes softening any wrinkles around the eyes and a little more skin softening if needed.

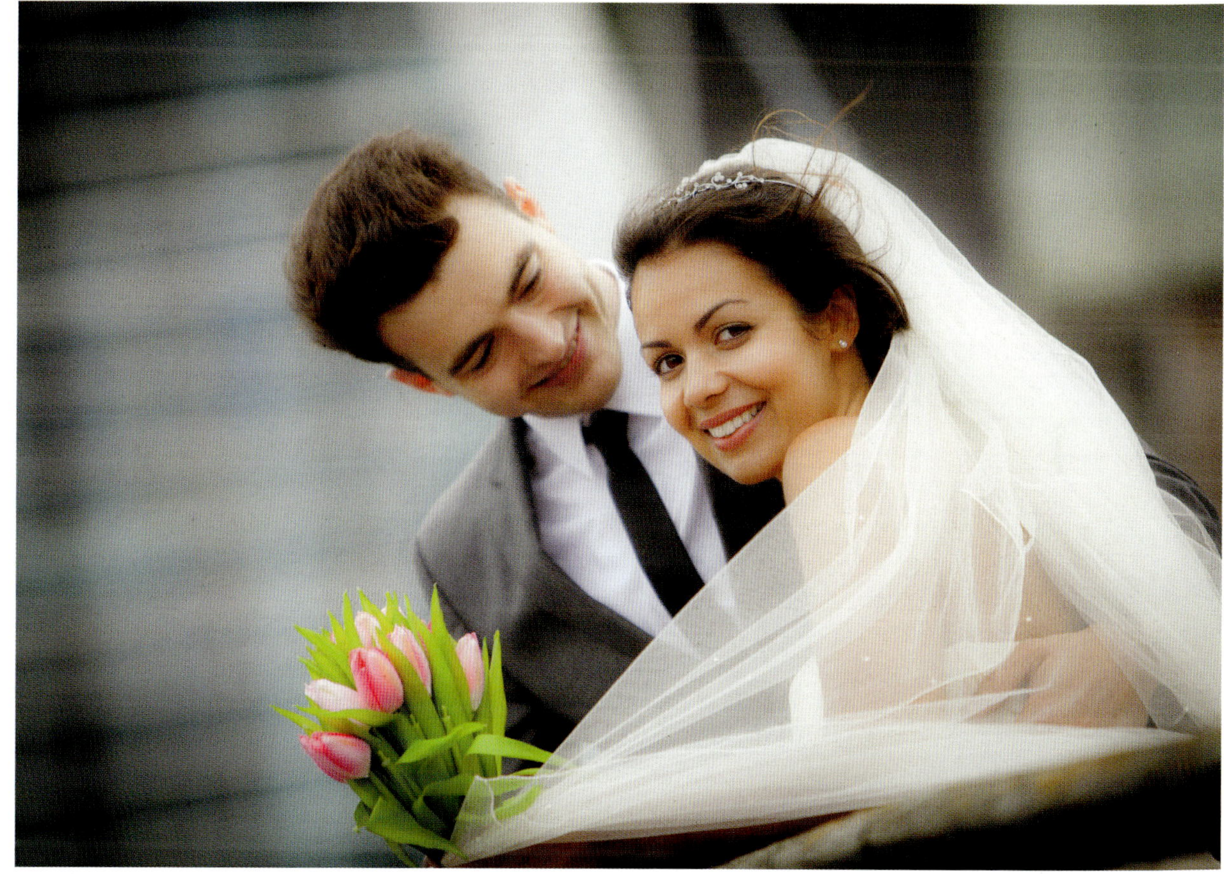

Right: The final finished image, ready to be included in the album.

Graduated skies

Adding graduated skies to an image was once something you could only do on the camera, using graduated neutral density (ND) or color filters to reduce the bright sky for an acceptable exposure. Graduated ND filters still come in many exposure levels today, from 0.5 to 3 stops. However, with powerful programs we can now apply these effects in postproduction. The power of software such as ACR is that it enables you to apply a controlled gradient on a 16-bit Raw file, so you can retain valuable detail, as well as having the ability to go back and adjust the effect time after time.

To apply the effect, click on the Gradient tool on the tool bar, which will launch a new side panel with multiple sliders. The key sliders are the Exposure, Contrast, and Highlights controls along with the Color panel, which by default shows an "X," meaning no color.

To add the gradient to the sky, click just out of the image frame, drag your mouse down over the part of the image you wish to affect, then let go.

You can still make adjustments at this stage to the applied gradient using the sliders, or you have the option to create another. To delete the effect, click the spot control at either end of the gradient then press delete.

Below: The Gradient tool allows you to reduce the intensity of the sky exposure, as well as add some color if needed.

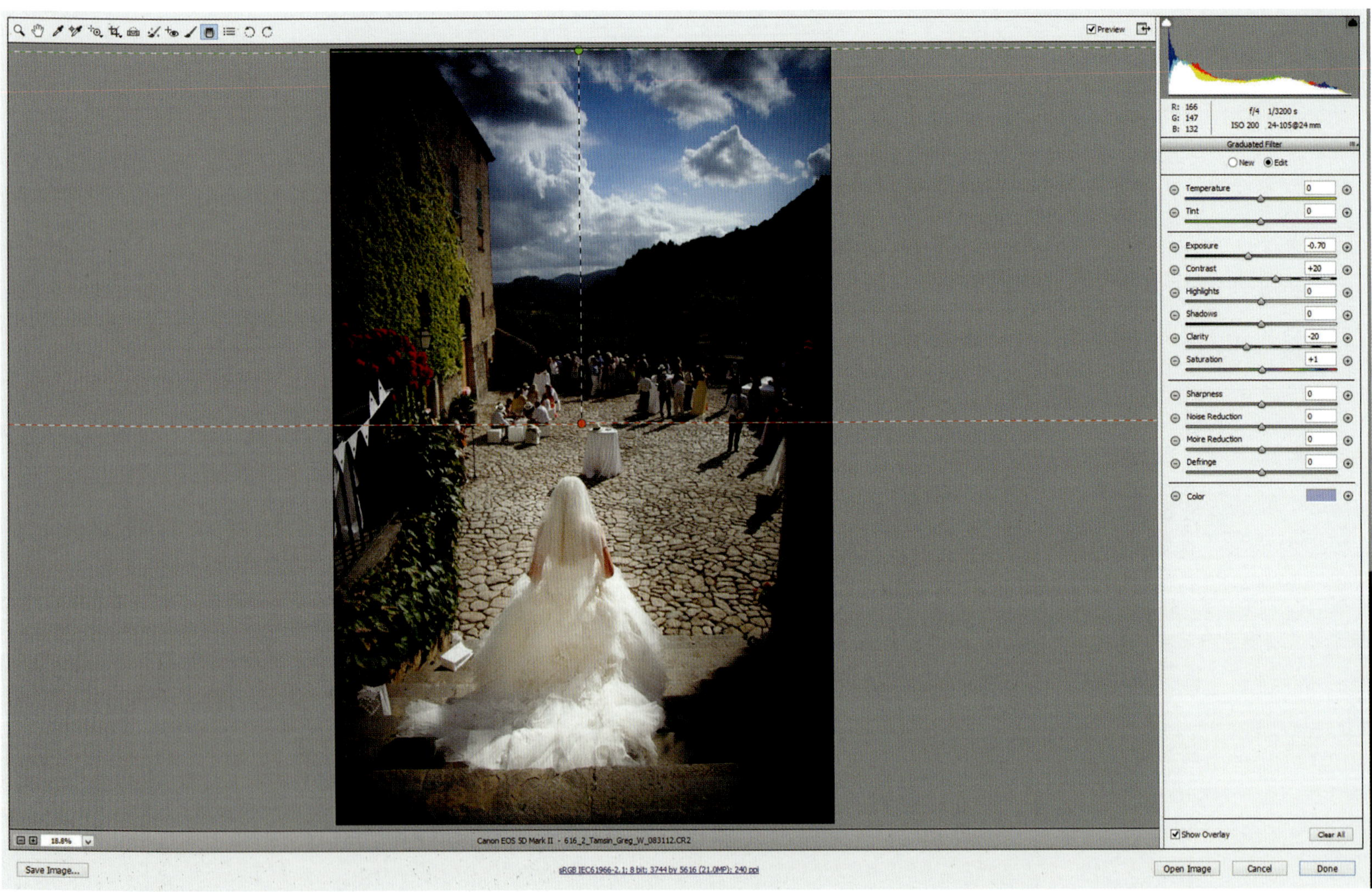

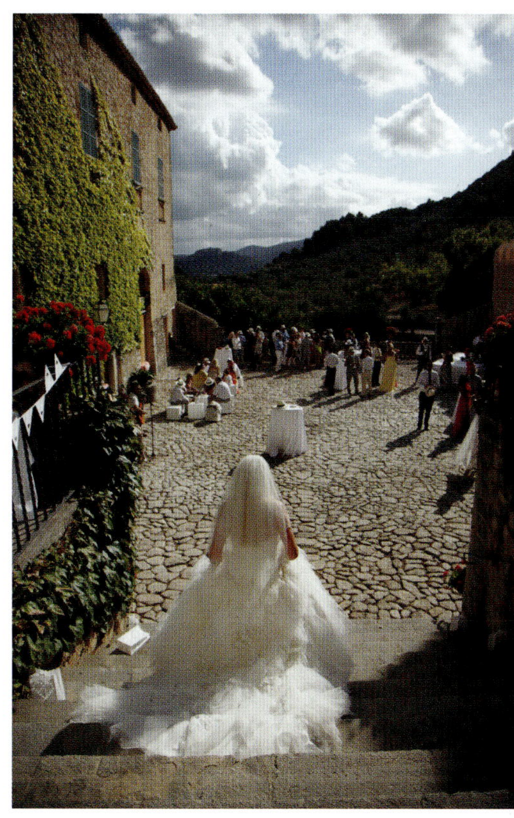

Above: As you can see in this "before" shot, the image has detail in the sky but needs a little gradient to push the clouds and color more.

Right: The finished image has had a gradient sky applied with a touch of blue, an increase in the contrast, and a reduction in clarity in the mid-tone sharpness to give a slight glow. In addition, the image has had a vignette applied to darken the edges, as well as a slight lightening of the dress using the adjustment tool.

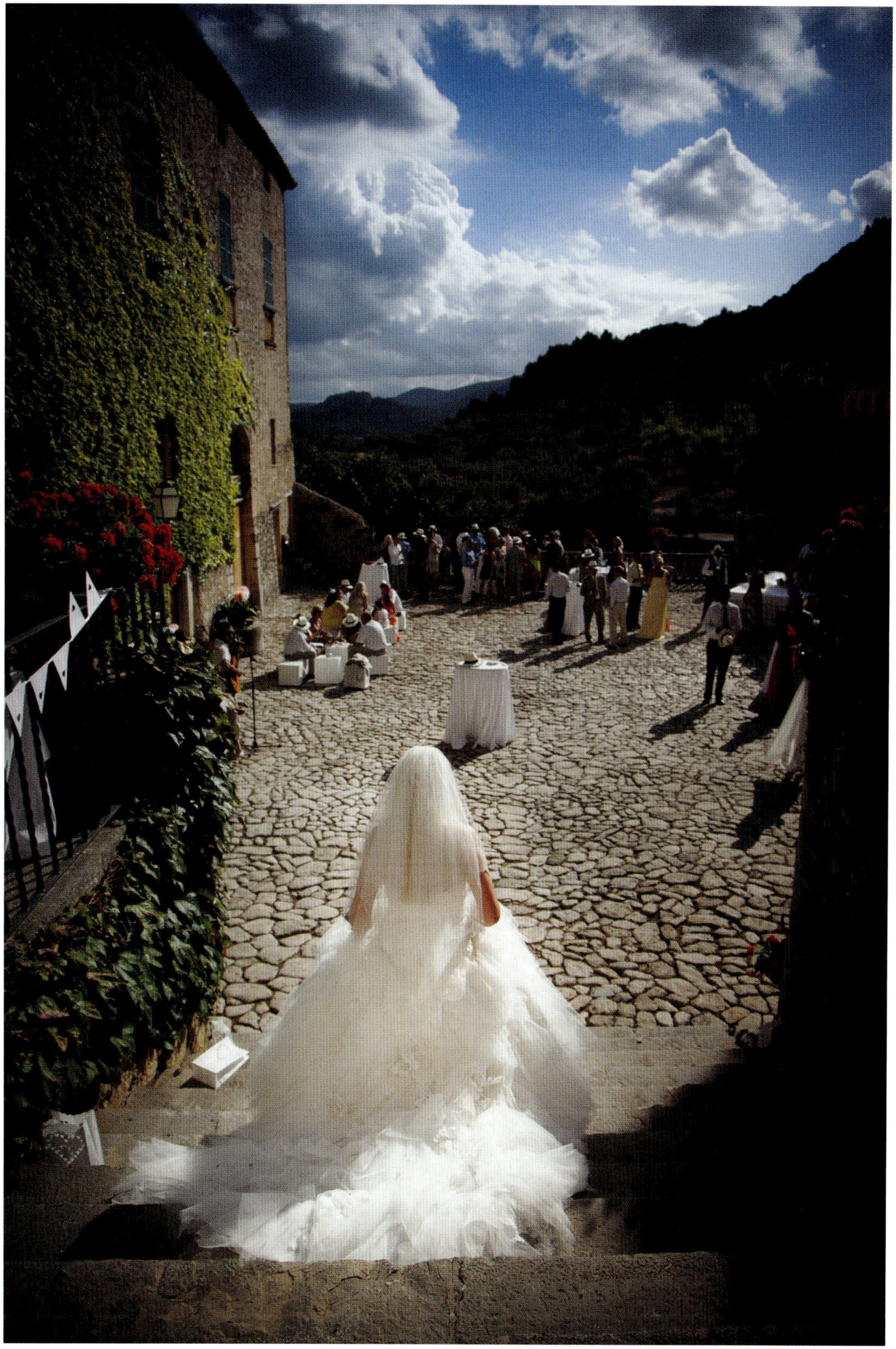

Photoshop Retouching

Actions

A fast, creative workflow is imperative when proofing for the client and designing wedding albums, so any time you can save using automation gives you more time for creativity.

Automation is one of the most powerful benefits of using a program such as Photoshop—different effects, once recorded, can be applied time after time to a single image or a whole folder of images. This means that Actions have to be an everyday part of your workflow.

You can set up Actions for the simplest or the most complicated effect, but the key is setting up Actions that are repeatable—I only wish I had this option back in the good old days of a darkroom. For over 16 years I have been using Actions to enhance my wedding images and, over the following pages, I will run through some basic and more creative effects that make great Actions.

Once you have added an Action, place it into a palette that, once saved, can be deleted and reloaded to save overfilling your Actions palette and filling up your screen working space. It is important to note that your Action sets can be lost until you save them. For instance, Photoshop will remember the Actions and where they are stored, but if you have to restart Photoshop because of a crash or an upgrade, your actions will be lost.

Actions can make workflow very easy, and they are ideal for repeatable, everyday tasks and effects. The Actions palette you see here has a combination of basic and creative effects that I apply to images. The colors can be applied to an Action button, making them easy to find amongst the crowd, and these can be collected together in groups of similar Actions.

CREATING A NEW ACTION

1 The first step in making an Action is to open the Actions palette. This is found under the top menu bar, under Window>Actions.

2 With the Actions palette open, click on the lines icon at the top right corner of the palette. This will open a new drop-down menu. As you can see, New Action and New Set are grayed out, so to access these we need to first deselect the Button mode.

3 Once Button mode is unchecked, the pallete will change. It will lose the colored button look, and be replaced by a small triangle, a toggle, with the name of the toggle. At the end of the line, you may see "F" followed by a number, which is the shortcut key that corresponds with your keyboard function keys.

4 To make a new Action, go back to the line icon on the Actions palette and select New Action from the menu. It is usually a good idea to first start a New Set, as this is where Actions are stored and saved. If you do not make a new set your Action will be added to the last in the list.

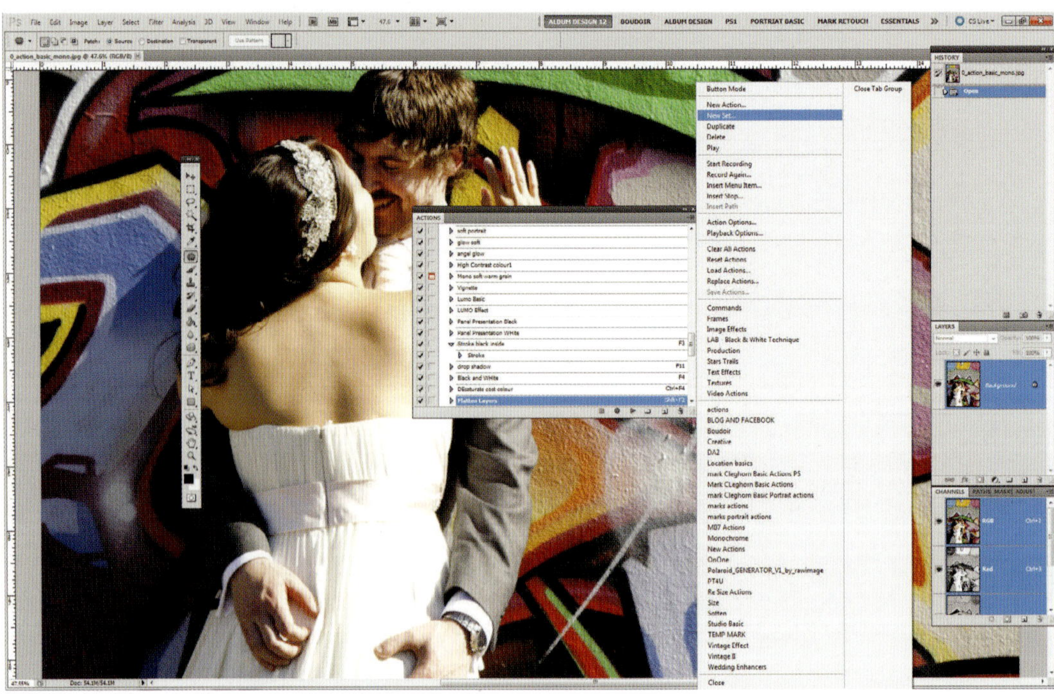

Above: Creating a new Action in Photoshop.

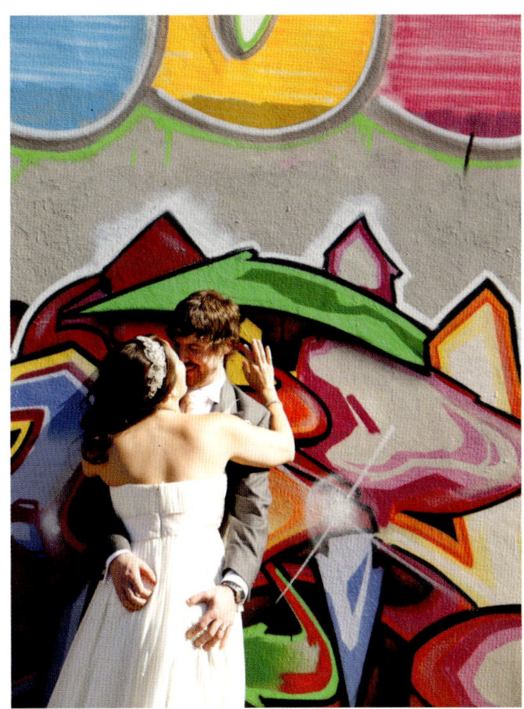

Black and white effect

First we need to name the action: "Black & White Basic." Then we need to select the set where it will belong, in this case the "Fashion Wedding & Print" set. Then we give the Action a shortcut—F4. Last, but not least, we select a color for when it is in Button mode—Yellow. The Action is now recording, as you will see from the red Record icon showing at the bottom of the palette.

Next, I am going to use the Channel Mixer to convert the image to mono. With the Channel Mixer panel open, check the Monochrome box, then set: Red +78, Green +22, Blue +0. Then press OK. These numbers should add up to 100, with one being left at +0.

The last step is to stop the Action recording by pressing the red Record icon on the Action palette. If you do not stop the recording it will just continue to record your actions. Remember to work fast with Actions once you have built a workflow palette, switching them to Button mode for speed and ease of use. Don't forget to assign a shortcut function key to the most used Actions, though, as this will make your life even easier.

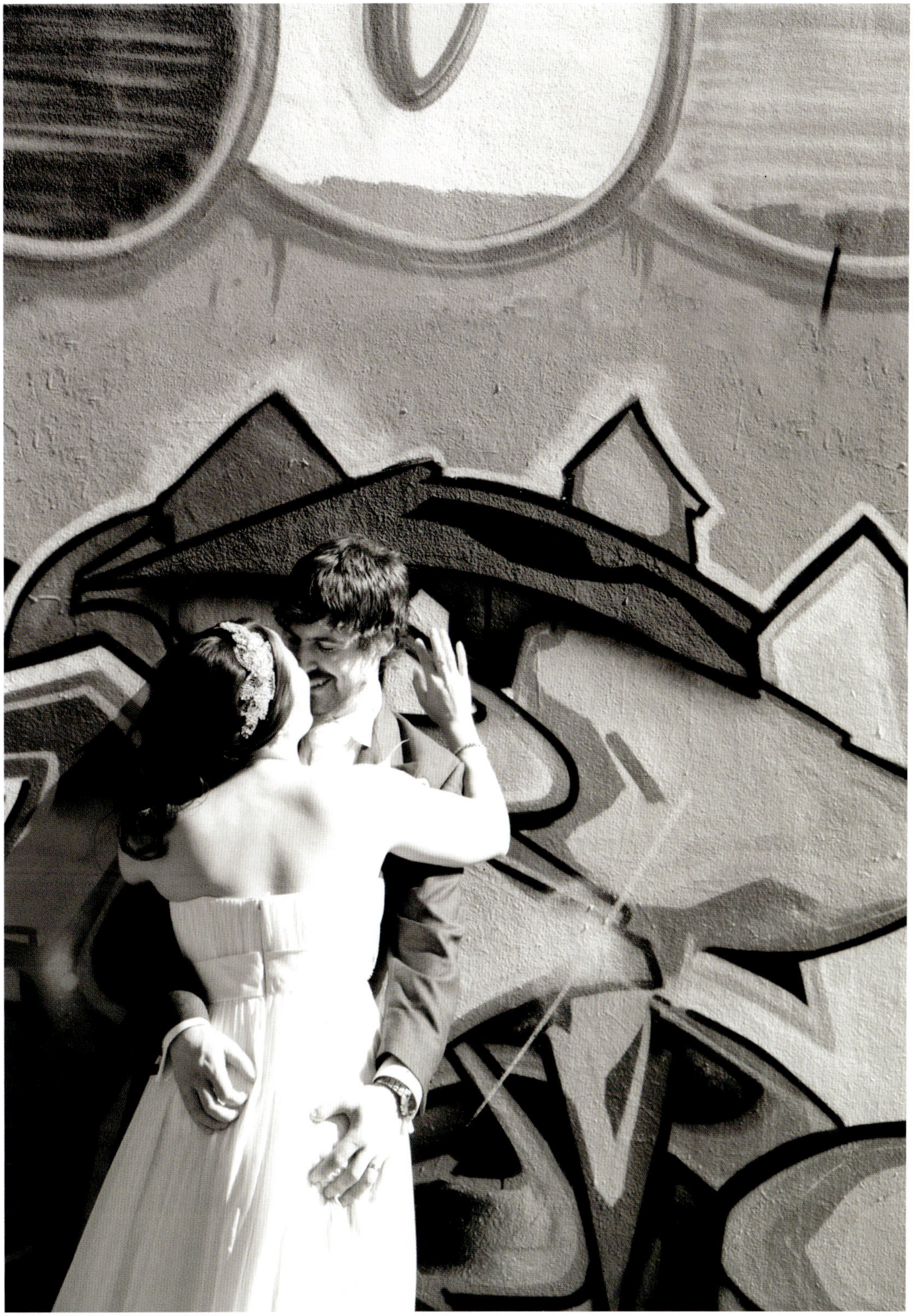

Above & above left: Before and after images showing a conversion from color to black and white.

Vintage effect

The vintage effect has become even more popular with brides since they began to see it in bridal magazines. This may still be an acquired taste, but when used with the correct couple and wedding styling, it will make an album stand out from the crowd.

The following vintage Action is best for images shot in a shaded area, with dappled lighting or backlight. The great thing about Actions is that if you don't like how one works with an image, you can just press your F12 key to revert back to the file you opened.

This Action is built using adjustment layers, which can be accessed from the Layers palette. Click on the half-moon icon at the bottom of the Layers palette and then click the relevant adjustment. Create a new Action as explained on page 162 and call it Classic Vintage, then the fun begins.

First of all, duplicate the layer, which can be achieved several ways, the most popular being to use either Control + J or, via the top menu,

Layer>Duplicate. Create a new Brightness/Contrast adjustment layer, and adjust the Contrast to +15. Then create a new Hue/Saturation adjustment layer, and adjust Saturation to +15.

Now create a new Curve adjustment layer. These adjustments are the most difficult to do. Click on the line curve and then set the values stated below. Each setting has two sets of numbers, representing the Output and the Input for one point on the curve: RGB Master adjustment, 60/25 and 255/ 219. To select the individual channel on the curve, press the black triangle next to the RGB: Red no adjustment, Green 70/55 and 205/189, Blue 57/2 and 238/255

Next, create a new Solid Color adjustment layer. For this action, we are going to add a slight purple tone overall, but this is where you could make slight alterations for slightly different Actions. For this effect, in the RGB settings type: Red 200, Green 000, Blue 255. Set the layer Opacity, found on the Layer palette, to 5%.

Before the next step, we need to make sure the colors on the Tool palette are reset to their default. To do this just press the letter D. Next create a new Gradient Map adjustment layer, and set Opacity of the layer to 20%.

Flatten your layers and stop the Action recording. Now test it on a few images. If you need to correct the contrast in images, it might be a good idea to build some further, simple Actions to slightly adjust the finished image.

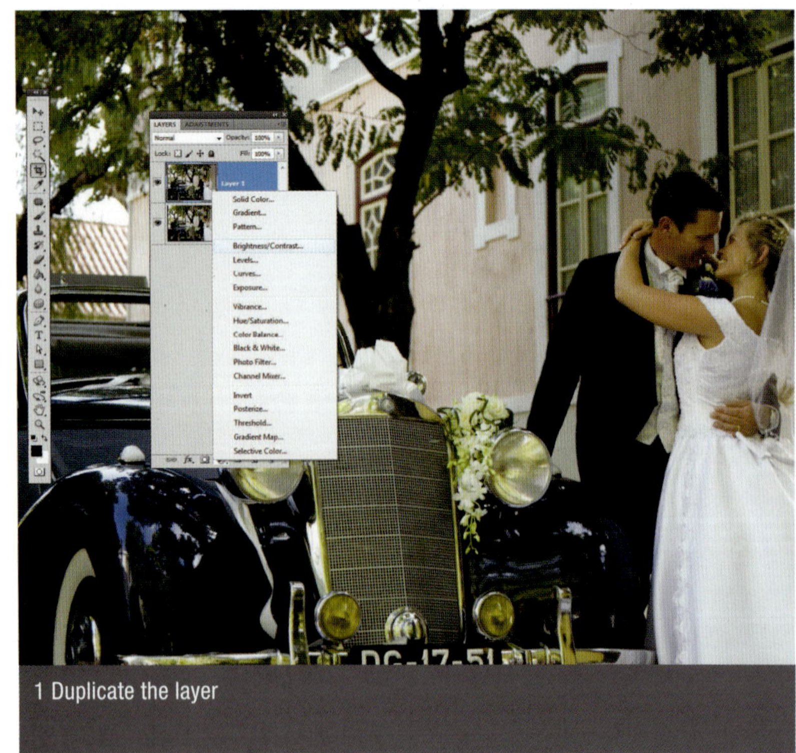

1 Duplicate the layer

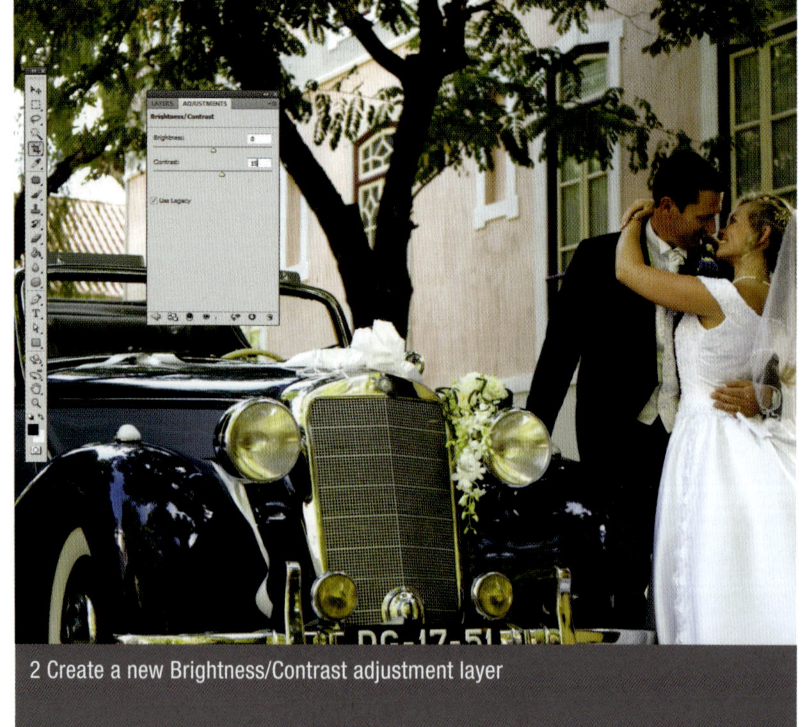

2 Create a new Brightness/Contrast adjustment layer

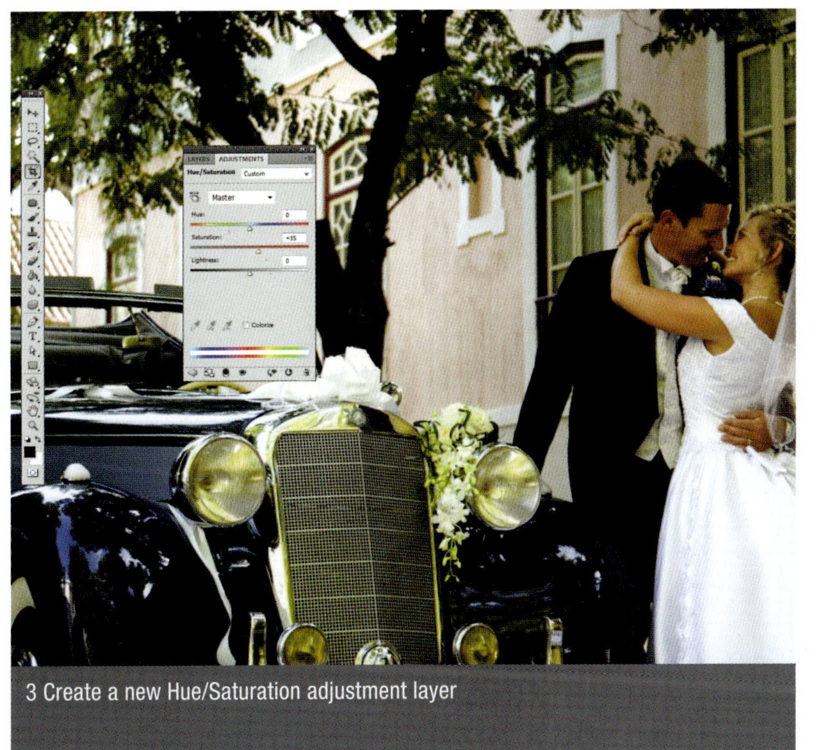

3 Create a new Hue/Saturation adjustment layer

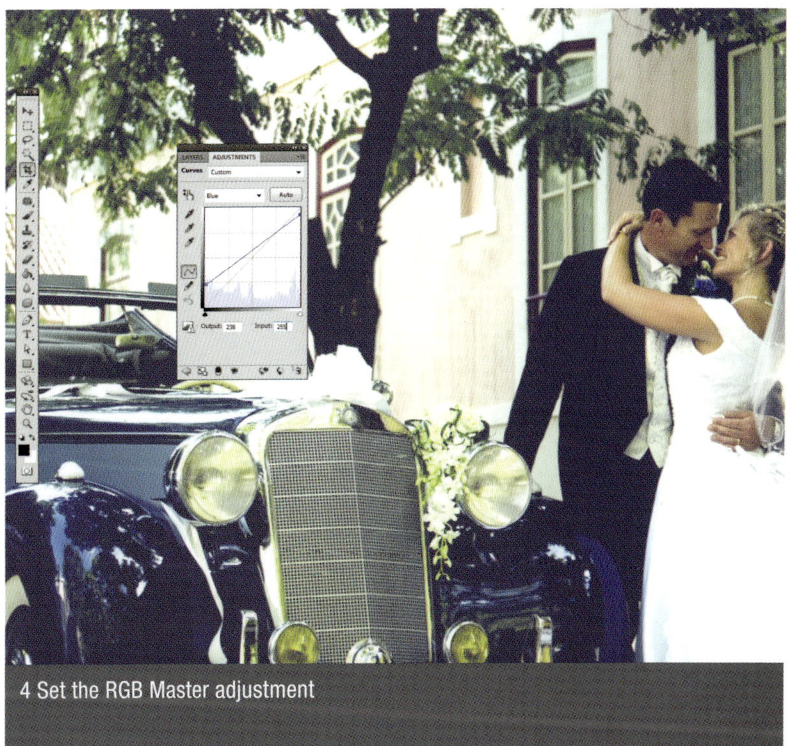

4 Set the RGB Master adjustment

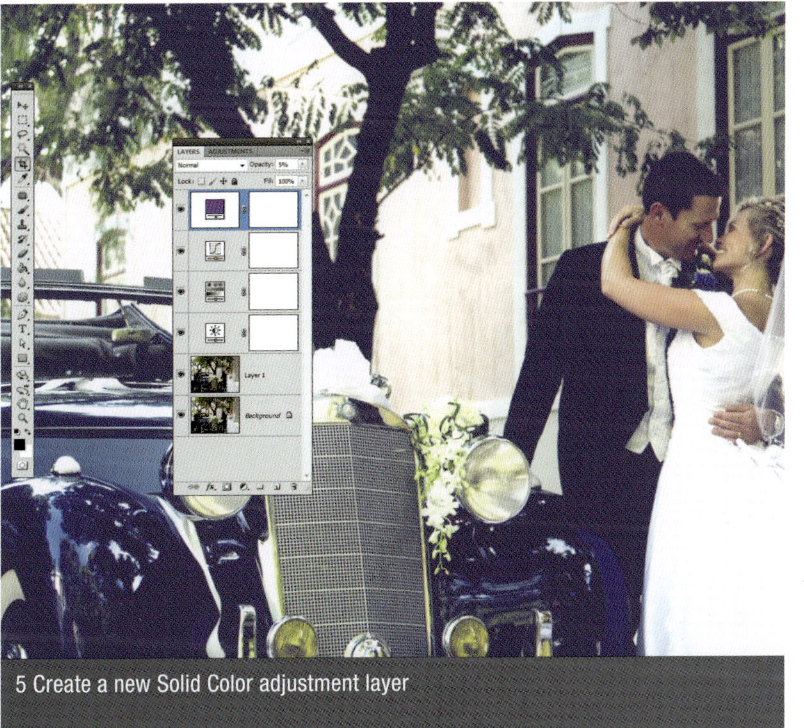

5 Create a new Solid Color adjustment layer

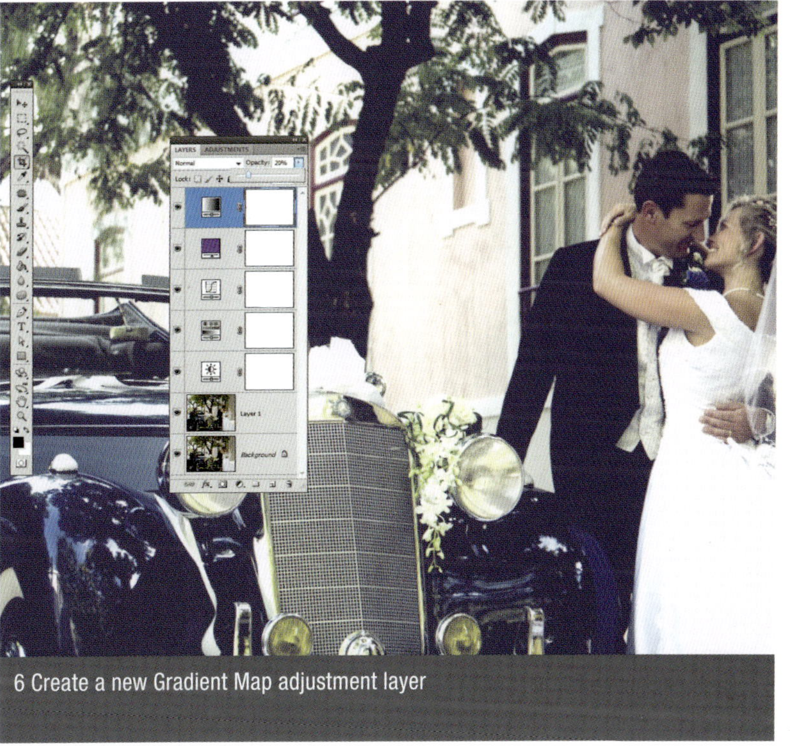

6 Create a new Gradient Map adjustment layer

Album Proofing

Proofing has changed for the working professional, as there is now no or little cost in producing proofs of the wedding images. In the film years, proofing was costly as it was reliant on expensive printing processes, whether with contact sheets or, more often, with fully finished prints. Now with the option of proof books, online proofing or via CD slideshow, the ability to shoot and show more could never be more of an attractive option as there is no real cost.

The wedding album has also changed a great deal in the last 20 years. Originally the only real album was an interleaf album—this used thick paper pages on which were stuck the finished photographs. In-between each page was a piece of tissue paper to stop the photographs sticking to each other, as well as protecting them from deterioration.

The interleaf album was superseded by the overlay album, which still remains popular today. The overlay album provides better protection for the print, as it uses a small pocket of air between the print and the page. It also offers a greater variety of opening sizes and custom page designs than the old interleaf album.

The photobook is the next generation of album, allowing the print alone to be mounted flush across the page. Long panoramic images can also be mounted. Modern print, ink, and glue technologies have stopped any deterioration of the prints, so that they can lie face-to-face for the first time.

Finally, the wedding photographer is now able to offer the custom storybook, in either hardback or softback covers. This type of album has always been available, but was just unaffordable for most with traditional ink print techniques. These albums allow the story of the day to be told, as the pages are thin enough for hundreds of images to be used in the layout without making the album too big and heavy.

Proof albums

Proof albums might seem old-fashioned in today's digital world, but I still love a proof book—it somehow brings the images to life and tells the story of the day. However, remember the client should pay extra for the book because it is an extra cost for you.

There are many online book companies to order from, but I prefer to use a one-stop shop, as long as the quality remains at a very high standard across the range of products. I use Loxley Colour, which is a British photo lab, for all my print production and, in recent years, for my albums and framing. They are able to deliver printed proof books of a very high standard at reasonable prices, and they offer the added benefit of online ordering and uploading. Other systems will vary, but the basic process of ordering a proof book are shown below.

For the proof, you do not need to use the full file size, so instead make a small copy using a Photoshop droplet, which reduces the image size to 2000 pixels along the longest edge. To resize your images in Photoshop, go to Image>Fit Image. Once the images are resized, it's an easy 10-step process to order.

ORDERING A PROOF BOOK

1 Launch the Loxley Designer Pro software for access to the order and design portal then click Next.

2 Choose the product category, in this case, Books, then click Next.

3 Choose the product, which is the Photo book Preview XL, and then click Next.

4 Next, choose the size and the orientation (portrait or landscape format) in which the proof book will be printed. Also, this is where you choose whether to add a filename, a copyright wash or both.

5 The next window is where you load your images, and this can be done either by selecting a folder of photographs or by selecting them individually, image by image.

6 In the next window you choose the font and font size for the text—to make sure that all your work has the same look and feel. You also see the basic cost for the book, as well as how much of the album you have used, and how much is left to fill, if you want to add more images. You will also see how many more images you can add without the price increasing.

7 The last step in the basic process is checking the images. You must do this to make sure all the images are in the right orientation.

8 When you press Next, you will be asked to give your project a name. Once you do this, you will enter the designer layout mode.

9 Designing the cover can be daunting, but as this is a Preview book I tend to use the same layout, and add my studio name and web site address on the back cover. The software allows you to create funky effects, and includes template layouts, as well as colored backgrounds and masks for blending images.

10 On the last page, put the "how to order" information, including your online gallery code, and the basic studio details.

Slideshows

The age of the slideshow is well and truly upon us. When I began to use digital slideshows for weddings in 2002, things were quite primitive—a simple fade-and-dissolve was not that difficult to set up, just time-consuming. Over time, several companies improved the software, but the world of slideshows has now changed, thanks to Animoto.

Animoto introduced their online software for the production of slideshows in 2008, and the service has improved ever since. Photographers are able to generate slick, full high-definition-quality video slideshows of their images, using a drag-and-drop interface and libraries of templates, visual effects, and licenced music. Different levels of account and payment entitle you to different levels of service and associated benefits.

Once the video slideshow is made, you can download it as an MP4 video to play on your web site and to sell to your client. This kind of presentation can set you apart from other photographers, especially if you use a tablet computer to show off your work to potential clients and at events. There is even the option of being able to download a file for burning to DVD. You can also share the video through social media, including Facebook, Twitter, SmugMug, Pinterest, and WordPress.

The procedure for making a video slideshow is simple. All you need to do is log on to the Animoto web site, choose a template style you like, drag and drop your images into an on-screen box, select a track of music from their library, and preview the video.

Creating a slideshow

Firstly, select your template style. There are over 65 templates to choose from at the time of publication, all with different design features and transitions. You can preview the style, as well as

going back and changing it at any stage, even after production.

Next, you'll need to upload your images. There are many ways to upload your images, including direct from Lightroom or your SmugMug account, or by dragging and dropping them from a folder on your computer.

Each video template comes with a different default soundtrack, but you can choose from a selection of thousands of tracks of different styles. You can add multiple text slides, as well as spotlight certain images, by showing them for longer or by using them as backgrounds.

At the preview stage, you can choose a name for the video and add a description. It is at this stage that you can decide to output the video you've created or carry on editing the slideshow by adding or deleting images or text slides.

The video takes about 2–3 minutes to produce, depending on the number of images. Use the Animoto web site to share your slideshows through Facebook or Twitter, to engage and generate more followers and potential clients.

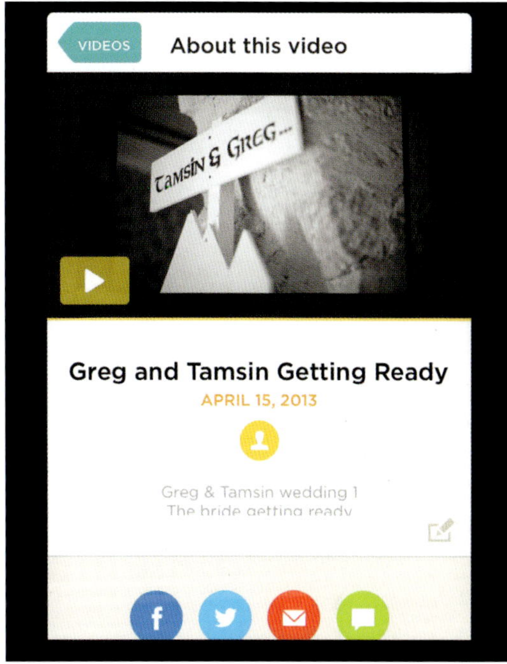

Above: A video slideshow on iPad.

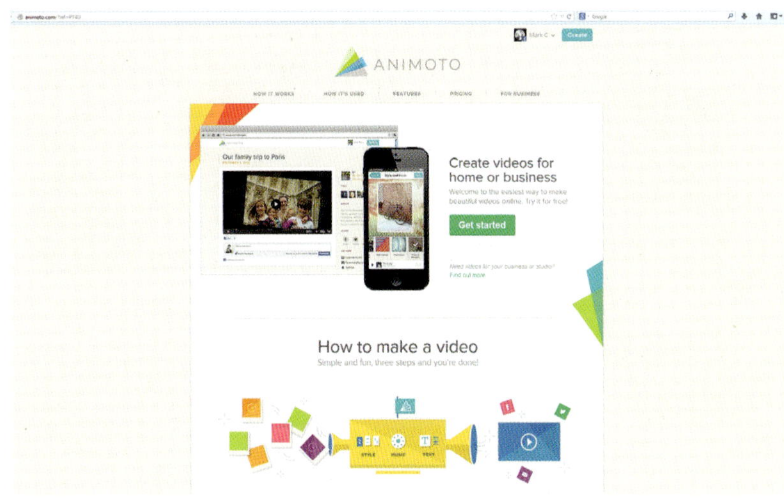

Above: The Animoto home screen.

Online Proofing

The most popular way to show images of a wedding to the bride and groom, and their friends and family, is via online proofing. You can still provide DVD proofs and printed proof albums but these will incur extra cost for the bride and groom, and as much as I prefer a proof book, an online gallery is a much cheaper way for your clients to view the images. An online gallery is also able to generate higher sales of images to the guests and family.

The company I currently use for providing online galleries is SmugMug, which is an online one-stop shop for my web site, storage, and sales, and for showing images. The SmugMug web sites are simple to set up, and come with a whole host of attractive templates. Once you get the hang of using the site, you can set up a fully functioning web site and viewing facility in just a few hours.

Once you've built your site, you just need to set up a new gallery for your client, and then upload the images directly into their gallery folder. You can then change the design of the gallery and add a price list. Security of your images is also covered, with options for watermarking and right-click protection, which prevents anyone—including clients—from downloading the images without paying for them.

For sales, I just email the client a link, give them the password, and then everyone who views the images can place their own order and pay online, all through the SmugMug portal. The images are then shipped directly to the client from a trusted photo lab.

SmugMug also offers lots of options for viewing, such as Event creation, which enables the client and their friends to collect their favorite images in their own personal gallery for sharing and purchasing.

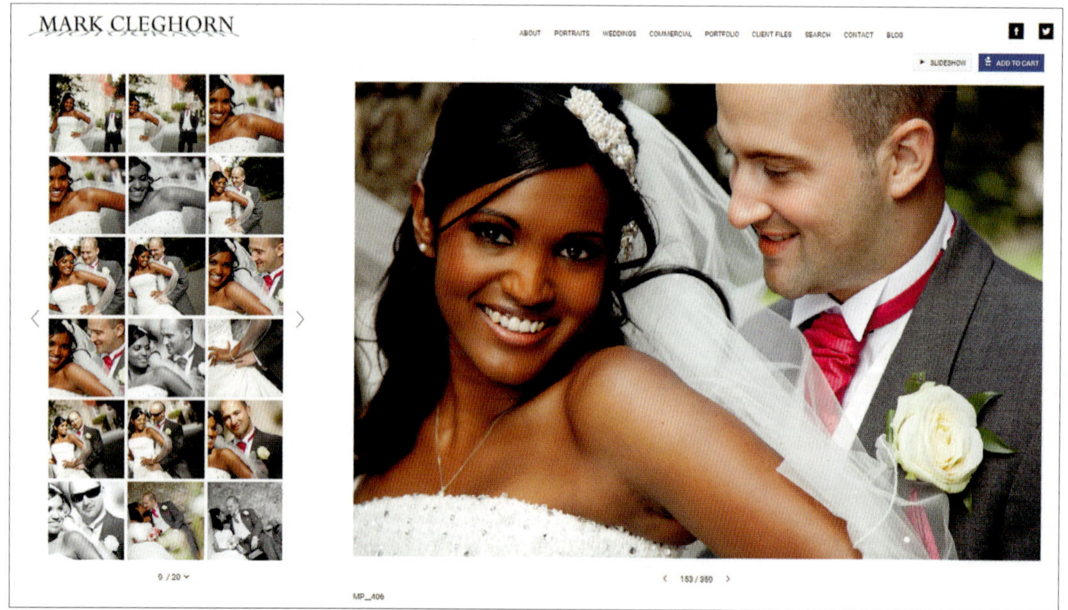

Above: Within the gallery you can protect your images in several ways, which include right-click protection. This stops a client from saving the image directly from the gallery.

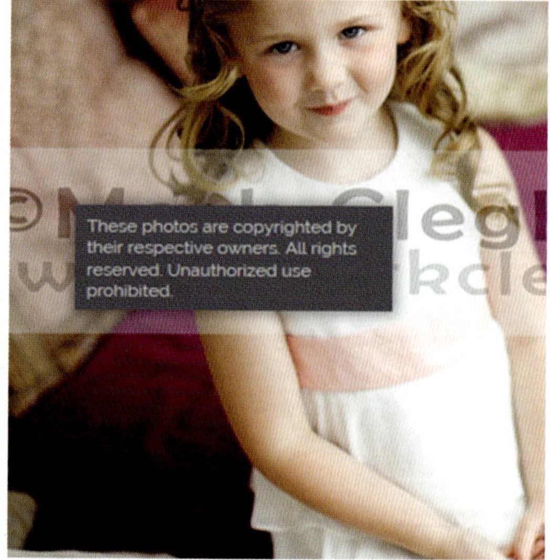

Above: You are also able to protect your images by watermarking them.

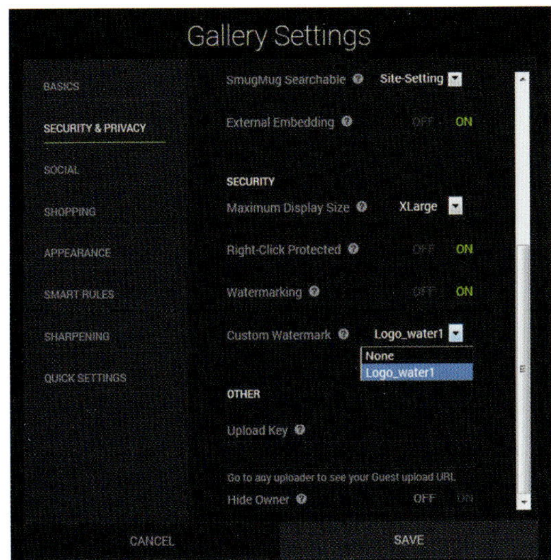

Above: Adding a watermark is a simple process within the gallery settings.

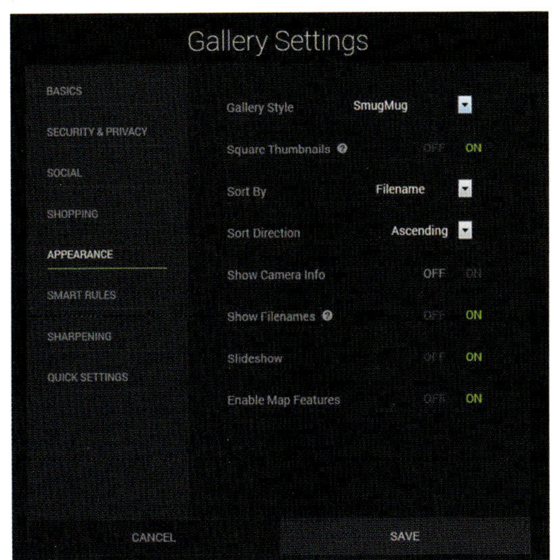

Above: While in gallery settings, you can set what the gallery looks like, as well as add the camera details, image file names, and change the order in which they appear in the gallery.

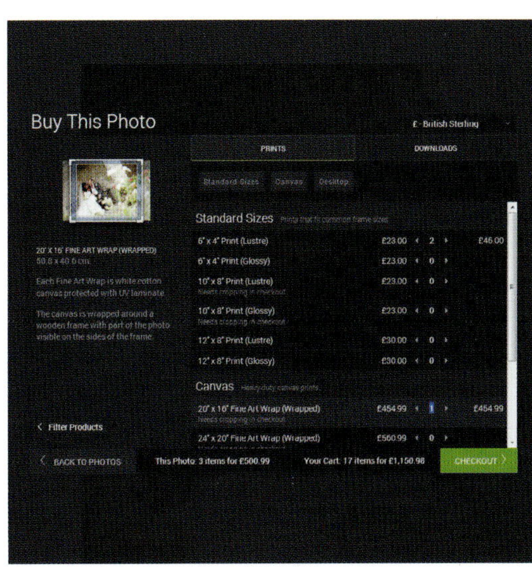

Above: To order an image, the client can select one image at a time and choose from your product ranges.

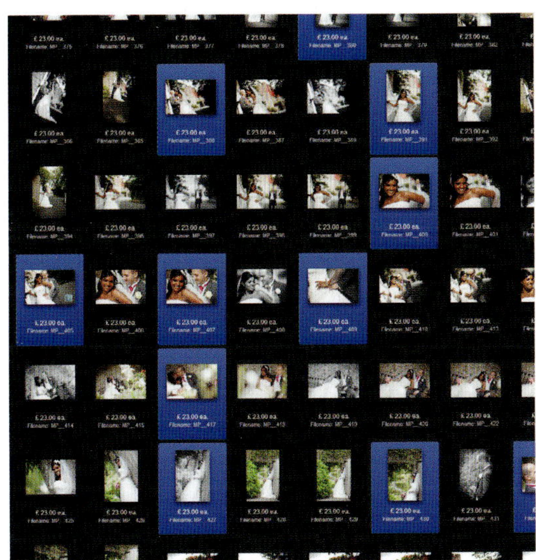

Above: Your client can view the gallery in a thumbnail style, making it easier to select multiple images for purchase at the same time.

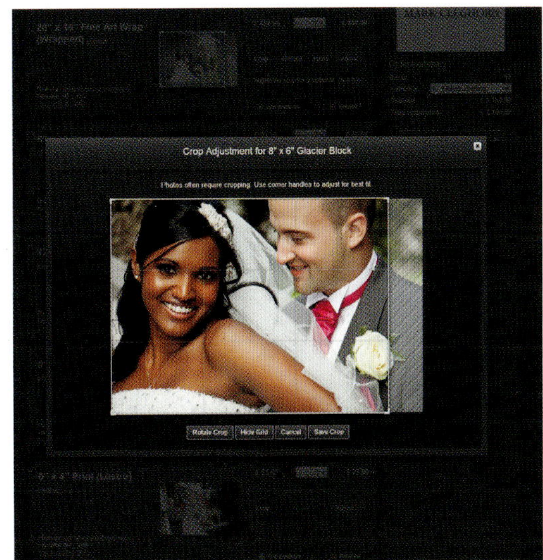

Above: At the checkout stage, the client can crop an image to their taste. I do have a print delay facility, which gives me seven days to review the online order before it goes to the photo lab.

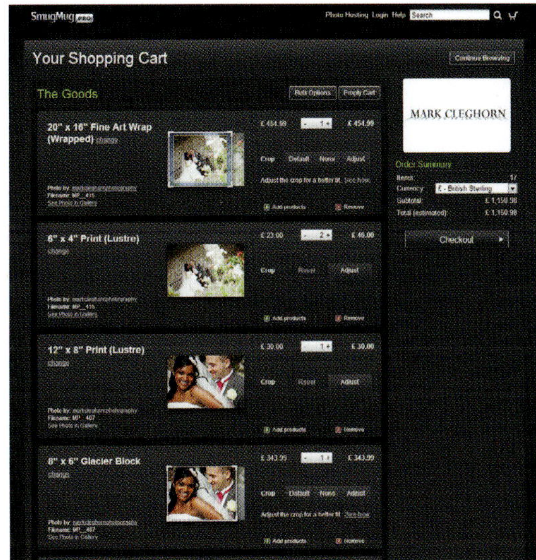

Above: The client pays SmugMug online directly, which takes all the hassle away of online payments. About 30 days later I receive payment, minus the print production costs and the SmugMug percentage.

Glossary

Aberration An imperfection in the image caused by imperfections in the optics of the lens.

Ambient light Light that originates from existing sources, whether natural or artificial, as opposed to those added by the photographer.

Aperture The opening in a lens through which light passes to expose the image sensor. The size of the aperture is denoted by f/numbers.

Aspect ratio The ratio of the width to the height of an image frame.

Autofocus (AF) A through-the-lens focusing system whereby focusing is achieved through activation of an electronic system in the camera rather than manually.

Backlighting Light coming from the far side of the subject, towards the camera lens.

Ball-and-socket head A type of tripod head with a sphere around which the head pivots, and a handle to lock it in place at the desired position.

Bounce flash Light from a flash unit that is bounced onto the subject—from a ceiling, wall, or reflector—to soften or hide shadows.

Bracketing Exposing a series of frames of the same subject at a series of slightly different exposures.

Buffer The in-camera memory that temporarily stores image data as it is processed and written to the memory card.

Burst rate The number of frames per second that a digital camera can record.

Burst size The maximum number of frames that a digital camera can shoot in a row before its buffer becomes full.

Center-weighted metering A metering system that takes the majority of its reading from the central portion of the frame, suitable for portraits or scenes where the subjects fill the center of the frame.

Color space A way of coding colors in terms of qualities such as lightness, saturation, and hue. Color spaces, such as Adobe RGB or sRGB, are device-independent and determine the color range you can work in.

Compression The way in which digital file sizes are reduced. There is usually some payoff between the quality of the image and the degree of compression.

Contrast This is a description of the extent to which adjacent areas of an image differ in brightness. It reflects the gradation between the highest and lowest luminance values.

Crop factor A numerical description of the magnification effect produced by using a camera with a smaller sensor than the "full-frame" standard with a particular lens.

Cropping Selecting and isolating part of an image with the aim of improving composition or fitting an image to the available space.

Depth of field The distance extending in front of and beyond the point of focus that is also perceived as being acceptably sharp. If an object is placed within this zone it will appear to be in focus.

Diffuser An object used to diffuse or soften light.

DSLR (Digital Single Lens Reflex) A camera that allows the user to view the scene through the lens using a mirror that directs the light to the viewfinder.

dpi (dots per inch) A measure of the resolution of a printed page.

Dynamic range The range of tones that can be registered by the camera sensor. A camera with a larger dynamic range will reveal more variation of tone—and therefore detail—in the brightest and darkest areas of the image.

Exposure The amount of light allowed to strike the image sensor when taking the photograph. This is controlled by altering the aperture size, the exposure time (shutter speed), and the sensitivity of the sensor (ISO). An exposure is also a term used for the process of taking a photograph.

Exposure compensation A level of adjustment given to auto-exposure settings. This is used to compensate for known inadequacies in the way a camera takes meter readings or records the image.

Fill-in flash Flash combined with daylight in an exposure. Used with naturally backlit or harshly sidelit or toplit subjects to prevent silhouettes forming, or to add extra light to shadow areas.

Filter A piece of colored or coated glass or plastic that is placed on the front or within the lens for creative or corrective reasons.

Flare Non-image-forming light that scatters within the lens system. This can create multi-colored circles or a loss in contrast.

Flash sync The flash sync speed is the fastest speed at which a camera with a focal plane shutter can work with flash.

Focal length The distance from the optical center of a lens to its focal point.

Frontlighting Light shining on the front surface of a subject. This can produce dull, lifeless photos, although it is good for picking out surface detail.

Hotshoe An accessory shoe with electrical contacts mounted over the optical axis, allowing synchronization between camera and flashgun.

Histogram A graph that reveals the number of pixels registering the various tones from white to black. It forms an illustration of the distribution of tones within the image.

Hue The attribute of color that enables it to be classed as red, green, blue, yellow, or purple. This is related to its spectral position.

Incident-light meter An exposure meter that measures the light falling on the subject, rather than the light reflected by the subject.

ISO The international standard for representing film sensitivity, this has been extended to the variable settings of digital sensors.

JPEG (Joint Photographic Experts Group) A widely used image file type involving some degree of compression to reduce file size.

LCD (Liquid Crystal Display) The screen on the back of a camera on which images and shooting information can be played back and reviewed.

Memory card A removable data storage device for digital cameras.

Metering Using a camera or light meter to calculate the amount of light that is falling on or being reflected from a scene to calculate the required exposure.

Monochrome A term for an image comprised only of variations of one tone (usually gray tones, when it equates to "black and white").

Noise Interference caused by stray electrical signals adversely affecting picture quality.

Overexposure A condition in which too much light reaches the sensor. Detail is lost in the highlights of the image.

Pan-and-tilt head A tripod head allowing movement in three axes.

Pixel Abbreviation of "picture element." Pixels are the smallest distinct bits of information that combine to form a digital image.

Prime lens A lens with a fixed focal length.

Raw A versatile and widely used digital file format in which shooting parameters are attached to the file, not applied to it.

Red-eye When photographing people using flash close to the optical axis, the light from the flash can bounce off the blood vessels in the retina of the eye causing the pupil to look red in the final image.

Red-eye reduction Some flash units can be set to fire a sequence of preflashes causing the pupil to contract and the amount of light reflected be diminished, reducing the appearance of red-eye.

Reflected-light meter A light meter measuring light reflected from, rather than light falling on, the surface of a subject.

Reflector A surface or accessory from which light is reflected for use in balancing the direction of a light source.

Resolution The number of pixels used to either capture or display an image, usually expressed in pixels per inch. The higher the resolution, the finer the detail in the image.

Saturation A description of the purity of a color and thus to some degree its intensity.

Shutter speed The length of time that the camera's shutter is open for, allowing light to reach the sensor. A slow shutter speed lets more light in, but increases risk of camera shake. A faster shutter speed freezes motion and decreases risk of camera shake.

Sidelighting Light striking the subject from the side, relative to the position of the camera.

Softbox A shoot-through attachment that softens the light from a studio flash unit.

Spot metering A system that measures from a small area in the center of the frame or under an autofocus point.

TIFF (Tagged Image File Format) A file format supported by virtually all image-editing applications. Unlike JPEGs, the files are not compressed.

Tone The lightness or darkness of a part of an image, or the shade of a color.

TTL (Through The Lens) metering A metering system built into the camera that measures light passing through the lens at the time of shooting.

Umbrella A flash attachment that diffuses the light.

Underexposure A condition in which too little light reaches sensor. There is detail lost in the areas of shadow in the exposure.

Vignetting Darkening of the corners of an image, due to an obstruction (usually caused by a filter or lens hood) or the optical quality of a lens.

White balance A function that allows the correct color balance to be recorded for any given lighting situation and applied to the image.

Zoom lens A lens offering a range of focal lengths.

Useful Web Sites

Photographers

Mark Cleghorn
www.markcleghorn.com

Photography tuition

The Photographer Academy
www.thephotographeracademy.com

Photographic equipment

Bowens www.bowens.co.uk
Quantum www.qtm.com
Canon www.canon.com
Elinchrom www.elinchrom.com
Expo Disk www.expoimaging.com
Honi www.honiphoto.com
Lastolite www.lastolite.com
Lexar www.lexar.com
Manfrotto www.manfrotto.com
Nikon www.nikon.com
Panasonic www.panasonic.com
Pocket Wizard www.pocketwizard.com
Ray Flash www.ray-flash.com
SanDisk www.sandisk.com
Sekonic www.sekonic.com
Sony www.sony.com

Software

Adobe
www.adobe.com

Photographic services

Photo web sites
SmugMug www.smugmug.com

Photo printing service
Loxley Colour www.loxleycolour.com

Cloud-based video creation service
Animoto www.animoto.com

Photography publications

Photogrqphy books and Expanded Camera Guides
AE Publications Ltd www.ammonitepress.com

Photography magazines
Black & White Photography magazine
Outdoor Photography magazine
www.thegmcgroup.com

Index

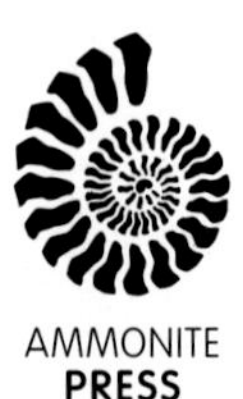

AMMONITE
PRESS

To place an order, or request a catalog, contact:
Ammonite Press
AE Publications Ltd, 166 High Street, Lewes, East Sussex, BN7 1XU, United Kingdom
Tel: +44 (0)1273 488006
www.ammonitepress.com